Sir Walter Scott

Familiar Letters of Sir Walter Scott

Vol. II

Sir Walter Scott

Familiar Letters of Sir Walter Scott
Vol. II

ISBN/EAN: 9783337105426

Printed in Europe, USA, Canada, Australia, Japan

Cover: Foto ©ninafisch / pixelio.de

More available books at **www.hansebooks.com**

FAMILIAR LETTERS

OF

SIR WALTER SCOTT

VOL. II

"In these far climes it was my lot
To meet the wondrous Michael Scott ;
   A wizard of such dreadful fame,
That when in Salamanca's cave,
Him listed his magic wand to wave,
   The bells would ring in Notre Dame !
Some of his skill he taught to me ;
And, Warrior, I could say to thee
The words that cleft Eildon hills in three,[1]
   And bridled the Tweed with a curb of stone :
But to speak them were a deadly sin ;
And for having but thought them my heart within,
   A treble penance must be done."

Lay of the Last Minstrel, Canto II.

[1] Once upon a time Michael Scott ordered a demon to divide the Eildon hill, then a single cone, into three. A single night "was sufficient to part its summit into the three picturesque peaks which it now bears."

"Where fair Tweed flows round holy Melrose
And Eildon slopes to the plain."

Eve of St John

EDINBURGH DAVID DOUGLAS.
1894.

CONTENTS.

VOL. II.

CHAPTER XIV.—1818.

v

CHAPTER XV.—1819.

CHAPTER XVI.—1820.

CHAPTER XVII.—1821.

CHAPTER XVIII.—1822.

CHAPTER XIX.—1823.

CHAPTER XX.—1824.

CONTENTS

CHAPTER XXI.—1825.

JANUARY—JUNE.

CHAPTER XXII.—1825.

JULY—AUGUST.—IRISH EXCURSION.

CHAPTER XXIII.—1825.
August—November.

CHAPTER XXIV.—1825.
November—December.

APPENDICES.

INDEX.

LETTERS

CHAPTER XIV

1818

EDINBURGH AND ABBOTSFORD

"Harp and carp, Thomas," she said ;
"Harp and carp along wi' me ;
And if ye dare to kiss my lips,
Sure of your bodie I will be."—

"Betide me weel, betide me woe,
That weird shall never daunton me."—
Syne he has kiss'd her rosy lips,
All underneath the Eildon Tree.

"Now, ye maun go wi' me," she said ;
"True Thomas, ye maun go wi' me ;
And ye maun serve me seven years,
Thro' weal or woe as may chance to be."

Thomas the Rhymer.

Buildings and rural affairs at Abbotsford.

Scottish Regalia Commission, February.

Handseling of the new house, October.

Accepts offer of Baronetcy, November.

Ballad, *Battle of Sempach*.

Account of Scottish Regalia, printed March 1818, published in 12mo, 1819, *Miscellanies*, vol. vii.

Tales of my Landlord, second series; *Heart of Midlothian*, 4 vols., published by Constable, June.

Essays on Provincial Antiquities of Scotland, 2 vols. 4to, 1819-26, London, Arch.

Contribution to Burt's *Letters*.

Contributions to Reviews—

Douglas on Military Bridges, *Quarterly Review*, No. 36, January.

Kirkton's Scottish History, *Quarterly Review*, No. 36, January.

Childe Harold, canto iv., *Quarterly Review*, No. 37, April.

Shelley's Frankenstein, *Blackwood*, March.

Gourgaud, *Blackwood*, November.

Maturin's Women, *Edinburgh Review*, No. 59, September.

CHAPTER XIV.

TO MORRITT.

MY DEAR MORRITT,—I was twice on the point of setting out for Rokeby last autumn, but in the one case the necessity of superintending a particular part of my building stopped me, and in the other mine old enemy the cramp grippet me by the pit of the stomach and gave it a cruel twist. Indeed this unhallowed disease seemed to constitute itself a monthly visitor of my frame. Happily, however, as the disorder became chronic it grew gradually less violent, ceased to affect my stomach so very acutely, and in its last visitation gave way to the use of anodynes, which used to be violently rejected while I was in a state of sufferance; so I have great hope it will shade away altogether.

Long may you enjoy your extended dominions.[1] I feel no slight interest in learning that Brignal Banks have been added to Rokeby, so that the whole exquisitely beautiful course of the Greta through its most romantic glades is subjected to your taste and judgment, and safe alike from waste and spoliation, and from the yet more formidable horrors of mistaken and misled beautifiers of creation. I claim a return of your congratulations; for *Vive la plume*, the public taste, or rather voracious appetite for fictitious narrative, has done for me what your kind, well-judging relative has performed for you, and has enabled

---

[1] Morritt's uncle had just purchased the estate of Brignal, for the purpose of adding it to Rokeby.

me to make a spacious accession of territory. Abbotsford now covers ten or twelve hundred acres, two or three hundred of which are such woodland as might make a figure in Lilliput; moreover my lake is but a millpond, my brooks but *sykes*, and even of Tweed, notwithstanding its romantic, poetical, and historical celebrity, it may truly be said *minuit presentia famam.* But what of that? every crow thinks her own egg [whitest], and I amuse myself as well as I can by laying the ground-work of future beauties in a tolerably waste region.

My neighbours in the meanwhile get, not beef and beer, poor fellows, but bannocks and buttermilk, by my frolics, which in these hard times they are right glad to come by; and when I want to realise what beauty is, I have only to come to Rokeby and enjoy your *present* and my *future.* . . .

. . . I trust you have read Rob[1] by this time. I did not much write-him *con amore*, and I think he smells of the cramp, as the Bishop of Grenada's sermon did of apoplexy. Above all, I had too much flax on my distaff, and as it did not consist with my patience or my plan to make a fourth volume I was obliged at last to draw a rough, coarse, and hasty thread. But the book is very well liked here, and has rub'd off in great stile. I have two stories on the anvil (a continuation of the *Tales of my Landlord*)[2] far superior to *Rob Roy* in point of interest.

---

[1] *Rob Roy* was published December 31st, 1817, and a copy sent to Morritt as a New Year's gift.

[2] Referring to the *Heart of Midlothian*, then running through the press under the guidance of James Ballantyne, to whom the following note was addressed:—

"DEAR JAMES,—I would be sorry the difference you complain of did not exist. You are to consider R[obertson] writes his letter [see W. N., vol. xii. pp. 144-5] in the strong hope of escaping himself, in the resolution of at least dying game,—in short, like a blackguard as he is. The circumstances of his friend's death, his own escape, and the affair of Porteous stir up those latent energies which have a very different and more striking character. If he had been a man of a regularly dignified cast of mind he could not have been in the

But my immediate labour has been in behalf of my friend
Terry, the comedian, in whom, on account of his sense,
information, and modesty I take a great interest. He has
named a child after me, and I am preparing a god-
father's gift in the shape of a drama.[1]   But godfathers, as
in the time of conjurors and fairies, may append what
conditions they please to their gifts, and mine is that as I
take no concern in the merit or in the emoluments of the
piece in case of success, so I shall only be damn'd by
proxy if damn'd I am. In a word, Terry takes his chance,
and I believe there will be no medium, for if it does
not succeed very decidedly, it will be damn'd most in-
fernally. I have tried to coax the public to relax some of
the rules of criticism, and to be amused with that medley
of tragic and comic which life presents us, not only in the
same course of action but in the same character. To
deprecate all rigidity of judgment, I introduce the mar-
vellous, the absurd, and something like the heroic, all to
make the gruel slab.[2]

Thus you see, as one good turn merits another, and
as Terry named his first-born after me, so I have named
my first-born drama after him. Keep this matter a dead
secret. Mrs. Scott and the bairns beg their kindest respects. I hope we shall meet on one side of the border
or the other this season. . . . My respects attend Miss
Morritt, and need I add how much I ever am, dear Morritt,
most truly yours,   WALTER SCOTT.

scrape. He is a Poins by nature and
habit, by strong circumstance a Moor
or a Bertram.—Yours, etc.   W. S.
   "The whole story must be mournful. There is no way of changing
the tone that I can discover, for it
is a mournful story. In fact it will
thrive the better, for novelty is half
the battle."
   [1] *The Doom of Devorgoil*, founded
on a Galloway tradition furnished
by Joseph Train. This melodrama
was never put upon the stage, nor
was it published until 1830, when
it appeared in an octavo volume
with *Auchendrane*. The legend
itself is told in a letter to Terry
with far greater power than in the
dramatic medley.—See *Life*, vol. v.
pp. 198-203.
   [2] "Make the gruel thick and
slab."—*Macbeth*, Act IV. sc. 1.

TO LADY LOUISA STUART.

EDINBURGH, *January 16th*, 1818.

MY DEAR LADY LOUISA,—I would have written to you long since but for the very melancholy event at Bothwell,[1] which, knowing the deep effect it would produce on your mind, I felt reluctant to touch upon. From the deep regret with which I myself look back to the virtues and talents of which we were so unexpectedly deprived, I can in some measure judge of the distress occasioned by that deprivation to the most beloved and intimate of her friends. It has never been my lot to see so much talent with such total absence, not merely of vanity, but even as it seem'd of the very consciousness of possessing it, and so much wit with such perfect good-nature and mildness of disposition. Amid the circle of friends whom I respected and loved some years since, fate has made many blanks never to be supplied, and none more regretted than Lady Douglas and the Duchess. I often look round and feel that I want motive and spirits to undertake the trifling tasks which used to give them pleasure. Though different in many things, they resembled each other eminently in precision and soundness of judgment upon men and manners, (which is seldom found in high rank, where opportunities of observation are limited considerably,) in active benevolence, and in manners which form the delight of society. It is in vain to hope that these blanks can be filled up, and I can only hope that those whom I have still remaining to set some value on my respect and attachment, will hold it higher than it might otherwise deserve from the recollection of those whom we jointly call'd friends. . . . The Duke comes to town on the 29th, and in a few days afterwards, I presume, will afford us his

---

[1] The death of Lady Douglas, June 1817.

presence at a very interesting research after the *Regalia*
of Scotland. I do not know if your Ladyship is aware
that the Crown, Sceptre, etc., of Scotland were at the date
of the Union deposited with great formality in a strong
chest, and the chest placed in what is call'd the Crown
room in the Castle of Edinburgh, there to be preserved for
the greater security. But notwithstanding the formality
of a public instrument, describing the Regalia and announcing the manner of their being deposited in the chest
aforesaid, and notwithstanding also a special article of the
Union declaring that these symbols of independent royalty
should never be removed from Scotland, it has been
always surmised that the Regalia, with our Peers and people
of quality, have at some time or other taken flight from
Edinburgh, and never stopped till they arrived in London
—whether they remained there or took another flight to
Hanover was left in alarming uncertainty. Some years
ago[1] a commission was granted to open the Crown room to
search for certain records which it was conjectured might
have been deposited there. They found no such records, and
being men rather of sound legal judgment than of irritable
imagination, they did not suffer themselves to be so much
interested by a huge chest, which was the only thing they
saw in the room, as to forget that in the eye of the law, a
chest lid is not a *door*, and that their commission only
enjoin'd them to enter the room, not to open the chest.
Accordingly, they left matters as they found them, and so
they remain at this day.[2] Now when I was in London I
was honoured with an interview at Carlton House, in
which it was my theme to speak about these Regalia,
and hence has in due time, and after all delays reasonably
to be expected, come down a commission to various
persons, my unworthy self included, to search for the
Regalia and report upon the state in which they may

---

[1] In 1794.   [2] See Cockburn's *Memorials*, p. 348.

be found. Now, don't you see us, Lady Louisa, Nobles, Officers of State, Governors, Generals, Crown Lawyers, and so forth, moving into the Crown room like the Committee appointed to search for and report upon the Cock Lane ghost—turning upon our heels and marching out again like the wise men of Gotham, without having found any thing but dust and cobwebs? As I maintain a correspondence with Mr. Jedediah Cleishbotham, I intend to recommend to him a tale founded upon an earlier adventure of these same Regalia. Your Ladyship remembers that in Charles II's. time (before his accession) these Regalia were kept in Dunottar Castle, and were (when it was besieged by the English) smuggled out by a clergyman's wife under a quantity of *hards*[1] of lint. They were buried in the old kirk at Kinneff, I think. Old Noll got some scent of them, and the minister and his wife were put to the torture, which they sustain'd with perfect constancy. At the Restoration they were restored also, and the fate of the persons concerned in their preservation was a striking instance of the partiality of a court. Keith, a younger son of the Earl Marischal, being governor of his father's Castle of Dunottar (though abroad when it was besieged) was made Earl of Kintore: Ogilvie of Barras (deputy governor), by whom the Castle was gallantly defended, was only made a baronet; and the minister and his wife, who had been the actual agents in the preservation of the Crown Jewels, and had their fingers and their knees disjointed for keeping the secret, got *Nothing at all*—"a goodly medicine for their aching bones."[2] I think this may be made a capital story, and Jedediah, without any sacrifice of his own opinions, may make his peace honourably with his Presbyterian friends if he can make a lively picture of a good divine of that persuasion and his good dame. The

---

[1] Hards or hardyn, the refuse of flax.

[2] *Troilus and Cressida*, Act v. sc. 2.

editing a new edition of Somers's tracts some years ago
made me wonderfully well acquainted with the little traits
which mark'd parties and characters in the 17th century,
and the embodying them is really an amusing task. Besides, I have the spirit of improvement strong on me, and
the rather that in these hard times it is of great consequence to my poor neighbours that I should carry on
my planting, hedging, and ditching. The very large
profits which have arisen from these smuggling adventures not only enable me to indulge myself with absolute
prudence and propriety, but moreover have enabled me
to make some very desirable purchases adjacent to
Abbotsford, which is now a valuable property.

Ever your most faithful and respectful humble servant,

WALTER SCOTT.

TO JOHN RICHARDSON.

EDINBURGH, 16th January 1818.

... I AM glad you liked the volumes[1] I sent you; it
is odd these things continue to have attraction, and very
odd how I should have been led into such a strain of
composition. But e'en so be it, for I might have laboured
long at anything intrinsically useful before I had extended
my domains at Abbotsford in the fashion I have done.
And I really think I may so far do some good by giving
striking, and, to the best of my information and abilities,
correct likenesses of characters long since passed away.

TO THE DUKE OF BUCCLEUCH.

EDINBURGH, 17th January 1818.

MY DEAR LORD,—The drama of the Iron Chest will
certainly be postponed until your Grace can be one of the

[1] Rob Roy.

dramatis personæ. We propose Wednesday, 4th February, for the fatal day, as it is a holiday (in some measure) at the Courts, and allows the legal part of the Commissioners to attend with ease. I intended to have asked your Grace to take an early beefsteak in Castle Street, but I find the Advocate is very desirous you should spend the day with him. . . . To use Lady Anne Hamilton's elegant phrase, your Grace must certainly be ashamed of yourself for laying out so much of your revenue in feeding a parcel of clod-hoppers, with their wives and squalling children, when you see how my Lord Darlington rewards public spirit and literary merit, in the person of Mr. Stone. I approve as much of his taste in expending his fortune as of his care in turning the most minute parts of it to annual profit. It would be long before your Grace, fond as you are of shooting, would have thought of converting Baliol's Tower, in the ruins of Barnard Castle, into a manufactory of partridge shot, although he makes about £30 a year by destroying one of the most curious vaulted roofs in England. "The Lord deliver me from Sir Harry Vane," said Cromwell, and he usually spoke to the purpose. The enormities of the Chinese room at Raby Castle ought not to be forgotten.

To return to the Regalia, we have agreed to say nothing of the precise day. It is possible we may have the fate of those sapient persons who went to the vault at Clerkenwell to speak with the Cock Lane ghost, of whose expedition Churchill has recorded—

> "Silent, all three went in—about
> All three turn'd, silent, and came out."

On these occasions the fewer spectators the better, and therefore to keep the laugh among ourselves we have agreed to say nothing of the day fixed.

The storm was tremendous here, and the Devil has plainly proved himself to be the prince of the power of the air, for he has blown the beautiful Gothic pinnacles off the tower of Bishop Sandford's Episcopal chapel, which have fallen on the roof and much damaged the building, and the wind has not stirred a stone of the ugly hulk of stone and lime which no one but the Devil or Edin^r bailies would have built upon the North Bridge. I am trembling for the fate of my tower at Abbotsford. Atkinson will triumph, for I preferred my own plan to his in finishing the battlements, alleging in my defence that the place was a Delilah of my imagination, not perhaps strictly *correct*, but, like Mrs. Samson, certainly very pretty.— Ever your Grace's truly obliged, and faithful,

WALTER SCOTT.

FROM LADY LOUISA STUART.

GLOUCESTER PLACE, *Feb.* 16, 1818.

. . . I HAVE read *Rob Roy* twice . . . and now I can fairly say I like it much, tho' possibly not *so* much as its elder brothers. The scale with me would be *Waverley, Old Mortality, Guy Mannering*—so far I am sure. I am not sure which of the three others I could positively prefer; there are striking beauties in each. In *Rob Roy* the painting of character is as vivid as in anything the author ever wrote: Rob himself, Die Vernon, Nicol Jarvie, Andrew Fairservice, not to speak of the Tory baronet and his cubs, or the Jesuit Rashleigh. The beginning and end, I am afraid, I quarrel with; the mercantile part is heavy, but some part always must be so to give what painters call relief, and beginnings signify little. Ends signify more. Now, I fear the end of this is huddled, as if the author were tired, and wanted to get rid of his personages as fast as he could, knocking them on the head without mercy. Die Vernon has what a Lord Bellamont (famous in my day and before it for profligacy and affectation)

used to call such "*a catastrophical countenance*" that one
cannot reconcile oneself to her being married and settled
like her sober neighbours. It is almost as bad as if Flora
M'Ivor had married the Colonel's nephew. This work
seems to me more sparing than the rest in descriptions
of scenery; however, it has one super-excellence where
Helen Macgregor appears to thrill one's blood and over-
power one's reason. You see I give my opinion (let it be
worth something or nothing) as if I were writing to a
person not supposed to be any way *sib* to the mysterious
Unknown: but it is because I believe you have too distinguishing a taste to relish all sugar and treacle. Goldsmith's metaphor was bad when he said—"Who peppers
the highest is surest to please," for flattery resembles neither
pepper nor salt. *Apropos* of the mystery, those who see
far into a mill-stone are now sure that the *Tales of my
Landlord* were written by a different person, and parts
of them by different hands. When they give their reasons
with a complacent delight in their own sagacity, I think
to myself, how often must I have talked as much wise
nonsense upon subjects which I knew nothing about. . . .
Very truly yours,   L. STUART.

TO LADY ABERCORN.

March 11 [1818].

MY DEAR LADY ABERCORN,—. . . I think you will not
doubt my deep and sincere commiseration in the great
sorrow with which you have lately been afflicted, and that
my sympathy is the greater, as it is one in which comfort
and consolation must for some time necessarily appear
intrusive.[1] What indeed can the wisest and most affectionate friend tell us, except that we must submit to evils
which are irremediable, and which are part of the tenure

[1] The Marquis of Abercorn died January 27, 1818.

by which we hold life, since we cannot pass our years here without parting from our dearest and most attached friends. I do not therefore waste words on a subject so painful, although I might claim a particular share in your sorrow, not only on account of the sincere interest I must always take in what concerns your Ladyship personally, but also in consideration of the eminent kindness which the regretted subject of your sorrow showed to my family, and his personal attention to myself. Many recollections, which I will not distress you, my dearest friend, by recapitulating, press upon me while I am writing to you.

My principal thoughts, however, are upon you. It is, I fear, scarce possible that I can in any point of view be of the slightest use to you, but if I can, do not forget you have a right by unremitted kindness and many active good offices to command anything which may be in my sphere. If your interest should chance to be involved in any of the affairs here, I hope you will allow me as an old friend to offer any assistance that may be in my power. To use any knowledge I have, either of these matters or of the law of the country in your behalf, would make my acquaintance with either valuable in my own eyes. At any rate, may I hope your Ladyship will let me hear from you when tranquillity and the state of your mind will permit? Believe me, if there is a moment in which a heart of good dispositions beats more warmly towards a friend, it is in the hours of their affliction. I have not ventured to write sooner, perhaps even this is too early, but it is easily thrown aside. I have however constantly heard of you through G. Wright and Mrs. Kemble.—I have the honour to be, with great respect and regard, dear Lady Marchioness, your most faithful and obedient servant,

WALTER SCOTT.

TO SOUTHEY.

ABBOTSFORD, *23rd March* [1818].

. . . Is there no chance of our meeting this year? You owe me two visits. . . . I want to show you my trees, which are Lilliputian, and my lake which is a mill-pond, and my cascade which is not made yet, and my new house, which looks like a thing you dream of. Sophia is much honoured and flattered by your recollection. She is a tall girl now, and a good useful housekeeper. She is keeping house for me here for the present, as the weather is too severe for Mrs. Scott to face the country till the sun comes earlier over the hill. I have also with me an old and faithful crony from the day we carried our satchels to school together, Capt. Adam Ferguson, the son of the historian. With the unceasing good spirits which find subject for exercise in the most trifling passages of human life, of which he is the most acute observer I have ever seen, he has borne and parried a world of misfortunes, which must have crushed any one possessed of less elasticity of spirit. Besides this unceasing fund of interest, I may converse at pleasure with my dogs and two yoke of huge oxen, who turn up the glebe with a grace altogether bucolical.[1] Or I may call in the aid of two or three country neighbours, and talk upon two subjects of common interest,—a circular saw which I have lately established as an experiment, and an intended railroad to connect us with the coal and lime works of Lothian. . . .

I saw Humboldt when I was at Paris, but was not made known to him. To you his acquirements must have been peculiarly interesting.[2] Capt. Basil Hall is with his father just now, and visits me often. I respect him and Capt. Maxwell much for their considerate conduct

---

[1] His yoke of oxen were named Og and Bashan.

[2] See Southey's *Life*, vol. iv. pp. 295-297.

to Loo Choo, which contrasted with Capt. Maxwell's
spirited behaviour at Canton, and his fortitude in the
desperate circumstances in which he was placed by the
loss of the *Alceste*, serves to show that moderation is
always connected with true valour. He gave a very
lively and interesting account of his interview with Bony
at St. Helena, in which the latter maintained his credit
as a charlatan. One trait was laughable enough: it related to the manners of the natives of Loo Choo. "What
arms have they?" said Bony. "None," answered Hall. "Ah,
you mean no fire-arms, but they have sword, bows, slings,
spears?" "No such thing, nor any other weapon so far
as we could discover." *Diable—pas même des poignards?*
A ridiculous counterpart to this story was, that when
Capt. Hall told it to old Vansittart,[1] he laughed heartily,
and immediately gave a similar proof of technicality by
admiring the simplicity of the savages, who could exist
without coin'd money or any other representative of value.
—Remember me most kindly to Mrs. Southey, and believe
me ever, my dear Southey, yours with true regard,

WALTER SCOTT.

TO MISS EDGEWORTH.

April 1818.

. . . I ASSURE you, dear Madam, there is no person in
the world of literature for whose name I have more sincere
respect, or in whose regard I esteem myself more highly
honoured, or whom I would have more pleasure in obliging. . . .

. . . You have had a merit transcendent in my eyes, of
raising your national character in the scale of public
estimation, and making the rest of the British Empire
acquainted with the peculiar and interesting character of

---

[1] The Chancellor of the Exchequer, afterwards Lord Bexley.

a people too long neglected and too severely oppressed. Public opinion, though ·a slow, is at length a sure, redresser of wrongs, and upon this, in respect to Ireland, you have produced a strong and abiding effect; and notwithstanding all the unfavourable circumstances which seem fated to retard the amelioration of Ireland, I cannot help thinking that writings which teach its natives their force and their weakness, and show to their fellow-subjects their real value and worth, must prepare both for a gradual but happy change. . . .

I do not rate the unknown author of our Scottish tales so high as to place him in the same rank either of merit or utility, and yet I think highly of many of his works, and expect to be gratified by those which are still promised from the same abundant and concealed source. ·

I do assure you I am quite an impartial judge upon the occasion, and that you do me too much honour in supposing that I have any interest in these narrations.

The whole story told (as Miss Baillie informed me) by a Sir Somebody Gordon about my having intimated to him my acquiescence in the report of my being the author of the *Antiquary* is so absolutely false that I do not even know such a person. . . .

TO THE SAME.

ABBOTSFORD, 10*th May* 1818.

IT was destined I was not to find the letter until I returned hither, for an unfortunate partiality for little cabinets and great cabinets, and all sorts of concealments and pigeon holes, makes it very difficult for me to know where any particular paper may happen to be. I regret that the delay this has occasioned may make me seem, what I would most unwillingly be thought, slack or careless in complying with your request. The letter contains an excellent and animated defence of Dr. Darwin, written with the spirit and feeling which your late respected relative was most likely to have exerted in behalf of a friend. Still, however, it does not appear to me to shake the powerful evidence that the lines in dispute were claimed by Miss Seward during Dr. Darwin's lifetime, and published as hers and with her name. After all, I do not think the verses very much worth struggling about. But the liberality of the letter does great honour (like everything he did) to Mr. E.'s memory. I found in the same drawer a letter of my own to Mr. Edgeworth, begun after my return from France and never finished,—a memorial among too many others how often I am misled by an unfortunate habit of procrastination into seeming indifferent to the kindness of my best friends. Latterly, indeed, that is, for the last twelve months, I have had very indifferent health to plead as an excuse for being an irregular correspondent. I began within these two last months to feel like myself again, so that I trust I shall not have that painful apology any longer. I am much obliged to you for thinking favourably of my attempts in poetry. They have one title to indulgent compassion, which is, that they are a sort of orphans for whom their ostrich parent cares most exceedingly little. In the earlier part of my literary life, partly from temper, partly from principle, having observed how very unhappy literary persons are made (not to say ridiculous into the bargain) by pitching their thoughts and happiness upon popular fame, I resolved to avoid at least that frailty, and think as little about my poems when committed to the public as I well could. It is only when you, Miss Edgeworth, or a few others whose talents and candour rank high with me, are kind enough to say that you receive pleasure from these poems, that I ever think of them with satisfaction, or indeed think of them at all. I have not read one of them since they were printed, excepting, last year, the *Lady of the Lake*, which I liked better than I expected, but not well enough to induce me to go through the rest; so I may say with Macbeth—

> "I am afraid to think of what I have done;
> Look on't again, I dare not."

This much of Matilda[1] I recollect, for that is not so easily forgotten, that she was attempted from the existing person and character of a lady who is now no more, so that I am particularly flattered with your distinguishing it from the others, which are in general mere shadows. Thus far have I written amidst the clank and clang produced by two noisy young borderers, my son and a cousin, who are wearing out a day by fencing with their naked broadswords to the eminent peril of their own heads, to animate which conflict a probationary piper is exercising a new and not over well-tuned pair of bagpipes. All this being literally the case, I really hardly know whether I am writing sense or nonsense. At least I must be comforted with the idea that my family is making a noise in the world. My rustic employments are so numerous, and require so much of my own eye, that I have no thoughts this season of quitting Scotland. If I can get away in winter I should like much to see Italy, but I fear I cannot do this very conveniently.

Ireland I trust I will one day visit, but I must first get my dominions here put into some sort of order. I have of late been rather an extensive planter and encloser in proportion to the extent of my property, and these operations require a good deal of personal superintendence. . . .

WALTER SCOTT.

FROM LADY LOUISA STUART.

SHEFFIELD PLACE, August 11th, 1818.

Now for it, dear Mr. Scott. I can speak to the purpose, as I have not only read it[2] myself, but am in a house

---

[1] Matilda in *Rokeby*.—See *Journal*, vol. i. p. 404.   [2] *Heart of Midlothian.*

where everybody is tearing it out of each other's hands, and talking of nothing else. So much for its success,—the more flattering because it overcomes a prejudice. People were beginning to say the author would wear himself out; it was going on too long in the same key, and no striking notes could possibly be produced. On the contrary, I think the interest is stronger here than in any of the former ones (always excepting my first love *Waverley*), and one may congratulate you upon having effected what many have tried to do and nobody yet succeeded in,— making the perfectly good character the most interesting. Of late days especially, since it has been the fashion to write moral and even religious novels, one might almost say of some of the wise good heroines what a lively girl once did to me of her well-meaning aunt, " Upon my word, she is enough to make anybody wicked." And, though beauty and talents are heaped on the right side, the writer in spite of himself is sure to put agreeableness on the wrong; the person from whose errors he means you should take warning runs away with your secret partiality in the meantime.

Had this very story been conducted by a common hand, Effie would have attracted all our concern and sympathy, Jeanie only cold approbation. Whereas Jeanie, without youth, beauty, genius, warm passions, or any other novel perfection, is here our object from beginning to end. This is " inlisting the affections in the cause of virtue " ten times more than ever Richardson did, for whose male and female pedants, all-excelling as they are, I never could care half so much as I found myself inclined to do for Jeanie before I finished the first volume. Is it possible that you had at all in your eye what my wishes pointed to, when I wrote to you last winter? If not, you will think the question strange; yet with all the differences of situation, improvement, refinement, etc., nay, with all the power to charm and dazzle, there was a strong likeness of character : the same steady attachment to rectitude, the same simplicity and singleness of heart, the same inward humility, the same forgetfulness of self, the same strong, plain, straightforward understanding always hitting exactly right. Superficial observers took for granted this last could not be where there was so much wit and taste, but thus it was notwithstanding. Let me dream that you designed this resemblance, whether you did or not; I would rather be indulged in the thought than set right, and I should like it the better for being so veiled by circumstances that the rest of the world would pass it without observation.

You know I tell you my opinion just as I should do to a third person, and I trust the freedom is not unwelcome. I was a little tired of your Edinburgh lawyers in the introduction; mere English people will be more so, as well as impatient of the passages alluding to Scotch law throughout. Mr. Saddletree will not entertain them. The latter part of the fourth volume unavoidably flags to a certain degree; after Jeanie is happily settled at Roseneath, we have no more to wish for. But the chief fault I have to find relates to the reappearance and shocking fate of the boy. I hear on all sides—"Oh, I do not like that." I cannot say what I would have had instead, but that I do not like either; it is a lame, huddled conclusion. I know you so well in it by the by! You grow tired yourself, want to get rid of the story, and hardly care how. Sir George Staunton finishes his career very fitly; he ought not to die in his bed, and for Jeanie's sake one would not have him hanged. It is unnatural, though, that he should ever have gone within twenty miles of the Tolbooth, or shown his face in the streets of Edinburgh, or dined at a public meeting, if the Lord Commissioner had been his brother. Here ends my *per contra* account. The opposite

page would make my letter too long if I entered equally
into particulars. Carlisle and Corby castles in *Waverley*
did not affect me more deeply than the prison and trial
scenes. The end of poor Madge Wildfire is also most
pathetic; the meeting at Muschat's Cairn most tremendous. Dumbiedikes and Rory Bean are delightful;
and I shall own that my old family prejudices were
secretly gratified by the light in which you place Uncle
John of Argyle, whom Mr. Coxe so ran down to please
Lord Orford. You have drawn him to the very life. I
heard so much of him in my youth, so many anecdotes,
so often—"as the Duke of Argyle used to say"—that I
really believe I am almost as good a judge as if 1 had seen
and lived with him. My grandfather dying very young
left his sons to the guardianship of their mother's brothers,
who placed my father at Eton school when he was seven
years old, and took him themselves in his holidays, while
their sister lived in Bute with her daughters. John
having a wife and family and country-seats in England,
my father was of course mostly under his roof, and had
the feelings of a son rather than a nephew towards him.
My grandmother Wortley too, as you may see by her letters,
particularly admired him; and my beloved mother has
told me that when she married (in 1737, the very time)
he was still remarkably handsome, with manners more
graceful and engaging than she ever saw in any one else,
the most agreeable person in conversation, the best teller
of a story. When fifty-seven thus captivates eighteen,
the natural powers of pleasing must be extraordinary.
You have likewise coloured Queen Caroline exactly right,
but I was bred up in another creed about Lady Suffolk,
of whom, as a very old deaf woman, I have some faint
recollection. My mother knew her intimately, and never
would allow she had been the King's mistress, though she
owned it was currently believed. She said he had just

enough liking for her to make the Queen very civil to her, and very jealous and spiteful; the rest remained always uncertain, at most,—like a similar scandal in our days, where I, for one, imagine love of seeming influence on one side, and love of lounging, of an easy house, and a good dinner on the other, to be all the criminal passions concerned. However, I confess my mother had that in herself which made her not ready to think the worst of her fellow-women.

Did you ever hear the history of John, Duke of Argyle's marriage, and constant attachment before and after, to a woman not handsomer or much more elegant than Jeanie Deans, though very unlike her in understanding? I can give it you, if you wish it, for it is at my fingers' ends. I was so much the youngest of a numerous family that I had no playfellow, and for that reason listened with all my ears to the grown people's conversation, most especially when my mother and the friends of her youth got upon old stories; nor did I lose my taste for them when I grew old enough to converse with her on equal terms, and inquire into particulars. Now I am an ancient tabby myself, I should be a great treasure of anecdote to anybody who had the same humour, but I meet with few who have. They read vulgar tales in books, Wraxall and so forth, what the footmen and maids only gave credit to at the moment, but they desire no further information. I dare swear many of your readers never heard of the Duke of Argyle before. "Pray who was Sir Robert Walpole?" they ask me, "and when did he live?"—or perhaps— "was not the great Lord Chatham in Queen Anne's days?"

Amongst the persons most pleased here is Lady Charlotte Lindsay. She has the true North humour and love of humour, and she does enjoy it heartily. They have, to help them, an exemplification on two legs in their country apothecary, whom you have painted over and over without the honour of knowing him; an old, dry, arguing, prosing

obstinate Scotchman, very shrewd, rather sarcastic, a
sturdy whig and presbyterian, *tirant un peu sur le démo-
crat.* Your books are bird-lime to him, however; he hovers
about the house to obtain a volume when others have done
with it. I long to ask him whether douce Davie was any
way sib to him. He acknowledges he would not now go
to Muschat's cairn at night for any money, he had such a
horror of it sixty years ago when a laddie. But I am
come to the end of my fourth page, and will not tire you
with any more scribbling. Let me inquire after your
family. My friend Sophia is now, I suppose, a young lady
at large, and her brother at the university; and the
younger ones much what I remember them. Pray give
my kindest compliments to Mrs. Scott, and ever believe
me, your much obliged and most sincere,   L. STUART.

P.S.—I should have found you out in that one paren-
thesis—"for the man was mortal, and had been a schoolmaster"—if I had known nothing and the whole world
had told me the contrary. Once more Adieu!

FROM LADY ABERCORN.

16th August [1818].

. . . SOME time ago I received the last 4 vols. of
Tales of my Landlord, "from *the Author.*" Who he is I
probably shall never know from himself, tho' with the
world I am inclined to suspect. All I can say is that the
first three vols. kept me in such a state of agitation and
interest that I could hardly get on with it. Certainly the
feeling was mixed with a severe pang, and as he who knew
how to rate the talents of the writer was not here to give
me his opinion, and to enjoy the perusal of the work, I
almost wished the book had never come out. I should
be sorry to think any one else but the one I imagine the
author had written them. . . .

TO LADY ABERCORN.

MELVILLE CASTLE, *10th Sept.* 1818.

MY DEAR LADY ABERCORN,—Your kind letter found me on my return to Abbotsford, which I had left for three weeks to make a short tour. I spent a week with the Duke of Buccleuch at his noble castle of Drumlanrig, where he is repairing, as fast as anything save time can do it, the devastation made by the late Duke of Queensberry. Imagine a man having the heart to cut at one time three or four hundred acres of noble wood which had stood for upwards of a century. Nothing but the lapse of another hundred years can make good the damage, but the present Duke has already planted double the quantity of wood, and the young plantations already begin to look *beautiful,* though the eye of this generation can never see them *grand.*

I also went to Rokeby to see my friend Morritt for a few days. In passing Bishop-Auckland we sent our names, according to form, with a request to see the Bishop of Durham's residence, and he was so good as to be *cicerone* himself, besides giving us an excellent breakfast. He is the finest old gentleman of his age I ever saw— smooth-faced and without wrinkles, perfect in eye and ear and intellect, and actually in his eighty-fifth year. One seldom sees extreme old age so agreeable.[1]

Since my return I have been busy with my farming matters, and with receiving visitors, chiefly travellers[2] who

---

[1] The Hon. Shute Barrington, who died in 1826.

[2] During the summer, Edward Everett, in his 24th year, came to Abbotsford, introduced by Gifford. His letters show how much he enjoyed the visit, and even forty years later the then distinguished scholar and orator wrote a glowing account of it to Mr. Allibone.—See *Dict. Eng. Lit.,* p. 1966.

The following letter to Sir Walter gives a pleasant idea of the inconveniences of great popularity :—

CAMBRIDGE, NEW ENGLAND,
28th March 1820.

DEAR SIR,—Just before I had the happiness of visiting Abbotsford, a party of ladies and gentlemen tra-

come to see Melrose. The pleasantest have been a Mr. and Mrs. Hamilton, of Dublin, the last a sister of the Duchess of Wellington, with the same simple and unaffected manners, but a good deal more liveliness than the Duchess seems to possess, or at least than I chanced to see her exhibit. The others were travelling esquires and bankers, and I don't know whom beside, for I think all England is upon a tour this fine season. I have come this length to spend a couple of quiet days with Lord Melville, who, with his Lady, have been residing here since the beginning of August. A peaceful day is a greater rarity to him than most folks, and so much for politics and ambition.[1]

I begged the publishers of these novels you inquire so much about to send you an early copy, as I thought it would amuse you. If your Ladyship has received also

velling into Scotland, and determined to see you, wandered into your enclosure and surprised you seated before your door, in that condition into which Horace says your great master Homer sometimes fell. This fact I have upon the authority of Miss Sophia, who came out and found them all standing round you in a ring, without breaking the quiet of your siesta. And it was a circumstance within my own observation, that two worthy pilgrims, who came down in the coach with me to Melrose, wandered over your estate for two days, in the design of falling in with you, and came at last near having their desire more than gratified; for we came bounding over the wall upon them, in pursuit of a poor hare, with the great deerhound in the van, in a manner to discompose the bows of the alarmed gentlemen. Resolved to save my friend, who offers you this, the chance of similar perils and étourderies, I have ventured to give him a regular letter of introduction. Pray receive with your usual kindness this fair New England shoot of the Old English stock, and persuade Mrs. Scott and Miss Sophia and Anne to take him up to the Mushroom Park, and the Spring of the World's end. If Urisk be still in existence I would solicit for my friend the privilege of being ungrowled at, an immunity I did not enjoy myself. Tell Miss Scott that her sugar almonds are in my desk before me, and Lady Anne that I still retain as faithfully as did ever Knight his Lady's favor, a bit of her sash, which I had the audacity to cut off. I am, dear sir, your obliged and affectionate servant, EDWARD EVERETT.

[1] In the course of a few weeks Lord and Lady Melville returned Scott's visit at Abbotsford.—*Life*, vol. v. p. 368.

one from the author, I apprehend you have been doubly provided.[1] I do not hear that they are ever like to be owned. I observe among other liberties the papers, in the lack of better subjects, choose to take with the affairs of literature, they are not contented with ascribing these novels to me, but are so good as to intimate that I am at this present moment writing a tragedy. I would much sooner write an opera for Punch's puppet-show.

That you, my dear friend, are pretty well in health I rejoice to hear. Time, the slow but sure comforter, must be the physician for other sorrows. . . . Life cannot be protracted without the pangs of surviving much that is valuable, and much that is dear to us. They must pass from us or we from them; such is the law of our existence, and the sad but quieting reflection that in our most acute deprivations we share but the general lot of mortality, is the only argument which on many occasions presents itself to the mourner's mind, or can be justly offered by others when recommending patience under affliction.

My own life is positively a blank, but a very agreeable one. The cultivation and improvement of my small estate has been for some years my chief amusement and occupation. I have given up all country sports to my son. . . . His younger brother shows much lively talent, and will, if spared, in all probability make some figure either in the law or in the diplomatic line; at present his age makes choice unnecessary. Mrs. Scott and Sophia send their best respects.

---

[1] Lady Abercorn a few years later, referring to *St. Ronan's Well*, writes to Scott, "By the way, the last was on my table the other day when Robert Gordon, Lord Aberdeen's brother, took it up, and upon opening it, he read 'from the Author;' he observed 'surely this is an avowal, since it comes from the author to you.' I said as I had had some of them sent before in that way, and at other times not, I concluded it done by the printer who sent me books at times, but that I, like the rest of the world, sometimes thought one thing and at others another,—that the handwriting was not yours, etc."

I am ashamed at sending you so stupid an epistle, but it shows my obedience at least to your commands, and that I ever am, dear Lady Abercorn, yours most sincerely and respectfully,   WALTER SCOTT.

TO HIS MOTHER.

ABBOTSFORD, 1*st October.*

I LEARN from your letter with great pleasure that you have heard from Tom. The letter he promised me is not yet arrived, but I trust I shall soon have it, of which I will not fail to acquaint you. We are all here very well, rejoicing in a favourable season, and the appearance of plenty. I am beginning to get rid of my workmen, to my great joy, for my improvements here have hitherto resembled Solomon's temple as little in the silence attending the erection as in the wisdom of the plan. In the meanwhile time draws on, and by and by we shall all meet once more in Edinburgh. I shall have regret in leaving this place, and among the few things make me look forward to the change with pleasure is the prospect of seeing you, I hope as well as when we last met on my flying visit.

Walter pronounces so anxiously for the army that I shall not cross him, for although it is not the line I would have wished *him* to have chosen, yet it is that which, but for circumstances, I would have preferred myself. Besides, I think him remarkably well qualified for the profession. He is a lad of determined courage, and at the same time of perfect good temper, so that I am not afraid of his not doing his duty, and at the same time confident he will not engage in private quarrels. Besides, he shows a talent for mathematics and drawing, as well as for the corresponding branches of natural philosophy, which will be useful to him in the army. It is singular that he would have preferred the engineers' service. But as promotion is very slow in that branch, I intend to get him a commission in the course of eighteen months or so in one of our steady old Scotch regiments, where I can have him well introduced to his commanding-officer, and placed a little under guardianship. When he is perfectly acquainted with his business, I trust, if I live, that in two or three years I may have interest enough to get him into the Quarter-masters' department, or else placed on the staff of some general officer of character and reputation. At least, such is the best plan I can at present form, and in all such cases we can but chuse the best and leave the rest to Providence.

Charlotte, the boys and girls beg to be remembered in all love and duty, and I am always, my dear mother, most affectionately and dutifully your obedient son,

WALTER SCOTT.

FROM LOCKHART.

23 MAITLAND ST., EDINR., *20th October* 1818.

MY DEAR SIR,—Altho' the petty squabbles of pamphlets[1] and magazines cannot very easily be supposed to have reached your ears among the hills at Abbotsford, yet it is possible that from our friend Mr. Ballantyne you may have heard something of a furious bickering in which Wilson and I hastily, and unnecessarily perhaps, have been somewhat engaged. The truth is that those foolish letters of ours were not written with any idea of their ever ceasing to be in MS., and that our conduct in taking any notice of the pamphlet itself was at the best very natural, and therefore may hope to be excused.

Had you happened to be in Edinburgh last week, unwilling as I should have been and must ever be, to intrude

---

[1] A pamphlet called *Hypocrisy Unveiled*, 8vo, Edin. 1818. — See *Life of Christopher North*, by Mrs. Gordon, vol. i. pp. 282-5.

upon you anything likely at all to disturb you, after the very kind notice with which you have been pleased to honour me,[1] I should certainly have been tempted to ask a little of your advice. The time is now gone by for doing so. Every attempt by fair means and *foul* (if any can in such a case be foul) to discover the author has utterly failed. The only person of importance enough to be at all cared about, upon whom any portion of the public suspicion fell, was Mr. Macvey Napier, and I have now before me an entire disavowal of all concern in the matter *upon his honour.*

In this situation of matters I have very little doubt your opinion must be that nothing further remains to be done by any of us—*in presenti* at least. To enter into a series of public denials or explanations in answer to the charges of an unseen and stupid calumniator cannot, I should think, be looked upon as advisable. But Wilson has, I believe, resolved to write to you upon the matter, and knowing as I do the situation of his mind, I thought it would be wrong in me to permit his letter to come to you without a few lines from me also, *commentationis causâ.*

Living in a house full of women—mother, wife, and sister —and perpetually teazed and irritated with the spectacle of their irritation (for what is in the newspapers can be concealed from no one), it is no wonder that one of his keen, ardent, and nervous temperament should have taken the whole matter to heart in a way apparently little worthy of his talents and judgment in other concerns. It is so, however; and in one word, his state has for some days, and sleepless nights, been such that his best friends here have not been entirely without suspicion and dread of something like incipient insanity. . . .

He will write to you in this frenzied state, and there

---

[1] See account of Lockhart and Wilson's first visit to Abbotsford in *Life*, v. pp. 368-393.

is no doubt as to the mode of your answer. But since you are to be troubled with the business at all, may I request that in case the strain of his letter should be as wild as I fear it may be, you would have the very great kindness to write to me, who am calm and *compos*, as well as to him. It is possible, however, that the very act of writing will restore him to his self-possession, and in that case I shall have no occasion to give you so much additional trouble. . . . Believe me, my dear sir, very sincerely yours,   J. G. LOCKHART.

TO LOCKHART.

ABBOTSFORD, 29*th October* [1818].

MY DEAR SIR,—I was favoured with your confidential letter and much obliged by it. Be assured of such advice or aid as I can give at any time you may require it. I am happy to say I have not heard from Wilson, so I hope the irritation of his mind on this unfortunate account has abated. I have not seen, and scarce heard of the libellous publication alluded to, but unquestionably your controversy is with persons who will not scruple to wield a sword unbated and envenomed. John Ballantyne mentioned to me the pamphlet as very abusive, but otherwise contemptibly written. I had not an opportunity to speak of it to his brother, the more prudent and steady person. I trust our friend will soon consider this sort of abuse as the natural attendant not only upon talents, but upon controversy both literary and political. It would be vain to preach total insensibility on such occasions, but a man should have as much as possible the *circum pectus æs triplex* of Horace. I did not approve of the personal and severe attack on Playfair, though extremely well written, and perhaps it is one consequence of such hostility that men of inferior literary consideration endeavour to distinguish themselves

in an alleged vindication of others, when in fact they only
seek to gratify their own envy and malignity, or to enhance
their no-importance. To some such source the late attack
may probably be traced,—obscure and therefore utterly
contemptible, especially if disavowed by those to whom you
have in vain endeavoured to trace it. I hope therefore
that Wilson will set his mind at rest. For yourself, with
your talents, natural and acquired, you have I trust a long
and splendid career before you, and you must expect that
it will be occasionally interrupted or even obscured by the
efforts of the envious or malevolent. The true antidote
consists in so bearing yourself both in life and in literature,
as to command the esteem and approbation of the good
and the wise, to whose opinion in the long-run that of the
rest of the world never fails to become conformable. I beg
you will always have recourse to me without scruple when
you think I can be of any use,—and believe me very much,
your faithful and obedient servant,   WALTER SCOTT.

I will take care to answer Wilson in the proper tone,
and will advise you of the tenor of his letter in case he
shall write to me.

TO MORRITT.

[*Nov.* 1818].

. . . I AGREE with you that the Conductors of the
Magazine[1] have acted inconsiderately and rashly in a
personal attack on Playfair. It gives too much occasion
to charge them with intolerance, for although Playfair has
never been suspected of orthodoxy, yet I know not that he
has upon any occasion made any attack on religion, and
consequently the dragging forward a charge of infidelity,
which cannot be proved from any overt act, sounds very
like personal scandal. The consequence has been an
answer in which both Wilson and Lockhart are severally

---

[1] *Blackwood's Magazine.*

charged with inconsistency, hypocrisy, and heaven knows
what, for I have not seen the pamphlet. Each of them
thought it necessary to write a personal challenge to the
anonymous author, who in a reply avows his resolution to
keep his incognito, grounding it upon their own refusal in
a similar case to give satisfaction to Mr. Leigh Hunt. The
person to whom the public ascribed the answer has denied
it upon his honour,—so these wars must be decided by ink,
not by blood.   I did acquaint the gentlemen that—

> When first they set this heavy stone a-rolling,
> 'Twould fall upon themselves.[1]

But I had the fate of Cassandra. I am sorry for this blunder,
because *hoc Illiacus velit.* But they are clever fellows and
will probably make a successful rally. It however must
make those who hold their names chary, shy of engaging
in a scuffle where it seems to be the object of each party
to rip all the follies of private life open for the amusement
of a gaping public. I know few people who have not glass
windows in their heads, in the sense which ought to prevent
them from flinging stones. I wish you would read the
article addressed to Playfair and give me your opinion. It
seems to me not sufficiently bottom'd on specific allegations
of assaults committed by him on Christianity. . . .

All my household send kind love to Miss Morritts.

FROM FRANCIS JEFFREY.

[*Nov.* 1818.]

MY DEAR SCOTT,—I prefix a draft for your lively little
article on *Women*[2] in No. 59 of the *Review*, and if you
knew how much pleasure I have in again addressing you
as a contributor to this work, you would wonder, as I do
myself, to find me dealing with you so shabbily. But

---

[1] See *Henry VIII.*, Act v. sc. 2.
[2] A criticism on Maturin's " Women " or *Pour et Contre.*

while I am most anxious, not only in my Editorial but in
my individual capacity, to have the chance of at least some
occasional assistance from you, I think it would be unworthy to mark it by a paltry addition to our usual rate
of pecuniary remuneration. If you would allow me to
inscribe you on the list of our contributors I should place
you at once in the rank of the *original founders* of the
work, who are settled with on a different footing, and
invested with a certain control, where they think it
necessary, over the proceedings of the Editor. I know
nobody whom I should like so well to have Viceroy over
me as you, and I am sure there is no one to whose advice
I should be so happy to resort in any case of perplexity.
I see obstacles, however, to this, which it is for you and
not at all for me to appreciate, only you will understand
that nothing will be so delightful to me as to have your
assistance—on any terms—except the feeling, which you
must allow me to retain, that I am most likely to be
indebted for it to your personal kindness to myself.
—Believe me always very faithfully and affectionately
yours,   F. JEFFREY.

CHAPTER XV

1819

EDINBURGH AND ABBOTSFORD

When the last Laird of Ravenswood to Ravenswood shall ride,
And woo a dead maiden to be his bride,
He shall stable his steed in the Kelpie's flow,
And his name shall be lost for ever moe.
                Caleb's Song—*Bride of Lammermoor.*

They've robed that maid so poor and pale
In silk and sandals rare,
And pearls for drops of frozen hail
Are glistening in her hair.
                Annot Lyle's Song—*Legend of Montrose.*

1819—AGE 48

Death of Charles, Duke of Buccleuch, 20th April.

Recurrence of Scott's illness, between March and July.

Death of Mrs. Scott's brother, Charles Carpenter.

Ivanhoe in preparation.

Son Walter joins the 18th Hussars, July.

Deaths of Mother, Uncle, and Aunt, December.

Ballad of *Noble Moringer.*

Sketch of Charles, Duke of Buccleuch, first printed in *Edinburgh Weekly Journal.*

Tales of my Landlord, 3rd series; *Bride of Lammermoor* and *Legend of Montrose,* in 4 vols. 12mo, published by Constable, June.

Ivanhoe, 3 vols. 12mo, published by Constable in December.

CHAPTER XV.

EDINBURGH, *March 5th*, 1819.

.. AFTER all, I cannot complain. I was told to expect a return of the complaint: it has kept away for a twelve-month, and now appears with mitigated features. And after so many years of the most robust health, how can I expect to go down hill without slipping now and then? I had a curious instance of health and strength enduring to the last within these few days. My very old friend and relation, Mr. Keith of Dunottar Castle, came to take a farewell visit of me, for such it proved, and so he seemed to think it, on Friday last. He was about 84, and told me he had been a young man all his life in point of health and constitution, and though he felt internal symptoms of decay, yet he had no objections to drink half a bottle of claret with a friend, and was otherwise in full possession of his mental and corporeal faculties, and only deprecated long illness and decay of mind. He took an unusually kind leave of me, went home, and died next day.

I am not the less obliged by your kind offer of quarters, that I do not find myself able to accept it on the present occasion. You will readily believe that I could be nowhere so happy or so much at home as with you, but I am chiefly in town to see if I can get Walter stuck into the army, and distance occasions such loss of time in your monstrous city that I must keep somewhere about Piccadilly or Pall Mall, where I will surely get accommodated in some quiet hotel or in lodgings, where I shall be near the agents and

37

public offices, for I have a notion I shall need some solicitation.[1] I hope to see you and two or three old friends very often, and I care not how little I see of the beau monde.[2] . . .

TO LOCKHART.

ABBOTSFORD, *23rd March* [1819].

MY DEAR SIR,—I am but just on my feet after a fourth very severe spasmodic affection, which held me from half-past six last night to half-past three this morning in a state little short of the extreme agony, during which time, to the infinite consternation of my terrified family, I *waltzed* with Madam Cramp to my own sad music.

> I sigh'd and howl'd,
> And groan'd and growl'd,
>   A wild and wondrous sound,

incapable of lying in one posture, yet unable to find any possible means of changing it. I thought of you amid all this agony, and of the great game which with your parts and principles lies before you in Scotland, and having been for very many years the only man of letters who at least stood by, if he could not support, the banner of ancient faith and loyalty, I was mentally bequeathing to you my baton like old Douglas—

> Take *thou* the vanguard of the three,
>   And bury me by the bracken bush,
> That grows upon yon lily lea.

I believe the women thought I was growing light-headed as they heard me repeat a rhyme apparently so little connected with my situation. I have much to say to you on these subjects, for which I hope we shall have a fit time; for, like old Sir Anthony Absolute, I hope still to

---

[1] Walter obtained a commission in the 18th Hussars in July.

[2] Scott's illness described in the following letters prevented his proposed visit to London.

live long and be very troublesome to you. Indeed the
surgeon could not help expressing his astonishment at the
great strength of my temperament, and I think had an
eye to my ribs as glorious hoops for a skeleton. And this
morning I am once more astonishingly well and enjoying
the exquisite Dr. Morris and his compeers. . . . The Duke
wants me to sit for a picture in his fine new library and
names Raeburn. I should like much better to sit to Allan,
but it is a sin to take up his time with chowderpates.

Adieu; my veins have been sluiced so often that they
give me pain in writing. Kindest compliments to Wilson:
the "Maga" is charming, manly, liberal, and spirited;
such principles, such talents, must at once atone for errors
or extravagances, and command respect where it will not
be readily yielded. The pleaders' portraits[1] are about the
best I ever read, and will preserve these three very remarkable and original men, for all of whom, however differing
in points whereon I wish we had agreed, I entertain not
only deep respect but sincere friendship and regard. Unquestionably Cranstoun in the days of our "Stove-hood"—
which I take to be a good phrase for the journeyman days
of young Scottish lawyers—was far the more likely of the
two to have risen by literature, and he made more than one
imperfect attempt that way. His extreme diffidence, the
narrowness of the family circumstances, and a proud
shyness which recoiled from the idea of a direct appeal to
the public, have been, I am convinced, the sole obstacles to
his embracing the primrose path of poetry, for a poet he is
intus et in cute.—Ever, my dear sir, most truly and
affectionately yours,　　　　　　　　WALTER SCOTT.

[1] *Peter's Letters to his Kinsfolk,*
it is understood, were written by
Lockhart and Wilson. There is no
first edition, and the second was
published in 3 vols. in October 1819;
but they had been partly printed in
the 23rd and 24th Nos. of *Blackwood's
Magazine,* and it is to these articles
that Scott refers. The Pleaders
were John Clerk, Cranstoun, and
Jeffrey, all afterwards Lords of
Session.

TO THE SAME.

April 1st.

. . . I HAVE much to say to you about Dr. Morris, being delighted with his proposal of publishing his tour. Should you spare me a day, as you promised, about the end of next week, I trust you will find me pretty *bobbish.* The Blucher brings you out and takes you back with the utmost convenience possible, being almost as convenient to Abbotsford as the Field Marshal to Europe. I want to give you the advantages of some of my experience respecting the state of our Scotch literature about twenty-five years since.

FROM LOCKHART.

EDINBURGH, *Saturday Evening, 3rd April.*

DEAR SIR, . . . I felt so much the kindness of your letter, which I received last week, that I should have answered it much sooner, had I not been apprehensive of troubling you during a season of illness. . . .

Without being fool enough to mistake some things you say for any other than the suggestions of a kind spirit that knows the value of encouragement, I could not be so affected as to deny that even as such they have afforded me much pleasure. I shall, unless you countermand me, come on Saturday, which is I understand one of the days on which the Blucher moves southward, and bring all my own ears and Dr. Morris's also, to catch what may drop from you concerning things so interesting to all, and so little understood by either of us.[1] . . .

I hope by the time I see you to find you entirely recovered from the effects of these distressing attacks. As soon as you are able to go out of doors, your best restorative will no doubt be the fresh air of your own Tweed. Believe me ever, my dear sir, your faithful and affectionate servant,   J. G. LOCKHART.

[1] See *Life*, vol. vi. pp. 100-103 for Scott's opinion of *Peter's Letters.*

TO JOANNA BAILLIE.

ABBOTSFORD, *17th April* 1819,

MY DEAR FRIEND,—Many thanks for your kind letter, which I would not answer till I could report myself a real convalescent. I now sleep o' nights (now and then) instead of counting the hours by assistance of a clock which never by any accident strikes right. Moreover I got abroad on my pony, Sybil Grey by name, and astonish the world by the spectre of death on the pale horse, for I am thin, exhausted, and ghastly to the last degree. But the cramp has so far mitigated its rigours as to return very seldom, and, what is much better, it gives way to immersion in the hot bath, when I lie as my grieve said, who is a great fisher, "like a haulded salmon," till the pain be gone. Do you remember enough of Clydeside to understand the simile, which took my fancy hugely. The salmon when frightened hide themselves under stones and in clefts of the rocks, where you may strike them with a spear, they lie so quiet, and this is called *haulding*, or taking their stronghold.

I am glad you are to do something for little Mrs. Harry Siddons. They have a fellow[1] in Edinburgh who plays Bailie Nicol Jarvie in Rob Roy with such truth and excellence that I never saw a part better, scarce so well, performed. He mixes the self-consequence, the vulgarity, the generosity, the irritability and the good-nature of the Glasgow citizen in the most delightful jumble. And in his conferences with Rob Roy there was something exquisite in his fear for the free-booter, his pride in being related to him, and his extreme desire to

---

[1] This inimitable personator of Nicol Jarvie was Charles Mackay, who was also successful in representing Dominie Sampson and Meg Dods in the dramatised versions of *Guy Mannering* and *St. Ronan's Well.* Sir William Allan painted his portrait in character, and Jedediah Cleishbotham wrote an amusing letter to "the Bailie," which may be seen in *Scott's Life*, vol. vi. p. 30. Mr. Mackay was a native of Glasgow, and died there in 1857.

intermeddle with, predominate over, and advise him, which I .thought would have made me expire with laughing. His despairing exclamation of "ah Rab! Rab!" after the other had been provoked into a tirade of Highland wrath, was quite irresistible. Would you think it—without a single performer out of their own troop, this picture of nature has from its absolute reality filled the house sixty times, and produced, it is said, above £3000 to the family, so that people will go to the theatre at Edinburgh if they have what they like to look at. To be sure, national predilections were all in favour of the piece.

I am glad the Bartleys come on well, and that you have a good opinion of the husband. I saw very little of him, but it seemed to me that Miss Smith had let herself down by marrying him; he appeared to have too much of the mere hacked player about him, but I readily admit I might be prejudiced. I hear a rumour that Mrs. Siddons means to be solicited out on the stage again. Surely she is not such an absolute jackass; she might return with as much credit if she had been a year in her winding-sheet. I should like if it were possible to anatomise Mrs. Siddons' intellect that we might discover in what her un-rivalled art consisted: she has not much sense, and still less sound taste, no reading but in her profession and with a view to the boards, and on the whole has always seemed to me a vain foolish woman spoiled (and no wonder) by unbounded adulation, to a degree that deserved praise tasted faint on her palate. And yet take her altogether, and where shall we see, I do not say her match, but anything within a hundred degrees of what she was in her zenith?

But it is against all my rules to write long letters. I enclose one of grateful thanks to your kind brother who took such care of me in my distress. His opinion gave me a confidence which I could have had in no other, and which was very necessary, considering the extreme pain as well as the bodily exhaustion which I sustained for several weeks. I wish you would all take a frisk down here this summer. We have plenty of room in Conundrum Castle, for so this place should be called, and a thousand pretty things to show you, some of them depending a good deal on the imagination. But you can make allowance for groves twelve inches high, and colours which the hand of time is to bring out on the landscape some twenty years hence. One of my great griefs, indeed my greatest, for not getting to town is, that I shall not see Miss Edgeworth, and I fear she will not visit Scotland. My kindest compliments attend Mrs. A. Baillie.—Ever most truly yours,

WALTER SCOTT.

TO TERRY.

EDINBURGH, *June 15th*, 1819.

MY DEAR TERRY,—I ought to have written to you long since, but no good news had I to send, and what signified telling you what I verily believed on my second relapse, that the timbers of the raft were hard strained and liable to part company after a little more tossing? The fact is, that though I know there was no immediate danger, yet the total derangement of all the functions of nature was such as must soon have worn out the strength of a Hercules. Fortunately a very intelligent man, Dr. Dick,[1] late physician to the East India Company, has put me on a very simple regimen by which I am already so very much benefited that I doubt not by perseverance I shall recover completely. The origin of the complaint, it seems, is some derangement in the gall leading to the formation of

---

[1] Of this skilful physician Sir John Sinclair tells a romantic story regarding his appointment as surgeon in the Company's service. —*Correspondence*, 2 vols. 8vo, London, 1831, vol. i. p. 144. A letter from Dr. Dick to Scott is given at page 53 of the present volume.

obstructions in the biliary ducts, whence arise cramps, fits of sickness, spasms, jaundice, and all the evils that have undone me. Calomel, not used in doses—which I had already employed in vain but in such very small quantities and so constantly as to maintain the effect of the mineral on the constitution, but not to bring on salivation— is, Lord love its heart, an absolute specific. Ten days' rigid attention to his directions have restored me to action and to appetite and to healthy digestion. I am now under the doom which Elbow denounces to Pompey: "Thou shalt continue, thou knave thou, thou shalt continue,"[1] and continue I will till I get quite round again. I am very greatly obliged to you for your kind attention about the armour, which I have no doubt is a great pennyworth. The catalogue you sent me contained no temptation except to naturalists. I enclose a draft for £50 (for there will be packing, discount, etc.,) to keep me out of debt to Mr. Bullock. If Addison's slippers and wig-box will serve you in your professional dress, pray accept them from me, for my curiosity leads chiefly to articles of armour; and Addison, I know not why, is personally no such favourite of mine as Sir Roger de Coverley should make him. I will send the measures correctly taken so soon as I get into the country. . . . I intended to be at Abbotsford to-day, but finding myself a little fagged with some previous business (the grasshopper being at present a burthen to me), I have put it off till to-morrow; on Wednesday I shall send the measurements, etc. I am sorry, not surprised, that the *H. of M. L.*[2] has done but so so,—better luck another time; if it does anything to do you good the end will be answered: the present set[3] (I hope you have your copy) will not

[1] *Measure for Measure*, Act II. sc. 1, varied.

[2] *Heart of Midlothian* dramatised by Terry.

[3] *Tales of My Landlord*, *Bride of Lammermoor*, and *Legend of Montrose*.

dramatise, but something else will by-and-by. I am delighted to hear that Mrs. Terry is mending in health: let her take great care of herself—that is the principal matter. As for Walter, he is the sprout of an oak. I subjoin an order for two copies of the Scottish scenery [1] (I have four at my disposal), one for yourself, one for Mr. Atkinson, to whom remember me gratefully and kindly. I must not write more at one brush, but remain, truly yours,   W. SCOTT.

FROM JOANNA BAILLIE.

HAMPSTEAD, *June 28th*, 1819.

. . . ALL the world since Sunday se'nnight have been busy reading the new *Tales of my Landlord*, and I feel myself covered with honour and glory in being therein mentioned in terms so very exalted.[2] I don't pretend to dive into mysteries, but I'm sure that Walter Scott his own self wrote the passage I allude to, tho' the Grand Cham of Tartary should have written all the rest; for there is nobody but him who takes any pleasure in praising me. I am, as we say in Clydesdale, very *vogie*[3] of it, tho' I try to behave myself as modestly as may be.

The *Bride of Lammermuir* is exceedingly and almost painfully interesting: the lovers there are the most engaging and interesting of all Jedediah Cleishbotham's lovers, and the tone of the whole, notwithstanding the lightening up of Caleb, who would make a most notable character in a farce, is so melancholy that it left a gloom upon my mind for a long time after I had finished the story. Tho' I do not wish to dwell upon this subject, there is one scene between the old hags, as they are pre-

---

[1] *Provincial Antiquities of Scotland.*

[2] See *W. N.*, vol. xiv. p. 176.

[3] Vogey or vogie, *i.e.* vain; highly pleased or satisfied.

paring to *straight* the corpse,[1] which struck me as fearfully natural and original; and before Mr. Cleishbotham or Pattieson give up writing tales, as has been so seriously threaten'd to the great dismay of thousands and tens of thousands of grateful and admiring readers, I would fain have him to give us a tale to be called the *Witch*.[2] It would be connected with much curious history of human nature, and of the times when so many people were executed for witchcraft, confessing the crime. I can see in the scene just mentioned a metaphysical view of the subject glimmering through the infernal dialogue of those hags, their own malevolence and envy associating them in their own imaginations with the devil; and this, pursued in the powerful and masterly manner in which it would be pursued by the author that you wot of, would be a most valuable and striking work. The author of *Marriage*,[3] or any other author whatever, cannot take this up, tho' they may pursue with some success the peculiar manners of the Scotch Highlanders. Pray let this matter be taken into consideration, for these said hags have created in me a prodigious hankering after it. The bewitching of Lord Torphichen's son caused the death of many reputed witches, both young and old, so the story need not be confined to

---

[1] "To straight the contorted limbs upon a board used for that melancholy purpose, to array the corpse in clean linen, and over that in its woollen shroud, were operations committed always to the old matrons of the village, and in which they found a singular and gloomy delight."—*Bride of Lammermoor*.

The knowledge of this custom gives significance to the grim prediction of Ailsie Gourlay respecting the Master of Ravenswood, "that hand of woman, or of man either, will never straught him—*Dead-deal will never be laid on his*

back."—*W. N.*, vol. xiv. pp. 226-228.

[2] See *Journal*, vol. ii. p. 10, and Joanna Baillie's tragedy *Witchcraft*.

[3] Miss Susan Ferrier — author of "the very lively work entitled *Marriage*," published anonymously in 1818, referred to by Scott in the postscript to the *Tales of my Landlord* as a "sister shadow." Miss Ferrier died in 1854 at Edinburgh, leaving a precious legacy to the world in her three books, *Marriage*, *Destiny*, and the *Inheritance*, full of the most piquant and humorous sketches of Scottish life and character.

old women. I can imagine a malevolent mind in those days
by degrees actually believing that it acted by power from
the devil, and to trace those steps would be very curious
and subtle, and give much insight into human nature. . . .

I think you are hard upon the elder and great Mrs.
Siddons. Her manner is too solemn and her voice too
deep for familiar society, and having her mind little stored
except with what is connected with her profession, and
thinking at the same [time] that every one who spoke to
her expected to hear her mouth utter some striking thing,
she uttered many things not very well suited to the
occasion; but I think she has a mind which has been
occupied in observing what passed within itself, and has
therefore drawn her acting from a deeper source than
actors generally do, besides her native talent for expressing
emotions; and I think she has a quick perception of humour
and character in others, at least she tells a humorous anecdote, notwithstanding her deep-toned voice, very drolly.
She was received in "Lady Randall," as you would read in
the papers, with the greatest warmth and respect, and I
have heard from those who sat near enough the stage to
hear and see well, that she acted with all her wonted power,
and still looked noble and beautiful. I heartily agree with
you that we shall never see her like again, or one
approaching within many degrees of her excellence. . . .

TO MORRITT.

ABBOTSFORD, 8th July 1819.

MY DEAR MORRITT,—I had your kind letter and am
very sensible of Colonel MacLeod's kindness in attending
to my health. I like the idea of Bohemia and its seven
Castles. I am fond of German literature and should find
much amusement at one of their watering-places. Above
all, I should be free from the pursuit of those alarming
hunters of wild animals so common at Harrogate, Chelten-

ham, and our English spas, who cannot suffer a poor *lion* like myself to come quietly thither for the benefit of his health without having a course at him, which to your sick lion is very oppressive. On the whole I incline to sit quiet at home this vacation. Under the directions of Dr. Dick, very celebrated for his knowledge of bilious disorders, I have taken and am continuing a course of calomel in very small doses, with excellent success, although the remedy produces both faintness and sickness in the operation. . . .

What say you to a rally over the border this summer? You will find Abbotsford enlarged in dimensions and improved in scenery. . . . I know little of the Maitland family by report—1 mean of the ladies—but report says what it does say very favourably. Lord Lauderdale treated, as I have heard, his countess and daughters like an absolute Bashaw. There was a strong feeling on this subject among the India House people (with whom Lady Lauderdale was connected by her father) when it was proposed to send him out to be Governor-General during the reign of the Talents. He kept the young ladies long in the background, to save expense and trouble, so that they are really little known here. Their mother is said to be an excellent woman. I hope the young lady Mr. Stanley has chosen will answer his hopes and yours.

Adieu, my dear Morritt—this is a long spell for me in my present state, for the very grasshopper is a burthen to me. Health and fraternity.—Yours ever,   WALTER SCOTT.

FROM LADY LOUISA STUART.

GLOUCESTER PLACE, *August* 11, 1819.

DEAR MR. SCOTT,—. . . Do not suppose, however, that I am at present reading the work [1] for the first time. I have

[1] *Bride of Lammermoor* and *Legend of Montrose*, regarding which Henry Mackenzie wrote to Scott on 5*th July* 1819:—"The opportune perusal of '*The 3rd Series of the Tales of my Landlord*' carried me away from my own feelings to sympathize with those fictitious ones so

had it by heart these five weeks. It possesses the same power of captivating the attention as its predecessors; one may find this or that fault, but who does not read on? The Master of Ravenswood is perhaps the best *lover* the author ever yet drew; and oh! how glad I was to hear the true notes of the old lyre in Annot Lyle's matin song![1] And why no more? Where are the good couple who concealed the Regalia from Cromwell's soldiers? I am sensible that the actor should always leave the stage before the spectator is tired, but I verily believe that nobody is tired. If no more exactly thus, however, may there be much more in some other way! Meanwhile I believe most people would say of the four-and-twenty volumes, what I have known the parents of large families do of their children: "You may think them a great many, yet there is not one we could spare." For my own part I acknowledge I am not a fair judge; all these writings, all the Author's works confessed and unconfessed, are so much associated in my mind with, not the earliest, but the pleasantest part of my life, that they awaken in me many feelings I could hardly explain to another. They are to me less like books, than like the letters one treasures up, "pleasant yet mournful to the soul," and I cannot open one of them without a thousand recollections that as time rolls on, grow precious, although they are often painful. Independent of this, how many hours of mine have they soothed and softened! and still

admirably delineated in that book. Now, although I dare not say you are the writer of those Tales, yet as you take a concern in their publication, it may be gratifying to the author and to you to know what a powerful lenitive they proved to a poor old invalid who formerly wrote Tales such as they were, however inferior to the Tales of my Landlord. I can sincerely assure you that I have followed the Apothecary's prescription 'bis sumendum,' and have read them a second time since I have become so much better (tho' still confined to my couch) as to be able to read them with a little more attention and with undiminished enjoyment." ...

[1] *Legend of Montrose*, W. N., xv. pp. 83-4.

do soothe and soften, for I can read them over and over again.

. . . It grieves me to think of all you have gone through. I am told you are not so careful of yourself as you should be, but I would fain suppose that arises from feeling an inward vigour still remaining, which sensation is one that promises a return of health.   For surely you would not be wilfully negligent of the welfare of all who love and depend upon you.   I cannot believe it. . . .

TO LADY LOUISA STUART.

ABBOTSFORD, 23rd *August* 1819.

MY DEAR LADY LOUISA,—Your very kind remembrance reached me two days since.   I have been dreadfully ill this summer; I mean in point of pain and exhaustion, for they say the complaint is seldom mortal.   However, when one can neither eat, drink, nor sleep for sheer agony, and is carried up and down like a log of wood, with hardly the power of lifting the hand to the head, one is not for the moment much comforted by the idea that an avenue so disagreeable does not terminate upon the last grand vista which closes mortal views.   As to care, I really take as much as I can, that is, I obey the injunctions of my physician as well as a man of mould may; but as all my friends prescribe for me, as a matter of course I must necessarily incur the bad reputation of neglecting many kindly meant hints, cautions, and recommendations, for which it may be some apology that they are totally irre-concilable with each other.   One person recommending a vegetable diet and no wine, another condemning me to butcher-meat, of which I eat but moderately at any time, and a long et cetera, concluding with bread, itself the very staff of life,—were I to obey both these injunctions there is some chance of my going without my dinner, which, now that I have recovered my appetite, would be no very pleasing prospect. Truth is, I swear by a certain Dr. Dick, long physician to the East India Company, who has discovered that calomel used in small quantities and for a length of time, is a specific in such derangements of the biliary vessels as I have suffered from. And assuredly persevering in his system has restored me to complete health for the present. On Wednesday I go to Langholm just to spend a few hours with Lord Montagu and the dear young ladies who are to be there on their return to England. My God, when I look back on what that family was when I had first the honour, among many high advantages I owe them, of forming your Ladyship's acquaintance at Dalkeith!

The last calamity has hurt me very much; it occasioned an immediate relapse, but that was of less consequence than a feeling which I have as if the horizon of my hopes and interests was narrowed around me. There were many things in which I only took an interest because they were the Duke's, and because they were the subject of conversation and correspondence betwixt us, and with which my connection is now ended. I have only once ventured up Yarrow. It was on some business, and I cannot tell you how severely I felt when my horse from long habit turned his head immediately to go to Bowhill. Your Ladyship was quite right in supposing I had tried to give some idea of the Duke's character. I feel it to be much colder than it would have been had I given vent to my own regrets, but I was addressing a public singularly ignorant of his merits, and to make the desired impression it was necessary to assume the tone of impartiality. I send a copy of the sketch, Mr. Ballantyne having thought proper to reprint it.

I am very glad your Ladyship found the tales in some degree worth your notice. It cost me a terrible effort to finish them, for between distress of mind and body I was unfit for literary composition. But in justice to my booksellers I was obliged to dictate while I was scarce able to speak for pain.[1] With better hope I am trying an antiquarian story; I mean one relating to old English times, which is a great amusement to me. I have laid aside a half-finished story on the dissolution of the Monasteries. When I print them I shall put them into different shapes, and publish them with different people and so run the one against the other. I have had a great event of sending my eldest son to join his regiment (the 18th Hussars), and one of these tales will be necessary to reimburse me for about £1200 or £1500 which his commission and outfit of all kinds cost me. It is better than mortgaging land for the same necessary purpose, as many a better man is obliged to do. . . .

I am in sad perplexity just now about a play of Joanna Baillie's[2] which she has sent to Mrs. Siddons (our manageress) to be acted in Edinburgh. It contains abundance of genius, and of fine poetry and passion; in short, abundance of all that one expects particularly from her. But then it is not well adapted for the stage, and many things cannot be represented in the way the author has conceived them. There is a coxcomb who turns out a man of courage and spirit. This is rather a comic than a tragic character. Then there is a child—an infant—a personage which, unless in the single instance of the pantomime termed the Virgin of the Sun,[3] has never succeeded. A wax-doll is ridiculous; a living infant more absurdly ludicrous. Now our friend desired Mrs. S. to show me this play, which she has not failed to do, intimating in a very delicate manner her own sense of its imperfection, but obviously wishing to shelter herself under my opinion. Now if I speak truth, and 'tis my occupation to be plain, I fear I shall hurt our

[1] See Ballantyne's note in *Journal*, vol. i. p. 409.

[2] *The Separation*: a tragedy now included in Joanna Baillie's dramas.

[3] An opera founded on Plumptre's translation of one of Kotzebue's plays, popular in London in the year 1812.

honoured friend or perhaps even offend her; and if I do
not, I suffer her to commit her well-earned fame as well
as her feelings to a certain risque, for whatever theatrical au-
diences may have been in former days, they are now such
a brutal assemblage that I am lost in astonishment at any
one submitting to their censure. I am really vexed about
this matter. But I have taken up enough of your time.—
Believe me, dear Lady Louisa, most truly and respectfully
your obliged servant,   WALTER SCOTT.

FROM DR. DICK.

TULLYMET, NEAR DUNKELD,
PERTHSHIRE, *Aug.* 23, 1819.

MY DEAR SIR,—I am this moment honoured and
delighted beyond expression with yours of the 6th inst.,
and regret that it was not in my power to answer it
sooner. I trust, however, that the delay is of no importance, as I could not give better directions for taking
the calomel than my good friend (for such I esteem
Dr. Clarkson) had given you already, and I hope by this
time he has advised you to leave it off altogether, for
though in general it be more safe to continue it rather
too long than too short a time where it agrees with the
constitution, yet from the very good account you give
of your state of health I think you may now safely dis-
continue it.

If any hints I gave Dr. Clarkson encouraged him to
go on with more confidence with the judicious plan of
treatment he had adopted, I shall always consider it as
one of the most pleasing circumstances of my life; but
to him, under God, the chief credit is due, and I consider
myself greatly indebted to him for his very kind and
ready communications.

Mrs. Dick and myself are highly flattered by your

kind invitation to take Abbotsford on our way to London, an honour of which the first and best in the nation would be very, very proud. I can figure to myself the exquisite pleasure of going to a place while inhabited by that proprietor for whose sake it will be visited with delight by thousands for many centuries to come, but to our grief, we have no longer any business in the south, and we now intend to pass our few remaining years (if any be yet in store for us) among our native mountains.

Judging from what was stated in the newspapers, I think the Queen died of the same disorder; it was coming on for more than a year, as she was at Bath on account of it before the death of the Princess Charlotte. I suspected what it was at the time, and always predicted the event, having had several opportunities of knowing the mode of treating the disorder by the physicians who attend her. At her age, the calomel might not save her life (though I have seen instances of older people being cured by it—of whom Sir Robert Preston of Valleyfield was one), but I was sure that we were not acquainted with any other medicine that could give her a chance of recovery.

I have to apologise for obtruding on you subjects so foreign to the purport of my writing, and have only to offer my grateful thanks for your intended present, which, however, I must beg leave to decline, because I am rewarded already a thousand-fold by being allowed the honour of prescribing for you, and by being assured, under your own hand, that you are so well. . . .

But if you will send me one volume of any kind, and write on it that it is from yourself, I shall consider it a great favour. I have the vanity to wish that my son and his descendants may have it to shew as a proof that I was honoured with the friendship of the author.

Sincerely wishing you long health and every happiness

this world can afford, I have the honour to be, with the greatest respect and admiration, my dear sir, your most obedient humble servant,　　　WILLIAM DICK.

I was sorry lately to see so little justice done to the memory of our poor friend Leyden in some of the Edinr. periodical publications. They ridicule the idea of comparing him to Sir William Jones as a linguist, but I believe he was the greater of the two, and I know he had a facility of acquiring languages that Sir William had no pretensions to. I was acquainted with both: Leyden was at times very idle, Sir William never. Sir Robert Chambers, who was Chief Justice in Bengal, assured me that for six years he was Vinerian Professor at Oxford he was intimate with Sir William and knew that he studied sixteen hours out of the twenty-four the whole time. When Sir William arrived as Judge in Calcutta, a friend of mine who was a very good Persian scholar was sitting with him when some learned Native Gentlemen came in to pay their respects to him. Sir William addressed them in Persian, as he thought, and after some time, one of them in a whisper to my friend said, " Tell Sir William that we do not understand English, but we know that he is a learned Persian, and I beg you will ask him to speak to us in that language." My friend smiled, but did not chuse to mortify the Judge.

Sir William was about a dozen years in Bengal, where the Hindustanee is the only language spoken by every class, and yet he never could speak a sentence in it. Leyden spoke it well, and understood it perfectly in less than two years. . . .

TO TERRY.

ABBOTSFORD, 28th September 1819.

MY DEAR TERRY,—I ought to have thanked you long since for your most acceptable present; the knife is by far the finest and fittest for the purpose that I ever saw, and shall henceforth be my constant companion. It has already sealed, or rather scored, the doom of sundry old firs in Moss' stripe, which might have cumbered the ground longer but for the irresistible temptation of marking them with this delightful implement. I have made John Goodfellow, the crooked tailor of Darnick, make a leather pocket to my jacket that the knife may escape the fate of its predecessor. The singularity of your having the kind purpose of presenting me with the very knife I wished for is one of these odd contingencies of which so many have happened to me both in important matters and trifles, that they would seem very singular if collected. The other day a learned American[1] (an uncommon animal also) told me of a collection of Spanish ballads published in Germany, which interested me very much. I looked through all catalogues for it in vain, when, behold, young Constable just returned from Germany comes out to pay me a visit with the book in his pocket which I was hunting for, designed as a present for me. You would, I know, be very much concerned to hear that Erskine[2] has lost his excellent and amiable wife. They were on a journey recommended by the physicians to the Lakes of Cumberland, and she was taken finally ill at Lowood,—a deplorable and irremediable loss to our poor friend; her case had, I think, been scarcely well understood, notwithstanding the best advice was of course resorted to. I will not dwell on this subject, so affecting in all its bearings. Another instance of mortality has taken place in my immediate neighbourhood. Poor old —— my brother Laird. . . . He sunk down before them a dead man, the contending passions of shame and

[1] It was George Ticknor, the historian of Spanish Literature, who recommended Depping's *Sammlung*. The little book is still at Abbotsford. For an account of Ticknor's visit, see his *Life and Letters*, vol. i. pp. 276-284.

[2] Lord Kinnedder.

anger and sorrow fairly burst the flood-gates of life. Was not this a truly dramatic exit?[1] He was talking much of selling his land a little before his death, but that prospect is now over for twenty years, his child being a minor, and only about a year old. So it will not be my fate in all probability to compleat Abbotsford on that side. This makes me look towards neighbour Nicol Milne, who is anxious to sell if he could get his price, as I am to buy if he would take mine. Walter's fortune would be better secured in land, and I have enough besides to manage it, trusting to health and future exertion. It would be an immense thing for Abbotsford, which would then be one of the best estates in this part of Teviotdale—worth probably £1800 or £2000 a year, and for beauty nothing would be so easy as to restore the old Lake at Faldonside, besides having the exclusive and compleat command of Cauldshields Loch. On the other hand, I must remember that gold may be bought too dear. I will acquaint you with the termination of this affair, which is at present *entre nous*. Prince Leopold honoured us with a visit a few days since, and was much pleased with Abbotsford, and especially with the Armoury, which by dint of the new acquisitions makes now a very handsome appearance. We use it much as a sitting room, being now compleated and in order. . . . Believe, dear Terry, that I am always most truly yours,

WALTER SCOTT.

TO LOCKHART.

ABBOTSFORD, 17*th October* 1819.

DEAR LOCKHART,—I agree with every word you write. In fact I was applied to to hold some intercourse with you

[1] See *Life*, vol. vi. p. 129.

last year on a similar topic,[1] but feeling no confidence that the matter would be creditably managed, I declined leading any of my friends into it. This is very different. Mr. Murray, being such as you describe him, would be an editor out of a thousand, and, if disposed to embark with us, would be much the better of having been in the enemy's camp. What Government will do I know not, but they cannot expect to obtain weight in the conflict if they set their soldiers to war on their own charges. I anticipate no difficulty in assuring him of a Kirk, and a good one. I have made Rae acquainted with your views, coinciding exactly with my own, and we shall meet on Friday I trust, with some chance of arranging this important matter. I should indeed have come to St. Catherine's at any rate, for my womankind have settled to see one day at least of the festival.—Believe me, very truly yours, WALTER SCOTT.

TO THE SAME.

ABBOTSFORD, *8th November* 1819.

MY DEAR SIR,—I got your two very interesting letters and am truly grieved to find you have not succeeded as could have been wished, more especially as I am convinced from the stile of Mr. Murray's letter, which I reinclose, that he was the very man we want. I own my own thoughts turn very strongly to our fat friend[2] in Saint John's Street; he is a thorough, well-principled, honourable man, and excepting his foolish rigg about Manchester,[3] which was a mere capriole from his having

[1] The Tory party in Scotland were at this time desirous of establishing a newspaper in Edinburgh, and the following letters to Lockhart relate to the attempt. Mr. James Murray was on the staff of the *Times* and declined the editorship, mainly because he was then in a position too responsible and lucrative to think of leaving London.

[2] Mr. James Ballantyne, who had been editor and proprietor for many years of *The Edinburgh Weekly Journal.*

[3] The "Peterloo" monster Reform meeting, 16th August 1819.

no one to advise or consult with, I have no notion that
his politics have been unsteady. After all, what we want
is a hulk to fire from, and his broad body might be cover
enough. He might conduct his own paper at the same
time with perfect ease, and as he fully understands all
the detail of the business, I should greatly prefer him to
any unpractised lad we might light on. If you should
approve of this, the question would be if he has time for
this additional occupation; for my own part I am clear
he has. Or it might be possible to lay hold on his weekly
paper, which has a certain circulation, and push it into the
shape we want, but this I think less advisable. As at any
rate he must be printer of the paper as a staunch Pittite,
etc., it may be worth while to speak to him on the subject,
saying nothing of the funds excepting that they will be
supplied by friends to the cause, and that he need not fear
being sent a warfare on his own charges. He writes a
good enough stile, and has often been happy in his opening articles; besides, I would very gladly do him a kindness.
I shall drop him a hint that you have some business of
consequence to mention to him, and I am well convinced
he will be upon honour whatever the issue of your conversation may be. I am obliged to break off in haste by
an invasion of the Southron.—Yours most truly,

WALTER SCOTT.

I shall be in town on Monday next. I have not enclosed Mr. Murray's letter as I send in a servant to-morrow
or next day.

TO THE SAME.

[Nov. 1819.]

MY DEAR SIR,—Finding an opportunity, I enclose Mr.
Murray's letter. In case Ballantyne will not answer, I have
some thoughts of Washington Irving—a very clever fellow

indeed, who I think might be had. He is a great friend of Walsh and has much humour and power of writing.— Yours truly,   W. Scott.

FROM WASHINGTON IRVING.[1]

London, *November 20th*, 1819.

I cannot express how much I am gratified by your letter. I had begun to feel as if I had taken an unwarrantable liberty, but somehow or other there is a genial sunshine about you that warms every creeping thing into heart and confidence. Your literary proposal both surprises and flatters me, as it evinces a much higher opinion of my talents and capacity than I possess myself. I am peculiarly unfitted for the post proposed. I have no strong political prejudices, for though born and brought up under a republican government, and thoroughly convinced that it is the best for my own country, yet I have a deep *poetical* veneration for the old institutions of this country, and should feel as sorry to see them injured or subverted, as to see Windsor Castle or Westminster Abbey demolished to make way for snug brick tenements. But I have a general dislike to politics. I have always shunned them in my own country, and have lately declined a lucrative post under my own government, and one that opened the door to promotion, merely because I was averse to political life or to being subjected to regular application, or local confinement.

My whole course of life has been desultory, and I am unfitted for any periodically recurring task, or any stipulated labour of body or mind. I have no command over my talents such as they are, am apt to be deserted

[1] It is curious now to imagine Washington Irving being requested to become editor of a Scottish newspaper. Scott's letter is not available, but Irving's characteristic reply has been preserved in the Abbotsford collection.

by them when I most want their assistance, and have
to watch the veerings of my mind as I would those of
a weather-cock.   Practice and training may bring me
more into rule, but at present I am as unfit for service
in the ranks, as one of my own country Indians or a
Don Cossack.   I must therefore keep on pretty much as
I have begun, writing when I can and not when I would.
I shall occasionally shift my residence, and trust to the
excitement of various scenes and objects to furnish me
with materials; though I hope, as I gain experience
and confidence, to be more copious and methodical.   I
am playing the Egotist, but I know no better mode of
answering your very kind proposal, than by showing
what a very good-for-nothing kind of being I am. . . .
Present my sincere regards to Mrs. Scott and the family,
and believe me most respectfully, your friend,

WASHINGTON IRVING.

TO LADY ABERCORN.

EDINBURGH, 25th November 1819.

MY DEAR FRIEND,—You do me great injustice in
supposing me capable of forgetting your unremitted kindness, so often actively exerted in my behalf.   I assure you,
my dear lady, I am incapable of such ingratitude, and
am but too happy when I can afford you any proof of the
warm recollection I entertain of former acts of kindness
and friendship.   But really, I wrote your Ladyship the
last letter which passed between us, and though your
silence ought to have been no reason for my not writing
again, yet, joined to the very bad state of my health last
summer, I trust you will receive it as an apology.   At
any rate I was only a ghost which waited but to be
spoken to, as this sheet of nonsense will testify.   I was
indeed very near being a ghost in serious earnest, but
after about three months' terrible suffering, the medical

treatment to which I was subjected seems to have eradicated the disorder, and I have now better health than I have enjoyed for several years. My recovery was so rapid that in July I was carried from my bed to the warm bath, unable to stir either foot or hand, and a fortnight afterwards I was able to ride on my pony.

I have not yet received the rank your Ladyship mentions, but it is near a twelvemonth since the Prince Regent intimated his unsolicited pleasure to confer it upon me, and I should have gone to town in summer for that purpose, but for my severe indisposition. I cannot now, with proper gratitude to the source from which this proposal comes, defer any longer my journey to town, where, I suppose, I shall be like Sir Andrew Aguecheek a knight (Bart., *cela s'entend*) dubbed with unhacked rapier and on carpet consideration.[1] As some witty fellow will quote Falstaff's speech on Sir Walter Blunt, "I like not such grinning honour as Sir Walter hath,"[2] pray remember I made this quotation first myself.

The *petit titre* is of little consequence to me, but as my son has embraced the army as a profession, it may be useful to him. . . . Walter is now at Cork with his regiment, the 18th Hussars. I had some regret in putting him into that Tom Fool dress, which is so unlike that of a British soldier. But beggars must not be chusers, and I was very desirous to get him into his profession as soon as possible. Mr. Wright would perhaps mention what I am sure your Ladyship would hear with pleasure, that my wife's brother has left my children a considerable fortune, which is at present liferented by his lady. The sum may be £40,000 or £50,000,[3] and it relieves me from some anxious thoughts, and permits me with justice to

---

[1] *Twelfth Night*, Act III. sc. 4.
[2] *First Henry Fourth*, Act v. sc. 1.
[3] Mr. Carpenter's estate appears to have realised only about half the amount expected.—See letter, *post*, p. 110.

my younger children to leave my landed property, which
is now valuable, to my eldest son, that if he be prudent
he may support his knighthood with decency and independence, if not with splendour.

About the novels you wrote of, I can tell you thus
much from good information, that the 4th series of *Tales
of My Landlord* are not by the author of the three former,
but a mere catchpenny of some hack author, and that
Ivanhoe by the author of *Waverley* will immediately
appear. Mr. Ballantyne the printer, who is a good judge,
speaks very highly of this romance. I will endeavour to
get you an early copy, and I could send it under an office
frank, did I know your Ladyship's direction in town ;
perhaps the best way would be to address it to the Bishop
of London.

The Duke of Buccleuch's death was indeed a very
severe blow to me. We had many feelings and pursuits in
common, and perhaps it is uncommon for two men so
different in rank to have lived more intimately and famili-
arly. But whatever the private loss may be to myself, that
of the country is incalculable. He employed nearly a
thousand day labourers, and had far the most extensive
following, as we call it, of any person I may almost say in
Scotland, all of which must be for some years in abeyance.
I have also lost a kind and hospitable neighbour in poor
Lord Somerville,[1] who lived within two miles of me, and
with whom I was on great habits of familiarity. I have
seen nothing of the Argyle family, and am indeed but
slightly acquainted with any of its members except my
old friend, Lady Charlotte,[2] who has made a sad mess of
it. Our Scottish proverb says there is no fool like an old
fool.

[1] This intimate friend and at one
time almost daily companion of
Scott, had left the Pavilion on the
Tweed, and gone abroad. He died
in 1819.

[2] Lady Charlotte Campbell had
lately married the Rev. Edward
Bury.

The western districts of Scotland, where the manufacturing interests prevail, are in a bad way. All the rest
of the country is steady enough, for the Scottish peasantry
are more attached to their lairds than is the general case
in England.

Adieu, my dear friend. I trust I shall have the pleasure
of seeing you when I am in London in January. My stay
there will be very short.—Believe me always, most truly
yours,   WALTER SCOTT.

TO MORRITT.

EDIN. [*December* 1819].

MY DEAR MORRITT,—We have had such a busy time of
it here that I have allowed to lie unanswered your kind
letter. The Devil seems to have come up amongst us un-
chained and bellowing for his prey. In fact, but that this
country possesses a sort of power of self-preservation which
seems incalculable, I would say we were on the verge of
civil war. In Glasgow the Volunteers drill by day and
the Radicals by night, and nothing but positive military
force keeps the people under. Men go about their ordinary
business with their musquets in their hands. The Master
Manufacturer dare hardly trust himself unarmed among
the workmen whom he feeds and pays, and all seems to
tend to an open rupture. They have in Glasgow about
three thousand steady Volunteers to keep ten times the
number of radicals in order, and the Volunteer regiment
here are desired to hold themselves in readiness to garrison
the Castle, as it is momently expected that all the military
may be sent to the west. Meanwhile the Loyalists are
arming fast. The Edinburgh Regiment is getting strong
and is very efficient, and they are raising sharp-shooters
and cavalry. A fine troop of the latter, all handsome
youths and well mounted, made me wish myself twenty

years younger, that I might join them again. The Highland chiefs have offered their clans. . . . The bills in
present dependence will do a great deal; certainly they
will bring the matter to this issue, that the disaffected
must instantly break out into open rebellion, or that they
will be gradually deserted by the doubtful, the timid, the
self-interested, and the fickle part of their adherents. I
should not be surprised if the despair and violence of some
of their leaders should induce them to try a scuffle for it.
But if they do not strike very soon they can have no hope
from insurrection, for all who have anything to lose have
become alarmed, and the force of property, however inert
in its general habits, is irresistible when called fully into
exercise by some strong impulse. We have constituted a
committee here to open a battery on the rascals with all
sorts of literature, grave and ludicrous. I have no faith
myself in the effect these paper pellets may produce
on the enemy, but they are supposed to encourage our
friends. I have let off a couple of *Visions*[1] at them; one
was published last week and made a strong sensation, the
other appears to-day, and I have a few more rockets of the
same description. I suppose I was instantly suspected, for
I was honoured with a letter reminding me of the fate
of Kotzebue. But they may fright boys with bugs, for
I fear none, as Grumio says.[2]

In the meantime my *Ivanhoe* is finished and will soon
kiss your hands. I am not sure whether it or the author
will reach you first, for I am to be in London before the
New Year, that is, if all remains quiet in this country.
We have a trial coming on of great interest. A landed
man and gentleman of ancient family, Mr. Kinloch of
Kinloch,[3] presided at a Radical meeting at Dundee in

---

[1] *The Visionary*, three essays in
the *Weekly Journal*, afterwards
published separately.

[2] *Taming of the Shrew*, Act I. sc. 2.

[3] See *Journal*, vol. i. p. 224,
Malachi's Letters.

which he made a most violent speech, exhorting the people to right themselves by arms in case the magistrates of Manchester, yeomanry, etc., were not *punished* (guilty or innocent). The same sentiment he embodied in resolutions, and the resolutions as well as notes of the speech in his own hand are in possession of the Crown Counsel.

17th December.

I have since received a very unexpected shock which I sustained on Tuesday last by my mother being struck with the palsy, which, though she still exists, must at the age of eighty-seven be fatal. What was sufficiently shocking, her brother, Dr. Rutherford, having visited her on Tuesday night and announcing to us that the blow must be fatal, died suddenly on the day following. My aunt, the only surviving member of the family of my maternal grandfather, is extremely ill. Amidst all this family distress we have enough to do with the public bustle. The Yeomanry are come back from Glasgow where all is quiet but the temper of the populace execrable.[1] In my country I have the pleasure to say that high and low are yet loyal. Scott of Gala and I have offered a body of three hundred or more, which, if accepted, may be useful about Carlisle. All Roxburghshire is very loyal. I send you this scrap of evil news and worse bodings. All my household desire their love to you. —Most truly yours, WALTER SCOTT.

[1] A shrewd observer, of the opposite party, writing some years after these exciting events remarks, " Edinburgh was as quiet as the grave or even as Peebles, yet matters were so managed that we were obliged to pass about a month as if an enemy had been drawing his lines round our very walls. The only curiosity of the affair now is the facility of spreading panic. . . . The whole affair was composed of three nearly equal parts, Popular discontent, Government exaggeration, and Public craze."—Cockburn's *Memorials.*

CHAPTER XVI

1820

EDINBURGH AND ABBOTSFORD

" How beautifully he varied his style of letter-writing according to the character and situation of his multifarious correspondents, the reader has already
been enabled to judge ; but to carry the same system into practice *at sight*, to
manage utter strangers, of many and widely different classes, in the same fashion,
and with the same effect, called for a quickness of observation, and fertility of
resource, such as no description can convey the slightest notion of to those who
never witnessed the thing for themselves. And all this was done without approach
to the unmanly trickery of what is called *catching the tone* of the person one
converses with."

Lockhart.

1820—AGE 49.

Visits London, March and April.

Portrait by Lawrence, and bust by Chantrey.

Baronetcy gazetted in April.

Marriage of his daughter Sophia, April.

Tendered Honorary degrees from Oxford and Cambridge.

Blair-Adam Club founded in June.

Visit of Sir H. Davy, Henry Mackenzie, and others, to Abbotsford.

Son Charles leaves for Mr. Williams' in Wales.

Elected President of the Royal Society, Edinburgh.

The Visionary, 3 Nos. 12mo, in January, political satires, first printed in *Edinburgh Weekly Journal*.

The Monastery, 3 vols. 12mo, published by Constable, March.

The Abbot, 3 vols. 12mo, published by Longman and Constable, Sept.

Lives of the Novelists in Ballantyne's Series.

Memorials of the Haliburtons in one vol. 4to, 30 copies privately printed.

Patrick Carey's Poems and Triolets, one vol. 4to, John Murray.

CHAPTER XVI.

EDINBURGH, 18th January 1820.

MY DEAREST FRIEND,—I owe you two long letters, but you are so gentle a creditor that as usual with all indulgent persons I have abused your patience. I had hoped ere now to have made an apology in person, but fate by a sudden and strange sweep has deprived me of three of my nearest and dearest relations within a very few days of each other, and without anything like pre-monition. My excellent mother, a person of rare talent and unparalleled spirits and good humour, having supported many domestic misfortunes with the patience arising from a genuine spirit of devotion, was in her usual health at the beginning of December, and in excellent spirits. Mr. and Mrs. Scott of Harden had paid her a visit on the Sunday, and were struck with the accuracy and vivacity with which at the age of eighty-seven she did the honours of her house, and entertained them with the stories of the olden time, of which few people knew so many or told them so well. The next day it pleased God to afflict her with a paralytic affection so decisive as to leave us no hope but for her speedy and easy removal. My uncle (her brother) Dr. Rutherford, well known to your brother Dr. Baillie, was on the second day of her illness just stepping into his carriage when about to visit her, when he also was arrested by the hand of fate, and with scarce an instant betwixt life and death sunk down a dead man in the arms of his youngest daughter. To close this strange concourse of calamity which has visited our devoted family, my aunt Miss Rutherford died two days after the Doctor, of a wasting illness which she had long complained of. And my mother was mercifully removed a few days afterwards. They were all persons of uncommon worth and talent, and to me all of them deservedly dear. Then their ages too were such as did not by any means render so sudden and strange a coincidence in their deaths at all probable. My mother (my grandfather's daughter by a first marriage) was as I have said eighty-seven, Dr. Rutherford was upwards of seventy, and his sister, the only one whose death could have been anticipated, was but fifty-seven. They were happy in this, that none of them knew of each other's death, which, much as they were attached to each other, we must account a blessing.

These events have necessarily delayed my journey to the South, and prevented my giving you an account in person of the commissions with which you kindly charged me. On conversing with Mrs. Siddons when I came to town, and on seeing her company, I could not think of trying " The Separation :"[1] the company is by no means strong in tragedy, and I own I could not have risqued reputation so dear to me as yours, upon imperfect playing. I read it twice to my family, and it drew tears each time, especially from poor Christie Rutherford, for whom ours have since flowed. . . .   WALTER SCOTT.

TO LADY ABERCORN.

EDINBURGH, 15th January 1820.

MY DEAR FRIEND,—I have great regret in mentioning to you the circumstances which have prevented my being

[1] One of Joanna Baillie's Dramas, ante, p. 52.

in town at this season, and have altered all my arrangements, since they have been of an unusually melancholy
nature. . . .

To take a more agreeable though still an egotistical
subject, in consequence of the bad disposition upon the
English frontier, we have determined to levy men, and,
as in the circumstances of my family distress I could not
attend myself, I ordered my Piper to play our Gathering
through the neighbouring hamlets, and I had in twenty-
four hours the offer of a hundred as handsome young
fellows as are to be seen anywhere, and I assure you I was
not a little flattered by their personal attachment to myself.
We propose they should wear green jackets and trousers,
with their own grey plaids, which they wear very gracefully, and the Scottish blue bonnet.   They are to be armed
with rifles, and are most of them excellent shots and well
accustomed to the hills.   I think, however, things are so
settled that our services will not be needed, as the discontent seems to be much abated, especially in Cumberland
and Northumberland, against which we might probably
have been detached.   The yeomen and agricultural interest all through Scotland has been very loyal and shewn
great energy.   About a thousand of the finest cavalry, of
that kind, which I ever saw, marched into Glasgow on the
morning of the apprehended rising, which their presence
altogether prevented.   The Scotch certainly seem to have a
natural turn for war, for they learn military discipline in
an incredibly short time, and are very fond of the exercise.
Our regiment would consist of 1000 men, chiefly shep-
herds. . . . Your Ladyship's truly faithful and affectionate
friend,   WALTER SCOTT.

FROM LADY LOUISA STUART.

DITTON PARK, *January* 16, 1820.

DEAR MR. SCOTT,—As Lord Montagu is answering a

letter of yours, I catch the opportunity of slipping in a little note, chiefly to say that everybody in this house has been reading an odd new kind of book called *Ivanhoe*, and nobody, as far as I have observed, has willingly laid it down again till finished. By this, I conclude its success will fully equal that of its predecessors, notwithstanding it has quite abandoned their ground and ploughed up a field hitherto untouched. The interest of it indeed is most powerful; few things in prose or verse seize upon one's mind so strongly, or are read with such breathless eagerness, as the storming of the castle related by Rebecca, and her trial at Templestowe. Few characters ever were so forcibly painted as hers: the Jew too, the Templar, the courtly knight De Bracy, the wavering inconstant wickedness of John, are all worthy of Shakespeare. And according to what has been alleged against the author in some other instances, the hero and the heroine are the people one cares least about. But provided one does but care enough about somebody, it is all one to me; and I think the cavil is like that against Milton for making the Devil his hero.

Yet I shall own I dislike one thing, the sudden death of Bois-Guilbert, and it is too much a *makeshift*. What really may (and does) happen to people of violent passions, breaking a blood-vessel, would have staggered the reader less and answered the purpose equally well, since in those days it would have alike seemed the judgment of God, and they would not have attempted to remedy the accident, even if they had known how.[1] I must not omit paying my tribute to Cedric, that worthy forefather of the genuine English country gentleman; he is admirable. . . .

[1] His correspondent was not aware that the sudden death of Mr. Elphinstone, a young advocate, on the floor of the Parliament House gave Scott the idea for the mode of removing Bois-Guilbert.— See *Life*, vi. p. 178.

TO LADY ABERCORN.

ABBOTSFORD, 15*th March* 1820.

MY DEAR FRIEND,— . . . I reckon I shall get to town about Wednesday, as I dare not travel night and day, as I used to do formerly. But I must be thankful, for my health is restored in a degree which it would have been great presumption to have hoped for at this time last year. In fact I never felt stronger in my life, but we have a proverb, " Burned bairns dread the fire." I am aware I must be cautious.

It is very true Sophia is going to be married, and to a young man of uncommon talents—indeed of as promising a character as I know. He is highly accomplished, a beautiful poet, and fine draughtsman, and what is better, of a most honourable and gentlemanlike disposition. He is handsome besides, and I like everything about him, except that he is more grave and retired than I (who have been all my life something of an *étourdi*) like particularly, but it is better than the opposite extreme. In point of situation they have enough to live upon, and " the world for the winning." He will probably rise high, as his family are rich, his talents excellent, and I have some interest : so I trust it will all do very well. Your Ladyship will see some beautiful lines of his writing in the last number of a very clever periodical publication called Blackwood's *Edinburgh Magazine*; it is published by Cadell and Davies, London. The verses are in an essay on the ballad poetry of the Spaniards, which he illustrates by some beautiful translations which—to speak truth—are much finer than the originals. I will show them to your Ladyship when I get to town, if you do not see them sooner. The youngster's name is John Gibson Lockhart; he comes of a good Lanarkshire family, and is very well connected. His father is a clergyman.

The times are very bad to be sure, and some of the

Ross-shire lairds have contrived to raise an insurrection among their tenants. I say *contrived*, for it positively requires a wonderful degree of oppression to turn these poor things against their landlords. They will manage it at last, however, and make us as bad as the south of Ireland. Non-residence is a horrid business. . . . Your Ladyship's much indebted and most faithful servant,

WALTER SCOTT.

TO HIS DAUGHTER.

LONDON, 23rd *April* [1820].[1]

MY DEAREST SOPHIA,—As I bring you down so much jewellery, etc., from one good friend and another—for Lady Compton sends a most beautiful necklace—I think you will be quite an Indian princess; so instead of adding to your trinkets, I send you on the other side a cheque for £50 for pocket money, etc., which you will find convenient in your new situation. . . . This will keep you always easy and teach you the comfort of having a few guineas at your own command. . . . This is my last letter, for I shall set off to-morrow and expect to be home on Thursday evening, although I may be "a borrower of the night for a

[1] The following extract from a letter by Croker to Lockhart, dated *April* 14th, 1820, shows the enthusiasm with which Sir Walter was received on this visit to London:—"He is so fêté that if he could dine three times a day he could not even then suffice to the anxiety of his friends to entertain him. Yesterday we went together to Woolwich to see the Arsenal and Congreve's rockets; and Sir Wm Congreve gave us afterwards a soldierlike dinner at the Repository. Sir Walter was greatly pleased with the rockets, and tho' it rained what is called cats and dogs all the while, the people flocked from far and near to see the great poet and greater novelist. The day before, Prince Leopold, the Prince of Hesse Homburg, some Ambassadors and such like grandees, had gone down to see the same sights, but they excited no curiosity, while everybody asked, 'but what day is Sir Walter to come?' Of all this he was unconscious, for Congreve and I thought that it would annoy him if he suspected that he was the object of attraction, so he thinks that that homage was paid to the rockets, which in fact was paid to a brighter, a higher, a purer, and more permanent light."

dark hour or twain."[1] As I am returning with the purpose
of performing one of the most interesting and solemn
duties which can be reserved for me in life, I feel desirous
to let no grass grow under my feet in the passage. All
friends here are well, and join in kindest love and best
wishes.—I remain always your affectionate father,

WALTER SCOTT.

TO LADY ABERCORN.

May [1820].

MY DEAR FRIEND,— . . . On Friday evening I gave
away Sophia to Mr. Lockhart.[2] They set off for Dunkeld,
and are to be at his father's house next Thursday. I own
my house seems lonely to me since she left us, but that
is a natural feeling which will soon wear off. I have every
reason to think I have consulted her happiness in the match,
as became the father of a most attached and dutiful daughter
who never in her life gave me five minutes' vexation. In
the meanwhile the words run strangely in my ear :—

> "Ah me ! the flower and blossom of my house
> The wind has blown away to other towers."

. . . I suppose by-and-by some kind suitor will carry off
my black-eyed maid, and then the old folks will be lonely
enough. But it is very wrong to grumble after having
had so much happiness in my family, and the change
which is like to take place being for their advantage. We
had a few friends with us after the couple had left us,
among others the Prince Gustavus of Sweden. . . . I cannot but think this young man will one day make a figure
in Europe. He has courage, spirit, and application, with
the utmost kindness and affability of manners. If Prince
Oscar does not sit the faster, my friend will have him out
of the saddle.[3]

[1] *Macbeth*, Act III. sc. 1.
[2] If the marriage took place on Friday it was on the 28th April, but
Lockhart says it was the 29th.   [3] See *Journal*, vol. i. pp. 385-6.

TO LOCKHART.

ABBOTSFORD, *Sunday.*

I HAD your kind remembrance from Perth, and rejoice
to find by a letter from Sophia to Anne, that you have
reached Germiston in all safety, and mean to be with us
in the end of this week; she mentions Friday or Saturday
—let us hope the earlier day, as we must be gone on
Monday, which will not, however, affect your motions, as
you can be comfortable here as long as you like. We . . .
hope to see Miss Lockhart, and Captain Lockhart if he is
not set forward to southern parts. Everything here is
looking delightful, especially since this mild rain has commenced, and Mama and Anne are impatient to see you.
The road from Lanark to Peebles is quite good though
a little hilly. As you pass look at the old Castle of
Drochills, built by Regent Morton, but never finished. It
is on the small river or stream which falls down on
Peebles. Neidpath, close by Peebles, is also worth looking at, though much destroyed by the old Duke of Q.
cutting all the fine old trees. I beg my kindest love
to Sophia, and Mrs. Scott and Anne join kindly in all
regards to your family, particularly my little friend Violet.[1]
—Yours most affectionately,   WALTER SCOTT.

TO MORRITT.

EDINBURGH, 19*th May* 1820.

MY DEAR MORRITT,— . . . I cannot feel that the
dignity inflicted on me has made the least difference
in my hopes, feelings, or thoughts. The king said some
very handsome things about it. Servants bow two inches
lower, a door opens three inches wider, and there it rests,
except that in Scotland my degree places me among the
old ladies at the head of the table and obliges me to carve,
at which office I am very awkward, and regret the real

[1] Mr. Lockhart's sister.

days of chivalry when all this labour devolved upon the
esquires. I had in London the great satisfaction of meeting Walter, who got leave of absence for that purpose, and
in order that he might be present at my daughter's
wedding. . . . To me, as it seems neither of my sons have
a strong literary turn, the society of a son-in-law possessed
of learning and talent must be a very great acquisition,
and relieve me from some anxiety with respect to a valuable
part of my fortune consisting of copyrights, etc., which
though advantageous in my lifetime might have been less
so at my decease, unless under the management of a
person acquainted with the nature of such property. All
I have to fear on Lockhart's part is a certain rashness,
which I trust has been the effect of youth and high spirits,
joined to lack of good advice, as he seems perfectly good-
humoured and very docile. So I trust your little friend
Sophia, who I know has an interest in your bosom, has a
very fair chance for such happiness as this motley world
can afford.

London I thought incredibly tiresome; I wanted my
sheet-anchors,—you and poor George Ellis,—by whom I
could ride at quiet moorings without mixing entirely with
the general vortex. The great lion—great in every sense—
was the gigantic Belzoni, the handsomest man (for a giant)
I ever saw or could suppose to myself. He is said completely to have overawed the Arabs, your old friends, by his
great strength, height, and energy. I had one delightful
evening in company with the Duke of Wellington, and
heard him fight over Waterloo and his other battles with
the greatest good humour. It is odd, he says, that the
most distinct writer on military affairs whose labours
he has perused is James II., in the warlike details given
in his own Memoirs. I have not read over these memoirs
lately, but I think I do not recollect much to justify the
eulogium of so great a master.

Things are pretty quiet in the West, but the poison remains to ferment and bubble when fitting opportunity offers. The unhappy dislocation which has taken place betwixt the Employer and those in his employment has been attended with very fatal consequences. Much of this is owing to the steam-engine. When the machinery was driven by water, the manufacturer had to seek out some sequestered spot where he could obtain a suitable fall of water, and then his workmen formed the inhabitants of a village around him, and he necessarily bestowed some attention less or more on their morals and on their necessities, had knowledge of their persons and characters, and exercised over them a salutary influence as over men depending on and intimately connected with him and his prospects. This is now quite changed: the manufactures are transferred to great towns, where a man may assemble five hundred workmen one week and dismiss them next, without having any further connection with them than to receive a week's work for a week's wages, nor any further solicitude about their future fate than if they were so many old shuttles. A superintendence of the workers considered as moral and rational beings is thus a matter totally unconnected with the employer's usual thoughts and cares. They have now seen the danger of suffering a great population to be thus entirely separated from the influence of their employers, and given over to the management of their own Societies, in which the cleverest and most impudent fellows always get the management of the others, and become bell-wethers in every sort of mischief. Some resolutions have been adopted respecting the employing only such men as have been either uniformly of loyal character or acknowledge their errors and withdraw from all treasonable meetings, associations, and committees.

The banks and monied men should use their influence, which is omnipotent with the manufacturers, to enforce the observance of these resolutions, so necessary for the general quiet. That such regulations would secure tranquillity is quite certain, for notwithstanding the general influence of example, the workmen in some of the greatest manufactures did not furnish a single recruit to Radicalism.

I do trust and pray that your next letter may bring me pleasant news of your household, whose welfare sits near my heart.—Ever, my dear Morritt, most truly yours,

WALTER SCOTT.

TO LADY ABERCORN.

EDINBURGH, 1*st* June 1820.

MY DEAR FRIEND,— . . . Sophia has taken possession of her own mansion, and is as bustling and important as may be in the exercise of all her newly acquired rights as the mistress of a household. She has scarce a guess how many cares and vexations she is taking upon herself, but it is lucky that in this changeable world youth at least can enjoy the present without being anxious for the future.

The report you have heard about the first volume is quite erroneous, unless the Second Sight be as common among the literati in London as it used formerly to be in the Hebrides. The fact is that not above one half is written,[1] so much have family affairs interfered with my literary amusements. Did you observe Lord Archibald Hamilton's tirade?[2] His Lordship is greatly mistaken if he supposes that I neglect any part of my official duties for the purpose of employing my time otherwise, for I believe no man ever discharged the duties of his office more regularly; and it has happened to me often not only to discharge my own, but take on myself those of my colleagues whom

[1] The *Monastery* was published in March and the *Abbot* in September.

[2] Lord Archibald was reported to have said in Parliament that Walter Scott wrote more books than any other man could read.

indisposition or other impediments prevented from attending to it themselves. And as to the mode in which I employ my leisure hours, I conceive I may answer my Lord Archie as the little child replied to the clergyman when he heard him asking his hearers in course of his discourse, why do you do this? and why will you do that? The child tired of this, and when he saw the clergyman looking to the pew as if addressing him in particular, could keep silence no longer but replied aloud, in answer to these repeated questions, "What's your business?"

I should be glad there was a change of court favour. Lady C. has scarce sense enough, as I am told, to support the character of Sultana in chief. As we must expect there should be such a person, it is much to be wished that she were gifted with prudence and moderation, and disposed to conduct such a matter with decency. I have seen a copy of Burnet's history with notes by Dean Swift written on the margin—severe enough of course.[1] Among others, Burnet happens to mention the celebrated Nell Gwyn, who he says, though she was a favourite, was never treated by Charles with the *decencies* of a mistress. "Quere," says the Dean on the margin, "what sort of decencies are these?" But begging pardon of the satirist, though the actual vice may be the same, the public scandal may be much lessen'd or greatly increased by the way in which this sort of persons conduct themselves, and the degree of avowal and *éclat* which is given to the connection. . . .

I should tell you Sophia and Lockhart are to have a little cottage at Abbotsford by way of summer quarters; it is about two miles from us, a good distance between the old and young poet, and being on my own estate we have a pleasant and private walk to connect us. . . .

Adieu, my dear Lady Abercorn. My best love to my

---

[1] See *Quarterly Review*, vol. i. pp. 176-7, for more of the Dean's comments. piquant *Marginalia* and Scott's comments.

pretty Lady Julia,[1] and believe me, with the most sincere
regard, your truly affectionate friend,

WALTER SCOTT.

TO HIS SON WALTER.

. . . I have little news to send you from this. The
weather has been vilely wet, scarce a day without rain,
good for nothing but ducks, and geese, and young trees.
Those in the cleughs at Abbotsford are coming on very
well. To-morrow I go there with Mr. and Mrs. John
Prevot *alias* Lockhart, to see what may be done in making
the little cottage at Burnfoot tenantable for their honours.
The situation you know is beautiful, and I have acquired
Heiton's grounds with the firwood for £2300, which bounds
Abbotsford completely on that side by laying it against
the Duke of Buccleuch's property. Said firwood was a
great roost for the black-cocks, of which Isaac Haig used
to knock down a good many there, which sport must now
have an end. Perhaps you may get over in August, though
I suppose you will be judged to have had your own share
of play in the spring. . . .

I am desirous to hear that you settle to reading and
to studying the languages a little. If you do not keep hold
of what you have gained, it is just throwing away all
the trouble you had to acquire it; and a very small and
short exercise is all which is necessary to enable you to
retain what is ever learned.

I should think this general distress would have made
good horses cheap, for generally when money becomes
scarce bargains may be gotten. Did you ever get the
books I sent you?

Mama, Charles, and Anne are all well; the enclosed
will speak for themselves. . . . Always your affectionate
father,   WALTER SCOTT.

[1] Lady Abercorn's youngest sister.

TO THE SAME.

EDIN^R., *27th June* [1820].

I HAD yesterday the great pleasure of a letter from Sir Thomas Brisbane, giving a very good account of your conduct both as an officer and gentleman, of which Colonel Murray has reported very favourably to him. Nothing, my dear boy, which earth has to give me can afford me so much pleasure as to know that you are doing your duty like a man of sense and honour, and qualifying yourself to serve your king and country, and do credit to the name you bear. So that Sir Thomas Brisbane's kindness in communicating intelligence so agreeable has given to all of us the most sincere pleasure. Meanwhile I beg you to mind your handwriting a little, as it gets worse and worse, like the pigs as they grow up, and remember what I have been so often telling you about the languages. Assuredly to have French and German at your finger-ends is of great consequence in your profession; as also the use of the pencil in habitually sketching from nature, and accustoming yourself to observe the surface of ground, and the advantages which it offers for military operations. Next to a good stout heart and a sound judgment, a good *eye* is of the greatest consequence for an officer of light troops, and that can only be acquired by practice. It would be of great use to you to read the King of Prussia's (old Frederick the Great) instructions to light troops. He was the first who reduced that important part of an army to system and principle. . . . I am your affectionate father,   WALTER SCOTT.

TO LADY ABERCORN.

July 1, 1820.

MY DEAR FRIEND,—The portrait is advancing by the pencil of a clever artist, and will I think be a likeness and a

tolerably good picture. I hope to get it sent up before I
leave town; at any rate I will have it finished so far as
sittings are concerned. If I look a little sleepy your kindness must excuse it, as I had to make my attendance on
the man of colours betwixt six and seven in the morning.[1]
About the 11th I go to Abbotsford for the rest of the
season, and truly glad I shall be to get out of this scene
of heat and dust and bad air and legal contention. It
is however a trifling penance to that which my betters
have to discharge in the House of Commons, where these
great folks' quarrel will make wild work and late sittings
for the rest of the Session of Parliament. I suspect the
poor Queen's head is turned by the huzzas of the mob,
which she possibly mistakes for the serious approbation
of the people of England. Whereas, if the truth was
known, I believe the ground of the huzzas is rather hatred
to the King than liking to her, and that they applaud her
as a certain great lady was once said to have been cheered
in the Dublin theatre with the cry, " Long may she live
to disgrace her husband ! " The opening of a green bag
with a seal upon it has, in itself, something very irritating
to public curiosity ;[2] and I suspect many a one is privately
glad we are to have the reading of all the scandal,
especially now that we have made [some show of] decent
reluctance to it. I own I have no great sympathy with
that extreme degree of delicacy which shrinks from the
discharge of justice and duty merely on account of objections founded upon delicacy. If the matter could have
been stifled earlier in the day, it would have been a great
comfort and saved the ears of the House much scandal

---

[1] This portrait, now in the possession of Lord Napier and Ettrick
at Thirlestane, was painted by John
Watson, better known as Sir John
Watson Gordon. For further details see letter of 2nd August in
present volume.

[2] The evidence against Queen
Caroline was enclosed in sealed
green bags which were laid upon
the table of the House of Lords and
Commons for investigation in 1820.

and the country some disgrace. But since the discussion has gone so far, I cannot see why these two great personages should remain, the one under the suspicion of subornation of perjury, false accusation, and I know not what, and the other under a charge of infamy and guilt, without the public knowing which is right, which wrong. . . .

My own motions are very uncertain, and will depend much on the manner in which I must dispose of my second son. He is come to that time of life when a year or two's absence from the paternal roof will be of great advantage to him. I beg my kindest respects to Lady Julia, and am always, dear Lady Abercorn, your truly affectionate friend, WALTER SCOTT.

FROM LOCKHART.

EDIN^R., *July* 20 [1820].

MY DEAR SIR,—I returned yesterday from Musselburgh in time to hear within two minutes of the election of Wilson.[1] He polled 21 to 8. . . . I believe he is now one of the happiest men in Britain, and like many others, chiefly of your making. I trust in God, and in his own high spirit, that he will do honour every way to the station. The arts resorted to against him, more particularly within the last few days, seem to have exceeded even the measure of Whig or Radical malice. . . .

All this however is now over, and it only makes his triumph the more complete. . . .

As Wilson will of course write you immediately and enclose you all the documents, I need not trouble you with any more of this at present.[2]

[1] John Wilson's election to the chair of Moral Philosophy in the University of Edinburgh.

[2] FROM PROFESSOR WILSON.

29*th July*, 53 QUEEN STREET.

MY DEAR SIR,—I have wished, but wished in vain, to write a few lines to you, expressive of my deep and everlasting gratitude, as intense as it becomes one human being to feel towards another, for your goodness on the late trying

Among other things that I wanted to speak to you about ere you left us was an imitation of Cranstoun's song on Packwood, which I had been amusing myself with in honour of *Blackwood*.[1] I trust, however, there is nothing in it which anybody can take amiss on general grounds, and as to the individual victims, they must be prepared to expect far worse. . . .

It is put in the person of the Glasgow Dentist, a vain idiot, who glories beyond measure in such fame as these things can bestow. I suppose it serves his trade. . . .

I suppose Mr. and Mrs. Skene have reached the

occasion. May I be able in a year or two to prove myself in some measure worthy of your opinion !

My enemies are still working against me with unabated ferocity. I sometimes cannot help thinking that they must have some other object in so doing than the mere impotent gratification of malice, though, my election being sure, I cannot reasonably foresee any evil brewing against the future. My mind however has scarcely recovered its serenity, for though it be natural for every man to over-rate his own importance, I must still think that I have suffered as severe a passion as ever afflicted any one in a similar situation.

I have not been able to direct my mind to my subject. Indeed, I determined on a fortnight's idleness or reverie, and on the 1st of August shall look into myself with a meditative eye. A month's reading and thinking may show me something I do not yet see, and in two other months I hope to compose thirty or forty lectures, such as they may be.

Have you anything to recommend during a leisure hour regarding books? or would you write me a letter or two on a plan of lectures?

I must refuse myself the delight of visiting Abbotsford, for the time is fearfully short, but I shall visit it in the thoughts of a grateful and affectionate heart.

With everything you say in your letter respecting retaliation, I do most deeply sympathise. Your will is law.

My kind friend Lockhart requested me to tell you that he too intended to leave the beasts in their own stye,'and the testimonium, admirable in spirit and vivacity of ingenuity, will I know be the last of that kind of composition in Maga. . . .

I have much to be happy about, and hope to triumph over all that is disagreeable and painful, by the exercise of patience, industry, and virtue.—I am, my dear sir, yours as I ought to be, JOHN WILSON.

[1] "The Testimonium, a prize poem by James Scott, Esq.," prefacing the 7th vol. of *Blackwood*. Packwood was an advertising cutler who "kept a poet on the premises." The lines referred to by Lockhart were written by George Cranstoun, afterwards Lord Corehouse, and reprinted in 1839 in the *Court of Session Garland*.

Pavilion ere now, so that you can be in no want of amusement, and that the *Abbot* will make his appearance in due season, and the sooner the better if he ends as he begins.[1]   Mr. Erskine, by the way, has seen the sheets of vol. i. and agrees with me perfectly that it at least equals *Waverley, Ivanhoe*, and the *Antiquary*.   I believe you have so much faith in his judgment that you will excuse me for mentioning this.

If I can get leisure enough at Germiston I mean to be very bold and begin the Roman story[2] I once talked to you about.   But I shall not say anything about it to anybody till I have written a volume and submitted it to your inspection.—Affectionately yours,

J. G. LOCKHART.

FROM THE SAME.

GERMISTON, *Tuesday evening, July 25th.*

MY DEAR SIR,— . . . Your letter has given me very great pain, and yet it has given me great pleasure also.   I wish I had trusted my own judgment, and then that foolish squib[3] would not have appeared, at least without your having seen it.   Wilson, however, by not writing as he promised and sending the documents to which I referred, has, I must hope, taken away from me a very considerable branch of the excuse pleadable in the mere *Corpus delicti.*

I am far from supposing indeed that anything of that sort could have at all affected your judgment as to the general points on which you touch, and in regard to these you may depend on my grateful and sacred attention to the hints your kindness has dictated.

I am sure Wilson is quite as sensible as he ought to be

---

[1] Published in September.
[2] *Valerius*, published in 1821.
[3] See note 1, page 85.   Scott's

letter of remonstrance referred to has not been preserved.

of the responsibility his new station confers on him, and will agree most entirely with the propriety of doing as you say he should do—*i.e.* dropping all connection with the skirmishing warfare of party politics.

I am not so great a fool as to covet a single-handed post of that sort, and besides have abundant weightier reasons (above all your desire thus distinctly expressed) for withdrawing myself at the same moment. But indeed I think neither of us have of late been great offenders, excepting only this last skit. I shall make it my business to communicate to Wilson immediately what I take to be your view of the whole subject, and trust the result both in his department and mine will be such as to satisfy you and your kind wishes for the welfare of us both.

. . . I rejoice to hear of the progress of the *Abbot*, and shall beg from James B. a sight of vol. ii. . . .

J. G. LOCKHART.

TO HIS SON WALTER.

ABBOTSFORD, 26th *July* [1820].

THAT you may not march like your namesake Walter the Pennyless (*Gautier sans sous*), I send you £50, being your August remittance, and I will make you a present of £20 of it over your allowance, providing you write me back word who Walter the Pennyless was, and where he marched to. I give you leave to consult your whole mess on this great historical question. Write to me at any rate that you have received this, and a previous cheque for £80 which I sent you for a horse, but which I suppose had not reached you upon the 19th, as you do not mention having received it. Be very pointed about mentioning sum and dates of bills received.

It can never be my wish, my dear Walter, that you should feel any stint, and on the other hand, your good sense will point out the necessity of your being a prudent manager, as in your service there are heavy demands for dress, etc., which can only be provided for by keeping a good look-out ahead, and recollecting that the money we have in pocket just now will be liable to future demands and contingencies, and must therefore be husbanded with due care.

I expect you always to be on honour with me in money matters, and not to run bills or incur debts without my knowledge, as I would, at any particular time, rather send assistance than you should get into those shuffling, underhand practices which ruin so many young men.— I am in some haste, yours very truly,   WALTER SCOTT.

TO HIS DAUGHTER.

ABBOTSFORD, 29*th July* [1820.]

MY DEAREST SOPHIA,—I had yesterday a very kind letter from Lockhart, who takes in good part the advice I ventured to give him about withdrawing from the personal skirmishes of the magazine,[1] which in his new and dignified character of a married man, and Wilson having become a professor, would not do so well as formerly. It flatters an old codger very much when he finds a young friend disposed to listen to him upon such an occasion, and so far as complete acquaintance with literary intrigue makes me a competent adviser, I have been long an experienced person.

He tells me you are going to Ireland for a trip if the weather permits. You will be delighted with the Giant's Causeway, and more so I think with the old castle of Dunluce, and the scenery of the adjacent cliffs at Kilrush. . . . —Always your affectionate father,

WALTER SCOTT.

[1] Blackwood's *Edinburgh Magazine.*

TO MORRITT.

[*July* 1820.]

MY DEAREST MORRITT,—Nothing could give me more
pleasure than the sight of your hand. I thought it likely
that I might not hear from you owing to the hurry of
your preparations for your proposed jaunt to the Continent,
but became truly uneasy when I understood from your
neighbour, Mr. Serjeant Hullock, that you had been
seriously unwell. I was just thinking whether I should not
write a few lines to my friend Mr. Dove[1] to make more
minute inquiries when your most welcome letter arrived
and set my mind much at ease. Nothing can give me
half the pleasure which the prospect of seeing you affords.
Pray come as soon as you can, and believe you cannot
come amiss: in truth we have no engagements, unless I
should go to Athole for two or three days to look at the
Duke's larch woods in the month of September, and
perhaps we might make out that tour together. At any
rate come as soon as you can. Will. Rose leads me from
his letters to expect him about this time; perhaps he will
pass by Rokeby—he brings his clown, my old acquaintance
Caliban, alongst with him. I expect Heber also, but his
motions are cruelly uncertain. However, when any one
comes to the door early in the morning, I always exclaim,
" There comes Heber after having travelled all night in the
Selkirk mail." With all this pleasant anticipation of most
welcome guests, it is necessary to notice that Abbotsford is
no more like the Abbotsford you knew it than the Rome
of Augustus was like the Rome of Numa. We have plenty
of little pigeon holes of bedrooms, plenty of mutton on the
hill and beef in the park, and salmon, and hares, and
grouse, and poultry, and so forth. And a parlour to eat
them in, the model of which I take to have been Mr.

---

[1] Mr. Morritt's attendant—sometimes playfully named, "Mr. Doo,"
the " Carrier pigeon," or " *Billet Doux.*"

Slender's own great chamber, which he makes the subject of asseveration when confirming his complaint against Falstaff. Above all, you shall not go through the night air to your bedroom, and should you find yourself at any time a little unwell we are within reach of very excellent advice. I think you are very prudent not to trust yourself on the Continent this year. When one feels so far an invalid as to wish to be within reach of the faculty, one is sadly off in France and Italy, where the Sangrados are of such low reputation that it were a shame even to be killed by them. The same causes which should make you stay here do not occur in your nephew's case, whose object will be, I presume, a quiet residence for some time in a mild climate. He is so amiable and so clever a youth that I trust his constitution, as often happens, will be confirmed by care and mild air at the early and hazardous period, and that he will add strong health to the *mens sana et divinior*. Forgive me if I talk a little Latin: the Principal of Harford[1] College is here, so, like the Justice in *Every Man out of his Humour*, who hands down his great old two-handled sword when Bobadil comes before him,[2] I have been gathering the scraps and fragments of my wretched learning to fit myself for such worshipful society. He is, however, a very gentlemanlike, well-informed man, and as I propose to send Charles one day to Harford, I am fain to pay him all the attention I can. A writer's place to India is better than fighting on at the Bar here, amidst all the dissipation which naturally distracts a lad's attention before business comes to fix and arrest it.[3]

I have very good accounts of Walter from Sir Thomas Brisbane, who commands the Cork district, and who finds him an alert, intelligent officer, minding his duty and liked

---

[1] East India College, Haileybury.
[2] Act v. sc. 1.
[3] It was Scott's intention at this time to allow Charles to enter the Indian service.

well by his Colonel and brother officers: completely steady
and gentlemanlike in his conduct, which is all one can
wish, and a great deal too, of a youth of nineteen left so
much to his own handling.

Lockhart is very much what you will like when you
come to know him—much genius and a distinguished
scholar, very handsome in face and person, and only wanting something of the *usage de monde*; I mean there is a
little want of ease in his manners in society. He does not
laugh as thou doest, Anthony—this is, however, speaking
critically, for he is neither conceited nor negligent in his
manner. His powers of personal satire are what I most
dread on his own account; it is an odious accomplishment, and most dangerous, and I trust I have prevailed
on him to turn his mind to something better.

John Wilson, author of the *Isle of Palms*, etc., has
been just made Professor of Moral Philosophy in spite
of the most desperate and unfair efforts by the Whigs,
who had recourse to all sorts of poisoned weapons to
oppose him. It is odd the rage these gentlemen have
for superintending education. They consider it as their
own province, and set their mark on it as Sancho did
on the cowheel; then their geese are all swans, and the
Tory swans are all geese, and they puff the one and
slander the other without mood or mercy. But we gave
them a day's kemping for once, and carried the election
by 21 against 8. I was obliged to canvas personally and
stoutly among the bailies and deacons, and if Wilson
fulfils the high promise which his talents and eloquence
have made, and which it only requires the concentration
of his mind on one important subject in order to realise,
I shall think I have done both Edinburgh and literature
some service. With great amiability he had (having an
easy fortune, and living for himself) some youthful follies
to look back upon, . . . all of which were most indus-

triously raised up and placed in array against the most
satisfactory proofs of sound principle, gentlemanlike conduct, and generosity of sentiment.   Such is party.

Your old friends here will be most delighted to see
you.   I feel my family diminished, and am a little sorry
for myself.   The hubbub of poor Walter with his dogs
and his guns, and a lively buck or two of companions,
kept the house alive.   And Sophia's constant good humour
and good sense, and her legendary poems and music,
makes a sad blank.   To remedy the latter as much as the
matter will admit, she is to have a little cottage in a sweet
little glen of mine which you do not know as yet, with a
babbling brook in front, and a screen of trees to the eastward, quite a place for

> —— Lucy at the door to sing
> With russet gown and apron blue.

We will be within two miles of each other, so that the old
homme des lettres may see enough of the young folks
without any chance of too frequent intrusion.   Pray come
and help me with your taste in all these weighty matters,
and believe me, dear Morritt, most affectionately yours,

WALTER SCOTT.

I have not the slightest return of my last year's fearful
complaints.   I think the system is clear of the gall-stones
or whatever they were, and at no greater sacrifice of
creature-comforts than resigning John Barleycorn.

TO LADY ABERCORN.

ABBOTSFORD, MELROSE, *2nd August* 1820.

MY DEAR FRIEND,—It gives me great pleasure that
you received the books safe.   I did not see them before
they were sent off, for I am obliged to transact all these
matters by a confidential agent, besides that to write upon
them might, in case of their being opened by any curious

person, lead to inferences and conclusions which for the
present I would rather avoid. The picture is embarked
for Stratford Place. Please to give orders to have it
unpacked, because the painter is afraid that the colours,
being so recently laid on, may sustain injury if excluded
from the air. The dog which I am represented as holding
in my arms is a Highland terrier from Kintail, of a breed
very sensible, very faithful, and very ill-natured. It
sometimes tires or pretends to do so when I am on horseback, and whines to be taken up, where it sits before me
like a child, without any assistance.[1] . . .

I am satisfied your tour on the Continent is to be of
service to you, and as for troubles and confusion of a
public nature, who can presume to say that you are not
rather flying from them, than putting yourself in the way
of them ? . . . The K. is not well advised to do anything just
now which can attract public notice, and Lady —— is a
fool to make parade of her favour. Her predecessor
understood matters much better.

In this remote corner we are very quiet, and think of
nothing except the good harvest which Providence seems
about to send us, and which is one of the most promising
I ever saw. I have not yet had Crabbe here, but expect
him every moment. His manner is a singular mixture
of simplicity, shrewdness, and something like affectation,

---

[1] Alluding to *Ourisque*, whose
ejection from the parlour fireside
by the Liddesdale whelp *Ginger*
is so graphically described by Scott
to Terry,—see *Life*, vol. vii. p. 240.
Thenceforth *Ginger*, and her equally
peppery sister *Spice*, appear to
have taken possession of the library
and dining room, though Ourisque
continued to be Lady Scott's
favourite. Half a dozen years
later, when its kind mistress died,
Sir Walter told his daughter
Sophia that "it remained in the
room without stirring and without
tasting food for many hours, when
all of a sudden it transferred its
regard to Anne, left the fatal
room, and now lies on Anne's bed,
whom two days since she would
not allow to touch her. Its fond-
ness for me seemed quite like a
rational creature who had lost a
friend and sought consolation from
another." (14th May 1826.)

but his poetry shows what an acute observer of nature he
has been.   I think if he had cultivated the sublime
and the pathetic, instead of the satirical cast of poetry,
he must have stood very high (as indeed he does at any
rate) on the list of British poets.   His *Sir Eustace Grey*
and the *Hall of Justice* indicate prodigious talent.   I
shall be very glad indeed to see him on Tweedside.[1]

I expect Will. Rose also, but he is such a changeable
mortal that I do not know whether he will come or no.
Heber also, who I think is known to your Ladyship,
promised to be here, as also John Morritt of Rokeby.   So
that allowing besides for chance guests, of which I always
have a share, we are not like to be very lonely.   But we
have plenty of beef and mutton, and poultry and game,
and salmon and trouts, so those who do not depend on
French cookery need not at least fear famine.   Walter's
regiment has marched to Dublin; if he can execute any
commission there for your Ladyship he will esteem himself much honoured. . . . —My dear Lady Marchioness, your
truly faithful and affectionate friend,   WALTER SCOTT.

TO HIS SON WALTER.

ABBOTSFORD, 15*th August* 1820.

I ENCLOSE a letter of introduction to your Commander-
in-Chief from an intimate friend of his and mine, and
request you will lose no time in delivering it.   I observe
from a letter to Mama you are a little afraid of him as a
disciplinarian.   It is upon discipline however that the
utility of an army must always depend, and there was
never more reason for keeping officers in mind of their
duty than at present, when the troops of other countries
are setting the example of mutiny, and when in our own,

---

[1] Crabbe did not make out his visit to Scotland until August 1822.

the Guards it is said are not altogether to be trusted. Respecting Sir David Baird, besides being always a man of courage himself, and a successful general, it should never be forgotten that the army, Britain, and the world owe the Duke of Wellington entirely to him. The story is told differently, but this is the right edition. At the siege of Seringapatam, Lieutenant-Colonel Wellesley was ordered on a night attack on a battery which annoyed the besiegers,—a sort of field-work or redoubt; his guides were stupid or treacherous and misled the detachment, which actually dispersed in the darkness, and Lieutenant-Colonel Wellesley returned *alone* to the camp. Lord Lake,[1] who commanded, ordered Sir D. Baird to repair this mischance by an attack the next day on the same post, but Sir D. entreated him to give Lieutenant-Colonel Wellesley another chance to redeem the credit he had lost, observing truly that he was otherwise a lost man for ever. Lord Lake said he was happy Sir David had asked him to do what he could not have done himself, without subjecting himself to the imputation of doing more for the Governor-general's brother than he would for another officer. And so Lieutenant-Colonel Wellesley tried his luck again, succeeded, and rose to be the first General of Europe, and its saviour. . . .

You have never said if you bought the horse for which I remitted the money, and I suppose you have received mine covering a draft for £50. Have you found out Walter the Pennyless?[2] . . . Yours truly and affectionately,

WALTER SCOTT.

Maida still wears his collar or rather muzzle, except when he walks with me. He don't seem to mind it.

---

[1] A slip of the pen for Harris.— See Baird's *Life* (2 vols. 8vo, London, 1832), vol. i. pp. 191-4, for a fuller account of the incident.

[2] One of the leaders of the first crusade. Dr. Brewer's useful *Handbooks* were not then in existence unfortunately for the young soldier!

TO THE SAME.

ABBOTSFORD, *5th October* [1820].

. . . I AM very anxious about you in so gay a town as Dublin, and I make it my earnest request you will not go too deeply into the current of dissipation. What company you do keep let it always be the best you can come at, and then you will be always picking up something of information along with amusement. I am obliged to Mr. Maturin for the civilities he has shewn you. He is a thoughtless genius, however, and I would not have [you] trust much to his counsels. . . .

You have never said anything of a draft for £80 to buy a second charger. I cannot suppose the money has miscarried, but I would be obliged to you to tell me whether the horse is bought or no—in short, to be explicit on the matter, which I have several times mentioned without receiving an answer. Pray write about it immediately, and also whether you have replaced your *dear* German. I shall think next year of realizing my original intention of procuring you leave to study at the military academy for some time, after you have become sufficiently acquainted with your regimental duty.

I shall be glad to hear that you have seen Sir David Baird. His fate was a singular one, in seeing Tippoo Sahib lie dead at his feet, after the said Tippoo had kept him so many months in a dungeon at [Seringapatam].[1]

[1] Sir David Baird had been a prisoner in Seringapatam for nearly four years (from 1780 until 1784), and treated with great cruelty by Tippoo. In 1799 Sir David stormed the city, and as he afterwards wrote, "ere the sweat had dried on his brow" he was superseded in the command by his junior officer Colonel Wellesley, to whom he had recently acted so chival- rously. The Duke on being asked in 1831 if he could explain why he, so young a man, was appointed over Baird's head, replied in a characteristic letter, in which he says, "I must say that I was the fit person to be selected."— Croker, vol. ii. p. 102. Sir David never forgot the indignity, though he knew and appreciated Welling- ton's military skill.

I have little news to send from this. We have had a great deal of company flying to and fro, some pleasant, some bores. Sophia's cottage is finished and looks very nice indeed,—I mean the mason-work is finished. It will be habitable next May. My last purchase has enclosed it very nearly on all hands.—I am always your affectionate father,   WALTER SCOTT.

TO LOCKHART.

ABBOTSFORD, 21st October 1820.

MY DEAR LOCKHART,—I received your letter, and your present embarrassment gives me the more concern, as considering it in every point of view I scarce know how to advise you. The best view of it is, that it is just at worst the loss of a certain number of hundred pounds, which industry and the exertion of talents like yours can always make up. I think the jury can hardly avoid finding damages due, but the exertions of counsel might bring them down to a trifle. It would be easy to produce very many instances of much worse being said of Inns, and so forth, than you have said of the Black Bull. But then a blot is not a blot till hit. And it would be difficult to shew that any inn-keeper had prosecuted for damages and been cast in his suit.

Topham's Letters from Edinburgh about 1772 might be appealed to; Johnson's tour through Scotland, Boswell's ditto, will readily occur to you as examples, and it is obvious that you had better refer to these books than to books of foreign travel. Out of Johnson much might surely be gleaned, and the character of the author,—no friend to any undue licence of the pen,—would be much in favour of your defence. About counsel I scarce know what to say. Erskine I have remarked with great grief has lost much of his energy since his great loss, and was even drooping before that event. But you are sure he will do his utmost. Cockburn is a good hand for a jury, but he is Master Totherside, and it is a case in which I should distrust even a man of honour where his feelings and his professional duties were working different tacks. Cranstoun would be the *ipsissimus* man, but I do not know where he is or whether he is come-at-able. In short I am able to suggest nothing better than you have proposed, namely Erskine and Forsyth.

The sale of the Inn I think a very strong point. In short, I think with management you will come through easy—not I fear triumphant. The worst is that the smallest sum of damages carries expenses. But at any rate I think (I know it will give you pleasure to be explicit on that point) that you have done all which you could to make up the matter, and ought not to have gone any further. I think it likely the Chief Commissioner may be a mediator—at least he and I are great personal friends, and I should think that might balance other prejudices. Pitmilly will be at least favourable, and Gillies is the only one I should think like to be much otherwise. But the matter must take its chance now, were that chance ten times worse, and it is to no purpose that I should vex you further with speculations, where I have no solid advice to offer. I think the conduct of the agent ought to be exposed.[1]

We went over the moor yesterday to Kippilaw in a pour-

[1] The case referred to in this letter was an action of damages raised by one Robertson, proprietor of the Black Bull Inn, Leith Street, Edinburgh, against the publisher of *Peter's Letters to his Kinsfolk*, in respect of a passage in vol. i. p. 4 of that work, in which the Black Bull was characterised as "a crowded, noisy, shabby, uncomfortable inn, frequented by all manner of stage-coaches and their contents, as my ears were well taught before morning." From a paragraph in the *Scotsman* newspaper of 28th October 1820, we learn that the case was set down for trial on 7th November, but was compromised by a payment to the inn-keeper of £400. The objectionable passage did not appear in the next edition of the book.

ing day,—a great exertion of neighbourly kindness by which
the whole party have caught cold. Our love to Sophia.
We hear with sympathy the fate and apotheosis of pussy.
I wish you could have tarried to see Joanna Baillie.—Ever
yours very affectionately, WALTER SCOTT.

TO MORRITT.

8th December 1820.

DEAR MORRITT,—. . . Talking of science, hast any
philosophy in thee, Morritt? If you have, now is the time
to clear any doubts which may hang on your mind about
geology, phrenology, or anything terminating in *ology*, for
I am installed President of our northern Royal Society[1] in
place of Sir James Hall,

> And Log the second reigns like Log the first.

Being an anxious vindicator of prerogative in all established authorities, I am not likely to forsake my claim to
that which is thus happily vested in my own person, and
therefore uphold myself to be a better judge how the world
is made than if I had been a Cocker, and capable *ex officio*
and without either hesitation or study to resolve all doubts
about stones flung from the moon, spots in the sun, green
pastures at the pole, and all the other arcana of nature.
Meantime I have only thought it necessary to get up for my
inaugural oration the well-worn opinion of Mr. Jenkinson in
the *Vicar of Wakefield* upon the cosmogony of the world.

I have yours of Monday, and therefore this letter shall
not await Mr. Scott's[2] motions.

> Stat Priami domus, stant alta mœnia Trojæ.

And why do they stand?—marry! because they had never
been attacked or in the least danger. The Sutors of Selkirk
never meditated the least injury to me or my dwelling, nor

---

[1] On November 27.
[2] A son of Sir Wm. Scott, Lord Stowell, then visiting Scotland.

was there the least disturbance or window-breaking even in the place itself. . . . Indeed I never can conceive a Selkirk mob so numerous but I would have met them beard to beard and driven them backward home before they came within two miles of Abbotsford. Who can be the author of this impertinent legend, which has not the slightest foundation of any kind, I cannot discover. I wrote to Mr. Pringle of Haining, to whose society it was falsely ascribed, and had yesterday a manly answer from him reprobating the infamous paragraph, which, far from originating with him or his, seems to have given him as much offence as it did me. All I know is that if the author be a responsible person, which I greatly doubt, he will do well to wear his nose in a case, for I will certainly have a pluck at it. . . . I have only to add that if a set of madmen had been so determined as to come four miles to attack my peaceful house, I would have fired from window and battlement and kept my castle while my castle could keep me.[1]

I have to write to Rose and others about this ridiculous yet vexatious hoax, so only send kind love to the young ladies and your nephew.—Yours most faithfully,

WALTER SCOTT.

TO LADY LOUISA STUART.

EDINBURGH, 14th December 1820.

MY DEAR LADY LOUISA,—Our family were not frightened on the occasion your kindness alludes to, for two excellent reasons; (1) they were and have been at Edinburgh since 12th November; (2) Abbotsford was never attacked by any human being. It is not easy to conjecture the purpose of this extraordinary and totally unfounded legend, whether merely an absurd hoax by one of those ingenious persons who mistake a dull lie for a good jest,

[1] Referring to a statement in the *Morning Post* London newspaper of Nov. 30th, 1820.

and who always remind me of the old laird of Pitmilly, who in his dotage used to walk about the streets of St. Andrews, and when any man asked him how he did, answered, "Ay, man, do ye ca' that wut?" or whether it has been some party trick of one side or other, as marvellously wise as the other is witty. A report here did Haining the great injustice to name him as the author, probably with the kind intention of bringing about another "Raeburn-meadow-spot," where his ancestor and mine fought a fatal duel.[1] He exculpated himself, however, in the most handsome manner. It would be a very desperate mob that would march four miles upon such an onslaught, and should such a whim seize the Sutors,

> Ils seront reçus,
> Biribi,
> A la façon de Barbarie,
> Mon amie.

However, having destroyed many a castle with my pen, I cannot complain that my own has been *Cossaqué* with the same harmless implement. The most agreeable compensation, however, has been the kind interest expressed by many friends, and in particular your Ladyship's valued letter. There are mischievous people with us as well as elsewhere, but the spirit is far from general, in evidence whereof the Queen was publicly burned in effigy upon the top of a hill near Melrose by a large concourse of farmers and labourers. Your excellent tact has exactly fixed on the point which has shocked many of the middle orders, namely, the bare-faced hypocrisy of the procession. I think the tide begins to turn. But Lord! what a stupid monster John Bull is, and how well he has chosen his natural emblem, for who but a brute of a bull that is driven frantic at sight of a red rag would run bellowing

---

[1] Between Walter Scott and Mark Pringle in October 1707. See Craig Brown's *History of* *Selkirkshire*, 2 vols. 4to, Edinburgh, 1884, vol. ii. p. 83.

mad on such subjects as the Popish Plot of 1682, or more lately on such worthy topics as John Wilkes, Currency, Lord George Gordon, or Queen Caroline? This last business, though not the most atrocious hallucination, is certainly the most discreditable that has befallen John's understanding. It is a kind of going to the Devil with a dish-clout, or as upon former occasions the country was in danger of being blown up by a barrel of gunpowder, we at present run the risk of being suffocated by a brimstone match. Meanwhile I go on quietly with my own amusements.

I do not design any scandal about Queen Bess, whom I admire much, altho' like an old *true blue*, I have malice against her on Queen Mary's account. But I think I shall be very fair. The story is the tragedy of Leicester's first wife, and I have made it as far as my facilities would permit "a pleasant tragedy, stuffed with most pitiful mirth." The mournful termination is certainly an objection to the general reader and may hurt its popularity. I think when I had the pleasure of seeing you we had better subjects of conversation than the *on dits* about these tales, otherwise I would have given you the key to the report about Mr. Thomas Scott. My brother, who is a person, as Captain Bobadil says, very near if not altogether as well qualified as myself to entertain the public, undertook some time since to send me a tale of a wanderer from Europe commencing backsettler in America; and seriously, from his powers, which are of no ordinary calibre, whether for jest or earnest, together with such corrections or additions as I could have made, I have little doubt he could produce something very interesting. Mrs. Scott when she was here entered much into the idea, and I have no doubt has been spurring her husband to it in all ways direct and indirect, which has given rise to these distorted reports. But alas! indolence which blighted all my brother's fairer and earlier prospects has now twined itself so closely into all his habits that he chuses to think himself incapable of doing what, were he to do with the success of any of these preceding novels, would be worth a good deal of money, which his family much needs. . . .

My youngest son, who is very clever and very idle, I have sent to a learned clergyman of Lockhart's acquaintance, who was one of the head tutors at Winchester, to get more thoroughly grounded in classical learning, and to avoid the dissipation of Edinburgh. For two years Mr. Williams has undertaken to speak with him in Latin, and as everybody else talks Welsh he will have nobody to show off his miscellaneous information to, and thus a main obstacle to his improvement will be removed. It would be a pity any stumbling-block were left for him to break his shins over, for he has a most active mind and a good disposition.[1] Here is a formidable letter and little in it after all. Believe me, dear Lady Louisa, always most respectfully, your faithful humble servant,

WALTER SCOTT.

[1] Here is a description of Charles Scott which Mr. Lockhart received from a friend after his brother-in-law's arrival in the Principality :—

"YSTRASMEINIO, Jany. 2nd, 1821.

"I had the pleasure of seeing Charles Scott here the other day, with my brother-tandem, but better late than never. They came up to have some coursing, but I had little time to study my young friend's character, . . . nor is that necessary; for it is a perfectly open one. I have had hundreds of boys under my care, and to tell you the truth, quietly, I never saw a lad that I could love more. He has all the frankness of a Highlandman, and all the observation of his father. He calls the portrait of Sir W. S. in *Peter's Letters* a miserable caricature; but I mortified the modicum of vanity which he possesses by telling him that I should know his father's son, even from what he called a caricature; the open brow, the depth of the eyes, and the firm position of the under lip were not to be mistaken; but after all, I fancy he thinks himself a *handsome* likeness of his father. . . ."

CHAPTER XVII

1821

EDINBURGH AND ABBOTSFORD

"The dews of summer night did fall,
The moon, sweet Regent of the sky,
Silvered the walls of Cumnor Hall,
And many an oak that grew thereby.

"Full many a traveller oft hath sigh'd,
And pensive, wept the countess' fall,
As wandering onwards they 've espied
The haunted towers of Cumnor Hall."

Mickle.

1821—AGE 50

Scott visits London on Parliamentary business, February, March.

A grandchild, John Hugh, born February 14th.

Sir Adam Ferguson's marriage in April.

Death of John Ballantyne, 16th June.

Scott revisits London at the Coronation, 19th July, returning by Stratford-on-Avon.

Lieutenant Scott, 15th Hussars, goes to Germany, December.

Visitors at Abbotsford in summer, Mr. Erskine and daughter, Mrs. Carpenter in August.

Kenilworth, 3 vols. 12mo, published by Constable in January.

Letter to Lord Clarendon on the Royal Society of Literature, March. See Appendix No. II.

Account of the Coronation of George IV., July, printed in *Weekly Journal*.

Edits *Franck's Northern Memoirs*, 8vo, Constable.

Fountainhall's Diary, 4to, Constable, published 1822.

Private letters supposed to have been discovered in the repositories of a noble English family, privately printed; the origin of *The Fortunes of Nigel*.

The Pirate, 3 vols. 12mo, published by Constable, December.

CHAPTER XVII.

FROM MORRITT.

ROKEBY, *January 28th* [1821].

MY DEAR FRIEND,—I feel that I am leaving Rokeby in your debt, and before I set out for town, amongst other things I have to settle I may as well discharge my account by paying you a reasonable and no small return of thanks for *Kenilworth Castle*, which was duly delivered, read, re-read, and thumbed with great delight by our fireside. You know when I first heard that Queen Elizabeth was to be brought forward as a heroine of a novel how I trembled for her reputation. Well knowing your not over affectionate regard for that flower of maidenhood, I dreaded lest all her venerable admirers on this side of the Tweed would have been driven to despair by a portrait of her Majesty after the manner of Mr. Sharpe's ingenious sketches. The author, however, has been so very fair, and has allowed her so many of her real historical merits that I think he really has, like Squire Western, a fair right to demand that we should at least allow her to have been a b——.[1] I am not sure that I do not like and enjoy *Kenilworth* quite as much as any of its predecessors. I think it peculiarly happy in the variety and facility of its portraits, and the story is so interesting, and so out of the track of the common sources of novel interest that perhaps I like it better from its having so little of the commonplace heroes and heroines who adorn all other tales of the sort. I see that it has already produced a cheap edition of Mr. Laneham's[2] work, for which I am thankful, as I wanted

---

[1] *Tom Jones*, Book vii. chap. 5.
[2] *Kenilworth Illustrated*, etc. etc., royal 4to, Chiswick, 1821.

one, and I hope also that is a sign the book itself is popular which can sell such an illustration.   I am, as I said, setting out for town on Thursday with my whole caravan. . . .

You must, notwithstanding your employment as President of the Royal Society, Edinburgh, contrive to fulfil your promise of coming to me in the summer.   I am glad you bear that new honour so properly, and are ready to support your title to it with at least as much chance of a satisfactory scientific result as any of your predecessors.

Adieu ! Accept and give your circle our united regards, and believe me, cordially yours,   J. B. S. MORRITT.

TO HIS SON WALTER.

EDINBURGH, *4th February* [1821].

I ENCLOSE you a bill for £50, this being quarter day, but as that will not I fear clear your damages upon horse flesh, you may write to me what is necessary to put you straight with the world.   Remember to be as economical as you can, for besides the expense of building Chiefswood, and very ample improvements at Abbotsford, of which I trust you will one day reap the benefit, my brother proposes to send over to me his only son Walter, whom, both for regard to my living brother and my deceased father, I intend to get out to India as a Cadet, and must take upon myself the expense of his outfit.   So you must make your cash go as far as it will, and avoid unnecessary expenses. . . . Let me know how your cash stands, and see that on no account you get into debt; nothing is so uncomfortable and discreditable.   I bought last year an old brood mare and foal for the magnificent sum of nine pounds, merely to stock my grass in the wood at Huntly Burn.   The foal is now considered as one of the handsomest things in the country, and I have been offered £25 by a dealer, which for a year old is very high. If your regiment be within reach when he is fit for service, I will make you a present of him. He is quite tame and as playful as a kitten.

I desire you will take care of the jaundice; drink no wine, and eat nothing that is bilious for some time. You are naturally I think temperate in the use of wine, but you cannot always avoid it without strong resolution to the contrary. I wish I heard of you giving some part of the day to useful reading; that is a habit as well as other habits, and may be acquired or lost, and when it is lost a man cannot escape being a trifler through his whole life. Lockhart has had a foolish scrape.[1] . . . This cost Don Giovanni a flying journey to London, which gave us the more uneasiness that I am sorry to say Sophia is very unwell. . . . None of the family excepting myself knew the cause of his journey until it was all arranged and settled.

I have myself to go to London on very short notice, and shall set off the day after to-morrow. It is for the purpose of meeting Mrs. Carpenter, who is just arrived, and I cannot dispense with paying this token of respect to the memory of your Uncle as well as to herself.[2] . . . Your affectionate father,   WALTER SCOTT.

TO LOCKHART.

WATERLOO HOTEL,
JERMYN STREET, 15th February [1821].

MY DEAR LOCKHART,—I had yours yesterday, and it gave me much relief in so far as it states Sophia to be relieved of the cramp, which I have more horror of than the pain in the side, which I believe is incidental to her situation.

I saw Mr. Christie yesterday. You will see the friendly and ready zeal with which he met Scott's impudence both in his letter to Smith,[3] of which I highly approve, and in

---

[1] See p. 112.
[2] Mrs. Carpenter was a Scottish lady, a sister of General Fraser.
[3] Horatio Smith, one of the authors of *Rejected Addresses*.

his printed statement. There is no human being of my acquaintance but what thinks that all is done that can be done. It is unlucky, to be sure, that their champion has this bit of a cockhorse thrown in his way to ride off upon, but with Stoddart's explanation, yours, and Mr. Christie's, everybody must see that the mistake happened by the merest inadvertence.[1] You have now to attend to the *paullo majora,* and keep clear of magazine-mongers and scandal-jobbers in future.

I have seen Mrs. Carpenter's papers. There seems to be no doubt of the clause in the marriage contract which gives her *in property* the sum of £16,000, then invested in the 3 per cent. consols. The sum divisible among my family at her death when realised will approach to £20,000, which I think was about what I calculated upon when settling matters with Sophia's trustees; so she is about £5000 poorer than she had once some reason to hope for, but I suppose it will make no great odds either to her or you. You have not only independence but wealth in your power if you take the right road to it, but you must lay aside your frolics and gambades and take a manful journey-pace for a little while at least.

My love to Sophia. I will write her a long letter one of these odd-come-shortlys, but I am just now almost worried to death; witness this letter begun three days since, and only finished just now. Love to the Captain and Violet.—Yours most affectionately, WALTER SCOTT.

TO THE SAME.

[1821.]

MY DEAR LOCKHART,—I give you joy a hundred times of the acquisition you have made.[2] I am inexpressibly

---

[1] Referring to the fact that a paragraph had been prefixed to Mr. Lockhart's Statement, as published in the newspapers, not contained in the Statement previously sent to Mr. Scott.

[2] John Hugh, born on 14th Feb.

relieved on account of my dearest Sophia, who has had
such a grievous time of it. I trust in God her recovery
will be as perfect as her confinement has been tedious.
The utmost quiet is necessary for eight or ten days, but
this the ladies know how to regulate. I go down to Ditton
to-day to return on Monday; pray contrive amongst you
to let me hear from you daily, were it but a line, and tell
me if the boy that makes me grandsire is dark or fair, and
above all if he can *grip* hard as a Scott should.—Yours
affectionately,   WALTER SCOTT.

The Duke of Wellington, whom I take to be the
highest military authority in the world, pronounces you
can have nothing more to say to S. [Scott]. . . .

TO THE SAME.

WATERLOO HOTEL,
JERMYN STREET, 20th Feby. [1821].

MY DEAR LOCKHART,—Knowing you are aware of
Christie's meeting with Scott and its consequences, I
have but to say that I came to town yesterday and made
my way to Christie, who was lying quiet with the purpose
of starting in the evening for Calais, and waiting the event
on the other side of the Channel. I offered him all sort
of assistance in my power either by purse, recommendations, or otherwise, but had not the good fortune to hit
on anything that could be useful. He was a little dejected
about the business, but I left him much cheered, as he
indeed should be, for he behaved with the utmost moderation as well as gallantry, and had no honourable mode of
avoiding the sleeveless quarrel fixed on him. . . . Meantime
this event sums up the affair *cum tota sequela* never to
be again stirred. I suppose their seconds will agree on
some kind of statement when the wounded man's state is
determined. Mr. Wilson, who has been very attentive,
has been here just now and is on his way to Chalk farm,

where Scott still lies; he will write you this evening the last intelligence of his health. Scott's surgeon ran off and left him on the ground, and Patmore was in such agitation that the chief assistance the wounded man received was from Christie and his second. To all this there is a fine moral, but knowing how much you will suffer from the inconvenience to which your friend has been subjected, it would be cruel to say anything more about it. I saw Mrs. Christie bearing the matter very bravely indeed. I will call on her occasionally. Christie is I suppose in France ere now.[1]

[1] In consequence of a series of articles in the *London Magazine*, by its editor, Mr. John Scott, attributing to Mr. Lockhart various personal attacks in *Blackwood*, Mr. Lockhart went to London in the middle of January 1821, and endeavoured, through his friend Mr. J. H. Christie, barrister, to obtain an apology or satisfaction from Mr. Scott.

Scott offered to meet Lockhart if he would declare that he had never derived money from any connection, direct or indirect, with the management of *Blackwood's Magazine*, and that he had never stood in a situation giving him, directly or indirectly, a pecuniary interest in its sale. Lockhart declined giving this assurance to Scott, on the ground that he had no right to ask it; but a Statement which he circulated had prefixed to it a paragraph to the effect that he had occasionally contributed articles to *Blackwood's Magazine*, but that he was in no sense editor or conductor of it, and never derived any emolument whatever from any management of it. The copy of the Statement sent to Scott did not contain this paragraph, Lockhart having added it afterwards on the sugges-

tion of Mr. Stoddart, the conductor of the New Times, for the purpose of making the narrative more clear and intelligible to the public.

Lockhart remained in London till the end of January, and before leaving, he posted Scott as a coward. Scott having issued a Second Statement, this was replied to by Mr. Christie, and the result was a challenge from Scott to Christie. They met at Chalk Farm *at nine o'clock p.m.* on 16th February—by moonlight—Mr. Traill acting as Christie's second, and Mr. Patmore as second to Scott. It appears that in the first instance Christie fired in the air, but at the second fire his ball struck Scott, and the wound proved fatal on 27th February.

When Scott fell, Christie helped to convey him to a neighbouring house. In a letter to Lockhart, dated next day, he wrote: "This has been to me the most heart-rending transaction that has happened in my life, and I would most willingly have changed places with him. I cannot and shall not attempt to describe the horror I felt. I arranged with my second (Traill) that I should not fire at Scott unless in self-defence. Accordingly, I fired

A pleasanter subject is Sophia's happy extrication from
cramps and spasms by so acceptable an addition to your
family and mine. I shall be very desirous to see your
marmouset, which I dare say Sophia and you think the
finest thing that ever opened eyes on the world. God
maintain you in the opinion! Grandmama seems to have
seen with your eyes, and pronounces the child to be a
perfect beauty. However, be it what it will in future, it is
a most acceptable personage to yours affectionately,

WALTER SCOTT.

I have just heard that Scott is a good deal better. He
is not yet moved from Chalk farm.

TO THE SAME.

[LONDON,] February 24th, 1821.

MY DEAR LOCKHART,—I am truly glad to report Scott's
amended state. For two days there was little hope, the
inflammation and fever having been very high, and I . . .
was anxious for Christie, as there must have been a trial,
etc., though there could be no doubt of the issue.

Lady Compton got me the enclosed from the celebrated
Surgeon Guthrie who attends the wounded "Champion,"[1]

my first shot in the air. Before we
fired again, Traill protested that as
Mr. Scott had taken the usual aim
at me, I should not forego that
advantage again. I felt bound to
follow his advice for self-preservation, and my second shot took
effect."

Scott made the following statement to one of the surgeons who
attended him: "After the pistols
were reloaded and everything was
ready for a second fire, Mr. Traill
called out, 'Now Mr. Christie,
take your aim, and do not throw
away your advantage as you did
last time.' I called out immediately
'What! did not Mr. Christie fire
at me?' I was answered by Mr.
Patmore: 'You must not speak : you
have nothing now for it but firing.'"

At the Coroner's inquest a verdict
of wilful murder was returned
against Christie, Traill, and Patmore ; but they had left this country. Christie and Traill afterwards
surrendered, and were tried at the
Old Bailey before Chief Justice
Abbot and Mr. Justice Park on a
charge of wilful murder. After
hearing the evidence, the jury returned a verdict of not guilty.

[1] Mr. John Scott had been editor
of the "Champion" newspaper.

and she congratulates me on the prospect that S. will live. . . . So, all things considered, the affair seems to have terminated as well as one so untoward could do. I do not see how you can be blamed more than if Christie had been hurt by the bursting of a pistol ; it was a chance you could neither foresee nor prevent, when once the first impulse was given. I trust Scott will take warning, that Christie will get credit, and that you, when you have had such severe practical proof how impossible it is to calculate the event of such matters, and how unexpectedly their consequences may involve those whom we love and regard, will abstain from any indiscretion which can lead to future calamities of this sort. You have now the best possible opportunity to break off with the magazine, which will otherwise remain a snare and temptation to your love of satire, and I must needs say that you will not have public feeling nor the regard of your friends with you, should you be speedily the hero of such another scene. Forgive me pressing this. Christie and I talked over the matter anxiously. It is his opinion as well as mine, and if either has weight with you, you will not dally with this mother of mischief any more. I make this my most earnest entreaty to you, and as it agrees with that of all your friends and well-wishers, I trust it will not be made in vain. Do not *promise*, but *act*, and act at once, and with positive determination. Blackwood has plenty of people to carry on his magazine, but if it should drop I cannot think it fair to put the peace of a family, and the life not only of yourself but of others, in balance with any consideration connected with it. This is the last word I will ever write to you or say to you on the subject, for I am sensible my anxiety makes me importunate, for which I have only the excuse of a father's feelings to Sophia and yourself, which said, *Tace* shall be hereafter with me "Latin for a candle."

I rejoice to hear of Sophia's good health, and of the baby's stout and healthy condition. . . .

TO THOMAS SCOTT.

LONDON [*Feb. 25th*, and *March* 1821].

MY DEAR TOM,—I have great pleasure in observing from your letter of the 19th December that you have adopted the manly, though painful, resolution of letting my nephew Walter follow the plan of life that is most likely to make a man of him. Since I came here I have had the good fortune to obtain from Lord Sidmouth a promise of a Cadetship. . . . He will carry out the best recommendations of all kinds, so that with fortune and good behaviour he has the world for the winning, and I trust will prove a credit to us all and a comfort to you and Mrs. Scott. Pray send him as soon as you can, for there will be little enough time to give him the chance of shipping some useful knowledge before he goes to India. . . .

I have to announce to you the news that I am a grandfather, hoping to hear the like from you some of these days. . . .

I am living very gaily here amongst old friends and some new. I went to Court on Friday last, where the King received me like an old friend, and shook hands with me before the whole circle, which I am told is unusual. Thus shall it be done to him whom the King delighteth to honour. . . .

I have kept this letter by me till I can add that Walter's appointment is secure. . . . Yours affectionately,

WALTER SCOTT.

TO LOCKHART.

[LONDON] WATERLOO HOTEL, 28th *February* 1821.

MY DEAR LOCKHART,—After all the fair hopes that were entertained of Scott's recovery . . . he expired last night at ten o'clock. In this sad business you have at least the consolation that you could neither foresee nor prevent what has happened, and that it cannot affect you as a man of honour and spirit, though this unfortunate chance has happened.

I have a letter from Christie, and at his request shall undertake the painful task of writing to his father, who I find is a clergyman.[1] It is a duty difficult to discharge, because the considerations which would move other men cannot be urged to him. But I will certainly do anything in my power that may gratify Mr. C.

To-morrow I will call on Mrs. Christie. I hope her husband will be in no hurry to come home: it is best to let such things cool a little. I shall be glad to hear that you are bearing this matter as it must be borne, with manhood and resolution, for vain regrets avail nothing. There is much of my last letter which I would not have written, but that I confided in the certainty of Mr. Guthrie's favourable predictions. You are aware that I could not mean it unkindly. . . . Yours affectionately,   WALTER SCOTT.

TO ADAM FERGUSON.

LONDON, 6 *April* 1821.

MY DEAREST ADAM,—I have been on the eve of writing to you ever since I left Edinburgh, and now I am on the very verge of leaving London before I can accomplish my purpose. Your business has gone on well, but more slowly

---

[1] Sir Walter's letter to the Rev. Mr. Christie is unfortunately not accessible.

than I could have wished.[1] . . . It is, you know, settled to be neat £300, which will make a neat addition on a certain approaching occasion.

Talking of the aforesaid occasion, I am bringing down with me a tankard for *swipes*, which I hope you will find place for on your new sideboard. I have got a verse of *Auld Lang Syne* engraven on it, which I think applies as completely to you and me as to any two friends that ever were separated and met again.

I beg, if this finds you at Edinburgh, you will make my most respectful compliments to Mrs. L.[2] I propose myself the pleasure of being acquainted with her before she changes that name for one that is very dear to me. I think I shall be in Edinburgh about Wednesday 12th, per Blucher, for if I get to Selkirk on Monday night, I will sleep there and breakfast with Laidlaw the next day. I shall get a peep at Huntly Burn, Chiefswood, etc., and may perhaps see you there, though I rather suppose town has more attractions for you than usual. From this you will see that I propose to travel the west road in preference to the tiresome northern direct. You go faster also. I expect to be at Manchester to-morrow to dinner.[3] I propose to be at Edinburgh until the 16th or over, and then hey for Tweedside, where we will meet so soon as you will allow us. I am glad you got Gattonside, since that churlish laird behaved so [badly]. See what comes of his affection for you, cemented at the Barmecide drinking-party at Philiphaugh.

My dearest Adam, I should never end if I were to say half what I think, and feel, and hope, about your happiness upon this approaching change of state. "Better late thrive," —the proverb is somewhat musty; but though few bachelors had a more comfortable home than yours, still the

---

[1] Appointment as Keeper of the Regalia in Edinburgh Castle.

[2] Adam Ferguson and Mrs. Lyon

were married before the end of April.

[3] See Appendix No. II., p. 399 for letter to Hon. John Villiers.

company of a kind and affectionate wife is something more delightful than the nearest ties of kindred can afford. I am only afraid that some confounded chance may remove you further from us, which would be a severe blow to yours very affectionately,   WALTER SCOTT.

TO HIS SON WALTER.

LONDON, 6 *April* 1821.

YOUR name is put down for the Sandhurst establishment, but it will be necessary that you make the formal application through your Commanding Officer, as directed by the enclosed card. Although your name stands on the list, it will be a year and a half probably ere you get to Sandhurst; meanwhile you must study hard at mathematics, arithmetic, outlines of fortifications, drawing and languages. . . .

I send you a very diverting German romance, which I think will entertain you unless you have seen it before. I also send, on an office frank, a set of stone engravings very fit to copy of an evening, and besides, Mr. Milliken has charge for you of a great parcel of French Military books, particularly Jomini's *History of the French War*, which is reckoned a book of great merit.

These will serve to amuse your leisure in the solitary dignity of Commander of Cappoquin. I recommend them to your very particular care. Solitude is better than idle company. . . . Yours affectionately,   WALTER SCOTT.

TO HIS DAUGHTER.

ABBOTSFORD, 1*st May* 1821.

MY DEAR SOPHIA,—The report you have heard is very true. Walter's regiment is ordered for India, but I am negotiating an exchange for the Cornet in which I hope to succeed. His corps has given great offence by some improper and seditious language, and toasts which they drank at their mess. I understand Walter was not present on that occasion, but the officers seem but a disorderly set. . . . If he does not get an exchange, I will have him rather resign on half-pay, than go out in such society. But I trust to get him into a steadier corps.

The ass wishes to go himself, and talks of being absent for five or six years, when I will be bound not one of them sees British land again till their beards are grey. . . . Yours affectionately, WALTER SCOTT.

TO MORRITT.

EDINBURGH, 16th June [1821].

MY DEAR MORRITT,—My kindest and best thanks for the manner in which you have taken what my sincere affection prompted me to say, and so let that matter rest. . . .

I want you of all loves to get the Prince's box at Covent Garden, to see a man from Scotland, called Mackay, play the character of Bailie Nicol Jarvie in *Rob Roy*. You never saw anything better played in your life—it is indeed the life itself. He has drawn immense houses here by the exhibition, but perhaps it has too much of the modest reality of nature to please those who are not acquainted with the original; and Liston's imitation of the pig may, according to the old story, please more than the pig itself. Altogether Mackay's performance is very extraordinary, and if he could play anything else but half so well, he would be a very great fellow indeed. But the Bailie is his masterpiece. I believe he only intends to stay a day or two, so I pray you to be upon the outlook.

Rose seems to be wavering in his resolution, and though happy to see him if he comes, I shall not be sorry if he and the Gander[1] should seek more comfortable quarters than Saint Mary's Loch affords in this sort of weather, which is at once cold and hot, but neither mild nor genial.

Pray, my good Lord of Rokeby, be my very gracious good lord, and think of our pirated letters. It will be an admirable amusement for you, and I hold you accountable for two or three academical epistles of the period, full of thumping quotations of Greek and Latin in order to explain what needs no explanation and fortify sentiments which are indisputable. I pray you to think of this. I must write to Lady Louisa for further contributions, as we are about to go to press in good earnest.[2]—Yours always, with truth and affection,   WALTER SCOTT.

TO HIS SON WALTER.

EDINR., 6 *July* [1821].

. . . I SEE an account of your skirmish not very accurately stated in the newspapers. I suppose it not unlikely that you may have some trouble with the trials that may ensue, if any of the prisoners are recognised as having been active.

I hope and presume that your part of this very disagreeable business was executed with satisfaction to the Magistrates, as on the other hand you seem to have acted with the humanity which I would have expected and recommended to the poor misguided peasantry.

It must be an unpleasant thing to live in a country where the poor and the rich are in a state of disunion, which every now and then breaks out into such frays as these. Then gentlemen find it disagreeable to reside on

---

[1] David Hinves, Rose's attendant.

[2] For further details respecting this Pic-nic volume see *Life*, vol. vi. p. 409, and *Journal*, vol. ii. pp. 473-475.

their estates, and then comes the system of absenteeship with all its natural ill consequences. So there is in all these matters a degree of action and reaction,—the evil of the mutinous discontent of the people chasing the gentry from the country, and the non-residence of the gentry adding to and increasing the discontent of the people. It is far easier to see these evils than to suggest a remedy; but it is clear that any remedy that may be resorted to will be very long before it can operate effectually to the advantage of the body politic. One or perhaps two generations must pass away before any remedies which can be adopted shall have effectually operated. . . .

I have some idea of stepping up to London to see the coronation, tempted with the ease by which we can now make the journey in the steam-ship within sixty hours, and without any fatigue, thus beating the mail coach, with the full advantage of sleep and stretching of limbs. . . . I am always your affectionate father, WALTER SCOTT.

FROM JAMES HOGG.[1]

ALTRIVE LAKE [POSTMARK, *July 8th*, 1821].

DEAR SIR WALTER,—I received yours last night, which has put me in a terrible puzzle, so fain would I go to London. I have thought on it all this day, and sometimes with the tear in my eye when I found on calm reflection the thing to be next to impracticable. That great day at London is the next after St. Boswal's fair : if I were to run

---

[1] Scott went to London in July to be present at the Coronation of George IV., and he had, as is well known, obtained an invitation for the Ettrick Shepherd to accompany him. The latter declined the tempting offer in the following letter, in which one cannot help seeing that the "half-stocked" farm and money anxieties had more to do with the poor fellow's refusal than the charms of St. Boswell's Fair, though Scott jocularly said "he stood balancing the matter whether to go to the Coronation or the fair of St. Boswell,—and the fair carried it !"—*Life*, vol. vi. p. 359.

off privately and leave the market and my farm half stocked, I were judged mad beyond all hope of recovery. *I may not do it!* The thing is impossible. But as there is no man in his majesty's dominions admires his great talents for government and the energy and dignity of his administration so much as I do, I will write something at home. I will however endeavour to see you before you start.

I think you have done wrong about the money. You should just have said—" I cannot give away money, Hogg, not knowing who of my own family, may require it, whose right it is; but I lend you so much in your need on condition that you pay the interest punctually and the principal as soon as convenient." I was thinking to myself that I would have liked if you had taken security on the stock. I felt as if you would be a sort of guardian angel over it for me, and do so still. I feel as grateful as any creature can feel, but am scarcely satisfied with your mode of lending. However, it is all that I require in addition to my own at present, so Martinmas must care for itself. Sufficient for the day is the evil thereof.

If you were to procure me a pension from that Society you talk of, or any Society, you will get it as well and better without me than with me. You may at least say this for me, that there is not a more loyal bard in Britain, and that I have written more loyal and national ditties well known among our peasantry than perhaps all the bards of Scotland put together. Either the song of *Scotia's Glens* or that entitled *Caledonia* recited by Mr. James Ballantyne would, if well timed, procure me a pension at once. It is such a pity that the Coronation should have been at this juncture, or that I had not thought of it sooner, for much need have I to be in London. . . .

TO MISS EDGEWORTH.

3rd August 1821.

I AM equally gratified and surprised at your caring at all about the *bon papa* letter which has thus strangely fallen into your hands, and which I should have thought as uninteresting as possible to all but the writer and the young person to whom it was addressed. I suppose my young hussar had given it to some person who was fond, as is not uncommon, of collecting the parings of the nails of literary lions. He is just now on duty at a place called Cappoquin, and has had the bad fortune to be employed on some disagreeable rencontres concerning cutting of turf attended with the loss of several lives. I understand my youngster behaved steadily, and with humanity at the same time, but this is a horrid kind of warfare. As for my manuscript, all that can be said of it is, that it was once, like Mr. Page's greyhound, "good and fair," but that greyhound was outrun in Cotswold, as Slender informs us, and time and too much writing have reduced my once current half text to such *pieds de mouche*.as I am now framing for the exercise of your eyes. I fear my son will not even have the right to say his hand *has been* a fine one, for he writes a most military scrawl at present. He has a letter for you whenever his local situation and duty will permit him the honour of delivering it. I am just returned from London, where I had the curiosity to go for the coronation, which was really a pageant worth going a great way to see. I did not think there had been quite so much virtue in lace and cloth of gold as they displayed on this occasion. I am now returned to my own humble residence, to think over all this magnificence during my own solitary rides over hill and dale, "between the thorn and the slae," as our old songs have it. . . .[1]   WALTER SCOTT.

[1] Mrs. Joanna Baillie writes to Scott on the 3rd—"And now let me turn my thoughts to the pleasures of Abbotsford; you are now at your

TO HIS SON WALTER.

ABBOTSFORD, *7th August* [1821].

I HAVE but little time to write to you, but I wish to enclose the quarterly remittance of £50, which I suppose will be by this time sufficiently welcome. Your next remittance will be as usual in November. Your last letter was so vilely written that what betwixt pale ink and bad manuscript it was almost illegible. I wish you would take some pains with your hand. Mine is not a good one, but then it looks well, and was once a good one, whereas yours is from the beginning most calamitously bad.

Your letter found me in London, where I witnessed the Coronation, certainly one of the most brilliant spectacles which the British eye could witness. The splendour was beyond anything I could have conceived. I went to the subsequent levee, and there met Mr. Lesly, one of your officers, who seems a genteel-looking young man. I made up to him without introduction whenever I was sure of the uniform, and had all my inquiries after you satisfactorily answered. I missed Col. Murray, but wrote to thank him for all his civilities to you.

William Rose is now our guest, also Mrs. Carpenter. . . . Sophia is in her new Cottage and delighted with all the importance of her new situation, ordering old Cock-a-pistol[1] to change this and replace that, turning wash-houses into dairies, and dairies into pigsties, with all the solemn fuss of an old managing dowager like Mrs. Plummer herself.— I am always your affectionate father,   WALTER SCOTT.

own pleasant home telling your traveller's story, as no other creature can tell it, to your own family and friends, and this is delightful weather for the banks of the Tweed, and all out o' door recreations. Your young mama with the bairnie, and the furnishing of the cottage, and all are passing through my fancy, and a cheerful moving picture it makes."

[1] James Scott, a gardener; see *Life*, vol. viii. p. 230, *n.*

TO LOCKHART.

ABBOTSFORD, *Monday evening*.

MY DEAR LOCKHART,—I return the sheets. They are most classical and interesting at the same time, and cannot but produce a very deep sensation. I am quite delighted with the reality of your Romans.[1]

I send you Scoular's bust,[2] which I beg you to accept in token of the sincere affection and regard of yours truly,

WALTER SCOTT.

TO MISS EDGEWORTH.

October 1821.

. . . THE country looks very ill [here] till the leaf appears on the tree; from the end of May till October the weather is as fine as we can in general expect in our degree of latitude and in a mountainous country, and during the first six weeks of that space Edinburgh is a very pleasant residence. Our own motions are regulated by the sittings of the Supreme Court, which I must attend on officially. From this period till 12th March, with the exception of the Xmas holidays, I must necessarily be in Edinburgh; from 12th March to 12th May I reside at this place; again from 12th May to 12th July our courts call me to town, and the four succeeding months I usually pass here. I need not say the great pleasure which seeing you here will give Lady Scott and my family as well as myself, or with what pleasure we shall look forward to the accomplishment of your promise. I shall not account it a proper visit unless you pass a month at this place, and get acquainted with some of our Teviotdale worthies, who continue to be a very interesting and amusing set of country folks. Once a year I have a solemn coursing match, attended by a few intimate

---

[1] *Valerius*, a Roman story, published in 1821.

[2] A bust of Sir Walter by Wm. Scoular, esteemed a good likeness.

friends and neighbours, and about a score of stout yeomen, when we kill a highland bullock and realise the old scenes when

"'Twas merry in the hall. . . ."

It is a great deal for all parties that you have discovered the possibility that all may be one side for a season at least, and if there was no better result to the King's journey than that single temporary union of feelings and interests, it cannot have been made in vain.[1] I am glad he did not come here after the enthusiasm which the Irish displayed, since our colder and more reserved manners must have shewn to disadvantage. But the German Sourcrout and some of the not unwholesome bitters of London will sharpen his appetite for such fare as we can afford him. I should like to see old Holyrood in splendour for once, and something I suppose we shall be able to do, though what it will prove, no one can pretend to form [an idea].

My wife desires me to offer her particular respects, in which my daughter sincerely joins. My eldest and married daughter will be particularly delighted with the honour of being known to you. She is in her way a great mistress of Scots song and ballads, which she sings with more feeling than usual, though not favoured by nature with a very fine voice. . . .

TO WILLIAM STEWART ROSE.

EDIN., 18*th December* 1821.

MY DEAR ROSE,—Walter left me yesterday [2] on his new destination. . . . His only purpose in London is to make his bow to the Commander-in-Chief. . . .

I wish you, my good friend, to keep up your habits of

[1] Miss Edgeworth wrote Scott a long account of the success of the Royal visit to Ireland, "when the Orange and Green were first seen to entwine."

[2] For Berlin.

early hours, and it is on that account that I always fear the
exciting life of London for such an invalid as you are.   I
always feel myself in a sort of mental and bodily fever
during the month I stay in town.   "Orlando," I think,
notwithstanding his amorous name, will prove a useful
sedative; if you rise with daylight in this season and
take an hour or two daily at the desk, you will speedily
find the habit both easy and pleasant.   There is no doubt
it will be published and relished were it once in a finished
state, and then the printing and correcting proofs is a fine
fidgeting sort of occupation which keeps the spirits in a
little agitation without overworking them.[1]   In a word, as
the old song of the Boatswain's whistle most sweetly
moraliseth,

Labour's the price of our joys.

I am going to Abbotsford on Saturday to sign the downfall
of the old cottage and its verdant porch, which I shall not
do without a sigh.   I would write an elegy, but it is out of
fashion.   Byron has written and inscribed to me a Drama
entitled Cain.   He has been very great in his personifica-
tion of the evil principle under the name of Lucifer, who
speaks of course the language of the Manichean heresy.   It
is a most extraordinary piece of composition, and he seems
to me in many places fairly to have drawn the bow of
Milton.   I think however the work will not escape censure,
for it is scarce possible to make the Devil speak as the
Devil without giving offence.   I remember in some old
play where the apostate is to be raised, the mistress of the
house pleads hard for the carpets and hangings, and prays
that if he is to spit fire the conjuror will recommend to
him to use the chimney.   To which his Exorciser answers,
Assure yourself he shall [not] be raised in such unmannerly
fashion as to spit and sprawl about the room.   This, how-

---

[1] Mr. Rose's translation of Ariosto's *Orlando* was published in 8 vols
post 8vo, London, 1825-31.

ever, is a grace not easily prescribed, and I question whether our noble friend has brought up his friend sufficiently cleanly.

This has been a most stormy season: if castles have not toppled on their warders' heads, stacks of chimney have in many instances overwhelmed those they were built to shelter. Lady Scott and Anne send their kindest remembrances, also the brace of Lockharts. Your name and jokes are familiar in their mouths as household words, and among the charms of July when we think upon it we always reckon on the pleasure of your company.—I am always most affectionately yours,

WALTER SCOTT.

CHAPTER XVIII

1822

EDINBURGH AND ABBOTSFORD

The news has flown frae mouth to mouth,
The North for ance has bang'd the South ;
The deil a Scotsman's die o' drouth,
  Carle, now the King's come !

CHORUS.

Carle, now the King's come !
Carle, now the King's come !
Thou shalt dance, and I will sing
  Carle, now the King's come !

Auld England held him lang and fast ;
And Ireland had a joyfu' cast ;
But Scotland's turn is come at last—
  Carle, now the King's come :
        Occasional Pieces.

Visit of George IV. to Scotland in August.

Crabbe's visit to Scott.

Morritt's visit to Scott.

Death of Lord Kinnedder in August.

Fortunes of Nigel, 3 vols., published by Constable, 30th May.

Halidon Hill | a dramatic sketch, 8vo, published by Constable, June.

Poetry contained in *Waverley Novels*, June 1822.

Gwynne's Memoirs of the Civil Wars, 1653-4, published by Constable, 4to, Autumn.

Macduff's Cross in Miss Baillie's *Poetical Miscellanies*, 8vo, not published till July 1823.

CHAPTER XVIII.

GLOUCESTER PLACE, *January 10th, 1822.*

. . . Now for the *Pirate. Il ne déroge pas,* he has the
family features, the family spirit : the Norwegian manners,
traditions, and scenery put one's imagination upon a new
track, introduce one to a new world, which (according to
custom) one is made to see and understand as distinctly as
if one were transported to the spot, and viewed it with the
bodily eye. This gives the work a particular zest; while it
has the further merit of keeping curiosity alive, for the
discoveries to come are wholly unforeseen, the interest
never flags, nor is any part heavy to the reader. Everybody
will cry "mair meat," like the ghost to courteous King
Jamie, especially as we have fasted ever since *Kenilworth,*
and were unusually hungry. Many faults will be found
nevertheless; dull books alone have none. Norna is accused of being Meg Merrilies over again : to me the peculiar
superstitions of the country, Norna's early misfortunes, and
her tinge of insanity mark the difference very strongly.
She reminds me more of Roland Graeme's old Catholic
grandame. But my cavil is that you do not keep the
language and sentiments of Minna, Brenda, and perhaps
Mordaunt, so strictly down to the natural tone of their time
and place as you have done those of all their predecessors
heretofore. They talk above both. What business has
Brenda to be incredulous about witches and fairies, like a
well-educated young lady of the present day ? Neither
good sense nor gaiety of temper (as you labour to prove)

could have made her so in Shetland a hundred years ago.
Does not Roger North tell us that in Devonshire (*forbye
Shetland*) a Baronet at the head of the Grand Jury declared
to his brother the judge, that nobody could live in the
country if some old woman's witchcrafts were suffered to
go unpunished? It would be too hard to attack you for a
few petty anachronisms committed by Jack Bunce, who
quotes plays written long after his time; but no great
matter if he does. Knowing your ways, I own I have a
lurking suspicion that Cleveland's character improved upon
your hands, *chemin faisant*, that you did not at first
intend he should have so much good in him, or escape so
well, but that you took pity on him before you had done.
Do I guess right? I highly admire the final conclusion; a
happy one would have been vulgar commonplace. As it
is, Cleveland, Norna, and Minna all end with delicacy and
dignity. Norna's recovery of reason and turning to religion
is a beautiful trait, as well as Minna's calm, and still elevated,
alteration of opinions. I have mentioned the chief specks
I can discover through my microscope. If I am tired of
any personage I think it may be Triptolemus and his
plough; yet he goes down very well along with the rest,
and having eaten all up "to hide and hair," again I say
"*mair meat*, Sir Walter, *mair meat*."

TO MRS. THOMAS SCOTT.

10th Feb. 1822.

. . . I HAVE the pleasure to assure you of the good
health, amiable disposition, and fortunate progress of my
nephew, who is, without flattery, as fine a boy as ever
I saw in my life, as gay as a lark, and yet assiduously
attentive to all his little duties and lessons. Every one
is fond of him, and he seems quite happy; and when he
tires of home he goes down to Mrs. Lockhart, who likes

him as well as we do. His progress in mathematics and
natural philosophy gives satisfaction to his professors,
though the studies are rather abstruse for his years, but
I have secured him excellent assistance for an evening at
home. He is prudent beyond his time of life, which seems
the effect of early buffeting with the world. His health
is excellent. I send him to the riding-school every day,
to secure so much exercise. When the winter classes are
up he shall learn fencing for the same reason. The only
thing I have seen about him to call for a hint now and
then, is a turn for shrewd remark, bordering on satire
occasionally, which I think it best to check gently lest it
grow to a habit. Except this very trifling circumstance,
and which really rises out of the acuteness of his observation, for I cannot help laughing sometimes when it [would
be] right to lecture, I never saw a better-disposed or more
promising boy in my life, and you may rely on my doing
all that I can in his favour, not only for his parents' sake
but his own. . . .

TO MORRITT.

EDINBURGH, 18*th February* 1822.

MY DEAR MORRITT,—I have owed you a letter for some
time, chiefly because one of my *confrères* in the Parliament
House is afflicted with the gout and the other a novice in
the duty, which has produced a good deal of occupation for
my fingers, though as little as may be for my head. I
rejoice to think that among other plans you entertain
thoughts of a summer in Edinburgh. Pray let the needle
of your inclinations tremble no longer, neither traverse to
and fro on the shipman's card of uncertainty, but pointing
direct to the North with the due degree of polarity, do you
steer your course by it, and so northward ho ! You can

easily get a good handsome house here for the season *à très bon marché*, and we will ride, run, and boat, and show the ladies whatever is to be seen in our romantic vicinity. If our fat friend makes good his word, there will be plenty of gaieties for Miss Morritt, and Gathering of the Gael and cocking of bonnets and waving of plaids and masques in Holyrood, with much more that will not be seen every day. I cannot help thinking that for a season you would find this change very agreeable, and should Miss Morritt's health still require the sea air and sea-baths the drive is but short to Leith, where both can be constantly had. Pray give your thoughts to all this, and let the earnest wishes of a feal and trusty friend and comrade weigh something with you on the occasion. The smaller or butt-end of Abbotsford where we used to be so happy is now, as the sailor says, on its beam-ends—in the language of the land-lubbers it is prostrate on the ground to be rebuilt in better stile, but there is ample habitable room, such as it is, for all of you. Walter is safe at Berlin under Sir George Rose's protection. I hold by the true saying "untravelled youths have ever homely wits," and that for a young soldier to make his way in the military profession a more enlarged view of society is necessary than the mess of their regiment affords. The command of modern languages and the general knowledge at least of the world in its higher circles is very essential to a young man. It is attended to be sure with some risk, but Walter has hitherto been a regular and a steady lad, and I hope will continue so. From what the Duke of York said, we hope there is every chance of his getting into the active discharge of his profession again after 12 or 18 months' residence abroad.

I hear good accounts of your young soldier from Sir John Beresford, and sincerely hope he will turn out what you would wish him—indeed I think there can be little fear of it.

I am going to dine with Sir John Beresford to-day; we have met him very often, and he has dined with us. He is certainly one of the most open, joyous sons of the ocean that ever I met with in my life, likes everything and everybody, and makes sunshine wherever he comes. He is got into a villa of Lord Abercorn's[1] a good way out of town, which is not utterly so convenient, as I could wish to see much of them.

You must do a thing for me—I want to have your own arms—the simple coat and the Rokeby Arms—neatly drawn for the following purpose. I have made at one extremity of my new building a tower or rather turret, the parapet of which I mean to finish after the manner of the Mortham parapet, which I have always admired, and from the love and regard which I have for the place and its owner, I want to have your own coat and that of Rokeby sculptured on two shields; the turrets being octangular will have a shield on each face, and each shall bear the arms of some valued friend or relation, after the manner of the olden time. I want your paternal coat without quartering or impalement; the size ought to be as large as a card to prevent mistakes. I have no doubt you will be happy to contribute to the ornament of the Tower of the Shields. Pray forgive all this Tom Foolery. I have so little that is fanciful or poetical about my own "*individu*," that I must trick out my dwellings with something fantastical, otherwise the cerulean Nymphs and Swains will hold me nothing worth. This is all at present from, dear Morritt, your loving and affectionate friend,

WALTER SCOTT.

I go to Abbotsford on the 9th March, God willing, for two months.

[1] Duddingston House.

TO HIS SON WALTER.

EDINBURGH, *25th February.*

. . . There is no news here except that the final plans for Abbotsford are adjusted, and that the foundation stone will be laid this week. I might perhaps have acted more wisely in leaving you to complete a house which is just now large enough for the property. But I have some confidence in the good star which has accompanied me, and think that if I live I may yet add considerably to an estate which must, when the woods rise and the times mend, be of some value. With economy, good conduct, and attention to your profession you will be able to live there respectably; without those attributes it signifies very little how much or how little a man inherits from others. I have so good an opinion of your sense and firmness that I need not remind you of the value of independence, which cannot be obtained without occasionally denying oneself indulgences attended with unsuitable expence. You are no boy now, and have a pretty good guess what you have to trust to. . . .

I hope you will see the Baron de la Motte Fouqué, as I wish to know what like he is.

[*6th March.*]

. . . I think the route you have chosen a very good one. . . . Employ your eyes, my dear boy, in looking at what you may see that is worth remark. Fools go to market and return as foolish as they went. Do not be enrolled in that list of incurables. . . . I am always desirous you should see fields of battle, and if possible compare them with the plans, and become an intelligent and scientific soldier. You pass near Hanau, where the Bavarian General Wrede tried to *head* back Bony in his retreat from Leipsic. Leipsic will of course attract your particular attention, as the great battle there in 1814 might be said to decide the Continental war so far as Germany was concerned.

I formerly mentioned Töplitz, which is worth seeing both as the scene of Vandamme's surrender, and as being worthy of a visit from its own beauties. . . .

Let me know what the Duke of Cumberland says about your stay at Berlin, and whether, as I fear, he insists on your getting the uniform of his regiment. In short, tell me all you are doing, and especially all about your studies.—Always, my dear Walter, most affectionately yours,　　　　　　　　　　　　WALTER SCOTT.

TO LOCKHART.

ABBOTSFORD, *Thursday.*

MY DEAR LOCKHART,—Your melancholy but most kind and attentive letter gave me great grief. It seems but yesterday that poor Boswell, my old companion, was rejoicing in Castle Street with Mathews. I sincerely hope that this catastrophe will end the species of personal satire and abuse which has crept into our political discussions; the lives of brave and good citizens were given them for other purposes than to mingle in such unworthy affrays.

It was scarce possible that Stuart could end without fighting somebody, in the circumstances in which he was placed by his own conduct and that of others. The resentment of a desperado . . . is even more dangerous than that of a brave man.[1] The latter has a certain aim like a musquet when discharged, the other bursts like a bomb, and there is no saying when or where a fragment may strike. If any statements, etc., are published I should

---

[1] Referring to the duel between James Stuart of Dunearn and Sir A. Boswell, in which the latter was mortally wounded.

be glad to see them, or if any change should take place for the better or worse in poor Sir Alexander's health. Pray let David call at Lady B.'s with my anxious inquiries.[1] Love to Sophia and little baby.—Yours truly,

WALTER SCOTT.

TO MISS EDGEWORTH.

[N. D.]

DEAR MISS EDGEWORTH,—You do me too much honour in supposing me so deeply and personally interested in the publication of the novels in question. Not so the rest of your letter, which gives me the agreeable assurance that you and the young ladies, your sisters, are to visit Scotland early in May and will honour Abbotsford (never more honoured) in the first week of that month. Remember however this is only your first visit; otherwise we shall be strangely defrauded, as I must be in Edinburgh on the 12th when our Courts resume their sittings, so I trust we will have, if we can contrive to make Abbotsford tolerably agreeable, the pleasure of seeing you there again when the autumn vacation sets me at freedom for four months after 12th July. You will find me like King Corney[2] busied with pulling down and building up. There is however enough of lodging, such as it is, having an actual roof on it, for I had the sense to build half of my house before I pulled the rest down, so we shall be well enough, though amid lime and dust and stones, good store.

---

[1] Mr. Lockhart wrote Sir Walter that Boswell died at three o'clock on the afternoon of Wednesday, March 27th, having been almost always in a state of stupor since the meeting, and he adds the emphatic statement:—"I hope I need not say how cordially I enter into the hope you express, that this bloody lesson may be a sufficient and a lasting one. I can never be sufficiently grateful for the advice which kept *me* from having any hand in all these newspaper skirmishes. Wilson also is totally free from any concern in any of them, and for this I am sure he also feels himself chiefly indebted to your counsel."

[2] A notable character in Miss Edgeworth's *Ormond*.

Lady Scott, "thof unknown," offers her kind respects, and I am glad I shall have my daughter Sophia with me, who, as well as her younger sister and brother, is very eager to make your acquaintance. They are neither of them at all made-up or *got-up*, and rather under than over educated. I was so terrified for their becoming lionesses at second-hand that I left them in a good measure to their natural gifts. Both are naturally shrewd and sensible, and the elder has a sort of quiet and sincere enthusiasm about her own country which will entertain you.—Always, with the greatest truth and respect, your most faithful and obliged, WALTER SCOTT.

TO MORRITT.

EDINBURGH, *25th June.*

MY DEAR MORRITT,—I am truly ashamed of my long silence, but as the parrot said, *I have thought not the less* upon you and yours. My only apology is that *Nigel* had to be finished hastily, and a good deal of official business occasioning some work for my pen at the same time. I learn with great regret the delicacy of Miss Morritt's health, which trenches so cruelly on your plans of happiness and amusement. My own hope is that with attention for a year or two, and a resolute retreat from late hours and raqueting, under whatever amiable temptation, the health of so young a person may be completely confirmed, but her age joined to the delicacy of her constitution certainly requires caution. I trust your northern motions will not be long delayed, for the air of our country turns moister and ruder as the long nights approach. Our motions are to be as follows. I stay here officially till 12th July, and on that day retreat to the rising towers of Abbotsford, which begin to make a distinguished figure on Tweedside. There I intend to abide till the beginning

of September, when I am half inclined to take a turn with
the Skenes to the Highlands, and go see Glengarry's
people pitch the bar, and so forth, upon his birthday.
This excursion may last a fortnight, as we cannot pass
Dunkeld, to which I have been often asked.[1] This done,
I will return to my Lares with the purpose of never again
quitting them till the Session calls me to town on 12th
November. It is needless to say how happy I shall be to
receive you and yours at any time consistent or inconsistent with these arrangements, for I shall not balance
betwixt the pleasure of seeing you at home and that of
witnessing broken heads at the Chieftain's castle. Our
room, though diminished by removal of the little old
cottage, is quite enough for your accommodation, taking it,
as I know you will do, with the same goodwill which offers
it. My motions are however apt to be deranged by an
event which though very precarious seems not yet to be
out of the cards. Yesterday official notice came hither
that the King was to be in Edinburgh about the 12th
August—though scarce with the purpose of going to the
moors I would think. To-day a similar official communication makes us aware that his medical advisers are
averse to his undertaking such a journey, which by land
must be indeed a serious matter, and that the plan is
suspended. There is something odd in all this, and I wish
it were well explained. Lord Melville is as much aware as
any man, of the impolicy of exciting public expectation on
such a subject merely to disappoint it the next day, and
yet he seems to have been forced to it by circumstances.
I wish our Sovereign may not be in an irritable and
changeable state of mind, which Heaven forfend. Perhaps
he may come down your way and take you in your form
at Rokeby, for he will surely have too much taste to pass
without seeing the Greta-walk.

To examine the Duke of Athole's plantations.

You ask me about poor Mr. Stuart.[1] I know nothing
of him personally. His father, still alive, is a foolish old
man who has spent his whole life in finding out a North-
west passage to heaven, and after trying many sects, has
settled in what he calls the Universal Church of Christ,
which consists of himself, his housekeeper, one of the
maids, and a foot-boy. The butler is said to be in a hopeful way, but is not yet converted. All this argues a touch
of madness, which, as they come of a very respectable
family in Fife (where all the gentry are a little crazy), is
not improbable. He, the son, was in early life refused
something or other, which set him up of course as a violent
Foxite, making speeches at dinners, county meetings, and
so forth, and lately he made himself more conspicuously
ridiculous by proposing himself, with his own vote and no
other to support him, as the County Member. This made
him a subject of ridicule to the Tories here, and in a
ridiculous article on the Queen's supposed and then
expected visit to Scotland some scribbler said that nobody
was like to visit her "*of a higher degree than Mr. James
Stuart*" or some such trash. Stuart went to the Printer,
one Mr. Stevenson, in point of birth rather above his trade,
and I believe a decent kind of man. Stuart proceeded at
first in all the forms with him; friends met on both sides,
and it ended in the printer referring Mr. Stuart to a

[1] One sees here how political
prejudice warped even the sound
judgment of Scott.   The friends
of Stuart described him in very
different terms.   His trial took
place on June 10th, 1822, and his
acquittal was hailed as a triumph
by the Whig party. Jeffrey and
Cockburn were his counsel, and the
latter records that "his injuries,
his gentleness, his firmness, his
sensibility, and the necessity he
was under of acting as he did, were
all brought out by irresistible evidence," and "that he had now got
so noble a character that if he cut
a throat every day nobody would
believe it!" A full report of the
trial was published in 8vo, 1822.
Mr. Stuart afterwards wrote
Three years in North America,
and   subsequently   edited   the
London Courier; he died in 1849.
Readers who care to inquire
further into this wretched newspaper quarrel will find ample
materials in *Lockhart*, *Cockburn*,
and *Kennedy*.

person who he said acted as Editor of the paper, and would at once inform him of the name of the author of the paragraph, providing he would say his intentions were personal. Mr. Stuart would not take the course pointed out, but declared he held the printer liable to him personally, and having procured the assistance of two stout men, whom he fetched from Fife on purpose, he fell upon Stevenson in the street and struck him a blow or two, his adherents holding the man by the arms, who nevertheless, though surprised and unprepared, contrived to return the injury pretty effectually. Stevenson instantly challenged Mr. Stuart, who declared he considered it beneath him to give him the meeting—a consideration which certainly ought to have prevented his offering any personal aggression. Stevenson " posted " him, and there the matter stood still as between them.

Stuart was now under the necessity of fighting somebody, as every one cried shame on his cowardice and violence. He tried it with the Advocate, under pretence that he was security for the *Beacon* Newspaper with some other Tory gentlemen for £100 each. But this was too absurd to hold water.

I was then very anxious our friends should have let Stuart be still, as a thoroughly degraded man whom there was much danger but no honour in meddling with. But Sir Alexr., poor fellow, had a great aptitude at writing clever squibs, and introduced this man's name into several of them. A quarrel among the Proprietors of the Paper in which they were published—not the *Beacon* but one called the *Sentinel* at Glasgow—made one rascal give up the papers of the concern to Stuart, and thus he had the means of compelling Sir Alexr. into the field. Boswell, poor fellow, complained it was hard he should be made the dish-clout to wipe up the stains of such a man, but he had in fact [driven] him to it by meddling with him. I under-

stand he was even disposed to decline fighting with Stuart
as a disgraced man, and to turn on Lord Rosslyn.[1] But as
he had given the provocation, I suppose he did not find
that possible.

I trust the matter will end here; but we Scotch are a
very hot generation, and though we do not flash up in an
instant like Paddy, our resentments are much more
enduring, and Boswell's death will be long remembered
and perhaps revenged.[2]

I have only to add that I shall be delighted to see your
young gentlemen. I have seen the fathers of both in
Portland Place, and also as I think their grandfather; at
least I remember old Mr. Wilbraham Bootle. I remember
pestering them about Lathom House, so gallantly defended
by the Countess of Derby. By the way, can you tell me
anything about it? it falls in my way obliquely in the
successor of *Nigel*.

I send a copy of *Halidon Hill* with this.—Believe me
yours truly,   WALTER SCOTT.

---

[1] Stuart's second.

[2] The bitterness of political feeling, however, was not confined to
one party, and after Stuart's acquittal his friends (on the 25th June)
brought the conduct of the Crown
officials in Scotland before Parliament, on a motion for the appointment of a Committee of Inquiry.
The Hon. James Abercromby,
afterwards Speaker of the House
of Commons, and subsequently
first Lord Dunfermline, was the
mover, and though it was defeated
by a majority of 25 in a House of
215, the charges made and the
language used by Mr. Abercromby
regarding the Crown officers gave
great offence, and were resented
so hotly by Mr. John Hope, son of
the Lord President, and long afterwards Lord Justice Clerk, and his
friend Mr. W. Menzies, advocate,
afterwards a Judge at the Cape of
Good Hope, that Mr. Abercromby
accompanied by Lord Althorp
instantly set out for Scotland for
the purpose of challenging one or
both of his assailants. A warrant
from the Speaker arrested his
progress at Penrith, and he returned to Westminster, his purpose happily frustrated by this
timely interference.

The two young Advocates were
summoned to the Bar of the House
for Breach of Privilege.—(See
Letters on Scotland by Kennedy,
8vo, London, p. 63; Cockburn's
Memorials, p. 312; and *Parliamentary Proceedings, July* and *August*
1822. .

TO JOANNA BAILLIE.

EDINBURGH, *Saturday* [*July*].

MY DEAR FRIEND,—This accompanies your Godchild,[1] which I wish for both our sakes was a better production, and so far more worthy of your kind acceptance. I know as little about the division of a drama as the spinster about the division of a battle, to use Iago's simile. But this I know, that if they should think to bring on the stage what subject and mode of treatment render alike unfit for it, I shall not grieve at any circumstance which may accelerate its downfall. I will not fail to be forthcoming with my contribution long before you think of going to press. I have a subject in my head, but I will not name it in case my muse should once more run away with me. The defeat of Halidon Hill will enable me to send my nephew Walter, who has devolved on my care like a child of adoption, "accoutred like a Thane." I sincerely hope your adventure will be splendidly successful in behalf of your protégé. I am just returned from a tour of two or three days, which has become a kind of annual custom, the Chief Baron, late Serjeant Shepherd, and Lord Commissioner (William Adam), Adam Ferguson, William Clerk, and myself scouring the country in search of old castles and antiquities,—a curious employment for a set of old lawyers who are in danger of becoming matters of antiquity themselves, if their researches are not soon cut short. With kindest remembrances to your sister and friends, I remain ever most truly yours, while

WALTER SCOTT.

TO JOHN WILSON CROKER.[2]

ABBOTSFORD, *Thursday*.

MY DEAR CROKER,—What have you been doing this fifty years? We had a jolly day or two with your Dean

[1] *Halidon Hill*, originally intended as a contribution to Joanna Baillie's Pic-nic volume, see *post*, p. 157.

[2] Printed in *Life*, vol. vii. p. 87.

Cannon at Edinburgh.[1] He promised me a call if he returned through the Borders; but I suppose passed in the midst of the royal turmoil, or perhaps got tired of sheep's head and haggis in the Pass of Killickrankie. He was wrong if he did, for even Win Jenkins herself discovered that where there were heads there must be bodies, and my forest haunch of mutton is no way to be sneezed at.—Ever yours, WALTER SCOTT.

[1] The "Dean," introduced by Croker in the following letter, was the original of the Rector of Fuddle-cum-Pipes in Theodore Hook's novel of *Maxwell*.

ADMIRALTY, *June 29th*, 1822.

MY DEAR SCOTT,—A friend of mine is going to Scotland, and I cannot refuse him the chance of seeing that which is the best worth seeing in Scotland. His name is Cannon, his profession the Church, his office therein one of the King's Chaplains, his chief delight good music and a good dinner, his chief talent, besides those exercised on the premises, a certain original drollery and knowledge of mankind which in a quiet way I have not seen equalled.

When he grows intimate he is a most entertaining companion, but he will complain if you do not give him cucumber to his turbot. His epicurism need not however alarm a less elegant table than yours, for instead of a fillet de volaille au suprème and a bottle of Mousseux, he has limited his more sober liking to a roast leg of mutton and a pint of port. If his welcome be hearty, he may even be prevailed upon to eat a bit of toasted cheese in the second course, and perhaps to make some progress on the other pint.

He has lived with all the world in *their* and *his* several times and seasons, and from his Majesty King George the Fourth down to that theatrical Sovereign, Edmund of Drury, he can tell you something personal of every man who has lived in our London society these last 30 years.

You will thank me for introducing him to you, but you will be angry that his stay in your city will be too short. If you want a pleasant companion, seat him at your table. If you want to hear Handel in perfection, place him at your pianoforte. If you want an excellent sermon, get him into one of your pulpits, and if you want to hear a good growl, walk him fast up the Castle hill on a hot day, and bring him down again to dinner of French fricassees and a cruet-sized pint of small claret.

I trust I have said enough to introduce my friend into your society for once—his ulterior visits I leave in his own hands.—Ever, my dear Scott, yours affectionately.

J. W. CROKER.

P.S. In our Society he is called the Dean—first because he ought to be one; and next because he is Dean of a certain fanciful order of knighthood, of which Sir Theodore Hook is the Grand Master. Let me know if by accident you hear him speak well of any human being.

FROM CRABBE.[1]

19 BREWER STREET,
GOLDEN SQUARE, *July 16th,* 1822.

DEAR SIR WALTER,—About two years since I asked your opinion whether a journey into Scotland would be of benefit to me in a disease which then oppressed me, and you very kindly advised the measure: the pain nevertheless was so severe that I was compelled to give up my purpose upon the very eve of the attempt.

I am now in London with the same strong desire of seeing Edinburgh, and without that degree of pain which forbade the visit before, but that must depend upon Sir Walter Scott: to go thither and return without seeing you would disgrace me so much that I must make it a condition of the journey.

Still, however, I am aware of the intolerable tax which this kind of visitation would be to you, and therefore I mean to be modest in my expectations. Let me see you, if so it may be, for one day in any place to which I can be conveyed, and I will content myself with gazing on your wonders and works at Edinburgh, and return a greater man by all the information I can retain, and perhaps a happier by all the pleasures I have enjoyed.

Will you, sir, do me the favour to write so much as will signify whether I may expect to find you, and where, for though I am very unwilling to create you trouble or engross any portion of your time, yet if I take my journey into Scotland, I must see you.—Yours, dear Sir Walter, most truly and with all respect,   GEO. CRABBE.

[1] Crabbe's poetry charmed Scott in his boyhood and soothed him in his last illness. As early as Oct. 1809 he wrote the author of *Sir Eustace Grey* that for twenty years previously his poems had delighted him. The two bards did not meet until 1820, when Scott was in London. Crabbe agreed to come to Abbotsford in August (*ante,* p. 90), but the visit was not made until two years later, when, unfortunately for both poets, it took place during the King's visit to Edinburgh.

TO LOCKHART.

[*August* 1822.]

DEAR LOCKHART,—I want you of all loves to come up and take a little charge of the excellent old Crabbe. I have written to Lord Kinnedder for the same purpose. He is agitated by the infamous reports of a vile madman to a degree which I think will kill him, and unfortunately his friends in this bustle cannot easily support him—'Fia and you will dine here of course. W. S.

TO WILLIAM STEWART ROSE.

ABBOTSFORD, MELROSE, *4th September* 1822.

MY DEAR ROSE,—Your breach of appointment distressed me more from the cause than the effect. For immediately after I had received your letter came the visit of his Majesty, with such a row in its train as might be truly termed Royal in all senses of the word. We were obliged to go to town, and when there I found every [thing] in such confusion that the Coronation (and that was pretty well) was calm water compared to it. The *purblind* is a king you know among the blind, and the very little I know of courts and court-like matters, with some other considerations, occasioned my being constituted a sort of adviser-general in the matter of ceremonial and so forth. Such a month of toil I never had, and trust never to have again, for from seven in the morning till midnight my house was like a cried fair, and your old acquaintance Turner counted sixty calls in one day. Amongst other charges I had that of all the clans, consisting of about 300 wild Highlanders completely armed, so that the house rung with broadswords and targets and pipes from daybreak to sunset. I had all sorts of difficulties to smooth, and all sorts of scruples to reconcile, and all sorts of quarrels to accommodate, and was in close and constant communication for the whole time with every kind of society, besides processions and all the public bodies in Scotland from the peers down to porters. I speak according to the letter. Fortunately the will of all being excellent, we contrived that the whole demeanour of the population should be the most regular and imposing which you ever saw, so that I was fully overpaid for my fatiguing exertions by seeing the country and city make the most striking appearance that perhaps any people ever did before a prince. There was on one day sixty thousand people at least drawn up on the streets of Edinburgh, without the least appearance, I do not say of riot, but even of crowding or inconvenience. All stood perfectly firm, and until the King passed, quite silent, while his progress was marked by a rolling cheer which accompanied him from the palace to the castle, each body taking it up when he came in front of them, for they were all separated into their own different classes and crafts, an excellent receipt for ensuring good order among the most riotously disposed.

In the midst of all this hurly-burly who of all birds in the air, or rather of all fishes in the sea, should be my guest but Crabbe the poet?[1]   He is such a sly hound that I never could find out whether he was pleased or no, but astonished he certainly was. I found him in the parlour one morning with two High Chiefs of the West Highlands whom he (hearing them speak together in Gaelic) regretted he could not address in French, which he thought would be more germane to their comprehension than English. Morritt was also present during a considerable part of these solemnities. It happened miserably enough for my

---

[1] In the admirable Memoir of Crabbe by his son, a book too little read, there is an interesting account of this visit by Mr. Lockhart, to whom Scott had consigned his venerable friend, pp. 270-281.

feelings, that in the midst of all this festivity and of the active pull at the oar which I had taken, my poor friend Will. Erskine, Lord Kinnedder, permitted an unfounded scandal of an intrigue with a married woman to sit so close to his sensitive feelings that (his frame having been much wasted by previous decline of health) it terminated in a fever on his spirits. He was much bled to keep down the delirium, and died, I think partly, if not chiefly, in consequence of the exhaustion. I suffered so much from this affliction, and the necessity of drowning it in secret, that I became extremely feverish myself, and had the disorder not terminated in a general rash or outstriking over my whole body I should have had a squeak for it. As it was, I came off with a fit of the mange, and it was a good escape. I did not wish for you in the midst of all this racquet of mirth and war, for I know how you hate bores, and the whole herd from —— downward were loose on the occasion. I send enclosed a letter to your brother, to whom I owe so much for his kind attention to Walter, for which the young Hussar is sincerely grateful. I am deeply sorry for the late severe infliction on the Baronet,[1] —perhaps one which a parent can feel most, for our sons are removed from us, while our daughters form the every-day sunshine of our house.

Let me hear how Orlando goes on, and what says the sapient Hinves.—And believe me, very truly yours,

WALTER SCOTT.

Game is quite plenty here, and no one to kill it but Tom Purdie[2] in the way of pot and spit.

[1] Sir George Rose, ambassador to Prussia.

[2] Those who wish to have an idea of the appearance and manner of Scott's faithful henchman at this date will find it in *Redgauntlet*, in the representation of Cristal Nixon at the cottage by the Solway at Brokenburn.

TO MORRITT.

ABBOTSFORD, *7th Sept.*

MY DEAR MORRITT,—This is quick firing for so lazy a correspondent as I am, but I hasten to explain how my southern tour has gone off for the instant. I had intended for Liverpool to hear Canning's farewell speech, and had my place taken, etc., when, lo! I was particularly commanded to Dalkeith,[1] which I could not gracefully disobey. . . . But besides this, *inter nos*, the edge of my desire towards Liverpool was much taken off by the private knowledge that Canning had had an interview with Brougham, who was invited to Mr. Bolton's. Now this gives rise to strange conjectures, and though I think no man's general principles are sounder than Canning's, yet in his minor movements I could never entirely acquit him of something like finesse. It was owing to this that the manly plainness of Castlereagh (poor fellow) baffled his extraordinary talents in the race of ambition. If this meeting with Brougham was meant to intimate a hint of a possible coalition just in order to quicken movements elsewhere, it was singular bad taste.

Thus much I believe, that everything is yet open, or was so when the King left Scotland. Now, such being the case, I do not much approve of "packing and peeling," as our law calls it, with the opposite party, and, knowing no more of the matter than is apparent, I should not have been flattered by going 200 miles in honour of a man who was finessing in this manner. This softens my disappointment *quoad* Liverpool. Let me know if you hear anything more of this. I would give sixpence it was a lie; if true, *que diable alloit-il faire dans cette galère?*[2] The

---

[1] Where the King was residing.

[2] Morritt's explanation of the meeting between Canning and Brougham came in due course. ". . . By the by I can, from a re-cent communication of Wilbraham's of Lathom, clear up your query about Canning's manœuvring in the summer, tho' you perhaps are already satisfied, and consider-

worst is, it kept me from Rokeby, for my intention was to have taken you on my return; as I could only have stayed two days at most, it does not greatly signify.

In point of order, decorum, etc., the civic banquet of Edin[r] greatly exceeded the Coronation dinner.[1] Our bailies are Roman senators in behaviour compared to the London aldermen, who broke their ranks in the procession to charge the turtle and venison. The Duke's[2] speech was delivered like a school-boy, and lest we should not be aware of his folly, he spoke it twice over in great trepidation, and yet with an air of his usual assumption. . . .

His Whig friends, whom I scrutinised closely, showed great signs of distressful impatience, and Lauderdale covered his face with his hands. There was no applause, but a gentle murmur, which only respect for time and place prevented from being a decided hiss. In fact, though only drunk as the premier peer, and along with his brethren, he chose to consider the compliment as exclusively his own, and regulated his speech accordingly. The Duke of Athole and Earl Morton were both about to reply, but this extraordinary debate in the Upper House was luckily checked. I wish you had seen old Ben-ie-Gloe[3] in particular. Morton got up and turned his back on the orator, and all the other peers seemed much annoyed· I wish you joy of the vicinity of the Duke of Sussex,

ing his subsequent elevation the subject is already mouldy. The interview with Brougham was not political, or at all brought about by himself. His friend Bolton had for years invited the lawyers of the Northern Circuit to dine, etc., at Storrs on Windermere. Since Brougham's conduct at the Westmoreland election he had been at feud with him, and felt, I believe, awkward at having made it personal. He wished to include Brougham in his invitation, and Canning being consulted very sensibly declared that his own presence could not constitute an objection to this pacific proposal. They all met, and Canning took his seat between Brougham and Scarlett, and made himself as agreeable as possible. This is what I think of such good example. I wish it was more common. . . ."

[1] In London.

[2] The Duke of Hamilton.

[3] The Duke of Athole.

especially of the certainty of not meeting him. I hope
Rose will come on. Does Sir George come with him?
I know he is in Britain at present. We have lots of
[moor-fowl], and plenty of partridges and black-cock;
indeed I never saw game so abundant at Abbotsford.

My kindest love to the dear young ladies, whom I love
better, if possible, that they love Scotland. There is something selfish in this too, for if they love it you will come
the oftener to see it, *et puis.* I wish you would send me
a copy of Miss Fanshawe's *Charade on a Pillion*;[1] my
memory begins to fail. I heard you repeat it twice at
least, and only remember one half of it, which is a great
vexation. All my household greet yours.—Always yours
affectionately,   WALTER SCOTT.

TO LADY ABERCORN.

ABBOTSFORD, MELROSE, 13*th September* 1822.

MY DEAR FRIEND,—By your last, received about a
month since, I observe you have not received a letter
from me which was directed to Rome. It is of little
consequence otherwise than as shewing that I am incapable of forgetting your constant kindness and your
friendship, now of so many years' standing. . . .

I imagine how you must have suffered from the
astounding news of Lord Londonderry's death, and how
much you must have felt for poor Lady Londonderry,
whom I learned to know as a friend of your Ladyship's,
and afterwards liked for her own sake and in gratitude
for the kindness she shewed me at Paris. The whole
circumstances of that most melancholy affair were so
unlike his calm, steady, courageous, and self-possessed

---

[1] See *Literary Remains of Catherine Fanshawe*, sm. 8vo, Lond. 1876.
This witty poetess, best known
to the present generation by her
"Enigma on the Letter H," died in
1834. See also Mitford's *Recollections* for an appreciative sketch,
pp. 143-153.

mind that for a long time I could scarce believe the manner of his death. And yet I remember his once telling seriously, and with great minuteness, the particulars of an apparition which he thought he had seen. It was a naked child which he saw slip out of the grate of a bedroom while he looked at the decaying fire. It increased at every step it advanced towards him, until he got up out of bed and advanced, when it retreated before him, and again diminished in size till it went into the fireplace and disappeared. I could not tell what to make of so wild a story, told by a man whose habits were equally remote from quizzing or from inventing a mere tale of wonder. The truth is now plain that the vision had been the creation of a temporary access of his constitutional infirmity. It is curious that Lord Londonderry was the only man I ever heard affirm that he had seen an apparition, excepting Lord Erskine, a person of so flighty a character that one does not wonder at anything he could say. The loss of Lord Londonderry will be severely felt by the Administration, as he [was] personally very acceptable to the King, and had deservedly great weight with the House of Commons, chiefly from his imperturbable temper and well-known courage.

We have had a singular scene in Scotland, the visit of the King to Edinburgh, which was like the awaking of Abou Hassan to a dream of Sovereignty. It went off very well—indeed surprisingly so, considering we had no time whatever for preparation, scarce a fortnight being allowed us to prepare for what was such a very new and uncommon occurrence. I believe, however, the shortness of warning was so far lucky that it saved us from committing any premeditated act of absurdity, and the nature of the Scots people being stiff and haughty and distant prevented anything like intrusion. From the highest to the lowest, they were anxious to know what was proper to be done, and to do it when they learned, as well for their own sakes as the King's. It was a very curious thing to see the whole roads and streets lined with so many thousands of people who were (even the very meanest) all dressed in something like decent attire, and each considering himself obviously as a part of the spectacle, and as having the national reputation dependent to a certain degree on his own behaviour. I thought I knew my countrymen well, and recommended the absence of all military, except the guard of honour, but to be sure they went far beyond my idea, for I have seen far more rudeness and crowding in the drawing-room at St. James's than I saw amongst an immense mob of all descriptions of people. But I will say for Saunders, that no one knows better how to behave well, and that when he is riotous and contumacious it is really from *malice prepense*.

A number of Highland clans came down, of whom I got an especial charge, which was rather an anxious one when you consider they were armed to the teeth with sword and target, pistol and dagger, and full of prejudices and jealousies concerning their particular claims of distinction. They all behaved very well, however, and from their wild and picturesque appearance added prodigiously to the effect of the various processions. The enthusiasm with which the King was received was extraordinary, and yet it was mingled on several occasions with a sort of *retenue* quite characteristic of the people. On Sunday, for example, when he went in state to church, all uncovered when he passed, but not a single shout, I may say not a single whisper, was heard—their idea of the solemnity due to the Sabbath being inconsistent with any noisy rejoicing. The King told me himself that the silence of such an immense concourse of people, and for such a cause, seemed to him the most impressive thing he ever witnessed. On the whole, he was delighted with the people, and they with him, and all was so prudently managed (which to your Ladyship who know courts so well will seem rather surprising) that nothing happened or transpired to mar the impression which his good humour and good manners made on his northern subjects. We had all a monstrous deal to do, and I myself had nearly died in the cause, as I took an inflammatory complaint owing to fatigue and over-exertion. . . .

I wish you could have seen the ancient front of Holy-rood Palace, alive as it was with all the Scottish officers of state and of the crown in their rich antique dresses, and the singularity of so many plaids and plumes and shields and drawn broad-swords, all under banners that had not seen the sun since 1745. The readiness of all the country to take arms was very singular. You saw children of ten and twelve years old with target and broad-sword, and one little [fellow], the son of the Chief of MacGregor, was very indignant when I laughed at him.[1]

---

[1] During the Royal visit Scott did not forget to prefer a request to the King that the "auld murdress Mons Meg" might be returned to her place in Edinburgh Castle. That the request was not forgotten by Sir R. Peel is shewn by the following notes, though the ponderous gun was not sent back from London until March 1829.—See *Journal*, vol. ii. pp. 247·8 :—

(*Private.*)

LULWORTH CASTLE, *Sept.* 22*nd*, 1822.

MY DEAR SIR WALTER,—A wish you expressed for the restoration of *Old Meg* to the Castle of Edinburgh did not escape me, and on my return to London I commenced a treaty with the Duke of Wellington, which was broken off by his abrupt departure for other more complicated negotiations.

He sent me, however, a parting line from Dover, which I do not send you *officially*, but in *confidence*, and rather to allay your own private anxieties about the old Lady than to authorise you positively to announce her intended departure from the Tower. I fear the show-man more than the King, but great as will be the difficulties in selecting a trustworthy Deputy and in determining the rate at which *Meg* shall be shown in Edinburgh, etc. etc. etc., I still hope that the King and the Duke of Wellington will prevail.—Ever most truly,

ROBERT PEEL.

DUKE OF WELLINGTON TO
SIR ROBERT PEEL.

DOVER, *Sept.* 18*th*, 1822.

MY DEAR PEEL,—I have omitted to answer you respecting *Old Meg*. This gun is in the Tower, and is one of the principal articles of

This bustle occupied us till the beginning of this month, since when I have lived the life of a *cow* in this place, that is, eating, drinking, and lying on the grass. The weather now turns too cold for this indulgence, and I must take more active exercise. Of domestic news I have little or none. My family are quite well. Walter is still at Berlin, or rather for the present at Dresden, studying the great art of war. I intend to go there in Spring 1823 to fetch him home, and hope I will have time to return by Vienna and the North of Italy. It is a pity to miss Rome, but I am not very classical and time will not serve me. Perhaps I may have the great pleasure of seeing you if you still remain on the Continent. I observe the Kembles have left Lausanne for a tour in Italy, and I conclude you have had the pleasure of their society; if so, pray remember me to them both.

I have little more to add, my dear Lady Abercorn, excepting the anxious wish to hear from you and to hear that you are easy and amused. Our friends Sir John and Lady Beresford now inhabit Duddingston House, and we see them often. . . . Always, my dear Lady, your very sincere and affectionate friend,   WALTER SCOTT.

FROM CHARLES LAMB.

EAST INDIA HOUSE, LONDON, *29th October* 1822.

DEAR SIR,—I have to acknowledge your kind attention to my application to Mr. Haydon. I have transmitted your draft to Mr. G[odwin]'s committee as an anonymous contribution through me. Mr. Haydon desires his thanks

Singleton's Show. But I shall have no objection to its being sent to Edinburgh Castle; nor will Singleton, I should think, if he is allowed to appoint a Deputy to show it to the inhabitants of Edinburgh. You may tell Sir Walter Scott that it shall be sent to Edinburgh, but I must get the King's orders to remove it from the Tower, which I will do as soon as I return to England. . . .—Believe me, ever yours very sincerely,

WELLINGTON.

and best respects to you, but was desirous that I should write to you on this occasion. I cannot pass over your kind expressions as to myself. It is not likely that I shall ever find myself in Scotland, but should the event ever happen, I should be proud to pay my respects to you in your own land. My disparagement of heaths and highlands—if I said any such thing in half earnest,—you must put down as a piece of the old Vulpine policy. I must make the most of the spot I am chained to, and console myself for my flat destiny as well as I am able. I know very well our mole-hills are not mountains, but I must cocker them up and make them look as big and as handsome as I can, that we may both be satisfied. Allow me to express the pleasure I feel on an occasion given me of writing to you, and to subscribe myself, dear sir, your obliged and respectful servant,

CHARLES LAMB.[1]

---

[1] The foregoing is what "Elia" refers to as "the respectful letter" in the brief note to Haydon (No. 193 of Canon Ainger's choice edition of Lamb's *Letters*). Godwin had been turned out of his house in Skinner Street for arrears of rent. Lamb on hearing of his misfortune sent him £50 in May, and was now endeavouring to obtain from friends £300 or £400, the sum required to relieve the philosophic author of *Political Justice* from a threatened execution. Haydon himself in a few weeks had his own house stripped by his creditors, and his next application to Scott was dated from the King's Bench Prison.

Scott's letter enclosing £10 will be found in *Haydon's Correspondence*, 2 vols. 8vo, London, 1874, vol. i. p. 356.

CHAPTER XIX

1823

EDINBURGH AND ABBOTSFORD

"And wha may ye be, gin ye speer,
  That brings your auld-world clavers here?
Troth if there's ony body near
          That kens the roads,
I'll haud ye Burgundy to Beer
          He kens Meg Dods."
                    Epilogue to *St. Ronan's Well*.

First symptoms of apoplexy in winter of 1822-3.

Elected a member of THE CLUB and also the Roxburgh Club.

Chosen by the Royal Academy, London, as Professor of Ancient History.

Bannatyne Club founded.

Miss Edgeworth's visit to Abbotsford, July.

Peveril of the Peak, 4 vols., published by Constable in January.

Quentin Durward, 3 vols., published by Constable in June.

Essay on Romance.

"Macduff's Cross," for Miss Baillie's Picnic vol.

St. Ronan's Well, 3 vols., published by Constable in December.

CHAPTER XIX.

ABBOTSFORD, *January 8th,* 1823.

MY DEAREST FRIEND,—I finished my hasty transcript only yesterday and send it under Mr. Freeling's cover; you must correct it yourself, for I did not much care to look at it again. I believe it may put you in mind of the old song—

> Thus said the old Man
> To the oak tree,
> Sair fail'd, hinny,
> Since I kenn'd thee.
> When I was young and souple
> I could loup a dike,
> Now I am auld and fail'd
> I canna step a sike.

But I will say nothing of my sense of its deficiency, and nothing of my regret that it is not better, lest I should be supposed to call forth civil contradiction. If I cared anything for poetical reputation, I might be supposed entitled to claim credit for an heroic act of friendship in sacrificing it to your wishes, but as it was never a point for which I much valued myself I cannot claim your thanks even on this score. I send enclosed a cheque, which, though a small one, is worth more than my poetical contribution.[1]

---

[1] Macduff's Cross now in *Poetical Works,* vol. xii. pp. 97-111.—Originally contributed to *Poetical Miscellanies,* London, 8vo, 1822, edited by Miss Baillie to help a friend. How splendidly she succeeded is shown in the following extract from her letter to Scott, July 1st, 1823:—

"I wrote you a short and hurried

Builders and planners have drain'd my purse, otherwise the luck penny should have been better worth your
acceptance. You cannot imagine how smart Abbotsford
looks with its turrets and queer old-fashioned architecture.
I sincerely hope you will one day alter your cruel resolution and come to us here, and for a longer time,—not to
say better weather than the last. I had the whole of my
books (no small quantity) to remove since I came here, as
I had the mortification to find they were suffering by damp.
You can scarce imagine such a labour, as every volume
pass'd through my own hand, as the zealous ignorance of
my assistants was like to be more prejudicial than useful.

TO MORRITT.

[11 *January* 1823.]

MY DEAR MORRITT,—I write a few hasty lines to say
nothing will give us more pleasure than to receive Miss
Morritt and her friend in Edinburgh as kindly as we
have the means to do; in short, your sister, whom I remember with great pleasure upon a former visit at Rokeby,
will be as if she were mine, and, as the Eastern folks conclude, What can I say more? I hope she will allow us

letter at the time I sent you the
first copy of my collected Poems,
and did not thank you half enough
for the very powerful and friendly
assistance which I received from
you in that troublesome business.
Pray believe that I did not feel
the less grateful on that account,
and accept now of my most hearty
acknowledgments. Your name
helped me beforehand, and 'Mac-
Duff's Cross,' which has been very
much admired by a great proportion of my readers, helped me
well afterwards. In short, I took
hold of your strong arm at the
very beginning, and leaning upon
that, put forth my hand and
caught at all the rest of the
Poetical Brotherhood likely to do
me any good. And great good has
come of it, for after paying all
expenses of printing, etc., which
came to £313 or £330, I forget
which, we have realized for my
friend two thousand two hundred
per cent. stock, and when we have
sold all the copies intended for
Indian subscribers, we shall add
better than two hundred more."
. . .

our blunt Scotch habits of asking folks to small parties,
and on short invitations, which methinks should be York-
shire too.

I have little to tell you of late, otherwise I should have
written. I suffered terribly after we met with a sort of
cutaneous eruption—dare not to suspect the tartan—
which most funnily broke out on my body after a feverish
crise during H. Majesty's reception here. I believe hurry,
anxiety of mind, and high living for the time had brought
me to the said base pass, but I literally had a very wild
rash all over me half the time, which I manfully endured,
rather than back out of the scrape I was in.

I fear you will think P.,[1] which I hope you have long
since received, *sent l'apoplexie*. Sooth to say, I tired of it
most d——, and Ballantyne mutinied me to make me put
more strength and spirit into a fourth volume which
(needs must go, when the Devil, typographically speaking,
drives) I wrote in 14 days as much too fast as the others
were too slow. I hope to do much better things in my
next, having an admirable little corner of history fresh in
my head where the vulgar dogs of imitators have no sense
to follow me. My idea is, strictly *entre nous*, the adventures of a young Scotchman going to France to be an archer
of the Scots Guard, *tempore Ludovici* xi^{mi}. You who
study Philip de Commines will easily imagine what a *carte
de pays* I have before me.

I have had the self-denial to refuse to meet the Beresfords at Newton Don, which is an excellent house, but
totally without *morning*; breakfast at 11 or 12, and so forth,
which deranges all my habits, who like to rise by peep of
day, dine at five, drink a few good glasses, and to bed
betwixt 11 and 12. But this was not the reason of my
stay; but having twenty things to do in my new premises,
I declined going down to my old paternal mansion of

[1] *Peveril of the Peak*, in 4 volumes.

Mertoun, so dared not stir elsewhere for fear of losing cast. I hope to see the Beresfords here in summer, when I have made arrangements to blow them up with gas, to astonish them with bells rung on the true pop-gun principle by the action of air alone, without the vulgar intervention of wire, and to do everything else which the President of a Royal Society, whether in Laputa or elsewhere, ought to do to distinguish him from the vulgar.

I suppose the meeting of Brougham and Canning was much like that of the Diable Boiteux and his enemy, who vowed friendship, embraced, and were more bitter foes than ever from that moment. The Whigs, however, take all the advantage, and boldly say terms were proposed. Although I knew this to be a lie, yet I wish Canning had kept out of the rencontre; for tho' liberality is an excellent thing, you should be sure that it is reciprocally disinterested, and the time was singularly unlucky.

I am looking to get Walter into his profession again— no easy task. He is still at Berlin, or Dresden, I am at this moment uncertain which, and I think he will be home in a month or two, as I have renounced the idea of going to seek him. My works here being of a conundrumical description require a good deal of my attention, and I must prepare other works to make these go on well. Charles is in Wales with Mr. Williams, and going on, I hope, pretty well—at least his master is pleased with him. I hope to see Rokeby in summer *cum toto corpore dominii de Abbotsford.* The Lockharts are now living on the babble and smiles of their single hope, which sometimes gives me uneasiness, for a failure, where a failure is so easy and probable, will make them too miserable.

I am delighted to hear Lady Louisa is so well. God knows an unusual fatality appears to have haunted her in

respect of the loss of friends, which has in her case taken
place so frequently and by such strange accidents that it
seems a fatality. I will write to her soon. By the by,
dearest Morritt, writing turns terribly embarrassing to me,
from the failure of eyesight. What a terrible thing blind-
ness, or even extreme obtusity of sight, would be to me!
But God's will be done. I have had more service of my
eyes than most people. Love to my pretty and kind
sweethearts, your nieces, and believe me, most truly yours,

W. SCOTT.

FROM LADY LOUISA STUART.

GLOUCESTER PLACE, *February 6th*, 1823.

—I care not for *Anachro*—(what's your Greek word?)
Event and date may dance the Lays at will ;
But, pray you, leave men's characters unaltered,
Nor make the heroine, firm in duty's cause,
A fierce revengeful fury—This is new ;
In *him* unwonted, and unwarranted ;
And never trust me if I like its savour—
——Sirs, I smell Whiggery—An 'twere not He
I'd think a change of colours hard at hand,
Th' old honest faith forsaken—

Old Play.

To this tune sing the Ladies Scott and I. In looking
for Waldron's *Isle of Man* we chanced to light upon a
modern description of it inscribed to Mr. Curwen, M.P.
for Carlisle. The author, one David Robertson, says
that the Earl of Derby justly suffered death, and calls
Christian's surrender of the island "an act of generosity."
We verily believe "*the great Unknown*" has been
pilfering from this respectable work. His detaining the
poor Countess a few years from her grave (like a child
kept up beyond bed-time) might be endured; but to
paint her as if she had gone down to the regions below

and returned to earth half a fiend, is so intolerable [1] that he richly deserves she should haunt him,—not in her own majestic shape, but in the virago form he has given her. And under favour, was not she a very good Protestant till she fell into his hands? Madame de Sévigné speaks of her heretic neighbour " *la bonne Tarente*," mother of the la Tremouilles; and surely the Countess of Derby's maternal grandfather, William, Prince of Orange, would not have married his daughter into a Catholic family.

As for her kinswoman the Lady Peveril, we cannot deny the Unknown's right to do what he pleased with her, his creature and private property; yet considering how he had made us love and respect her, it is a little hard upon us to find her at last quitting the stage with a lie in her mouth, invented on purpose to cheat and chouse her worthy husband—when Charles the Second was there too ready to say *le roy le veut* and cut short all objections. Who knows but he loved matchmaking as well as another Prince, who they say does not dislike being thought to resemble him in some points of his character? However, in all this I recognise the old habit of a friend of mine growing tired before any of his readers, huddling up a conclusion anyhow, and so kicking the book out of his way; which is a provoking trick, though one must bear it, rather than not *have* his book, with all its faults on its head.

The best amends he can make is to give us another as soon as may be. So much for *Peveril*. . . .

TO ADAM FERGUSON.

CASTLE STREET, 11*th February* 1823.

MY DEAREST ADAM,—. . . I was much interested by the account of your distresses, as well as by some details from

[1] See *Peveril of the Peak.*

Will. Laidlaw, who describes himself as swimming through the snow, on the back of old Cameronian Davie Deans, like a leviathan through the waters. We have been in a strange pickle here, the clerks of court only able to make their way in a noble *hack*, with four horses, like the magistrates on the race-course, and that addition of dignity, purchased by much subtraction from safety, for how we have escaped overturn is to me wonderful. I found Shanksnaigie[1] (bad as is my specimen of that stud) the only way of moving by which I could get out to dinner and so forth. In short, we have made so many visits to the North Pole of late, that I think the weather of that zone is come to return our calls; *now*, the thaw seems fairly commenced, and we have floods to apprehend instead of wreaths. But laying all this aside, I will speak to the serious business of your epistle. . . .

My wife and Anne send love and compliments of all kinds. This is the 11th February, so in a month, 11th March, I will hope, health, etc., allowing, we will be at Abbotsford. I beg my respects to Miss Wells, Mrs. Jobson, and Miss Jobson. When you can, write me a letter, telling me what you are about; it gives me a smell of Tweedside. Huxley and Walter are, I suppose, sticking somewhere in the snow, but *where* God knows. . . . Yours very truly,

WALTER SCOTT.

TO HIS SON WALTER.

EDINBURGH, 13*th February* 1823.

THE black seal is owing to the death of my Uncle Thomas, near Jedburgh, at the advanced age of 94. . . .

I have given up thoughts of the Continent in Spring, Mama's health having been much impaired during the

---

[1] Shanksnaigie or shanksmare—a Scottish phrase for using one's own legs in travelling.

winter by an asthmatic complaint, which even threatened water on the chest, with swelling at the extremities. These very unpleasant symptoms have induced her to take great care of herself, and I am happy to say they have in a great measure disappeared; but she is not by any means in that state of health which would make it easy for me to leave her in Anne's sole charge. It is now my wish to get you again into the service, for which purpose I expect you to return early in Spring. You had better make your route home by the Low Countries, that you may see a little more of the world. But I do not wish you to stop anywhere unless just to see what may be worth seeing. . . . I do not limit you in the point of expence, desiring you should have what is reasonable, and trusting to your own good sense for wishing to have no more. I also leave to your own discretion the time of setting off, only wishing it to be as early as you can make it suit your arrangements. If you do not get into service again immediately, you must put up with old papa and mama for a little while, and may find many ways to employ your time usefully. Indeed I should be very glad to have you here for a little while, as mama's illness requires her mind to be amused, and Anne and I are not equal at all times to the task. Do not mention her illness in your answer, for she does not like to have it alluded to.

The snow hereabouts has been something beyond all remembrance, lying in many places ten and twelve feet deep,—where blown up, much deeper; all communication stopped on every point, and no less than twelve mails due at the Edinburgh post-office. The communication is now partly open, but letters come without the coaches, being carried on horseback. In the midst of all this, Major Huxley has, the Lord knows how, fought his way on to London, like an old soldier, with my nephew Walter. The last came off at his examination with flying colours, and is now safely installed at Addiscombe, the Indian military seminary for engineers, where, for about £50 per annum, he has the advantage of the best masters, board, bed, clothing, and every other expence supplied by the Company, any further advance on the part of his friends, even for pocket money, being not only unnecessary, but strictly prohibited. If he lives and labours, I trust the poor boy will do well.

Lockhart and Sophia are well—little baby excellently well—and friends in general so. I think there will be some stir in the army, and if you were once in it again, and had served a sufficient time, you might stand as fair as others to get a troop or company, in which case you would be tolerably independent of my support, save for some odd turn or occasion. I am told to get on just now would be a very great matter indeed for you.—I am always, Dearest Walter, your affectionate father,   WALTER SCOTT.

FROM MISS EDGEWORTH.

EDGEWORTHSTOWN, *April 10th*, 1823.

"AND July shall be the time."[1] Does Sir Walter Scott remember writing those words? They have never gone out of my mind since I read them. But three-quarters of a year have passed since he wrote them, perhaps some circumstances may have changed his views for July, and it is but fair to ask this plain question, and to assure him that I shall make my convenience suit his whatever it may be. I can never forget the politeness and kindness with which he first accepted of our offered visit, and then allowed me to change the time to another year.

Pray, my dear Sir, consult Lady Scott before you answer me, and let me be quite sure that we do not interfere with any of her plans or yours by our visit. As the trouble of female guests generally falls most heavily upon the lady of the house, let Lady Scott have upon this occasion a double

---

[1] See *Life*, vol. vii. p. 34.

casting vote. Here follows our present plan—but observe it may be changed or modified as you please—no measures are taken yet, and you are the first and only person I write to of our Scotch friends. I propose to be with two of my young sisters, Harriet and Sophy, at the Giant's Causeway the first week in June—I should say the first of June if I had not almost a superstitious horror of *pinning* (a gentleman would say *tying*) myself to a day. . . .

TO MISS EDGEWORTH.

My dear Miss Edgeworth,—Nothing will give Lady Scott and myself more pleasure than your redeeming the kind pledge which your letter gives us, and coming here in summer. The time you propose is the very best to see the country, and affords the best prospect of what we can least promise—fair weather. Your scheme for the Giant's Causeway and Glasgow is admirably planned, and we will hope to see you in Edinburgh about the second week in June. We cannot offer you quarters in Castle Street, because the house does not afford them, but we hope you will bestow on us as much of the time which the natives will leave at your disposal as you possibly can. I will arrange a highland tour for you, which shall command all the objects of chief attraction excepting those which are very remote. In fact Lady Mary Wortley's remark is true in the highlands as elsewhere, namely, that the finest scenery always occurs where the mountains break down upon the more level country. I dare not promise myself the great pleasure of going with you further than perhaps a stage or two, for although we are not kept very close to duty in my official situation, yet, one of my colleagues being terribly subject to be laid aside with the gout, I dare not go far from Edinburgh while the Courts are sitting, in case of his being laid up.

The 12th of July dismisses me to my ruralities for four months, and we will count the days till it brings your party to Abbotsford. We hope you will protract your stay long beyond the little shabby week you talk of. Lady Scott bids me say that if she had twenty votes they would all say come and tarry. We have not a romantic country to show, yet when you have seen enough of lakes, rocks, mountains, and waterfalls, Teviotdale is a very *loveable* district, and full of historical remembrances. Your own chaise would be a convenience, your horses rather an encumbrance. Through all the Lowlands you get jades that would rival Knockecroghery's[1] own self, and when you go to the Highlands you get a driver and pair of horses on the job, who knows all the proper places to stop at, and is often no bad cicerone. A strange driver and strange horses in Highland inns are a great pest, though matters are much mended now since I and my brown palfrey often messed together on the same straw, fed on the same oat cakes, and drank small ale out of the same bicker. Everything is now very decent, and no adventures to be met withal, even for three ladies travelling without a squire. As the old song complains—

"*Scotland* is turned to *England* now."[2]

Pray write me a line before you set out. Lady Scott and my daughters offer their sincere respects, and congratulate themselves on the prospect of knowing you and the young ladies. . . .

TO MORRITT.

ABBOTSFORD, 11*th May* 1823.

MY DEAR MORRITT,— . . . I congratulate you sincerely on the good news you have from your nephew. One

---

[1] An Irish horse, described in Miss Edgeworth's *Ennui.*
[2] See *The Turnimspike* in Herd, vol. i. pp. 186-8.

should never judge of a lad's character from any little extravagancies in temper or opinions exhibited during the first dawn of the passions, when they begin to feel themselves men, yet have neither masculine judgment nor experience. The army is perhaps the best school for romance, the worst for libertinism. My hussar arrived two days since at midnight, and occasioned a grand council of night-caps to welcome him, for our household were all at rest—

> "Each one fast asleep in bed,"

as sings the bard of Christabel. He is much confirmed in person and improved in manners by his residence abroad, and expresses with becoming gratitude his infinite obligations to Sir George Rose, who took a paternal charge of him, for which I cannot be sufficiently thankful. He now speaks and converses very differently from the young cornet whose views were much limited by the circle of his regimental mess, and has got over an awkward shyness which those who did not know him might have thought sullenness.

> "Mon âne parle, et même il parle bien."

We must meet somehow this season. Rose comes to Scotland in July. Pray detain him till the 12th, then come to Abbotsford with him and we will *hoicks* back with you again to Rokeby.

My house is enlarged much beyond what is necessary, but Constable's voice says, like the cackle of the hens to the old woman, as translated by the children in Scotland—

> "Buy tobacco—buy tobacco—I 'll pay a'."

All here, including Skene, join in kindest remembrances to you and the young ladies. We go to Edinburgh to-morrow for the two months of the summer session.—
Yours ever,
                              WALTER SCOTT.

TO THE SAME.

EDINR., *25th June* [1823].

My DEAR MORRITT,—I have both your kind letters, which I delayed answering until I should see, according to our Scotch phrase, how bowls are to run this season, and whether I could possibly promise myself the pleasure of a raid of Rokeby. I find however on computation, that this very pleasant matter must be put off' till next year. I have a monstrous deal to do at Abbotsford, and besides expect one or two birds of passage in the course of July and August, who intend to rest their wearied wing at Abbotsford. I wish to heaven Lady Alvanley [1] and Miss Ardens would be of that party. I have not seen them since 1815, when their presence contributed so much to make Paris delightful. I trust in God your charming young friend will experience all the advantage you can desire from the milder climate of the south. Ours is the only bad thing about our country. I myself am insensible to cold and rawness, but I see the young people even of Scotland sinking daily under pulmonary or stomach disorders, exasperated by the rigour of our northern seasons. I think we have made our houses too comfortable in comparison to the state of the external air, and yet the Russian rushes from his vapour bath into the extremities of a polar climate. Wherever the fault lies the consequences are too obvious. My friend Hector MacDonald has just lost a fourth son, who like his brothers died at the age when he should have entered the world, and he has now only one left of five most hopeful young men—a sad business. Upon the whole this has been a most unhealthy season, and the aged and weak have been swept off at an awful rate. All our household have been ill except myself.

[1] Lady Alvanley, widow of Lord Chief-Justice Alvanley, came to Scotland to visit Sir Walter Scott, and died in Edinburgh in January 1825; she was buried in Holyrood.

Walter has had a tough touch of fever and ague, but seems now quite re-established. He stays with me but a short time. . . .

Miss Edgeworth is here, very lively and entertaining, and acting well up to the character one forms from her compositions. In person I can never free myself from the recollections of Whippity Stourie, the fairy[1] so much renowned in Scottish nurseries. Her proposed visit to Abbotsford, after she has whisked through the Highlands, is one of the circumstances which oblige me to stick fast at Abbotsford for the next two months.

All here join in kindest and best love to the young ladies and to Miss Morritt, whose residence in Edinburgh this last winter gave us so much pleasure.—Always, dear Morritt, sincerely yours, WALTER SCOTT.

TO MRS. HUGHES.[2]

ABBOTSFORD, *July 26th*, 1823.

. . . I WAS much entertained with your account of the Lions of Leamington; the learned Doctor Parr[3] is certainly

---

[1] See Lockhart's letter on Miss Edgeworth in Mrs. Gordon's *Christopher North:* and *Life*, vol. vii. p. 177.

[2] Mrs. Hughes—an early friend of Scott's, and Mr. Lockhart testifies, "a more affectionate one he never possessed"—was the wife of Dr. Hughes, one of the canons-residentiary of St. Paul's, London. Her son was John Hughes of Oriel College, author of the *Itinerary of the Rhine*, so highly praised in the Introduction to *Quentin Durward*, and her grandson is the genial and accomplished author of *Tom Brown's School Days*.

[3] Dr. Samuel Parr, of whom Mrs. Hughes had written: "There is a very respectable Menagerie of Leamington Lions (to use the Oxford term) at present. That 'old original lion, which cannot be tamed by the hand of man '—Dr. Parr—resides about four miles from hence, and frequently drives over to snuff up the incense of his worshippers: he moves in a sort of Juggernaut procession up and down the street, dressed in a black velvet fancy great-coat, with a very small triangular hat exactly like those worn by the London coachmen when they drive in state, perched on the top of his huge wig; out of this the broad disk of his fiery face, unsheltered from the sun and bronzed with the red dust of the road, gleams portentously like the sun struggling through a

one of the first order.   I saw him, to my astonishment, in
the streets of Edinburgh at a time when they were
deserted by all but tradesfolk and tourists, but when some
accidental business obliged me to come to town; I heard
a prodigious talking, and looking out saw the Doctor march,
like a turtle erect on his hinder claws, in full canonicals,
and surrounded by a sort of halo of satellites, male and
female, to whom he was laying down the law as if the
whole town was his own.   After all, it is very difficult to
be a lion in good society, if you happen to be at the
same time a beast of moderate bearing, and of common
sense.   The part played by the lion in the Spectator, who
fought on the stage with Nicoline, is much easier; if you
do not make some play, you are set down either for a
sulky or a paltry animal, and if you do, there is generally
something very absurd in it.   For my part, who am sometimes called upon to be a lion, I always form myself on
the model of that noble animal who was so unnecessarily
disturbed by the knight of the woeful countenance; "he
rose up, turned himself round in his caravan, showed
himself, front and rear, then licked his moustachios with
a yard of tongue, yawned most formidably, and then lay
down in peace."   Pray tell your son to practise this in
time, against his claws and mane attain the due of
notoriety.   I have a great notion they will grow rapidly.
. . . I am ever, dear Mrs. Hughes, your faithful friend,

WALTER SCOTT.

thunder cloud: his voice roars and echoes through the whole street, as he notices his numerous acquaintance, who, cap in hand, approach in their turn and pay their homage: there is so much display and paltry vanity in all this that I cannot connect such *Charlatanerie* with my idea of a great *mind*.   I love to see old age *venerable*, and really he makes it farcical.   understand that he is much subdued since his absurd conduct respecting the Queen, which has lowered the credit of this prophet even in his own country."

TO WILLIAM STEWART ROSE.

ABBOTSFORD, *Sunday Morning.*

MY DEAR ROSE,—Yours brings the joyous news of your safe arrival in the Land of Cakes. Your chamber here is inviolate, come who may; you have escaped the quintessence of bores in the best-humoured of all Irishmen and the dullest of created beings. I never found your apophthegm more true, that a Bore must have something estimable about him, for, if it had not been for his extreme humility and good-nature, I was on the eve of instituting family prayers, for the purpose of expatiating on Sir Walter Riddell's text—"Remove thy foot from thy neighbour's house, lest he grow weary of thee and so hate thee." The great Hogg found his lair at Abbotsford on Friday, Lockhart bringing him here like a pig in a string, for which the lady of the mansion sent him little thanks, she not thinking the hog's pearls (qu. Perils[1]) an apology for his freedoms. I am to be from home on Friday and Saturday next. . . . But you know that if your shooting arrangements, or any others, include these days, at Abbotsford you have the ladies and Lockhart to make much of you, so come as soon as you can. About the 25th I go for two days to Drumlanrig. As for food, we must take what the gods send us, but there is a turtle come hither—

> " And if we could but get it dressed,
> Which will be right uneasy,
> I would lay baith my legs in pawn,
> We 'll have a feast to please ye."

I wish Lord and Lady Minto and Lady Anna Maria would come over and assist at ridding of this nuisance. The arrival has shaken Lady Scott's nerves excessively, for first the brute must be killed, which shocks her humanity,

---

[1] *The Three Perils of Woman—Love, Leasing, and Jealousy,* by James Hogg, had just been published.

and secondly it must be dressed, which I foresee is to prove
embarrassing to her culinary associate.—Yours ever,

WALTER SCOTT.

TO JOHN RICHARDSON.

Oct. or Nov. 1823.

I HAVE been cumbered with many things which have
prevented my thanking you for two kind letters, one accom-
panying two or three little delilahs of the shelves, which
I am grateful for. I will bind the quaint labours of the old
piscators Whiteney and Barker with the immortal Walton, of
whom they have just printed a new and highly ornamental
edition, with some very pretty plates. I envy you your
German tour, and always think time may give me such an
enjoyment. *Sed fugit—interea fugit irrevocabile tempus.*

The death of Dr. Baillie is a great deprivation to our
excellent friend. I had a most kind letter from her
announcing the event. There is a sort of firmness which
arises even out of the extent of such a calamity, much
like that which enables men to start up and exert themselves after receiving a dreadful fall; the extent of the
injury received is not perceived till long after. I am truly
concerned about Joanna, for she is not strong, and likely
to suffer under the excess of her feeling. He is himself
an inestimable loss to society, and especially for his total
contempt of that science of humbug by which so many of
his brethren make fortunes. He always put me in mind
of Johnson's beautiful lines, though made for a humbler
practitioner :—

> " When fainting nature call'd for aid,
>   And hovering Death prepared the blow,
>   His powerful remedy display'd
>   The force of art without the show." [1]

---

[1] Slightly changed from the fourth verse of Lines on the death of
Mr. Robert Levett.

. . . Charles is still between three and four years from that era.[1] He goes to Oxford next year, and, I am induced to hope from his present tutor, Mr. Williams, who has never flattered me about him, with the information requisite to make proficiency, and a strong disposition to be a reading man. If so, I shall have succeeded very happily in my boys. . . .

Abbotsford has cost me a mint of money without much return as yet. But after all, it is the surest way of settling a family, if one can do without borrowing money or incurring interest. Sweet Abbotsford has thrust its lofty turrets into the skies since you saw it, and I will scarce forgive you unless you make it a comfortable visit next season. It is, from the unusual combination of the garden and courtyard with the manor-house, a sort of romance in architecture,

> " A place to dream of, not to tell."

In fact, I have at last nearly completed a sort of vision I always had in my mind. All our rooms are moderate in size, except the library, which is forty feet by eighteen, yet will not hold my books without the assistance of my private room. Our Bannatyne Club goes on à *merveille*, only that at our *gaudeamus* this year we drank our wine *more majorum*, and our new judge, Lord Eldin, had a bad fall on the staircase, which has given rise to some bad jokes, as for instance, that to match Coke upon Littleton we have got Eldin upon Stair, and so forth. I did not get to my carriage without a stumble neither, but had no hurt, and being preses, was not sorry to have kept my senior in company. After all, we were, as you may believe, " no very fou, but gaily yet." It is said there is to be an act of sederunt prohibiting all judges from keeping company with Sir Samuel Shepherd and me. Pray, is Cockburn to send you his duplicates of this learned and thirsty body, for if not, you shall have mine.

[1] His majority.

Lady Scott joins in kind respects to Mrs. Richardson.
Pray come all down next summer and bring the babies.
—Always, my dear Richardson, yours truly,

WALTER SCOTT.

TO MISS EDGEWORTH.

[*November* 1823.]

THAT I have not my time so much at my command as
you, my dear Miss Edgeworth, would persuade me,[1] is
evident from this packet containing the two miniatures,
which has lain on my table several days waiting for the
few lines which you are now reading. I do not believe,
however, that any one can want time who has a strong
and forcible desire to make use of that which we all enjoy.
Two hours' rising in the morning before the rest of the
family are astir makes the greatest possible difference
between leisure and want of it. This space resolutely
employed will serve in the usual case to despatch much of
the business which is necessarily pressed upon every man,
and it is also a very healthy practice, for if you arise in

[1] Miss Edgeworth wrote on Oct. 12th: ". . . What time do you work? When do you write? Any court of judicature in or out of Christendom would acquit you of being the author of half the works laid to your charge upon the mere physical impossibility of the human hands penning so much in a given time, let alone the human head inventing so much." And on January 26, 1824, as to *St. Ronan's Well*—" We are all much happier than when I wrote to you last. My sister is much better, and she is able to listen to reading, and has much enjoyed the last of those Scottish novels in which you take so little interest that I am almost ashamed to mention them to you, and afraid to sink in your opinion by confessing how deeply it has interested and how much it has amused us all.—*till we come to the last 30 pages*, for which we all agree that the author deserves to be carbonadoed. When he and Touchwood had the game in their hands, how could he have the heart to throw it up and huddle the cards together in such a shameless manner, overturning table and all in haste to be after some new game?

". . . Touchwood is an admirable and new character—so is Mrs. Blower and capital Meg. Lady Penfeather, tho' a character old as affectation, is newly handled. The scenes in which Clara appears— the fitful lights and clouds of her partial insanity are drawn by a master's hand. So is the touch of insanity in the brother's character in the last shudderingly fine scene."

the morning you secure sound and refreshing sleep during
the earlier part of the night.   It is not many years since
I adopted this practice, and I am sorry for it, but late
hours at night made me formerly averse to quit my couch
in the morning.   By constitution I require a great deal of
sleep, seven hours at least; and if I have not, I am sure to
indemnify myself by a nap during the day.

Were you not much shocked at poor Lord Hopetoun's
death?[1] We saw him so well and so happy in his paternal
palace with all his flourishing family, the husband of a
beautiful woman, lord of a noble estate, a great name in war,
and in peace looked up to by a large body of his countrymen as their natural head and leader, and all this has passed
away and left but mourning and sorrow behind it.   I think
I shall never forget our visit to Hopetoun House. . . .

Caraboo[2] reached me safe, and is a most delightful
personage.   She was obviously slightly touched with insanity, and possessed of all the cunning which often belongs
to such dispositions.   It is curious how often the great
impostors who have driven their success to the verge of
incredibility, seem to have been in a certain degree insane.

No one completely possessed of a rational judgment
can possibly guess the extent of popular credulity.   They
are like regular doctors, who fail to carry their point now
and then, by giving medicine in quantities too moderate,
when empirics are successful by wholesale and triumphant
doses.   It is more humbling to think that utter and
egregious folly will have the same success as madness in
enabling people to gull the world.   This wretched Poyais
Cacique is a mixture of knave and fool, in which the
latter greatly predominates, yet you see how he has been
able to impose the grossest deceits upon his cautious
countrymen, and that in spite of warning.

[1] On 27th August 1823.   vol. ii. p. 163, for an account of
[2] See Hone's *Every Day Book*,   this singular female impostor.

We had our great harvest home supper on Walter's birthday as usual, and all the natives, young and old, danced till four in the morning. Whisky *à discrétion*, but no drunkenness, unless amongst two or three of the old jockies, who, being past dancing, consoled themselves with punch. The festivity much enlivened by the news that an old retainer of mine, John Scott, called the Turk, had beat all the wild Macraws at a wrestling match in Kintail, flinging Duncan above Donald and plaid over bonnet in such a style as has not been seen since Culloden. The champion was one of my stoutest men, a great dancer at the Kirn suppers, where he used to dance reels with Sophia and Anne, never sinking into the ordinary dancing step but *cutting* most resolutely from the beginning to the end. His father, the old Turk, shakes his head and wishes him better gifts. I will send to Liddesdale to see to get a good puppy for you, and keep it till it has had the distemper, so fatal to the canine race, and fatal to them, as it strangely happens, always in proportion to the purity of the breed. Vaccination is said greatly to mitigate the virulence of the disease. Spice will I think recover. She has got her agility again, and her appetite, but still wheezes strangely, and I should fear the consequences of cold. I would not like Dr. King to have a creature to become attached to, and then to lose it.

I really did not write the additions to Shulagaroo:[1] I found them in a curious little collection of Dumfriesshire songs, made by Charles Kirkpatrick Sharpe, and which he has printed, but for distribution only. It is easy to account for the song having strayed into Dumfriesshire from Ireland. If your brother looks sharp about among the Irish labourers I daresay he will find more of it. Love to Misses Harriet and Sophia. I do not think the miniature does the former justice, yet it is like. Lady Scott sends

---

[1] Forming No. xiv. of "*A Ballad Book*," republished in 8vo, 1880.

kindest wishes, in which Anne joins, and has the grace to write besides. I beg my compliments to your brother and am, dear Miss Edgeworth, most faithfully yours,

WALTER SCOTT.

TO TERRY.

ABBOTSFORD, 22 *December* 1823.

DEAR TERRY,—I enclose a letter to poor Theodore Hook,[1] which pray give into his own hands. If, as Lieutenant Bowling says, "a small spill of cash" was wanted there on such an immediate and distressing pinch, I have £50 at his service, but of this I of course can say nothing till I shall hear from you how his matters stand. It will be an eternal shame if they leave the poor fellow in the lurch after all he has done, and yet there is so much *candour* (or want of pluck) in those principally benefited by his exertions, that my fears rather outweigh

[1] In reply to a letter from Hook, dated *December 17th*, 1823:—

DEAR SIR,—I am sure you will pardon my writing to you, which I do because having taken a kind interest in my welfare I feel bound to let you know my *progress* in the world.

The Government have arrested me for £12,000—the debt undecided —part of it in dispute. I was stripped of everything five years since on the same account by Extent, deprived of my office, sent home under an illegal warrant and a military guard, and all for conduct arising out of an incorrect account which *had been audited and passed* for two years.

Mr. Croker has left town, and I have no communication with the Government, who have gone to work in the ordinary way of business. It is curious that the suspicion under which I have laboured of being a literary partisan, and the hidden vindicator of my King and Constitution, and which has roused such a host of enemies, should have failed in securing something like a proportionate body of friends amongst those who really ought to appreciate the power of *that weapon* which has so irritated the opposing party.

I have no object, as I before said, in stating my case to you, except that you should have an accurate account of the fate of one who most deeply feels your kindness, and in hopes of retaining the support which on former occasions you have shown yourself so willing to afford me.

I once more request you to forgive this intrusion, and that you will believe me to remain, dear sir, your obliged and faithful servant,

THEODORE HOOK.

my hopes on his account.   Yet surely the commercial value of the speculation itself must be considerable.   And I should think there are many friends who with prudent management might be induced to "put five pounds in a sartain place."

We are here for Christmas, but deprived of Sophia by a return of an illness indicative of those cursed cramps which attended her last confinement, in a gentler degree however, and which I hope will give way before the proper treatment.

We expect Walter daily; . . . Charles goes to enter at Oxford, though he does not become resident till next Autumn. . . .

I expect our old friend Russell[1] here one of these days. We have been playing tragedy in Edinburgh.   Sir Giles[2] I saw, and he was very judicious and respectable, but still his features are comic in their natural expression, and he seems to be conscious of this, from the bad habit he has of contracting and sharpening them into a tragical contortion of aspect.   I hope he may succeed however, for he is a good fellow, and clever to boot; I will try and insinuate to him to stick by the sock. . . .

---

[1] James Russell, a clever comedian, who preferred oddly enough such parts as Richard III. and Shylock.

[2] In Massinger's comedy, *New Way to Pay Old Debts*.

CHAPTER XX

1824

EDINBURGH AND ABBOTSFORD

" For all our men were very very merry,
    And all our men were drinking ;
    There were two men of mine,
    Three men of thine,
    And three that belong'd to old Sir Thom o' Lyne ;
    As they went to the ferry, they were very very merry ;
    And all our men were drinking."
                                    Wandering Willie's Catch.

Son Charles at Oxford.

Autumn guests — Lady Alvanley, Lady Compton, Mrs. Coutts, etc.

Maida's death and epitaph, October.

Christmas festivities at Abbotsford.

Redgauntlet, 3 vols., published by Constable in June.

Second edition of *Swift's Life and Works*, 19 vols. 8vo, published by Constable.

Tribute to the memory of Lord Byron in *Weekly Journal*.

Contribution to *Quarterly Review—Lady Suffolk's Letters*, January 1824, No. 60.

CHAPTER XX.

EDINBURGH, *5th February* 1824.

. . . IF you have seen little Russell he will tell you
how our Christmas gambols came off gaily, and how they
danced in the new library till moonlight and starlight and
gaslight went out.[1] The entrance hall with its blazonry,
carved oak panels, and huge freestone chimney-pieces,
with such pieces of old armour as can be handsomely
stow'd there, will be quite baronial. The outer court,
with its screen and carved work, looks very antique.

The command of time which your absence from the
Haymarket [allows] may be advantageously disposed of
here; indeed as you come down with a new halo of
London fame, I think it might be very successful, for
theatrical attraction always depends more on popularity
than on real merit. Besides, you have now several parts
of your own, which always infers novelty, and with a
little help from friends and James Ballantyne's blarney,
I have little doubt of the campaign, and I will be personally responsible for a good benefit. I speak this confidently,
because circumstances have forced me into wider connections of every kind than perhaps I could have wished,
and a friend like you should take the full benefit. . . .

My present labours [2]—but tell it not to one mortal
ear—comprehend two narratives in about two volumes
each; they may perhaps intrude on vol. 3rd. I intend

[1] See *Life*, vol. vii. p. 252.
[2] *Redgauntlet*, published in June,
and *The Tales of the Crusaders*,
published in 1825.

you shall have this, which I think will be highly dramatic, as soon as printed, and as nothing can come out till the other vols. are both written and printed, you will have ample time to dramatize it before any intruder can possibly interfere.

I am very much pleased to hear of your theatrical history, which I think is capable of being rendered much more agreeable than in any shape it has yet taken. To guide you in a trifling point about my own theatrical collection, please note that I have got Mrs. G. A. Bellamy and Mrs. Sumbel Wells.[1] If you are anxious to trace the root of Sir Anthony Absolute, whose humour is well maintained in *Percy Mallory*,[2] pray look into Cowley's old comedy of the *Guardian*, afterwards altered into the *Cutter of Coleman Street*, where you find the first sketch of the knight in Truman Senior. I am morally certain Sheridan had read this piece and taken the hint. I am truly glad that poor Theodore's[3] affairs are looking up; it would be terrible to think he should be deserted, but I hope he will look about him and push the matter to a settlement, for should he not get a *quietus* now, it may leave him open to oppression when the Whigs come in, and I know these worthy gentlemen so well as to believe they would not neglect to use them. A thousand kind compliments to Mrs. Terry and nursery, not forgetting Walter. If I live to see him fit to go out in the world, it shall go hard but I lend a hand to the launch; the Engineer Department of the East India Company offers great advantages for young people who have a turn for drawing and mathematics. . . .—Yours always,

WALTER SCOTT.

---

[1] The autobiographies of both ladies are noted in the Abbotsford Library catalogue.

[2] An anonymous novel by the author of *Pen Owen*. The author was the Rev. James Hook, afterwards Dean of Worcester.

[3] Theodore Hook, *ante*, p. 182.

FROM LADY ABERCORN.

PARIS, *February 19th*, 1824.

.. I WOULD have bet all I possess when we parted
last in Stratford Place that I should have had constant
letters from you, yet three years are gone over and three
letters have I received. Is this like the friend of my
heart? Now for a word about *St. Ronan's Well.* It
interested me to such a degree that when it concluded I
could have destroyed the book, the author, and the
whole village, and if you can but find out who the author
is, tell him never again to end his novels so unfortunately;
weak nerves cannot bear it. I like the whole book; it,
like all the rest of those novels, makes one feel at home
and a party concerned. No one but that Unknown ever
could have the same power. I hear he has entered into
an agreement to furnish 3 novels a year for 3 years,
and is to get for that £10,000 a year. I wish he could
hear how much he interests every creature in all countries.
Every one reads these novels, and talks of them quite as
much as the people do in England; and though some of
them are more admired than others, yet they are all of
them favourites. People are still as curious as ever to
find out the Author. I express the same curiosity, but
agree with all that since Junius no secret ever was so
well kept. I heard the other day from G. Wright, who
seems to say there is now no doubt but W. S. is the
author. Pray tell me do you *believe* he has entered into
that agreement for £10,000 a year for three years?

. . . And I want the engravings you promised me of
the novels—do, my *good* (no, *good* you do not deserve)
friend, send them to me as soon as possible—and above
all the engraving of Lawrence's picture. I am become a
connoisseur in statues—that I learned from that ever-to-
be-regretted Canova. If you thought but half as well of

me as he did, I should have known more about you since
we parted than I do. I received the last letter but one
that he ever wrote, but I will not reproach you for broken
promises—perhaps you will be good in future. . . . God
bless you, my dear Sir Walter, most affectionately yours,

A. ABERCORN.

TO LADY ABERCORN.

CASTLE STREET, EDINBURGH, *March 4th*, 1824.

MY DEAREST LADY,—We have an old phrase in Scotland about taking the first word of *flyting* (scolding)—that
is to say, being the first to complain when we happen to
have given some reason to be complained of. Now I really
think that I can see a little of this policy in your Ladyship's letter with which I am just favoured. I wrote
a very long letter addressed to Rome, and I had
never the pleasure of hearing that it ever reached its
destination. Now I would be most unreasonable to wish
you, my dear friend, to bestow much leisure upon me
and my letters; but then you are to consider that you
are not at present stationary, but travelling a good deal,
and that my letters would be less worth reading even
than at present, if they [did] not contain many things
that I should be sorry fell into any hand other than the
honoured ones for which they are intended. So that you
must really have the goodness, by a line or two at least,—
for I do not insist upon long letters—to let me know in
the first place how you are, and then that you have
received my letter, and that I am to continue the same
address or use another one. Remember, my dear friend,
that when you form the *impossible* conjecture that I have
forgotten *you*, it may with much more justice occur to
me that there is a great probability, arguing from your
silence, that *you* have forgotten *me*,—an idea which

would not surprise me, though it would certainly give
me much pain; for which reason your Ladyship may be
well assured I will not rashly entertain it. So I hope, my
dear friend, that this of ours is a sort of commercial
treaty, not with respect to bulk, but with respect to value;
for I will willingly allow one line from your Ladyship to
stand as a full requital for a page of mine—only you
must send one to tell me how you are, what you are
doing, and that you have received my letter and wish
to hear from me again. Now this is a treaty which only
waits for your Ladyship's ratification to be most faithfully
observed by me, since God knows there are few in the
world, and these turning daily fewer, whose commands
I would be more willing and anxious not only to obey,
but to anticipate. And let me hope I have at present in
some degree explained the cause of my late silence as
being only the consequence of that on the part of Lady
Abercorn.

You may rely upon it, I think, that the author of the
novels you mention would never enter into any bargain as to
producing a certain number of volumes within a given time.
No creature can be entitled to reckon upon such a flow
of spirits and regular continuation of good health, and I
believe an attempt to comply with such a contract as the
newspapers have invented would be a very dangerous task
both to body and mind. The labour must be great enough
as it is, and attended with much tear and wear of constitution and of intellect. Besides the supposed recompense,
large as it is, would not be adequate to the author's profits
in an ordinary way of publication. Two odd things have
happened in consequence of the pertinacity with which
the public have so erroneously posted me as the author of
these novels—the first is that I got a letter from America
accusing me of having encouraged that report for a large
sum of money in order to conceal the real author whose

name it was supposed would be obnoxious to the public. This was good enough, but a better incident still is the publication of a German novel professing to be translated from the English, and bearing my name at full length on the title-page.[1] So that I must not only bear my own faults, and in the opinion of many, those of that unknown gentleman, but also all the devices with which the invention of others continues to load either him or myself.

Your kind inquiries about my family, I can, thank God, answer generally speaking in very agreeable terms. Your Ladyship's acquaintance, Walter, is now again on full pay, and Lieutenant in the 15th Hussars. He has been, since his return from the Continent, by the Duke of York's favour a student in the advanced class of officers who are allowed to reside at the Royal Military College at Sandhurst.

My younger son Charles is now with us. He has entered at Brazenose, but does not go to Oxford to reside until the October term. If I do not deceive myself, and I think I can judge impartially even on so tender a point, he is a young man of high promise; from being very volatile and idle, he has, since he resided for three years with a learned clergyman in England, become a keen student and a promising scholar, and full of that sort of pride which looks to future distinction. My daughter Lockhart has been rather unfortunate; her eldest child came to this world rather too early, and though a pretty, clever, and very engaging infant, alarms me a little from the slenderness of its frame, and a sort of delicacy of health sometimes connected with premature development of intellect. Sophia was again confined about two months ago, but lost her infant, and has had but a slow and precarious recovery, which indeed is yet far from complete. This is at present the only shade in our domestic horizon. My black-eyed lassie is dancing away merrily, and I believe generally

[1] *Walladmor*, Berlin, 1824.

thought handsome, but her hour, if it ever comes, is not come yet.

You may not have heard of poor Tom's death, in whom one leading fault, thoughtlessness, blemished so many good and noble qualities. His eldest daughter is married to Major Huxley of the 70th regiment, a very gentleman-like man, who was in Britain last year. Tom's widow is returned here with two younger daughters, very good-looking girls, and the younger (about thirteen years old) very clever and amusing. The elder has refused some good matches in Canada, which her mother seems rather to regret. The girls, though hurried during the great part of their life along with a marching regiment, are so modest, well-bred, and accomplished that I was proposing to advertise His Majesty's 70th regiment as an excellent boarding-school for young ladies. To be sure their father and mother, both well qualified for the task, bestowed constant pains to improve their understandings and manners. I must add, to complete my account of this family, that the only son, Walter, whom I have in a certain degree adopted into my own family, is one of the Cadets for the Engineer service of the East India Company, and as such is following out his studies at the Company's College at Addiscombe, where this class of their students receive instruction. Walter, my nephew, whose talents for arithmetic and mathematics are of a most uncommon kind, has fought himself up, though much younger than most of the students, to the top of the class, gained mathematical prizes, and is promoted to the rank of one of the officers of the Corps of Cadets. This promises very well, for if he lives and continues to attend to his studies, he will get ready promotion if he leaves college with the report of his superiors in his favour, and the Engineer Department, when followed by a man of talent, is one of the best lines in India.

As your Ladyship has the advantage of Canning's all-powerful franks I send a book of my son-in-law Lockhart's upon Spanish literature, which I think you will like. He is a most unexceptionable friend and husband, very clever, very learned, and very handsome—addicted to satire though, by which he has made himself enemies. He has written several things which are, I think, very clever.

I would with pleasure send you the supposed print from Lawrence's picture, but none such has yet appeared. Indeed the picture remains unfinished, the costume having never been settled. I don't like a real good picture to be quite in a modern dress, ours being the most unpicturesque possible. I might to be sure take the plaid about me, as I sometimes do at public meetings of the Celtic Society. But I am no Highlander by birth or connection, and to take their dress looks like assuming their character, which I would not do, holding that of my own province more highly. So that this important matter being undecided, the picture is unfinished and probably will remain so, for I have little idea of again visiting London. Why should I? All whom I knew and loved are dead or dispersed, and even in 1821 I felt it quite an altered world. We are not sensible of these changes in the same degree as they affect the scenes in which we move, for new objects spring up to which we become attached, though not with the same feelings. But the changes made by time are strikingly felt when we return to a place from which we have been absent for many years.

I wish you would come to Scotland when you revisit Britain. You are fond of travelling, and I would hope to detain you a few days or weeks at Abbotsford, which has grown by degrees from a cottage into a manor-house, too large perhaps for the property. Do, dear Lady Abercorn, think of this, and I will travel with you and show you the lions wherever you would like to go.

I hasten to close this scrawl, which justifies what I have sometimes thought, that I neither know how to begin a letter nor how to end one.

Believe me, with the greatest respect and affection, your Ladyship's ever obliged and grateful,

WALTER SCOTT.

TO HIS SON WALTER.

9th March 1824.

. . . SOMETHING has happened last week which I can only hint to you in a mystical sort of way. You must know Sir Adam and Lady Ferguson brought their niece, Miss Jobson, here to dinner, who seems a very sweet, pleasant young woman, and has none of the conceit of an heiress about her. Now Sir Adam made a sort of explanation to me of his and his lady's views towards the young lady, to understand the nature of which, I beg you to read over the *first scene* of the *Merry Wives of Windsor*, supposing yourself Mr. Abraham Slender, that I am representing the worshipful Justice Shallow, and our friend Sir Adam Sir Hugh Evans, and that a lady already named is sweet Mistress Anne Page. I understand she is to pass the summer or part of it at Gattonside House, and if you have courage to make the attempt you will have plenty opportunity, and, as Sir Adam thinks, a fair chance of success. I need not point out the great advantages on the lady's side, but there are some on ours also, which would make the match not so remarkable, though there were as many wooing at her as at Tibbie Fowler of the Glen, renowned in song. But she has seen a little of the world now, and I understand has a good deal of steadiness of character.

Now if you think this matter worth prosecuting, it will

be necessary that you be at Abbotsford in the summer, and I have no doubt that leave may be obtained by me from Sir Alexr. Hope if he succeeds to the establishment. I have only to add that Sir Hugh Evans is of opinion that Mr. Slender will not be crossed by the influence of any Mr. Fenton.

Seriously, if you can make up your mind on this matter, and render yourself acceptable, in my opinion you may do worse.   There are no unpleasant stipulations of any kind, and you would pursue your profession with the advantage of a comfortable independence.   I am to suppose that our friends Sir A. and Lady F. would not have come so far forward in a matter which had not a face of probability.

You know I have always treated you with the utmost confidence, and therefore expect the same in return, and that I would do everything in my power to contribute to your happiness.

I will match your old officer of the African Corps with Henry Cranstoun, who has been here telling long stories out of Gil Blas and Joe Miller as if they were the newest and wittiest things in the world; and to mend the matter cats have no terrors for him, for old Hinse has sat staring him in the face this half hour.

Mama is pretty well, and Anne as usual.   Soph is getting stouter, and her child is also better.

Probably the usual term of vacation will suit well enough to come down, instead of employing it in sketching in Kent.   But whatever be your resolution, we have agreed to say nothing of it until the time approaches, but let the Lockharts and every one else suppose that you stay all the summer in England, as originally intended.

If you desire to break off the matter entirely, you will let me know immediately, and I shall inform Sir Hugh Evans that Master Slender is a second Lord Henry—

> "His thoughts were still on honour bent ;
> He never stoop'd to love ;
> No lady in the land has power
> His frozen heart to move."

Yours most affectionately,   WALTER SCOTT.

"Five hundred pounds and possibilities are goot gifts,"
says Sir Hugh Evans.

FROM LADY LOUISA STUART.

GLOUCESTER PLACE, *March 26th*, 1824.

DEAR SIR WALTER,—How ungrateful you must have
thought me for returning you no thanks, as you probably
sent me *St. Ronan's Well* a great while ago! But the fact
is, it came only last week,—I suppose because directed to
South Street, Grosvenor Square, a place I never inhabited,
tho' to be sure born and bred in its near neighbourhood.
I am equally gratified by the proof of your kind remembrance. You will readily conclude I had the book by
heart long before; it is not so much my favourite as
certain of its predecessors, yet still I can see the author's
hand in it, *et c'est tout dire*. Meg Dods, the meeting, and
the last scene between Clara and her brother, are marked
with the true stamp, not to be matched or mistaken. Is
the Siege of Ptolemais really on the anvil, or announced,
to carry on Josiah Cargill's history? I heartily hope the
former, for I should have high expectations from it, the
Crusades being a subject worthy of such a pen; and in this
respect my appetite grows by what it feeds on, perhaps
from wanting, more and more, something to steal my
thoughts away from painful contemplation. My employment for above a year past has been watching the progress
of decrepitude in my nearest surviving relations, seeing
reason ebb and imbecility creep on in those I once looked
up to. By the time I have done with this, the failure will

most likely begin in myself. I often feel that my own mind will give way the sooner, from the effect the constant observation of other minds in a wavering state has upon it. . . .

TO LADY LOUISA STUART.

ABBOTSFORD, MELROSE [*April 4th*, 1824].

MY DEAR LADY LOUISA,—I think very little of the volumes I sent your Ladyship, and were I not a builder and a buyer of books and land, would long since have resigned the office of standing public tale-teller. But . while it is worth a great many thousand pounds a year, what mortal wight can refrain from labouring his brains? I think the next will consist of two tales, one of which will be an extract from the Crusade history. Your late and present melancholy occupation, my dear Lady Louisa, are the penance we pay for having enjoyed in earlier days the countenance and protection of friends and relations older than ourselves, and I know by experience how sad it is to see those whom we love gradually weeded away from the world in which we are left. In my youth I gained much of the limited information of which I may be possessed by keeping company with those older and wiser than myself, and I sigh when I think of the great number of excellent persons with whom I had some intimacy that are now no more. Still there is some comfort that those who have lived in youth with the aged may be said to have collected the wisdom of two generations instead of one. . . . I have Lord Castlereagh here with me on a visit—a very fine good humoured young man, but they must have been mad if they sent a young man of his rank to Edinr. to study. It is positively the idlest place I know for a young man of immediate consequence and future expectations. My sons have nothing of the first, and very little of the second, and yet merely as smart young men and reasonable partners

in a quadrille, they have so many provocations to idleness
that I am always delighted to get them out of Edinr. though
at the expense of losing their society. I am delighted
my dear little half god-daughter is turning out beautiful.
I was at her christening, poor soul, and took the oaths as
representing I forget whom. That was in the time when
Dalkeith was Dalkeith; how changed, alas! I was forced
there the other day by some people who wanted to see the
house, and I felt as if it would have done me a great deal
of good to have set my manhood aside, to get into a corner
and cry like a schoolboy. Every bit of furniture, now
looking old and paltry, had some story and recollections
about it, and the deserted gallery, which I have seen so
happily filled, seemed waste and desolate like Moore's

> " Banquet hall deserted,
> Whose followers are dead,
> Whose odours fled,
> And all but I departed."

But it avails not either sighing or moralising; to have
known the good and the great, the wise and the witty, is
still on the whole a pleasing reflection, though saddened
by the thought that their voices are silent and their halls
empty. I have been building by degrees a home which
I long to show Lady Louisa Stuart, because it is a good
deal out of the common run,—neither castle nor priory,
but an attempt at the old manor-house of a comfortable
country family. I have gambolled a little in the entrance
hall, which I knew was not in very good taste when I
did it; but why should a gentleman not be a little
fantastic as Tony Lumpkin says, " If so be he is in a con-
catenation accordingly." [1] . . .—I am always, my dear Lady
Louisa, your truly obliged and grateful humble servant,

WALTER SCOTT.

[1] Tony Lumpkin, however, does not make use of this favourite expression of Scott's, but Goldsmith puts it into the mouth of one of Tony's boon companions at the " Three Pigeons."—*She Stoops to Conquer.*

TO LADY ABERCORN.

JEDBURGH, *April 21st*, 1824.

MY DEAR LADY ABERCORN,—I must not allow any rust to gather on the chain of friendship (to use an Indian expression) which your Ladyship has been so kind as to brighten by your kind letter of 20 March, which reached my hand about a fortnight ago. I am truly sorry you should stay at Paris when you find that it does not suit with your health.

In winter and spring I should suppose Paris cold. When I was there in August 1815 I felt it unsupportably warm, and was unusually listless and inactive during the middle of the day on that account. I wish you could have quitted the French capital immediately, and tried what early hours and quiet would have done for you upon Tweedside, which the inhabitants think the healthiest residence in the world. But I fear your return to Rome for the winter will put this out of the question for this season. Really in the short period of fine weather Scotland has much to interest and amuse strangers, but for eight months in the year the climate is so rough and so uncertain that it requires to be a native to endure it, and even amongst ourselves complaints of the lungs are too common and very fatal; yet it is not excess of cold which we have to complain of, but rather the variable quality of the atmosphere around us. For instance, all this last winter there was but one day when they could collect ice for the ice-house at Abbotsford. Most fortunately, or to speak more properly, most providentially, the gardener being an alert person, had the ice-house filled on that occasion, which has been the means of saving the life of one of my best friends and nearest neighbours, John Scott of Gala. He had been thrown down a precipice while hunting, but though his head was dreadfully cut, no damage to the skull was apprehended. But after three or four days a fever of such intensity came on that the pulse mounted to 150, and could only be kept under by the constant application of ice to the patient's head, to which the physicians, who were long in total despair, ascribe his present progress towards recovery. Had we not fortunately been able to supply the remedy, there was none to be had nearer than Edinburgh, for none of our neighbours had been upon the alert as we were. Thus you see, dear Lady, that ice may be a great rarity, and a matter of high consequence to boot in this northern climate of ours, severe as I acknowledge it to be. It was not many weeks before this accident that I had like to have had a bad accident on the same hill, called the Meiglet, and on a similar occasion. I had turned out to see the fox break cover, which I often do when the hounds are in my neighbourhood, and had dismounted from my pony to run down the hill, which was too precipitous for riding, supporting myself on the shoulder of one of our strong forest yeomen, when some stones giving way I fell very awkwardly with my leg under me. Luckily the man whom I held by was a Hercules for strength, and though my fall dragged him at length atop of me, yet his resistance made my descent gradual, and I came off with a slight sprain instead of a broken leg. I promise you I will keep the brow of the Meiglet in future. Your Ladyship is to suppose my health is pretty good, since I am risking my precious limbs in such frolics. My ordinary health is very good. It is, indeed, as confirmed as I ever possessed it in my most vigorous days, but I use a great deal of exercise, and rise early in order to diminish some tendency to become more of the alderman than I should like to be. Perhaps your Ladyship may have seen my father, who was rather corpulent towards the end of his life, though originally a very fine active man. My lameness would,

I fear, become more inconvenient were I to get too much *embonpoint*.

Your Ladyship asks me about my sister-in-law's talents. They consist in strong sense and knowledge of the world, with an unusual fortitude in encountering and surmounting distresses and dangers of which it has been her hard lot to encounter many. But she has no literary turn, beyond reading and liking a book in the ordinary way. She has had much distress lately in her family—dangerously ill herself, and now seriously alarmed on account of her youngest daughter, a girl of most uncommon talent. Whatever she has been taught since she came to Europe she has excelled in, and in America she contrived to manage the squaws or Indian women by threatening to prophesy evil to them. Once or twice some things she threatened them with came out true, and of course that was enough to establish her reputation, till her mother, coming to the knowledge of the source of her ascendency (she was then about ten years old), put a stop to her predictions. From this you may see she has a peculiar character. This was very like some of her father's oddities. But I fear we shall lose the poor child. She has had a violent fever, and now is extremely weak—a severe trial to her mother, who now has this addition to the many unpleasant circumstances attending her return to her native country. But I trust the poor girl will yet be preserved.

I can easily conceive that Soult's collection of pictures must be magnificent. He had the readiest mode of collecting them during his Spanish campaigns, and however nefarious such modes of acquisition are, still they have been the common cause of transference where the arts are concerned, for many long years. And one cannot but be pleased to see the works of such masters as Velasquez and Murillo pass from the obscurity of Spanish chateaux and convents, into countries where they can be seen,

admired, and appreciated. In one respect Bonaparte's collection was of use, in making these noble works of art, which
once occupied the Louvre, easily accessible. But there was,
I think, little taste in the manner in which they were
arranged, since out of 800 fine pictures you never saw above
30 or 40, and the spoliation which brought them there was
perpetually mixed with one's admiration of the things themselves. I have forgiven him, however (since he is dead), for
this and many other offences. He was a strange mingled
phantom of grandeur and terror, and a little meanness
withal, as ever bestrode the destinies of the world, and his
own close was as extraordinary as his rise. I wish we had
given him a more gentlemanlike keeper than him to whom
he was intrusted.[1] But it is only for our own sakes I could
have wished this, for to him the confinement would have
been the same, whether the bars of his cage were gilded or
not. Sir Pulteney Malcolm tells me escape was never out
of his head. I should not have believed him had he said
otherwise, and as it was his keeper's business to *keep* him
fast, the irritation of the devices of the captive encountering with the precautions of the officer appointed to prevent
his escape, must have always given rise to scenes unpleasing to contemplate. He might have been a great
man, and was only a great soldier. He might have been
the benefactor of the human race, and he was the cause
of more blood being spilled than had flowed for an hundred years before. He lowered the standard of virtue
and public feeling among the French, and soiled their
soldierly character by associating it with perfidy and dishonour. Still I think the sufferings attending his double
fall are a great atonement for the faults of his character.
By the way, I was reading a very clever memoir of the
campaign of 1814 by a Baron Fain (I think),[2] one of his

[1] Sir Hudson Lowe.

[2] *Manuscrit de Baron Fain*, an English translation in 8vo, was published in London, 1823.

aides-de-camp.   It is clear to me that his successes during that awful struggle, which he supported with so much talent and against so much odds, were the ultimate cause of his refusing peace on the one hand, and, on the other, of the allies, and in particular the Emperor of Austria, insisting on his dethronement.   Thus his high military talents through which he rose were also the cause of his fall.

I do not understand the controversy between the Duke of Hamilton and Lord Stanley, nor can I answer your Ladyship's question how the titles came to go to the heirs general instead of the heirs male in the Abercorn line, but I believe there was a surrender and a new creation.   I speak at random about it.   I know the Dukedom of Chatelherault, decidedly a male fief, was always considered to belong to the Abercorn family.

I will make a parcel of one or two of Lockhart's books and send them to Sir Coutts Trotter to wait your arrival in town, in case they cannot be safely sent to Paris.   I cannot say I like his last;[1] it is full of power, but disagreeable, and ends vilely ill.   I do not believe he writes in *Blackwood's Magazine*, though it continues to flourish. It is too much of a party publication, and I think it is a pity for him to interfere in matters where you make very bitter enemies and only lukewarm friends.   He is just now in London; Sophia at her father-in-law's recovering strength fast, as does her baby; they are recommended to try sea-bathing, and Mrs. Lockhart, who is as fond of her as if she were her own daughter, proposes to take her to Largs or Helensburgh, or some other place on the Firth of Clyde, for that purpose.

I think the length of this epistle about nothing will make your Ladyship dread such a correspondent in future; if it is *very* dull indeed, the apology must be the congenial stupidity of my present situation, at a circuit town,

---

[1] *Matthew Wald.*

and in attendance upon the judge during his residence there. We have very little criminal business to attend to on this progress, but in return make a great deal to do with what we have. Yesterday we contrived to spin out, by a trial of several hours, respecting the theft of a piece of cheese (it had not the dignity of a whole one) by two wretched boys; to-day having positively nothing to do, the Judge has walked away to the top of the next mountain, and I sit down to bestow my tediousness, like Dogberry, on my dear Lady Marchioness. I must however at length release you, with the assurance that I am always, dear Lady Abercorn, your most faithful, most obliged, humble servant,   WALTER SCOTT.

I set off to-night, thank heaven, and will be borrower of the said night for a dark hour or twain, rather than stay here any longer. . . .

TO THE SAME.

EDINBURGH, 4th June 1824.

MY DEAREST LADY ABERCORN,—Your kind letter of the 20th May reached me yesterday, so that it is probable that by writing in what is called course of post,—not my wont I confess,—this may kiss your hands before the 15th June, when you propose leaving Paris. I am truly sorry to think there is no chance of my seeing your Ladyship, which I should look forward to with so much pleasure. It is just about the time when we look with some confidence to a few weeks' settled weather in Scotland, where there really is nothing to complain of except the uncertainty and severity of the climate, so that if you could have extended your tour a little northward, I think I could have promised your Ladyship some amusement among our hills and glens of green bracken.

I have been terribly distressed at poor Byron's death.

In talents he was unequalled, and his faults were those rather of a bizarre temper arising from an eager and irritable nervous habit, than any depravity of disposition. He was devoid of selfishness, which I take to be the basest ingredient in the human composition. He was generous, humane, and noble-minded, when passion did not blind him. The worst I ever saw about him was that he rather liked indifferent company, than that of those with whom he must from character and talent have necessarily conversed more upon an equality. I believe much of his affected misanthropy, for I never thought it real, was founded upon instances of ingratitude and selfishness experienced at the hands of those from whom better could not have been expected. During the disagreement between him and his lady, the hubbub raised by the public reminded me of the mischievous boys who pretend to chase runaway horses—

> And roar stop, stop them, till they're hoarse ;
> But mean to drive them faster.

Man and wife will hardly make the mutual sacrifices which are necessary to make them friends, when the whole public of London are hallooing about them. Sir Frederick Adam's last letters state that poor Byron's loss will be inestimably felt by the Greeks. He had influence with their chiefs, which he employed in recommending moderation in their councils, and humanity in their actions,— very contrary doctrines to those preached by some hot-headed folks from this part of the world. The worst of the Turks is their religion, which embraces the doctrine of fatalism to the most blighting and withering extent, under which the human mind can never become progressive, and so they remain the same Turks which they were in the days of Mahomet the Magnificent.

Lockhart is not author of the books you mentioned.[1]

---

[1] *Annals of the Parish, Ayrshire Legatees*, etc. etc.

A Mr. Galt, who has tried literature in several other modes and all unsuccessfully, had the merit at length of writing them, and discovering a degree of talent which no one conceived could belong to him. Lockhart however wrote one or two tales of fiction uncommonly powerful in incident and language. His first was called the Confessions of Adam Blair, a Scotch clergyman who succumbs to strong temptation, and according to the rigorous morality of the Presbyterian Church suffers degradation. There is, I think, a want of taste in printing some part of the story something too broadly, but perhaps that was unavoidable in telling such a tale. It is written with prodigious power. A gayer book which he wrote some time ago entitled " Reginald Dalton," had great success, and he very lately wrote a little volume called " Matthew Wald," which is a painful tale, very forcibly told; the worst is that there is no resting-place—nothing but misery from the title-page to the finis.

I have been spending two days last week with old Lord Haddington, who although a Hamilton is not, I think, much known to your Ladyship.[1] A stroke of an apoplectic nature, and the violent bleeding to which he was in consequence subjected, has given him a constant giddiness, so that he leans on two servants when walking. But it has left untouched one of the best arranged and most powerful memories I ever remarked in any one. He got on the subject of the Suffolk letters,[2] on which he could certainly write a most entertaining commentary, for he has all the vivacity and gaiety of youth mixed with the extensive experience of old age. It must be owned that if our forefathers were not in fact worse than we are in point of

[1] Charles, eighth Earl, who died four years later. A specimen of Lord Haddington's humorous stories is given in a note to the raid of Caleb Balderston in *The Bride of Lammermoor*.

[2] *Lady Suffolk's Letters* [edited by J. W. Croker], 2 vols. 8vo, London, 1823, reviewed by Scott in the *Quarterly* for January 1824.

morals, they were at least less decent in their impropriety, and the same may be said of our foremothers. I always thought the beautiful Miss Bellenden, mother of the old Duke of Argyle and Lord Frederick Campbell, was a very exemplary person, but certainly the jokes which seem to have passed current between her and Lady Suffolk were of a very free description. Well I am getting into scandal, though somewhat antiquated, so I will write no more at present. Trusting your Ladyship will honour me with a line from Fulham, where you will find something lying for you, believe me always, dear Lady Abercorn, your truly obliged and grateful friend,   WALTER SCOTT.

FROM LADY LOUISA STUART.

GLOUCESTER PLACE, 29th June 1824.

DEAR SIR WALTER,—I ought to have thanked you for *Redgauntlet* a fortnight ago, but I stayed to read it, and then to read it again. It has taken my fancy very particularly, though (not to flatter you) I could almost wonder why: for there is no story in it, no love, no hero—unless Redgauntlet himself, who would be such a one as the Devil in Milton; yet in spite of all these wants, the interest is so strong one cannot lay it down, and I prophesy for it a great deal of mauling and abuse, and a second edition before the maulers know where they are. I do not pretend, however, to relish your Grimgribber of Scotch law; those may who understand it.

The Pretender's imperious mistress conjured up a thousand recollections of her sister, good Mrs. Catherine Walkinshaw, the Princess Dowager's bedchamber woman—in my younger days the most eminent managing gossip in London, always busy about somebody's affairs, the adviser of every Scotch family, the protectress of every raw young Scotchman the confidante and assistant of all match-

making mammas, Scotch or English. I have the portly
figure before me with her long lace ruffles, her gold snuff-
box, and her double chin. My eldest brother, who knew
the sister at Paris, where she resided with her daughter in
a convent, described her as a complete Frenchwoman,
retaining no mark of her own country; but Catherine was
a genuine old wife. My father would have made her old
with a witness, for he maintained he first came up from
Scotland seated on her lap. The woman really not being
many years older than he, the fact was disputed with him
as impossible, and probably related to some other person.
Surely there are varieties of the human species that die
away and are lost, like golden pippins and clove gilly-
flowers. The Catherine Walkinshaw class seems extinct:
at least I know no such general undertakers at present.
And perhaps the world does just as well without them.

You will rejoice, and that heartily, to hear of Mr.
Morritt's return home, in better hopes and spirits than
could have been expected. . . .

Your comfortable long letter was not thrown away, I
assure you; it made amends for the long silence preceding it, which however required no apology. I am
always delighted to hear from you, but take it as a
godsend when I can get it without claiming it as a right,
because I know you have something else to do in every
hour of the four-and-twenty, independent of writing Red-
gauntlets and Sieges of Ptolemais. What you say of poor
Dalkeith would be a shining passage in a work of fiction,
exactly from being so just and true. I do not like even to
think of that gallery cold and silent. I shall never see it
again; you will, probably, and see it filled with a new
race of beings much excelling the old, as your sons will
tell you. You wonder Lord Castlereagh was placed at
Edinburgh. I have a notion he made rather a forced *exit*
from Oxford, found the gates of Cambridge barred, and

resorted to our university as a *pis-aller*. I do not listen
to tattle much and usually lame a story, but there was
some *esclandre* or other, and he a party concerned in it,
which sent him to sow the remainder of his wild oats in
North Britain: no great advantage to the natives by the
by, tho' the young man may turn out very well in the
end.

I believe you will have the Montagus in Scotland ere
long. My friend Miss Murray, who has been staying with
me (off and on) for some months, talks of going next week
in the steam-packet. I shall be a sad lonely being without her. I read her the legend of Steenie Steenson the
other night, and we agreed that it was in the author's very
best manner. I felt disappointed, though, at Wandering
Willie's not coming forward more effectually after that
very interesting scene of using old times as a sort of
telegraph. I thought he was to be a prime agent, and
then I heard no more of him; that is to say, the aforesaid
author grew tired and flung the cards into the bag as
fast as he could. I know his provoking ways. But once
more, When shall we have the Crusades?

Next to demanding a letter from you, the most
audacious thing is to plague you with a very long one, and
I am afraid four pages may be so termed when they
contain little worth saying. But beyond the four I will
not go. Remember me kindly to Lady Scott and Mrs.
Lockhart, and ever believe me yours with the sincerest
regard,   L. STUART.

TO LADY ABERCORN.

ABBOTSFORD, *August 1st,* 1824.

MY DEAREST FRIEND,—Your letter gave me great
pleasure, as I was beginning to be anxious on your account:
the papers had apprised me of the very melancholy news

from Stanmore,[1] in which I sympathise sincerely. I do not well know whether such is really the dispensation of good and evil, or whether our attention is more powerfully attracted by family distress when it comes upon those whom we know to be kind and amiable, but it always seems to me that those domestic deprivations happen most frequently in the quarter where they are most keenly felt, and such is eminently the case with Lord Aberdeen. He has, however, a strong mind and many resources. . . .

After all, it is a cruel thing this dancing away again from old England after seeing so few friends, but I suppose it must be; it is the worse for me, as I intend to be in town in spring if circumstances will permit.

Nothing can interest me more than the last verses of poor [Byron], born as he was for something so noble, and only prevented from attaining the highest point in public esteem by the faults which I think flowed from a morbid temperament, which like the slave in the triumphal chariot so often accompanies genius, to humble her and her triumphs. The unfinished state of the lines, the heartfelt pressure of care and unhappiness under which they are written, and the longing for closing the scene by an honourable death, render them as melancholy and as impressive as any verses I ever read in my life. There are one or two errors of the pen, I should suppose, which render it difficult to make out the sense of particular passages.[2]

We expected rather an appalling visit, for little folks, from the Duchess of Buckingham, but her Grace found the seas of the Hebrides so rough (for she went as far as Dunvegan Castle) that she broke her purpose of trying

---

[1] The death of Lady Jane Gordon, Lord Aberdeen's eldest daughter.

[2] Lady Abercorn in her latest letter enclosed the touching verses referred to, beginning—
"'Tis time this heart should be unmoved."

They had been sent to her host the Bishop of London by a correspondent in Greece.—See Byron's *Poems*, royal 8vo ed., p. 577,—"On this day I complete my thirty-sixth year. Missolonghi, January 22nd, 1824."

the mainland. I never saw her, but have heard she is intelligent and amiable. I expect a more interesting visitor, however, than even this dignified guest, and that is my friend and former ward Countess Compton, who is a highly accomplished and most agreeable woman. I think your Ladyship never met her. She has promised to come with all the *bairns*, and I have engaged, by a wild and un-usual road through our pastoral hills, to guide them here in person from Moffat, performing in one day's journey what usually requires three.

I can easily conceive your Ladyship must have been amused with Basil Hall, and struck with the very direct and almost abrupt mode in which he always prosecutes his object of inquiry. He has written an excellent book,[1] full of practical good sense and sound views, and I admire how as a traveller he has said so much about the manners of the people, yet avoided any breach of the confidence of private society, upon which travellers think themselves entitled to trample merely because they are travellers.

As to the book you inquire about, I greatly doubt its seeing the light till November;[2] it is going on, but in-terrupted by various amusements and occupations. My son Walter came down on me two days ago rather un-expectedly. He had much the appearance of a wild Arab, being burnt black with the late sunny days which he had spent in sketching and making military drawings in Kent, and having chosen to let his moustaches and beard attain a formidable growth. He has really a most Saracenic appearance, and were not Kamehameha departed, I should certainly have passed him off for King of the Sandwich Islands at a review of the yeomanry which we attend to-day. By the way, was it not a foolish fuss they made

---

[1] Basil Hall's *Journal*, written on the coasts of Chili, Peru, etc., in 2 vols. 8vo, had just been published.

[2] *Tales of the Crusaders*, by the author of *Waverley*, 4 vols., pub-lished in 1825.

about these poor savages, besides cramming them to death as children do their pets?[1]

Our gracious Sovereign has been very civil to me, desiring Wilkie to introduce my ancient figure in a large picture he is painting for his Majesty of his reception at Holyrood. My younger son also figures as one of the Knight Marshal's pages of honour, so there will be enough of us. Like you, I admire his Royal constancy: there was an idea that that was all over, but habits become inveterate at a certain period of life. Now here is a long letter, and as little in it to the purpose as three sides of paper and a bit of another can be well supposed to contain. It is time to stop.—Believe me, my dear Lady Marchioness, always most affectionately and respectfully yours, WALTER SCOTT.

FROM GIFFORD.[2]

JAMES STREET, 29th August 1824.

MY DEAR SIR WALTER,—Nothing ever gave me greater pleasure than the timely renewal of your kindness. With you I began my laborious career, and pleasant it was to fall in with you again at its conclusion. Poor George [Ellis]! I thought of him—the third in our little band.

Things have fallen out sadly with me: still, however, I am more than thankful, for it is miraculous that with such a paper-constitution I should last so long. I am, however, become so feeble that I can no longer sustain, poor Atlas that I am! the incumbent weight, and Murray

[1] Referring to the Hawaian King and Queen, who died in London in July 1824.

[2] This is the closing letter written by the redoubtable editor of the *Quarterly* to his old ally, before demitting his charge on the publication of No. 60. Mr. Coleridge, afterwards Sir John Taylor Coleridge, one of the judges of the King's Bench, was Gifford's successor, and edited the four or five following Nos. in 1825-26. The correspondence indicates that the arrangement was only a temporary one between Mr. Murray and Mr. Coleridge for the convenience of both parties.—See note, *post*, p. 374. Wm. Gifford died in 1826.

has to seek for a new supporter of this unwieldy frame. Yet I will do what I can, and so I have promised him.

I am greatly pleased with your little article.[1] Murray wished for an extract or two, which I made, and shall be happy to find that you do not disapprove of them.

I thank you for your former letter, which I had the pleasure of receiving from the hands of Mr. Lockhart: but alas! calling on me is next to calling on an Egyptian mummy, unless for the rarity. A man might have visited Tithonus formerly with some profit, for that venerable shadow had a *voice* at least, but I have nothing.

I heard of you once as being far from well, but the subsequent accounts have all been cheering, and long I trust they will continue so.

I am just returned from Ramsgate, whither I was despatched by my doctor to pick up a little breath. In this I failed, but I am evidently returned somewhat stronger, if strength can be predicated of that which has no strength. . . .

Shall I beg you to make my kindest compliments to Mr. Lockhart?—I am, dear Sir Walter, ever yours faithfully and affectionately,   WM. GIFFORD.

TO JOHN RICHARDSON.[2]

DRUMLANRIG, THORNHILL, *29th August* [1824].

. . . YOURS of the 12th reached me only about the 20th. Since that time I have been a-cruising about, down to Lees to meet Mrs. Coutts, then through the hills to spend a day or two with my young chief and his excellent uncle at this fine old place. How you would luxuriate in the fine dashing stream of the Nith, and the grand old

---

[1] In No. 60, *The Correspondence of Lady Suffolk.*

[2] At this time on a tour in the Highlands with his friend Henry Cockburn. Richardson replied from Bonaly, near Edinburgh, that he hoped to be at Abbotsford on the 29th September.

building, now recovering its mantle of green, of which old
Q.'s rapacity had divested it. I could scold you for not
coming to Abbotsford, *cum tota sequela*, as we say that
practise the law. . . . Our house is now as ample as I
could wish it, and I hope it has not lost its quality of being
like the tent of the fairy Perizade, capable of stretching
so as to accommodate all friends. I hope Mrs. Richardson
and you, with Mr. and Mrs. Bell, will carve us out a comfortable visit towards the end of September or beginning
of October. . . .

I want your opinion of my house, library, etc., and in
reward you shall kill as many fine fish in the Ashestiel
water as you can wish for. It is but a morning's ride from
us. I am not sure I should give you leave at this very
moment to kill quite so large a trout as the last,[1] for fear
of the effect on Tom Purdie's weakened nerves. Seriously,
I have almost lost my poor Sancho Panza by a sudden
and most violent inflammatory complaint, augmented by
his obstinacy in persisting in going to the moors with
my sons on the 12th August. He has swam for his life,
and during his delirium it was most melancholy to hear the
poor fellow, sometimes hunting his dogs as if he were on
the hill, and sometimes talking as if he were walking with
me in the plantations. I thought of Joanna's exclamation,
"Alas, poor heart, thy thoughts stray far from home."
He is now out of danger, or probably I should not have
been here.

I rely I shall hear from you when your plans are
matured. About the middle of September we shall be
rather throng, but towards the beginning of October I
know of no visit can interfere with yours, and certainly
know none from which Lady Scott and I will anticipate
so much pleasure. If you take us on your return it will
be just so far on your way, but then it casts your visit

[1] See *Journal*, vol. ii. p. 28, note, for the story.

into the "sear and yellow leaf," and deprives us of good days and fishing weather.

But consult your own convenience, only pray come and oblige yours truly,   · · · WALTER SCOTT.

TO MISS EDGEWORTH.

[ABBOTSFORD, *October* 1824.]

MY DEAR MISS EDGEWORTH,—Your philosophical friends, or friend's friends,[1] arrived safe at Abbotsford, and of course were received as we would receive every friend of yours. As the Gods have not made me philosophical, I was happy to invoke the assistance of my neighbour Dr. Brewster, an excellent fellow who talked geology, and mineralogy, and all other ologies with them to their hearts' content. . . . The tide of English tourists seems now to have abated, and I see few but country neighbours. We have been deprived of a visit from your distinguished countryman and my old friend, Mr. Canning. He had proposed to be with us for two or three days on his tour through Scotland, when behold poor old Louis L'Inévitable meets with Death, a personage still more inevitable than himself, and so ended my hopes of a good day's laughing with a Secretary of State after the manner of Auld Lang Syne. To mend this disappointment I have got so deaf in one ear that I do not believe Mr. Canning's sharpest jests would pierce the organ. The affection came so suddenly that I am told it will depart with as little ceremony. Meantime I have to turn my head like a mandarin when any one speaks to me, so as to get the organ which still performs its duty within the line of conversation. All the rest of our little household are as well as our kind Irish friends could wish. Sophia is getting stout and healthy, which inferreth that little Johnie is getting stout and healthy also, for their good or indifferent health seems to depend most regularly on each other.

[1] Mr. Marcet and M. Prévost from Geneva.

We have been inundated by friends, all or most of whom were such as are most welcome, because they came to renew old friendships. Such were Lady Alvanley and her two daughters, whom I had passed many a merry day with in Paris, and my friend and ward Lady Compton, with her mother, sisters, and children. On the back of this came the mistress of millions, Mrs. Thomas Coutts, whom I would gladly have seen at some other time when I could have made her Lady of the ascendant, for her husband, a relation of my father, had been at all times kind and liberal to me in some dealings which I had with him. However, I could not help the matter, so I e'en let rank and wealth fight it out their own way.[1] Then we had Leslie, an artist of great eminence to whom I had promised to sit for my picture—a promise which he made me fulfil to the letter, so that I was as much bored of my chair as ever was Speaker of the House of Commons. Your Irish Oratrix seems to have been a most extraordinary personage. I wonder how green Erin comes by that profusion of elegant expression which never leaves them dry whether in mirth or in sorrow, and differs so much from the dry, sarcastic shrewdness of the Scot, and the Bullishness of John Bull. The Irish, one would think, should at least have something akin to the Highlander, who is decidedly of the same nation, and speaks the same language. Yet the Highlander, unless when his

[1] MISS EDGEWORTH TO SCOTT.
"*October* 11*th*, 1824.

"It is true that there is always something in the misfortunes of our best friends that is not disagreeable to us. Certainly I rejoice, my dear Sir Walter, that you were so inundated with visitors this season, since you made the inundation and all its consequences so entertaining to me. I wish I had been by to see 'Rank and Wealth' fighting it out, and you sitting by, *not* to judge the prize,

—with your innocent look, which I could never see without laughing internally. There is a humorously demure composure at times in the drawn-down corners of your mouth, and a lurking humour in your eyes, when you vainly attempt to expel from them all expression save that of perfectly polite submission, which no portrait could represent." Mr. Lockhart gives an amusing account of the party at Abbotsford in the 8th vol. of the *Life*, but places it in 1825 instead of 1824.

spirits are roused by bodily exercise, is a grave, proud, stiff animal, his language sometimes poetical but never by any chance humorous, and his demeanour often polite and obliging, but never intimating any sense or expression of humour. Who can solve this difficulty if you cannot?

Mrs. Fox will now have got accustomed to the novelty of being called Mrs. Fox, and must be in quiet possession of all the privileges and authorities of matrimony. I remember my wife's great plague for a long time was the necessity of ordering dinner, and divers embarrassments about the gooses and turkeys, of which she used to complain heavily. Pray remember us both kindly to her and to Miss Harriet. Would you think of Scotland next year? If we could ensure such a season as the last, it would be truly enchanting. Anne sends kind love and respects. She has the grace to send a letter to Miss Harriet which I have the pleasure to enclose. Little Spice has got quite well again notwithstanding Miss Harriet's ominous dream. Always most respectfully and truly yours,   WALTER SCOTT.[1]

TO THE SAME.

[*15th October* 1824.]

. . . I WAS really vexed about Lord Forbes's politeness being so ungraciously requited, but the truth is that owing to some omission in the communication betwixt

---

[1] The venerable Lord Moncreiff, on reading the foregoing letters to and from Miss Edgeworth, writes me on August 30th, 1893, that they form a singular corroboration of an anecdote which Lord Cockburn gave him :—" Cockburn happened to be at Abbotsford at a time when Lady Grey, the wife of Earl Grey, was a guest in the house. Shortly before dinner was announced another visitor arrived in the person of the Duchess of St. Albans (formerly Mrs. Coutts), and Scott was troubled as to the precedence of the two ladies. Cockburn was applied to, but declined to give an opinion. Scott contrived to commence one of his diverting anecdotes, and to engage the attention of both ladies, and when dinner was announced, as if in a fit of absence, he continued his tale, and offered one arm to one and the other to the other, and carried them off to dinner in this fashion, still crooning over his story."

Abbotsford and Castle St., I did not receive the card with
which he honoured me till a general gaol-delivery of all
parcels and letters at the latter place, when it arrived with
a whole lot of tradesmen's advertisements, intimations of
public meetings, petitions to the charitable, and other
affairs belonging to the twopenny post-bag, with which the
stupidity of our old housekeeper had most unworthily
associated it. . . . As I have every respect to Lord Forbes
for many different reasons, may I request you will express
to him my sincere regret for not having seen him, and my
sorrow for the unlucky circumstances which made me
appear thankless to his courtesy? . . . I have been always
particularly intimate with the Forbeses from my infancy,
since the excellent old Lord (Scottish Lord I mean) with
his wife and most of his family used weekly to dine at my
father's always of a Sunday, and on the same bill of fare,
which would now be thought a curious one to invite a
nobleman to. In the first place there was sheep's head
broth, and said sheep's head itself, the reason being that
the sheep's head, which requires much boiling, was put on
the night before and the dressing of the beef-steaks
occupied the least possible time, and thus the necessity of
employing servants on the Sabbath-day was diminished
as much as possible. Then there was a bottle or two
of special wine, which no wine-merchant had fitted for
the market, and there was a sermon read, during which
one part of the children were sleeping and the other
pinching and kicking them to make them keep awake.
And there is an old Presbyterian Sabbath for you in
Edinburgh. . . .

We all go to Chiefswood to-day to dinner, and to-
morrow they come to the hall house for (I hope) the
remainder of our autumn vacation. When weather turns
chilly and nights long, it is best to follow the example
of the black-cocks, who always pack together in October.

All loves attend you and Miss Harriet, and I trust they will bear water carriage even if you send them across the sea to Mrs. Fox. . . .

Adieu, my dogs are impatient to see me take my pilgrim's staff, and the sun is smiling fairly though the snow lies sprinkled on the glens. Who cares for snow? So yelp not, Ginger and Spice, and keep out of the way of that which is hotter than yourselves, the hot sealing-wax which I will presently make use of. . . .—Always yours,   WALTER SCOTT.

TO HIS SON WALTER.

[ABBOTSFORD, 22 *October* 1824.]

. . . ALL has jogged on in the old way since you left us, without any event of consequence, unless it be the death of poor old Mai, who departed quietly and without a struggle, just when I became apprehensive it would be necessary from the failure of his limbs to have helped him from the stage. The other dogs are all well, and Spice quite recovered. . . .

Here is Maida's epitaph inscribed under his figure at the door beneath which he now lies buried. I hope you are still classical enough to construe it:—

> " Maidæ marmorea dormis sub imagine Maida
> Ad januam domini sit tibi terra levis." [1]

George Thomson said grace yesterday, and gave us it like a tether, not forgetting something about the dominion which was given us over the fowls of the air and beasts of the field, which was a kind of apology for the business of the day. [2] . . .—I am always, yours affectionately,   WALTER SCOTT.

[1] Thus Englished by an eminent hand :—

" Beneath the sculptured form which late you wore

Sleep soundly, Maida, at your master's door."

See *Life*, vol. vii. pp. 276-281.

[2] The Abbotsford Hunt.

TO MRS. HUGHES.

ABBOTSFORD, *Nov.* 14, 1824.

My DEAR MRS. HUGHES,— . . . I am very much indebted to Mr. Hughes for his kindness to Charles, of which
I hope the youngster will endeavour to deserve the con-
tinuance.   Charles is clever enough, but has alternations
of indolence of which I am somewhat afraid, knowing from
experience how fatal it is to the acquisition of knowledge,
even when associated with the power of working hard at
particular times.

Pray when you see Dr. Stoddart recommend me to him
very kindly.   You would see in Byron's "Conversations"
that I was led to imitate the style of Coleridge's *Christabel*
in the *Lay of the last Minstrel*; it is very true, and Dr.
Stoddart was the person who introduced to me that
singular composition by reciting some stanzas of it many
years since in my cottage at Lasswade.   Byron seems to
have thought I had a hand in some ill-natured review
of Coleridge's wild and wondrous tale, which was entirely
a mistake.   He might have remembered, by the way, that
it was I who first introduced his Lordship to the fragment,
with a view to interest him in Coleridge's fate, and in the
play he was then bringing forward.

I agree with you that Lord and Lady Byron were not
well suited, yet I am not much disposed to throw blame
exclusively on either.   Unhappily Byron's distinguished
talents and high imaginations were mixed with inequality
of spirits, increased by early habits of uncontrolled
indulgence of every whim which occurred to him at
such moments; this is a bad ingredient for family happiness, where after all "bear and forbear" must be the
motto.   From what I saw personally of Lord Byron,
I was always of opinion that if a great and worthy
object, capable and deserving to engross his attention,

should ever occupy his mind, or should present itself to his pursuit—in other words, if an ill-directed love of pleasure had been exchanged for a well-directed love of action, he would have made a figure as distinguished in the page of history as he must make in that of literature. He pursued the freedom of Greece, as I am well assured, on the truest and most rational principles, desiring to unite the whole efforts of the country in the task of liberating them from the rod of their oppressor, instead of dividing them into factions by insisting upon all persons subscribing some fantastic political creed. It pleased God to cut off this extraordinary man before he could accomplish anything very considerable in the task he had undertaken. The night has come upon him in which no man can work; and so much to teach us to improve our time. After all I have not seen these celebrated "Conversations,"[1] but from what I see in the papers, and from what I know of Lord Byron, I conceive Captain Medwin to have been an accurate reporter. But all men talk loosely in their ordinary conversation, and of course much will remain to be corrected and deducted both in matters of opinion and matters of fact.

Here is a long stupid letter. I have been sitting to Wilkie these two days past. *Sedet et in eternum sedebit.* Ask the Doctor for the English; but this was a very particular occasion, being by royal command, to be introduced as a personage at the reception of Holyrood. . . . —Most truly yours,   WALTER SCOTT.

TO HIS SON CHARLES.

EDINBURGH, 1*st December* 1824.

MY DEAR CHARLES,—I write chiefly at present to say that with every wish to yield to whatever suits your

---

[1] Capt. Medwin's *Conversations with Lord Byron at Pisa in* 1821-2. 2 vols. 8vo, London, 1824.

comfort, I do not think it advisable that you should
leave Oxford in the short Christmas vacation, as you
propose in a letter to Sophia. Nothing suffers so much
by interruption as a course of study; it is in fact just
stopping the stone while it is running down hill, and
giving yourself all the trouble of putting it again in
motion, after it has lost the impulse which it had acquired. I am aware you propose to read in Wales, but
as the only object of your leaving college would be to
find amusement, I rather fear that to that amusement
study is in much danger of being postponed. You will
meet with many men, and these by no means such as
can be termed either indolent or dissipated, who will
conceive their business at college well enough done if
they can go creditably through the ordinary studies.
This may do very well for men of independent fortune,
or who have a direct entrée into some profitable branch
of business, or are assured from family connection of
preferment in some profession. But *you*, my dear Charles,
must be *distinguished*; it will not do to be moderate. I
could have got you a good appointment in India, where
you might have had plenty of field sports and made
money in due time, but on your affording me proofs
when under Mr. Williams, that you were both willing
and able to acquire knowledge, I was readily induced
to change your destination. God knows if I have chosen
for the best, but this I am certain, that you, like every
youth of sufficiently quick talent, have the matter much
in your own power. Solitude and *ennui* you must
endure as others have done before you, and there is this
advantage in both, that they make study a resource
instead of a duty. The greatest scholars always have
been formed in situations where there was least temptation
to dissipation,—I do not mean that which is mischievous
and criminal, but the mere amusements, in themselves

indifferent or even laudable, which withdraw the mind from serious duty. I beg you therefore to remain *inter silvas academi*, although they are at the present season both lonely and leafless. We shall think of you with regret at Christmas, but we will be comforted with thinking that you are collecting in your solitary chambers the means of making yourself an honour to us all, and are paying an apprentice fee to knowledge and distinction. . . .

TO MRS. HUGHES.

EDINBURGH, *December 26th*, 1824.

MY DEAR MRS. HUGHES,—If I have been tardy in expressing my sense of your kindness, I have a formidable excuse. Our good town, as Edinburgh has been fondly denominated, was on fire for three days in the course of last week, and much of what your zeal and activity investigated will never more be seen by human eye. The whole of the Parliament Square, excepting that building occupied by our supreme courts, has been either burnt to the ground or mined by the means necessarily resorted to to prevent the fire spreading to the courts and the princely library of the faculty of Advocates. The tenements destroyed were (exclusive of castles and towers) probably the highest houses in the world built for human habitation, and the sight of them in a full blaze, while spirit vaults and the like sent a strange, wild, unearthly flame from the caverns of the earth to aid the grosser fires which were fed by the timbers of the buildings, made a sight unequalled on earth, whatever it may be in the place that is never mentioned to ears polite. The south side of the Tron Church caught fire, though 300 yards from the conflagration, and the upper part, which was of wood, was

burnt to ashes before our eyes, without the possibility
of saving it. Many hundred families lost all, but the
charity of their fellow-citizens has flow'd in such a stream
that we justly fear it may prove rather too large a premium
for future carelessness, unless managed with more discretion than our awaken'd feelings are like to be in union
with. Poor Will. Allan the painter is burned out, but he
fortunately saved most of his pictures, particularly a noble
painting of the death of Regent Murray, which he was just
finishing for the Duke of Bedford. James Hall, brother of
Captain Basil Hall, made some sketches of this extraordinary scene, which are to be lithographed, and I will
send you a copy, though it can suggest but a faint idea of
the horrible original. The means used to bring down the
ruins, which continued to stand menacing a fall every
moment, was also a very striking scene. Part were mined
and blown up, part pull'd down by a combination of
mechanical powers, operations on which I attended with
deep interest. Upon the whole, I believe the conflagration
will be followed by its own advantages, as such evils
generally are. A large space is cleared, which though in
old times it contained the abodes of the learned, the noble,
and the gay, has latterly become the cells of misery and
often of vice. I trust a good use will be made of the
opportunity, and might say something of the Phœnix, but
the emblem has been rather worn out by the prologues to
the opening of Drury Lane.

I owe you a thousand thanks for the transcript respecting poor Byron's conversations! He was much of a
crammer—that is, sometimes told his bottleholders a sort
of romance for which he seriously claimed no credit. I
always suspected the duels to be escapades of this kind, if
Captain Medwin rightly understood what he said, and if
Lord Byron was not speaking of boxing-matches at school.
We must have heard if he had fought twice or been second

in many affairs of honour; they do not occur among men
of note so frequently as to escape notice, and the world
had been long anxious to learn all they could of Byron. I
know he was like to have fought at Malta, but it went off
as such things often do. Mr. Hughes has shown up Mr.
and Mrs. Bull in fine style;[1] "the lay of the one-horse
chay" was an event to be celebrated by the fine arts in
poetry as well as painting, and well has my friend John
performed his part in both departments. Carey's poems
are with Blackwood, to be forwarded by the first opportunity. I wish Mr. John Hughes could have seen Lockhart
on duty on the morning of the fire,—wet to the skin and
elegant, with a naked sword in his hand, the very picture
of a distressed hero in a strolling party's tragedy. For my
part, I felt rather sorry for myself when I heard the Rouse
of the Yeomanry blown at dead of night, which I had so
often obeyed on like occasions, and saw my old corps drawn
up "by torch and trumpet fast arrayed." It is when we
find ourselves unable to do our more youthful feats, that
we feel our better days gone by. Lady Scott and Anne
join in kind wishes to you and the excellent Doctor. . . .—
Your ever obliged and faithful friend,

WALTER SCOTT.

[1] The Magic Lay of the One-horse Chay.—See *Blackwood*, xvi. p. 440-2.

CHAPTER XXI

1825

JANUARY—JUNE

EDINBURGH AND ABBOTSFORD

Of this Mabel is a story by tradition of undoubted verity, that in Sir William Bradshaw's absence (being ten years away in the wars) she married a Welsh Knight. Sir William returning from the wars came in a Palmer's habit amongst the poor to Haigh, who, when she saw, and conjecturing that he favoured her former husband, wept, for which the Knight chastised her : at which Sir William went and made himself known to his tenants, in which space the Knight fled ; but near to Newton Park Sir William overtook him and slew him. The said dame Mabel was enjoined by her confessor to do penances by going onest every week barefoot and bare-legged to a cross near Wigan, from Haigh, whilst she lived, and is called Mabb Cross to this day ; and their monument lyes in Wigan Church. . . .—A.D. 1315.

Origin of *The Betrothed—Tales of the Crusaders.*

FAMILY ANNALS AND LITERARY WORK

1825—AGE 54

Marriage of his son Walter on February 3.

Excursion to Ireland—July and August.

Visitors at Abbotsford—Mrs. Coutts and Moore, etc.

"Journal" commenced, 20th November.

Christmas at Abbotsford.

Mr. and Mrs. Lockhart leave Chiefswood for London, December.

Tales of Crusaders (*Betrothed* and *Talisman*) 4 vols. published by Constable in June.

Life of Bonaparte projected.

Introduction and Notes to *Memoirs of Madame La Rochejaquelin.*

Song of *Bonnie Dundee.*

Contribution to *Quarterly Review*— *Pepys' Diary*, March 1826, No. 66.

CHAPTER XXI.

[*Jan. 22d,* 1825.]

MY DEAR CHARLES,—You have been silent a long while, which is rather disagreeable. Your allowance is not quite due, being payable at the four quarters, 2d February, 15th May, 2d August, 15th November, but you may anticipate a few days and draw on Messrs. Coutts, London, for £75, being your quarter's allowance, which I have advised them to honour. Regulate your expenses well, for loose and careless habits are easily acquired and ill to get rid of.

You will have heard of Walter's approaching nuptials from sister Anne. I have settled Abbotsford on Walter and his heirs-male by this or any subsequent wife; failing these, it goes to you and your heirs-male, because I think it right that the distinction of rank, however moderate, should have something to support it. Should your heirs-male not exist, or become extinct, there will be an end of the Baronets of Abbotsford, as there has been of the Four Monarchies of the world, and the estate may go for me where the law will carry it.

Lochore—about £1200 a year—will be settled on the heir of the marriage, with £20,000 for the younger children. Abbotsford is computed at £50,000, so the match is not an unequal one, only the bride's fortune is in possession—the bridegroom's, excepting his commission and an annuity of £300, in expectance. But they will have enough for all the comforts, and even for most of the elegancies of life.

Walter being thus provided for will enable me to attend to Mama's provisions, and to yours and your sisters', more than I could otherwise have done.

They will be married I think at Gattonside, take up a week's solitary blessedness at Abbotsford, then to London for a few days, and then to join the King's Hussars at Cork. Perhaps they may make a détour in their journey to see you, and you will shew your new sister the lions of the University.

There being no game worth sending at this season, Mama is to send you some tea, and I will add two dozen port and one dozen old sherry, which I fancy is all that you keep in your *cellar* at once. It will serve to drink your brother's good health on this happy occasion. All join in greetings.—Yours affectionately,   WALTER SCOTT.

TO MRS. HUGHES.

EDINBURGH, *January 23rd*, 1825.

MY DEAR AND GOOD FRIEND,—I have a hundred apologies to make for my ungracious silence : but my news may allow for it. My son is just about to be married : the young lady is a very considerable heiress, a Miss Jobson of Lochore, with at least £50,000 in land and landed property, which, as Sir Hugh Evans says, "is good gifts:" she has better gifts in sound sense and cheerful temper and excellent principles, being brought up by her mother, who, though rather straitly laced in her Presbyterian stays, is a very worthy woman in excellent sound old-fashioned Scottish principles, which like massive old plate have as much bullion in them as would suffice ten thousand modern plated trinkets. She is very pretty both in form and face, but so *little* as to make almost a ludicrous contrast to her Hussar, who rises six feet two inches at least. She is timid almost to awkwardness, and tho' she has

walked the course as a wealthy heiress for two years, no
one ever heard of her having a flirtation. Truth is, there
had been some little kindness between the young folks
about two years ago, and though they had not met again
till lately, yet hearing much of each other through Lady
Ferguson, the wife of my old friend Sir Adam, they had
neither of them it seems forgotten their intercourse, but had
in our Scottish phrase (which I think a good one) *thought
on* till our Christmas gambols brought out little Cupid
with his linstock and fired the mine: and the Hussar
with his mustachios and his schnurbart was found to
have snapp'd up the prize which Lord and Laird had been
trying for. The poor lassie has agreed to follow the camp:
the mother has on this sole account rather acquiesced
than consented to the match, and truly I cannot blame
the good lady, considering that her only child is to
exchange two good houses, one in Edinburgh and one at
Lochore, for the accommodations of a barrack. In Ireland
they will at least be safe within their guarded walls, however inconvenient, whereas in lodgings they would have
little more comfort, and in certain events, which God avert,
might be exposed to danger. I cannot but picture to myself poor little Jane, with her little innocent pensive-looking
face, looking with surprise at her quarters, where mats and
horse-cloths must supply the place of carpets, and arm-
racks garnished with pistols, sabres, and carabines, and
adorned with the caricature drawings of good Mr. Lieutenant, serve the purpose of all decoration: but then if she
manages well she may always secure good society even
within the regiment: two or three of the officers are respectably married, and the little heiress' fortune, giving
her the means of kindness in sharing her extra accommodation of carriages, etc., with those who are less in the
way of commanding them, may make her a person of as
much importance as even the Colonel's wife, if he has one.

Walter is to get a troop shortly, which will entitle him to better quarters. But a very knowing lady of my acquaintance assures me on her own experience that your "bonny bride" is diverted with all these occurrences so long as she is secure of her Cavalier's affections, and that ladies who have been most delicately bred up are, like blood-horses, most capable of meeting and enduring fatigue, spirit doing for them what habit and insensibility do for the more ignoble. Still the old song rings in my ears, the first verse of which has been already exemplified in our love affair :—

> "My Bonnie Lizzie Baillie,
>   I 'll row you in my plaidie
> If you will gang alang wi' me
>   And be a soldier's ladie.
>
> My Bonnie Lizzie Baillie,
>   Your Mother canna want ye,
> Sae let the trooper gang his lane
>   And carry his ain portmanty."

But mark the sequel :—

> "She wadna hae an English Lord
>   Nor be a Highland Ladie,
> But she's awa wi' a *Border Scot*
>   And he's row'd her in his Plaidie.
>
> She hadna gane a mile or twa
>   When O but she was weary,
> She aften looked back and said
>   Farewell to Castle Carie."

However, we must hope that these little recollections will neither be distressing nor too frequent; for myself I can safely say few things would have made me more happy than my son's establishment in life so early. Though acquainted with camps and courts, and those the licentious courts of Dresden and Berlin, I know his principles to be steady and even severe, and therefore am sure he will love and cherish this poor thing who has behaved through the whole transaction with a modesty, candour, and generosity, which deserve everything on his part.

Here is a long and selfish letter, but you are a mother, and moreover my dear and partial friend; besides, joy as well as sorrow makes us selfish.—Believe me, in either, my dear Mrs. Hughes, ever faithfully yours,

WALTER SCOTT.

My kindest compliments to the excellent Doctor and Mr. Hughes. About the 3d or 4th of February there will be a young lady of Abbotsford; luckily the original dame has the *petit titre*, and so escapes being Mrs. Scott, senior. What shall we do if Walter one morning gets the Companionship of the Bath? I never *will* be *old* Sir Walter. These are rare castles in the air.

TO MISS EDGEWORTH.

I HAVE been long silent, my dear Miss Edgeworth, and like most ungrateful folks have neglected my kind friend till I have a favour to ask. This however you must excuse in consideration of much business and decaying eyes, which in these misty days begin to feel the effects of former watchful nights spent at the desk. Not that they are so bad neither, but they begin to require the aid of spectacles, to which I reconcile myself with such a sense of declension as the old highland warrior braved, who complains of attending the meeting of his clan

"With a crutch in the hand where the broadsword should be."

... In short, Cupid mingled with our Christmas gambols, and we learned with some surprise one fine morning that the lady had agreed to carry the young hussar's knapsack. But although the town, which is a very pretty little town, had surrendered, the citadel, in the person of the old mother, continued to make a desperate though hopeless defence. It was in vain that I,—liking the girl very much for the modest and unpretending way which she had

walked the way as an heiress, and flattered you may
believe by a preference to my son, long given and frankly
and generously avowed with a firmness which made a
strong contrast to the extreme timidity of her general de-
portment, which is shy almost to awkwardness,—and every
friend and relation she has in the world joined to overcome
the good mother's prejudices, which resolve into this, that
my son is a soldier and a hussar, and must be a rake of
course.   Everything else she allows to be unexceptionable.
A worthy clergyman, one of the great guns, as they call
them, has with twelve olive texts almost persuaded her
into a conviction that she is acting wrong, and she has
yielded after the manner of Brabantio; so deeds, etc., are
all on the anvil settling who are to be the future lords of
Abbotsford and Lochore. . . .

Walter's military leave must be very short; so the
wedding will come on speedily, and soon after he must
start for Ireland; and with your consent the first resting-
place [will be Edgeworthstown].   They will put you in
mind of the old ballad—

> " I have learn'd my gay goss-hawk
> Right well to back a steed ;
> And I have learn'd my turtle dove
> As weel to write and read ;
> And I have learn'd my gay goss-hawk
> To wield both bow and brand ;
> And sae have I my turtle dove
> To plait gold with her hand."

Now this turtle dove of mine must be your guest for
four or five days or more, for Walter must go on to join
his regiment at Cork and make some preparations for her
accommodation in his barracks; a sore change, I fear, for
a creature on whom air has scarce been suffered to breathe.
She *has* undertaken it, however; for what will not woman
undertake for the man she loves and who loves her?   I am
sure that with you she will have quiet kindness, instead of

that feverish attention which, like an over-heated hot-house, withers the little flowers which it is meant to call into bloom; and I know that after a day or two of silence and brief answers and causeless fear of strangers, she will be opening her budget of female accomplishments, and bartering Scotch tunes for Irish ones with the young ladies. The story of her mother is of course for your own private ear; but I am always desirous to point out tender points where such exist, lest they be pressed on by some unlucky accident. I once hurt an officer who was showing me the ground at Waterloo by riding rather rashly against him, which hurt, as well as the pain I felt, might have been spared had the young soldier's modesty allowed him to tell me that he was still suffering from a wound in the action. This long story might have been spared by using the hackney coachmen's phrase of a *raw*, but the comparison would have been slovenly. Let me hear from you if it be quite convenient for you to receive this leaguer lady, and at the same time what you are doing about your new work. Your reasons for being anonymous are very strong, as they affect your own feelings; for my own part I think you ought to snap your fingers at the critics, and be sure the world would be at your back. But female authors, as I have observed in my friend Mrs. Baillie, have the same sensitiveness and deference for censure which our masculine nerves are apt to hold too cheap. I saw Mr. Butler twice or thrice, and was much pleased with him. Love to my dear Harriet. I am sure she will be kind to my poor little Jane, and remember that all have not had her own advantages. . . .

It is time to conclude, and it shall be in character from an old ballad, with a trivial alteration—

"My bonnie little Jeanie, etc., etc."

W. S.

TO HIS DAUGHTER-IN-LAW.

ALBYN CLUB ROOM, *4th February.*

My dearest Love,—I thought it quite unnecessary to embarrass your departure yesterday by any attempt to express my own feelings; in fact I do not much like that people should witness that sort of agitation in myself. You would not doubt, however, that my good wishes and blessings, as well as Lady Scott's, follow you both faster than your carriage could drive. God make you happy in each other, my dearest loves, and it will be the greatest pleasure which Heaven can reserve for me to witness it.

I had an extremely affecting interview with Mrs. Jobson after you left, and I am perfectly sure that she now looks upon an event which appeared so unpleasing at its first aspect, with different eyes and with hopes of happiness for you and comfort to herself. You may rely on our paying her every attention which seems acceptable, as I think it is perhaps the way in which I can best convince *you* of my affectionate regard.

No mastiff was ever so tired of his chain—I should say more correctly no turnspit was ever so weary of his wheel—as I am of the Court of Session, which prevents me coming out early next week and being with you for a few quiet days. After Saturday 12th they cannot detain me; and if I cannot come off sooner, I will be with you that night at latest.

Our bridal party went off as merrily as possible; even the good-humoured Colonel forgot his disappointment, poor fellow! I hope he will be more lucky in his own affairs than he has been in yours, for at the *fatal* ball you jostled him out of the cotillion, and on the more fatal 3rd February he was left out of the ceremonial. He sang " Begone, dull care," notwithstanding, and even volunteered "Jolly, Jolly, Jolly!" in the drawing-room, with some very moderate assistance from my good old claret.

This is our town news; send me some from the country when you can collect any—whether the dogs are well; whether they have bit your maid's heels yet; whether you see Sir Adam, as he proposed, on Sunday; and—awful question—what you mean to give him for dinner? I hope you were duly carried over the threshold of the hall. Compliments to the hussar, and believe me, my darling Jane, your affectionate father,

WALTER SCOTT.

TO MISS EDGEWORTH.

ABBOTSFORD [*February 14th*, 1825].

MY DEAR MISS EDGEWORTH,—Your kind letter assured me of what required small assurance, that my dear little Jane will find warm hearts and open arms to receive her at Edgeworthstown. She is a little body that has wrought herself about my affections very intimately, from a *leal truth* of character which she showed in the whole of our proceedings during this affair. . . . You will soon know more of her than I can, for ladies are capital at tracing out each other's characters, which are rather too evanescent for us. They were married on 3rd February, and came here to reside quietly for a little.

Since I joined them on the 10th we have seen the Scotts of Harden and the Fergusons, and my little landlady did the honours of her chateau with very pretty embarrassment. My wife was detained by a bad cold. We join them in Edinburgh to-morrow, and in four or five days afterwards they set out for London, and then for green Erin. I conceive they will be at Edgeworthstown about the 20th; but Walter will write as soon as he has his foot on the sod. I could have wished to have kept them longer here, for Jane seemed to take very kindly some trifling hints I gave her, and I am sure I could have cured some of her little deficiencies in the *usage de monde*, as she showed great readiness and good-humoured shrewdness in catching a hint. This however in good society is easily acquired. I am greatly indebted to Mrs. Edgeworth's extreme kindness in offering such a desirable place of refuge for my little wanderer. . . .

I parted from Abbotsford with great regret; for Auld Reekie, as we fondly call her, is covered in mist and smoke —very picturesque indeed, but far from being agreeable in other respects. You have leave to continue in the country all the year—happy person! But happy you would be anywhere, who have such powers of amusing and entertaining at your own command and at the service of others.—Always, dear Miss E., yours with the most sincere regard,   WALTER SCOTT.

TO HIS SON CHARLES.

EDINBURGH, 17*th February* 1825.

MY DEAR CHARLES,—Walter, as Anne would inform you, is now "Benedick, the married man," and behaves with becoming dignity under his change of condition. They went to Abbotsford immediately after the marriage. I joined them there on the tenth, and found them living very comfortably and quietly, as if they had been housekeepers for ten years. The people had a dinner one day and a dance the next, so that you may suppose the wedding made some noise in the parish.

We remained at Abbotsford till Tuesday, when we returned together bodily, and since that have been feasting among our friends. Yesterday Mrs. Jobson gave us a very handsome dinner, and a party in the evening. . . . I like Jane very much; she speaks little, but what she says is sensible and to the purpose, and she possesses a degree of truth and candour which I have rarely met with, either in

man or woman. But you will soon judge for yourself, for
they propose to take Oxford on their way to London, and
set out on Tuesday next. I suppose they will reach you
about the 26th, and conclude you will have the pleasure
of shewing them the wonders of Alma Mater, and that
Mr. Surtees will render them the same assistance. . . .

Joy and grief mingle strangely together in this world.
I have lost my good and tried friend Charles Erskine.[1] He
died of an apoplectic fit. . . . The day before he died he
had written me a most kind letter on Walter's marriage,
begging to know the very day, as he meant, notwithstanding his regimen, to drink at least one bumper that day.
Alas! the day before the wedding was that of poor
Charles's burial.

I hope the studies are advancing actively. Your future
success in life will, in part at least, depend upon the figure
you make at college; wherefore, *incumbite remis*. God has
given you lively enough parts, but the improvement
depends upon yourself. Mama desires me to say that a
large hamper stocked with good things for luncheon went
to London by sea, to be forwarded down by some of the
waggons. I trust it will reach safe, and in time to give
our travellers some picking at your chambers, or rooms,
or whatever you call them. . . .

TO LADY LOUISA STUART.

[*21st Feby.* 1825.]

. . . AND now about the matter of the library.[2] I
only petition you in judgment to remember mercy, and
think how many antiquarian chops have slobbered over
the fiery trial, the doleful Auto da Fé, held by the relent-
less Curate and Barber,—how many pounds of pure gold
would be cheerfully given for the *Casts*, to speak in horse

---

[1] Charles Erskine, Sheriff-substitute of Selkirkshire.
[2] At Ditton Park.

jockey phrase, of the Don's library. Think of this, my
dearest friend, and do not let your excellent judgment
mislead you so far as to trust much to it in a matter
where value depends on anything rather than sense and
utility. Dread, my dear Lady Louisa, that in preferring
some comely quarto to a shabby duodecimo, your Ladyship may be rejecting the *editio princeps*. Consider that
in banishing some antiquated piece of *polissonnerie* you
may destroy the very work for which the author lost his
ears two centuries since, and which has become almost
priceless. Then there are so many reasons for not parting
with duplicates, for they may have a value in being tall,
or a value in being short, or perhaps in having the leaves
uncut, or some peculiar and interesting misprint in a
particular passage, that there is no end to the risque of
selection. So much for Bibliomania. But besides the
whims of the book-collectors, there are real and serious
reasons why books should not be discarded but with the
utmost caution. Many useless in themselves are curious
as marking manners. Many, neglected and run down
when they appeared, and ill spoken of by contemporary
critics, contain much nevertheless that is worthy of
notice and preservation. These fall asleep like the
chrysalis, and awaken to glitter in the sun of popularity
like the butterfly. I firmly believe I could bring myself
to send nothing to the bookstalls excepting school-books
and ordinary editions of English Classics, and that should
be done with great caution. I do not condemn banishment to the garret, or your Ladyship's more honourable
species of relegation, as the civilians call it, by placing
them on the upper shelves, which will have this additional
advantage, that there may be some chance of getting an
old antiquary's neck broken in clambering up to examine
them. But actually parting with them is very hazardous.
I remember when Dibdin, that eminent Bibliomaniac,

went down to Lincoln, and offered in the kindest manner
a few of the best and most readable modern authors for
some of their antiquarian treasures, they allowed him
to take, I think, sixteen volumes, and were confounded
with his liberality in sending books to the extent of £300,
or so, in exchange.   But Dib., like Tam o' Shanter,

"Kenn'd what was what fou brawly."

The *Lincoln Nosegay*, as it was called, was sold for
£1800, and the consequence was, that when the Bibliomaniac went down to repeat his researches, he was
indignantly refused admission by the affronted parsons.
I think here be feuds!   Adieu, however, dear Lady Louisa.
One thing I am sure of, that if the formation or reforma-
tion of a library depended upon high talent, united with
extensive information, the most correct taste, and the
purest principle, there could not be such a heaven-born
librarian as she of Ditton.   But you know what old Noll
said to a man who threatened to take the sense of the
House upon some particular point?   "Well," answered
Noll, perfectly conscious he was in the wrong, "do so if
you will, and I'll take the *nonsense* of the House, and see
which will have the best of it."   Remember me most kindly
to Lord and Lady Montagu. . . .   The little Buccleuch
turns out a goodly youth, with fine points of sense and
generosity about him.   A better selected course of reading,
and still more of conversation, will do very much for him,
and I think Mr. Blakeney will accomplish this.—Always,
dear Lady Louisa, your truly honoured and obliged,

WALTER SCOTT.

TO MRS. THOMAS SCOTT.[1]

February 1825.

CHEER up, my dear sister, much dearer to me in
adversity than when in prosperity our haughty natures

[1] Then residing in Ayr.

made us understand each other less. It would have been better for us all had we been more mutually confidential, and in this I take the blame to myself, the elder and more experienced; but while we are on this side the dark flood, there is time for repairing as well as repenting of errors committed in the pride of youth and inexperience. Our young folks were wedded on the 3rd, and reached Abbotsford safely in the evening of the same day, as we heard from Dalgleish, who was sent to get things ready. We had some squally weather with the poor old lady, but it subsided into sunshine and calm at last, and all is smooth water. Her opposition had this good effect, that I had an opportunity of seeing little Jane, poor body, in several interesting and affecting situations, which raised my opinion highly of her candour and simplicity, mixed as it showed itself with much delicacy, good sense, and firmness. She made the happiest face I ever witnessed when she saw her mother and me kiss and shake hands, and really, to use a hackneyed phrase, looked for the moment like an angel. I trust they will be happy. Their fortune is equal at present to all the comforts and most of the elegancies of life, with the power of contributing to the wants of others. Eventually, it will be equal to the rank they will be called on to sustain. All this supposes good management. . . . Now, the happy time I have to look forward to is when I can assemble my children and nieces and mamas at Abbotsford, and play love in the chair among all my pretty bodies. My kindest love to Anne and Eliza. As she has lost Captain Basil, I intend to send her a gingerbread captain, with a fine gilt sword, if he should cost me sixpence; I don't mind expense. He shall be a Captain of the Navy, too, for I remember the old sign "Gingerbread sea and land" as it stood in Snap Hall in Leith Walk. Mama and the girls join me in love. Oh for an hour of you on

Wednesday! Mrs. J[obson] dines with us *en famille.* I can answer for my part, but unless Sophia can administer strong potions of her honey and oil, what the devil will become of Lady S. and Anne, with the Beatrice spirit of the one, and the unnecessary sincerity of the other!

TO HIS DAUGHTER-IN-LAW.

EDINR., 1st *March* 1825.

YOU must suppose, my dearest Jane, that the departure of those for whom we have been anxiously interested for so many weeks, has made us feel rather dull here. For my part, every morning I awake I think on the verse in Cymbeline,—

> "The bird is flown
> That we have made so much of."

The enclosed piece of paper will add a pen-feather to my pretty bird's wing, since fly away she must. You have only to put your name on the back and Walter will get the contents for you. I meant to have bought a set of tea-plate for you, but perhaps the most convenient, though least genteel way, is to send you the vile mammon of unrighteousness, and leave you to put it to the use most convenient in making up your *kit,*—a military phrase for which you have an interpreter at hand. And here I ought to stop, for I have twenty letters to write. But like all old papas, I would rather read nonsense to my children than play *genteel, sensible,* and *clever,* with half the world beside. After all, this propensity requires some apology. For I know there is such a thing as *inflicting* kindness, and that officious affection is sometimes as troublesome as a blistering plaster, which, while it is doing perhaps some good, is giving all the while a great deal of plague and vexation to the patient. . . .

On the other hand remember it is our bargain that you

are never so much as to mend a pen when you write me, or think a moment either about subject or about expression. Sometimes, perhaps, I shall suggest topics, as I did in my last, which you answered so faithfully from Abbotsford. I will however be extremely prudent in this. For instance, I may ask you if you liked Warwick Castle, or if you thought it belonged to the class of old chateaux, which your classical neighbour calls *stupit things*. But on the other hand, I will be careful *not* to inquire whether you were very glad to be rid of papa and his old stories, as you passed the Border land, and whether you did not feel his absence quite as great a relief as when you found that a certain good friend was only going to escort us as far as Darnick toll, and had no intention of being *kirked* along with us. Neither will I be so inquisitive as to ask how often Rebecca and Pixie were turned into the coach with you, while the gallant Captain, like the man in the little clock called the Dutch Weather House, turned out to smoke his cigar *al fresco* upon the box.

But you will expect news instead of asking it, and the best I have to tell you is, that all were well at Shandwick Place and Castle Street by the last accounts.

On the night of Tuesday broke out another dreadful fire in the High Street. I was wakened at midnight with the ringing of bells and beating of drums, and then I saw the sky entirely red with flame. I could not help dressing myself and going to the scene of action, where there was a most horrible confusion. I met our pet skeleton Major Stisted of the Royals, and getting with him through the guards, I got a fine view of the fire, which destroyed all the tenements on the opposite side of the street from that where I had my post. The sight was terribly grand. This is one divertisement we have had since your departure. Another is an excellent exhibition of Italian puppets, extremely well managed. We went to see it, and I wished for you often, as the exhibition was extremely comic. A restive mule which flung its rider was extremely well managed, and not less so a coach run away with by the horses, but the last might have awakened recollections of the tragical accident which befell your own chariot.

Since I began this letter I have been over to fulfil an old promise, which carried me for two days to Sir Robert Preston's at Valleyfield, on your side of the water. We had charming weather, and I visited the old monastery of Culross, which has been a magnificent place. Moreover, there are at Valleyfield the finest gardens I ever saw in Scotland, and to crown all, Sir Robert gave me some fine old carved oak which had come from the church. I think it will make a beautiful back to a Gothic couch for Abbotsford. Adieu, my dearest Jane, you are tired and so am I.—Your affectionate father,   WALTER SCOTT.

TO HIS SON CHARLES.

EDINBURGH, 13th March 1825.

MY DEAR CHARLES,—I am very glad you like your new sister, who seems to me a sweet girl, sensible and affectionate, and if no dasher just the more likely to make a domestic connection happy. I suppose you swaggered about in great form at the head of your lions. Pray, how did they stand the critique of your Oxonian loungers, who are, I know, severe observers of lions of low degree, and whose manes and tails are not managed *comme il faut*?

Poor Elmsley,[1] I know him very well, and valued him as a most accomplished scholar. We have had a dreadful shock here, with the awful catastrophe of poor ——. He was the last man from whom an act so fatal was to have been anticipated, but there is insanity in the family, and

---

[1] Peter Elmsley, the distinguished Principal of St. Albans Hall, and Professor of Ancient History, had just died in Oxford. See *ante*, vol. i. p. 39.

he suffered grievous torture from an ill-cured wound. I
lived much with him at Paris, and always held him one of
the most sensible as well as agreeable men I ever knew.
But we hold our intellectual powers by a fearfully slight
tenure. When I saw him, about two months since, at
Penicuik, where I passed a day chiefly to meet him, I
thought him very gloomy, but did not wonder, as it was
the first time we had met since his wife's death, who was
also a great friend of ours. . . .—I am always, your affectionate father,

WALTER SCOTT.

TO HIS SON WALTER.

ABBOTSFORD, 19th March 1825.

I THINK I told you in my last that I meant to go
one day with Mr. Bayley to Lochore, and take Mr. Laidlaw
with me, as he was in town at the time. It is his opinion,
as well as mine, that this property, in which Jane's confidence and affection have given you so deep an interest, is
under excellent management, and rapidly improving in
value with the improvement of the times. Its value may
be at present held very low at £40,000, or from that to
£45,000, but if times hold good it will reach £50,000 as
readily as any estate in that country. The parks are particularly excellent, and it was a novelty to South country
bodies to hear of grass-land at £3 and so far as £4 per
acre. Allowing for the dead season of the year, the grounds
looked very well. There is a noble screen of thriving planting which forms a fine background to the House, and rises
nearly to the top of Benarty, and there is a great deal
more plantation and many full-grown trees. Upon the
whole it is a most gentlemanlike place—no railroads
needed there; you may send the cook-maid with the coal-
scuttle to dig out the coals she wants for the day; plenty

of limestone rock, and plenty of free-stone for the quarrying. I find Jane had ordered some spots of planting, which were stopp'd till her pleasure should be known. I took on me to say they should be proceeded with. I can assure you the places were chosen with great taste, though she was sly enough not to allow she knew anything about plantations, I suppose for fear she should hear more than enough upon that subject. I must not omit the game, which is plenty; I sprang several pheasants in my walks, for which you are obliged to the vicinity of the Lord Chief Commissioner, for as he had little corn last year the birds had come down upon Lochore. The gardener, John Macleod by name, reported to me that he had destroyed of vermin, two wild cats, eight household cats gone wild, four polecats, one of terrible size and weight, which I think must have been a marten, five weasels, three whittrets, besides sundry magpies. I exhorted him to continue to set the traps, assuring him it would be held good service. I did not wait to see how the parks let, and leave it to Mr. Bayley to write you about that and other matters of business. We were most comfortably lodged and accommodated during our stay, and everything seemed in perfection on my arrival yesterday. I will write her fully to Edgeworthstown. Jane's letter is like herself, sensible, pretty, and unaffected. I therefore conclude she writes easily, and would not willingly believe the contrary, because I should be sorry to think that our correspondence, so agreeable to me, was very troublesome to herself.

The Lockharts are lazy, and stay in town this spring, so we have only Mama and Anne at Abbotsford. Both join in kindest love to you and Jane.—Always your affectionate father,   WALTER SCOTT.

Write me precisely about the troop as soon as you can, and be sure to make your figures legible. I see you will be a little short, having had so much to pay for, but you know when you want £50 or £100 I would rather you would draw than get in debt; and above all, there can be no occasion for any economy which can trench on Jane's comforts.

TO MISS EDGEWORTH.

ABBOTSFORD, *March* 23, 1825.

MY DEAR MISS EDGEWORTH,—I calculate, as the Americans say, that this will find the Lady of Lochore with her black hussar at quiet moorings at Edgeworthstown, though I suppose the gentleman's stay will be very brief. I hope my dear little Jane will get over her fears, and show to such advantage as her quiet nature will permit, as with all her humility and shyness she has at the foundation a strong share both of principle and good sense, with fortitude where it is necessary. I am anxious to hear she is safe on your side of that vile channel, and under the protection of the kind friends who have offered her hospitality.

You wished to have, for a medical friend I think, one of Spice's puppies. I did not send you one, or indeed keep any of the first litter, which is seldom good for much, but she will have a family this Spring, and as the sire is of high fame and she herself one of the best-bred terriers in Scotland, I wish to know whether you still wish me to keep a whelp, and whether it should be male or female, or if you would prefer a brace. Spice is quite recovered of her asthma, notwithstanding Miss Harriet's most ominous dream. She despatches rats and vermin in the most knowing style, and is an extremely kind and sensible creature. She is a capital specimen of the

> "Fierce terriers wont in high-hill'd Liddesdale
> To storm the wild cat's lodge and badgers rough."

How does your literary undertaking come on?

TO HIS NEPHEW.

ABBOTSFORD, *23rd March* 1825.

MY DEAR WALTER,—I desired your cousin to look into your affairs and see what cash you needed, and by his report I send you a cheque for £30, to pay your tailor's bill and other inevitables. I learn you are living with economy on your pay, which is very right, and a good lesson to begin with. Walter would give you all the last Edinburgh and Abbotsford news. I fancy you did not see his *Cara Sposa*. I was visiting her Fifeshire property at her request since the Session rose, and it is a very fine estate indeed. Your cousin may think himself very fortunate in getting so handsome a property with a pretty and amiable young person. . . .

Let me know how you come on at your new institution, and what your motions are likely to be when you get your commission, and all about it. . . .

We are here, Anne, Lady Scott and I, rather lonely wanting all our natural beaux and useful persons, but we rub on as well as we can. Dogs, etc., are all in handsome enjoyment of their health, and the chateau is peaceful, though solitary and quiet compared to our Christmas rejoicings. Charles is at his College. If he gets for a day or two to London, perhaps you may meet him, for I daresay if your duty prevented your coming up, he would be desirous to go down. . . .

Mama and Anne send their best loves to you and wish you all luck in your studies. I suppose you will have some time to spend here ere you go to India. I should be very desirous that it was spent in acquiring as much insight as possible into the mysteries of civil engineering : pray lose no opportunity of looking into such subjects. They may be the making of your future.—Believe me always, dear Walter, your affectionate uncle,

WALTER SCOTT.

TO HIS DAUGHTER-IN-LAW.

ABBOTSFORD, 26 *March* 1825.

YOUR very attentive and kind letter from Dublin
reached me this morning, and gave me both great pleasure
and some vexation. The former greatly predominated,
for it told me my dear child was safely across the channel,
although after a rough passage. I wish I had been with
you to console you, for I am an excellent nurse to ladies on
shipboard, and a capital maker of negus and mulled wine,
and I daresay the Schwarzritter was too sick himself to
be of half the use he should have been. My vexation is
that you have not heard from us, though I have written
three times, once to Walter, Dublin, *poste restante*, and
twice to you. The first is on business, and I am surprised
he has not had it. It was in general to apprise him of the
terms on which he could agree with Captain Macalpine for
his Troop, and in addition to £2100 (I say two thousand
one hundred pounds) now deposited with Coutts for that
purpose, I would find him the overplus, which I think was
to be about £1500, for which we can afterwards arrange
together. Beg him to be very precise concerning what is
to be done in this matter, and *you* had better write me
than *he*, because paying money beyond regulation, though
every day done, is not strictly regular. I fear on succeeding in this great object you will lose your new acquaintance Mrs. Macalpine, whose manner you seem to be
pleased with.

My two letters addressed to you were both sent to
Edgeworthstown, not being aware of the alteration of your
motions; I hope Walter or you have written there, and
then the letters will be sent forward, as you may desire.
The receiving old-dated letters is, to be sure, like getting
old newspapers, which scarce reward the trouble of reading

them. But mine to you are full of little affectionate nonsense, which may amuse Walter and you, but are not quite fitted for other eyes, so I hope you will inquire after them. You must make out your visit to Edgeworthstown, when you get to Dublin, otherwise there will be little affronts and disappointments, and they are really valuable people from the kindness of their hearts as well as the distinguished talents of Miss Maria Edgeworth.

I observe you have seen my very honest, good-natured, and tiresome friend, one of the best creatures in the world, could he lay aside a rage for being a literary character, for which he has so very little qualification. But many clever people I know might envy him his good-natured and obliging disposition.

Mrs. Jobson is quite well and happy, and, as I hear from all quarters, in excellent spirits, which Walter ought to take as a great compliment, since it infers her perfect reliance on his care of a certain person who shall be nameless. I daresay she had her share in a fright which all Shandwick Place experienced from a melancholy accident two days since. An unlucky foot-boy of Colin Mackenzie's chose, during the absence of the family from town, to amuse himself by removing the *burner*, as it is called, from the gas-pipe in a small cellar in front of the house. Ask Walter if he knows of no young gentleman who has practised such a trick in his time ? The consequence was that the gas, having no exit by door or window, became inflammable, and when the unhappy urchin, instead of calling in proper assistance, came with a lighted candle to examine the mischief he had done, a terrific explosion took place, by which the poor thing was killed and a maid-servant much hurt. Though there required as much *malice prepense* to produce this catastrophe as in the very similar case of the monkey, which, while he put a match to the touch-hole of a cannon, peeped into the muzzle to see the

effect of the explosion, yet it will check for a time the use
of gas, which was becoming generally popular.

There is something of farce mingles with the most
serious events of life, and when I heard among other effects
of the explosion, that a butler in a neighbouring house
had lost the use of speech, I could not help thinking that
had Rebecca been in her old quarters, you would not have
sorrowed greatly if her talents for conversation had been
something impaired.

This I presume will find you at Cork, though there is
a fine uncertainty in all your motions, which put me
(beaks and claws out of the question) something in mind
of a partridge transported through the air by a hawk.
Your cautious qualification of *I believe*, added to your
announcing your journey to Cork for the next day, reminded me of an expression I found in an Irishman's love
letter, "I do not know, my dear, when I am going to the
highlands, but I will certainly know *before I set out*."
Pray write soon; let me know how you like or how you
endure your quarters and accommodation, and how you
like the regiment, and whether Walter looks well in his
uniform.   In my former letter I told you all about a 24
hours' visit to Lochore, but I forgot to say there was an
important personage in the family whose notice I courted
and who resisted every attempt at intimacy. I suppose he
was angry with me for being accessory to depriving him
of his mistress,—it was the large yard dog. Mama sends
kindest love. *Addio, amata bene,*   WALTER SCOTT.

TO MISS EDGEWORTH.

MY DEAR MISS EDGEWORTH,—I have not forgiven
Walter for his breach of appointment, which was very
thoughtless after having permitted me to give you so
much trouble. It is a very thoughtless thing in young
people to make engagements which they do not mean to

keep, and though I can pardon a young woman just from her mother's charge, I have no patience with a man who has seen the world and should know at least the rules of good breeding to the world in general, if not what was particularly due on this occasion. Their stay in London was prolonged to the very last minute, in order that he might attend a levee of the commander-in-chief. They had then a very stormy passage and fell in with the assizes, which made their journey very uncomfortable, for though it is quite right that, according to our old Latin brocard, arms should give way to the gown, yet petticoats do not owe the same deference. So I fancy that Jane had got frightened and afraid to quit convoy; at least this is all that I can make of it. She is lucky in finding a married lady of good manners following the drum, or rather the trumpet, in the same regiment, and they are both fond of music and play duets, which will help to keep concord between them. By-the-bye I should add that they separated from their heavy baggage, and perhaps it had the favourite gown in it. Who knows whether this might not be one spoke in the wheel? Walter used always to put me in mind of a character in a fairy tale called *L'homme qui cherche.* . . . Walter's moveables are often in this condition. He has just sent a pressing request, that a cartouche-box forgotten in Edinburgh shall be sent without delay to Dublin, and, what is worse, I rather suspect that two horses worth £200 are seeking their owner through the isle of Erin, or on the opposite shores of the sister kingdom. . . . I do most certainly intend to be at Dublin in the summer or autumn, and indubitably one of my earliest objects will be to visit my kind friends at Edgeworthstown, so that any lion lovers in the neighbourhood who may have been disappointed at not seeing the lion's cub, will be gratified by a sight of the old lion himself, though what can their curiosity desire when they have such a first-rate lioness at

their own door? . . . I have seen more irritable creatures
than myself bounce and shew [teeth] on these occasions,
but I know you at least agree with me and Snug the joiner,

> " That if one should as lion come in strife
> Into such place, 'twere pity of his life."

Depend upon it I will not fail to possess myself of the books
you recommend; it would be felony to neglect your opinion
of any, and high treason when Ireland is concerned.   Jane
writes me she has been much pleased with the domain of a
lady, Mrs. Newenham of Coolmere, near Cork, to whom they
had been introduced by Mrs. Scott of Harden.   She says
that property forms a very agreeable contrast to other places
which she has seen, where the proprietors are absentees.   I
am glad she carries her eyes about her. . . .

To return to my hopes of a visit to Edgeworthstown.
Beatrice is extremely desirous to be of the party, and so is
Lady Scott, but I am afraid of the health of the last,—not
so able as in her younger days to endure indifferent accommodation, and much given to be frightened where no
fear is.   I believe I must come alone, except I can bring
Lockhart with me.   Depend upon it that if Walter and
his little lady have not made the *amende honorable* by
going on their knees at Edgeworthstown before I appear,
it will be only that they may wish to shelter their bad
behaviour under my countenance.   Delighted I shall be
to see Ireland, but as for writing about it it would be
interfering with the office which her guardian spirit has
discharged, and will I trust continue to discharge to the
honour of her native land and the encouragement of
reciprocal kindness between its inhabitants and those of
the other island.   I have known many a poor Irish
labourer against whom fifteen years ago men's minds would
have been hardened by prejudice and preconception, who
has been treated with kindness as the countryman of the
postillion Jerry. . . .

TO HIS SON CHARLES.

ABBOTSFORD, 6*th April* (1825 ?).

MY DEAR CHARLES,—I am truly obliged to Doctor and
Mrs. Hughes for taking such kind care of you, and only
wish I had better means than mere thanks to offer in
requital. It was particularly obliging to introduce you
at Stowe, one of the first houses certainly in England,
and which has long retained that high character. There
is this advantage in the very first society, that it teaches
a young man to hold the low, strutting, straddling make-
believe sort of fashion which generally consists in caricaturing the manners of the great, or what they conceive
to be such, with the contempt such affectation deserves.
We should have been honoured by receiving the Duchess
of Buckingham, because we would have been sure that
in conferring on us the honour of her company, her Grace
would have come prepared to make our goodwill supply
any wants in the accommodation we had to offer . . .

Matters here go on as usual—only Tom Purdie has
had a dangerous fall from Sybil Grey, or rather with her,
as she rolled over him and bruised him. He is recovering
slowly and still uses a crutch.

How does your money come on? Look into your
affairs and let me know how you stand with the world,
for habits of debt are easily acquired, and are most fatal
to honour and independence of feeling; and I am always
willing to do what is reasonable to prevent any thing
of that kind. . . .

I am going to get you such a gun as Colonel Ferguson's—one of the best I ever saw. Do you prefer the
explosive lock or the old-fashioned prime and load?
Forrest at Jedburgh is the maker. I scarce ever saw
better gunsmith's work. . . .—I am always, dear Charles,
your affectionate father,　　　　WALTER SCOTT.

TO MRS. HUGHES.

ABBOTSFORD, *April* 12, 1825.

MY DEAR MRS HUGHES,—I should be worse than un-grateful did I not immediately communicate Lady Scott's gratitude as well as my own, for the kind and parental notice which the good Doctor, your son, and above all yourself have so kindly bestowed on our young Oxonian; his future welfare in life must depend so much upon the habits which he adopts during his present state of *free will*, as it may in some degree be called, that we cannot but account ourselves inexpressibly obliged and indebted to those who admit him into society alike favourable to his manners and his morals. I am sure he has that kind and affectionate disposition which will remember with deep gratitude the kindness you have shown him. I am afraid her Grace of Buckingham will think she has received a guest at your hand of rather an uncommon description at Stowe,—a wild boy from the Scottish hills improved by an education chiefly acquired amidst the mountains of Wales; however, he would not I think make his deficiencies very obtrusive, unless he has acquired a little more of the metal from which his College takes its name than he used to have before he became a *man* as he calls himself of Brazen Nose. He writes in the highest terms of delight with what he has seen at Stowe, and especially with the Duchess' kindness and affability, which he justly sets down to the patronage under which he made his *entrée*.

Touching the Clan Tartans, I have always understood those distinctions to be of considerable antiquity, though probably the distinction was neither so minute nor so invariably attended to as it is in general the custom to suppose. I have myself known many old people that were out in 1715, and I have understood that, generally speaking, the clan tartans were observed by the more

numerous and powerful names. But many used a sort
of brown and purple tartan, and there were more from
remote corners that had no tartan at all, nor plaids, but
a sort of dress worn by children in Scotland, and called
a *Polony* (polonaise, perhaps) which is just a jacket and
a petticoat all in one, buttoning down in front from the
throat to a palm's breadth above the knee. Very many
had no bonnet, their shaggy hair being tied back with
a thong or garter, and very many had neither hose nor
shoes. The custom of clan tartan arose very naturally—
the weaver was, after the smith and the carpenter, a man
of consequence, whose art was transmitted from father
to son, and when he lighted on what he thought a good
sett or mixture of the colours, he was unwilling to change,
and the clan of habit, in most instances, gradually became
attached to it, and adopted it as a sort of uniform of the
tribe. It is certain that in 1739, when the Black Watch,
or independent companies of Highlanders, were formed
into the 42nd Regiment, a doubt arose as to what tartan
they should wear, as hitherto the independent companies
had worn the colours of those officers who commanded
them. But none of these being entitled to a preference,
which others would probably have resented, there was
formed a new *sett*, composed out of different tartans, and
still known as the 42nd colour. Again, and in 1745, when
the Chevalier landed, he chose a tartan for himself, of a
colour different from any clan tartan which existed, to
avoid showing a predilection for any particular tribe; and
I have heard repeatedly that the Stewarts both of Athol
and Appin grumbled a little that he did not take the
colours of his own clan. Indeed, a moment's consideration
will show that if the distinction of clan tartan had not
existed at the time of the 1745, it could never have existed
at all: for there was neither time nor means to introduce
it at the time of the rising, when all came with such cloaths

as they had; nor was there a possibility of introducing such distinctions after 1745, when the dress was prohibited by Government under the penalty of imprisonment and transportation. The poor Highlanders were reduced to great distress by this law. Most of them, both unwilling and unable to obtain lowland dresses, endeavoured to elude the law by dyeing their Highland tartans to one colour—dark green, crimson, purple, or often black. I have seen them wearing such dresses myself as long since as 1785. I have no doubt that Mrs. Macleod dined with a party of gentlemen dressed without the least respect to clan colours, for it was no time to observe these distinctions when the plaid itself was an illegal garb. Her mother was not married till long after 1745, so she can have no personal recollection of what the Highlanders did before that period. By the way, the Macleods of Dunvegan might drink Charles's health, but they fought for King George, and were defeated by Lord Lewis Gordon at Inveraray. So much for Highland dress: I could say a great deal more, but it would only be tiresome. I must however add, that though I am sure I could show that the clan tartans were in use a great many years before 1745, I do not believe a word of the nonsense about every clan or name having a regular pattern which was undeviatingly adhered to; and the idea of assigning tartans to the Douglases, Hamiltons, and other great lowland families (who never wore tartan) has become so general that I am sure if the Duke of Buckingham had asked at some of the shops in Stirling or Edinburgh for his own family tartan, they would not have fail'd to assign him one.

As to the kissing affair, it was a great fashion among the Scots of the last generation, male and female. On the other hand, as every period has its own fanciful limits of decorum, I remember old people being much shocked at seeing the modern fashion of gentlemen affording the full protection of their arm in leaving the drawing-room with their fair partners, whereas old-fashioned etiquette only permitted such a slight junction of the finger and thumb as was allowed in the minuet. "I canna bide to see them *oxtering* the men that gate," was the observation of an old Scotch lady of fashion to me scarce a dozen years since.

I have been horribly ungrateful not to thank Mr. Berens very particularly for the sketches, especially poor Leyden's. It is, so far as I know, the only memorial of the features of one who lived too short time for his friends, his country, and general knowledge, and it recalls him to my recollection in the most lively colours. I beg my most particular thanks to Mr. Berens, and am scarce able to believe that this is the first time I have expressed them for a favour so deeply valued. I am much concerned about Charles's deafness, especially as he must rise in the world by his own exertions, to which such an infirmity is a great impediment. I have always thought that it was in some measure nervous, and depended much on his health and spirits. It is combined with a tendency to abstraction and absence of mind which, I have observed, it increases, as on the other hand, it is increased by this sort of mental deafness. I wish him to see and correspond with Charles Bell, from whose prescriptions he had formerly received help. Here is an unmerciful letter; but when I begin to write to a valued friend I never know when to leave off, and when I leave off I scarce know how to begin again. Lady Scott offers kindest and most grateful remembrances, and I beg to be most kindly remembered to the Doctor and Mr. Hughes. I am flattered that he thinks Charles worth his notice. . . .

As much of this valuable letter is intended to satisfy his Grace of Buckingham's curiosity about the Highland dress, I take the liberty of putting it under his cover; there remains ample room for a most interesting and curious dissertation on the gradual alterations which were introduced in the Highlands from the period of Montrose's wars, when they first began to make some figure in history, down to the present day. This will scarcely be done however, for the Highlanders contend for everything, and are under the great misapprehension of supposing they derive honour from manifest fables, whereas there is another sort of cold-blooded set of folks who will not allow them the merit which they certainly deserve. Thus far is certain, that this is the only case in which it might be shown how civilisation broke in on patriarchal habits. Many of the Highland chiefs in the earlier part of the eighteenth century had two distinct characters, that of an accomplished gentleman in London, and beyond the Highland line that of a chief of an almost independent tribe. No more room.—Ever yours,

WALTER SCOTT.

TO HIS SON WALTER.

ABBOTSFORD, 21st *April* (1825).

. . . NICOL is again talking of selling; but I doubt his making up his mind to taking any price that might be but moderately high, and I do not feel justified in making too great sacrifices. A good deal will depend on your own views and wishes. . . .

The Jew talks of forty thousand; but he is an absolute Hebrew, and once named 50,000, so I suppose he will come down. I am determined to lie by and say nothing. Meanwhile I should like to have your sentiments on the subject, and also to know what Jane thinks. If we had the heugh of Tweed from Ettrick foot to the Carraweel,[1] we would have a proper estate.

I hope this will find you comfortably settled at Dublin,

---

[1] A pool in the Tweed just above the Railway Bridge and below Gala foot,—swirls or eddies in the Tweed are called "weels."

and I want to know all about your ménage, whether your
horses have joined yet, and what is become of them—
whom you see, and who are kind to you.

Little news. . . . The weather is now charming and
things looking well. Ginger has puppies. Spice expects
presently to be confined.

I hope Jane continues to like the campaign. Her last
letter was a very pleasant and favourable account of
matters, and I suppose Dublin will greatly improve on
Cork. . . .—Yours affectionately,   WALTER SCOTT.

TO THE SAME.

ABBOTSFORD, 29th April 1825.

I OBSERVE from your last Jane is like to have a female
commanding officer, who I suppose will take the direction
of all the ladies belonging to the regiment. Seriously, I
hope she will be a companionable and ladylike person, as
I suppose she must be a person of some influence. I
suppose you are not sorry with the effects of "La belle
passion" on your redoubtable commandant, nor excessively
sorry that

> "Grim-visaged war hath smoothed his wrinkled front,
> And now instead of mounting barbed steeds
> To affright the souls of fearful adversaries,"

Or you may read—

> To fret the souls of lazy subalterns
> "He capers nimbly in a lady's chamber,
> To the lascivious soothings of a lute." [1]

If this quotation is rather threadbare, I cannot but think
it is happily applied.

We are all well here, and send love to Jane and you.
I want to know how you are settled at Dublin, and hope
Jane will take the trouble to write whenever she has
arranged herself comfortably. I will also desire to hear

[1] See *Richard III.* Act I. sc. 1.

from you how your arrangement proceeds with the Major, and tell me to whom the regulation money at Coutts' is to be paid—to the agents, I suppose. I shall be stationary here till after the eleventh May, when Edinburgh will be my address.—Always your affectionate father,

WALTER SCOTT.

TO HIS DAUGHTER-IN-LAW.

ABBOTSFORD, 3d *May* 1825.

. . . I EXPECT a long letter from you about Pat's capital and its gaieties. Take good care of your health among them, my love, for you know it is very precious to us all; and be gay in *moderation* that you may be gay *long*.

Lockhart was here two days since to attend the Circuit, and brought us news of little Johnie's complete recovery, to our great joy, in which I am sure Walter and you will sympathise. That child's delicate health is rather an assailable point in our domestic happiness, which I thank God has otherwise, humanly speaking, a very comfortable aspect.

I desired Mr. James Ballantyne to write by post to Walter when he remitted Major Lane's money as advised. I presume he did so, and the cash (£1500) having been sent on Saturday, 1st May, is this day at the gallant Major's credit in London. I hope this will immediately lead to your becoming " Mrs. Captain," which is always better than even "good Mistress Lieutenant." It is, as Hamlet says to the actress, being nearer Heaven by the altitude of a chopine. Let me know if you feel yourself taller on the occasion.

There is little news stirring with us, only a few days must carry us back to the fag of Edinburgh, as the session of the Court begins on the 12th; so pray after you receive this, address to Castle Street. . . .—Your affectionate father,   WALTER SCOTT.

TO HIS NEPHEW.

ABBOTSFORD, *5th May* [1825].

MY DEAR WALTER,—I have been an undutiful relation in not writing you some time past. About making up your kit, the first thing is to know accurately what it ought to consist of, for young men are strangely imposed on in this particular, sometimes wanting things which are essential, and often buying a quantity of what they have as little use for as a highlander for knee-buckles. It is also to be considered that you are not quite come to your size yet, and that clothes made exactly for your person just now, may not suit so well. It seems to me also to be of consequence, that you should have a few good books on engineering, both civil and military, and I wish you to get advice as to what are likely to be most useful. Get a business-like list of the cloaths, and another of the books and sundries necessary, and add the prices, and let me have them for my consideration. . . .

Walter is anxiously looking out for his troop, which we expect immediately, as the Major retires from bad health, and the hopeful arrangement is, that a certain Capt. Byam gets the Majority, and Walter Captain Byam's troop. Jane seems to take kindly to a military life, and writes in high spirits with all she has seen, and the attentions they have met with. By mixing in general society she will rub off a little of that reserve which is the great fault of her manner.

I conceive your mother and sisters will now have reached your uncle in safety. Their society cannot but be valuable to him in his precarious state of health, but I fear, unless that is considerably amended, the girls may find it a little gloomy. They are accustomed however to prefer duty to pleasure, and upon the whole the arrangement seems the most natural and most respectful, which could have been made for their comfort and protection.

I wish to hear from you what your own motions are likely to be—how long you stay at Chatham—and when your final departure is to be expected. I should be very desirous that your leisure, which must I suppose be short, should be employed in learning whatever may be necessary to forward and increase your stock of useful knowledge. In your profession, the best-informed man inevitably gets furthest forward.

How do you get on with Col. Pasley?

Lady Scott, Anne, and I are the only residents here, and to-day our solitude is cheered by James Scott with his pipes, and Maxpopple[1] with his pedigree. I have given the latter an office of about £300 which Charles Erskine, poor fellow, held under me, and which seems to have made poor Max very happy—for look you, sir, it is no easy matter to find meat and cloth for twelve small children.—I am, with kindest wishes from Lady Scott and Anne, always, my dear Walter, your affectionate uncle,

WALTER SCOTT.

TO HIS SON CHARLES.

EDINBURGH, 13th May.

MY DEAR CHARLES,—I desired Mr. Ballantyne to send you your full allowance, £75, which is due at or about this time; so put your house in order and remember you will have another remittance of £75 due three months after this, so that you can arrange your matters for regular payments

"Regardless of the wily tradesman's way,
    Who hushed in grim repose expects his Christmas prey."

I am glad to find a good report of you from Stowe. It

[1] William Scott, younger of Raeburn, appointed by Sir Walter to the Sheriffship-substitute of Selkirkshire.

always requires some tact to live with great folks, without either seeming to intrude on their intimacy, or observing an awkward degree of reserve; but a sense of propriety mixed with a desire to please points out the just medium.

I had a letter this morning from Jane, by which we learn the 15th have reached Dublin, where I suppose they will remain the best part of a twelvemonth. Walter and spouse have got half a house on Stephen's Green, a brother officer and his wife taking the other half. If there be not proper quarrelling among the domestics I shall wonder, but luckily there are two kitchens, so the cooks cannot scald each other with their ladles. Walter's address will be, 15th Hussars, Barracks, Dublin.

Little Walter is working hard at mining, sapping, and all the pioneering art: he seems from his letter to be in high spirits and happy.

Johnie Lockhart has been at Germiston for a few days with Sophia, and is much better. I calculate upon his recovery with the greater certainty that I am well assured there is no medical man within reach. Soph is rather too great an encourager of the art of Esculapius. Mama, Anne, and I came to town two days since, much grieved to leave Abbotsford in such high beauty; everything seemed bursting out into flowers and foliage, and such a choir of birds were never heard. The only interesting news is that Purdiana (Jenny, viz.) was to be married forthwith to George Fairbairn, with the entire approbation of the magnanimous.

I have ordered the gun to be made with percussion locks on the best principles. I believe Walter gets one from the same man, having destroyed his excellent Manton by neglect. I am sorry I gave the gun to him.

Mr. Chantrey the celebrated sculptor has been down here fixing the place for the King's statue, which is I believe to be the centre of George Street, opposite to Hanover Street, which will have a most noble effect, as the street sloping down both to Princes Street and Queen Street will show the statue relieved against the sky in approaching it from any division. It will be about 12 feet high exclusive of the pedestal, and pedestrian of course.

TO HIS DAUGHTER-IN-LAW.

EDINBURGH, 16th *May* 1825.

YOUR kind letter of the 9th reached me, my dearest Jane, just as I was beginning to think you a little lazy in your correspondence. It followed me from Abbotsford to town, where I arrived the last Tuesday with great reluctance, for leaving the country in its beauty is to me very like having a tooth drawn. Your motions being a little irregular owing to your marchings and counter-marchings, I see that you have not received your letters very regularly, but I suppose you have by this time got one from Mrs. Jobson, with a few lines from me. I had the pleasure to see Mrs. Jobson yesterday in perfect good health, and to assure her of yours. She and I both unite in being rather glad that the gay season is now near over in Dublin, as we are parentally afraid of your over-fatiguing yourself amid the hospitalities of the Irish Capital.

Servants are always the plagues of young housekeepers. You should part with either, or both, without a moment's ceremony, the instant they begin to give you trouble. I remember I used to be much hurt at the idea of parting with an old servant, but I have found from experience, that whenever they conceive themselves indispensable they become abominably tyrannical, and that the best way of compelling them to regular good behaviour is to change whenever they become troublesome, either by quarrelling with you or with each other. There never was so good a servant, but with good wages and kind treatment, you will always find as good a successor.

I wrote Walter about his promotion, which appears for the present to have miscarried. I hope an opportunity will soon offer of completing the matter.

Chantrey, the great sculptor, was with me a day before I left Abbotsford, and went off the happiest man in the world, having killed two salmon. I do not believe that the applause which he received for any of his fine works of art gave him more pleasure. He has made Lady Scott a present of the fine bust he cut of my poor noddle three years ago, and of which you probably have seen casts. It is reckoned (the subject out of the question) a very fine piece of sculpture, in point of execution. Chantrey himself is a right good John Bull, bland, and honest, and open, without any of the nonsensical affectation so common among artists.

I hope your housekeeping in St. Stephen's Green will go on well; it cannot be very different from people living in different families in the same hotel, and with respect to your servants, male and female, take my counsel—if you have an aching tooth have it drawn out—if a quarrelsome servant dismiss him or her. An empty house is always better than a bad tenant.

By the way, your late remove has brought you a good deal more within hail as the sailors say, besides giving us a sure direction, which for some time was rather uncertain. Let me know, my love, how the housekeeping goes on, and whether you keep your accompts accurately, and are a good manager. But no doubt you will give yourself an excellent character. I must come and see, I fancy.

Anne and Lady Scott send kindest love to Walter and you. I expect to hear from Walter daily.—Always yours, my dearest child, most affectionately,

WALTER SCOTT.

TO HIS SON WALTER.

EDINBURGH, 17th May 1825.

I PROPOSE to bring Anne with me, and perhaps Lock-hart, for Boots to pay postillions and so forth. But we need not litter up your house you know, as we can always get into a hotel. If Mama should alter her plan, I must leave Anne with her, which will be a disappointment to the young lady. Under the conditions above expressed, I expect to start about 12th July. As my stay must neces-sarily be short, I will like to see as much and visit as little as I can.

You say nothing about Nicol's property. I think he will come down to a moderate price if let alone, but I want to know what you yourself wish about it, for, as I formerly wrote you, it is more your affair than mine. By the way, I understand from Chantrey that there is a near prospect of a large and fine thoroughfare being made across London from North to South, terminating at the Museum on one extremity, and Waterloo Bridge on the other. This mag-nificent Bridge has been in a manner useless, and its toll unproductive, because there is no access to it, but if this goes on, it will become a great place of passage, and benefit the Stockholders accordingly. Chantrey says people are buying up shares. Now Jane holds equal to £10,000 stock in that concern, which may turn out a very good thing. I should not be surprised to see it much above *par*.

The Chief Commissioner has settled the 12th of June for our usual summer rally, and very handsomely proposes to occupy part of the time in setting off a good access to Lochore, the present one being a very circuitous and awk-ward approach. You need of course be in no hurry making the road, as you may make a bit now and then. But to have the power of making it will be an immense improve-ment to the place, both in comfort and in value. I wish to know what Jane thinks of this, that I may regulate what I have to say to Lord Chief Commissioner accordingly.

The kindest love of all the household attends Jane. I wrote to her yesterday, so have not much to say.—Always your affectionate father, WALTER SCOTT.

TO HIS NEPHEW.

EDINR., 17th May [1825].

MY DEAR WALTER,—I have your letter, and enclose a cheque for £25 to help out your pay and get the things you mention. Take particular care of the quality of the instruments which you purchase. Better give more to get them warranted good, and from first-rate makers, than pay less for them of an inferior order, as they are not easily replaced in India. You would have a letter from me directing you to get a list of your things required for out-fit, taking care to take good advice on what is really useful. I also mentioned that you would be the better, I thought, of some approved works on Engineering, both civil and military. I believe you will find that Robert Shortreed is getting on very well in the Engineer line, though in some respects an interloper, so I have great hopes for you who are regularly in the service. Omit no opportunity, my dear boy, of acquiring the knowledge necessary for availing yourself of opportunities which I have little doubt will occur to you, and let your thoughts and studies be turned as much as possible to science, both for civil and military purposes. I have a notion that you will find the first very useful. The last you learn as a matter of course.

I heard from Walter yesterday,—anxious about his troop, in which I hope he will succeed, as in the case of a Benedick, captain sounds better than *sub*, and besides Jane has better quarters. They have got a house at Stephen's Green however, and do not live in barracks just now.

I had a letter from your Mama from Cheltenham. Their journey was well made out. She, as well as I, was rather desirous you would bestow some pains on your handwriting, which is however getting firmer and better than it was. . . .—I am always, your affectionate uncle,

WALTER SCOTT.

And so good morrow to you, good Master Lieutenant.

TO MRS. THOMAS SCOTT.[1]

EDINR., 21st *May* 1825.

I MUST no longer delay to wish you and my nieces joy upon arriving at a home which will, I trust, prove more comfortable and more permanent than anywhere it has been your lot to inhabit lately. I wrote a long letter to Mr. David M'Culloch from Abbotsford, giving him joy of an event which I myself have thus far reason to regret, that it carries you so far out of my ken, and diminishes the chance which I have to be useful upon occasion. I enclose a cheque for £30, and you will have the goodness to mark it as a year's payment of interest on one of the girls' bills, to which interest I add £5, to help on the "Doctor's" musical studies, which little remittance will take place half-yearly, as I expect some day to be greatly the better of her proficiency in that accomplishment. I intended to send you the remittance before you removed from Scotland, but I was poor for the moment. The real road to ruin is, 1st, to have an improvable estate with a taste for building; 2ndly, to have your son marry a wealthy heiress, and call on you for outfit and marriage presents; and if over and above you can manage to have a troop to buy for him in a crack regiment of Cavalry, you will find the bottom of the purse with a vengeance. But there is always balm in Gilead for Clerks of Session, when quarter day is always coming round in its due time.

[1] Then at Cheltenham.

I should be happy, were it in my power to vary your groups of *yellow* gentlemen, by a happy mixture with some *blue* ladies; and whenever I hear that Lady Montagu, or any other proper person is coming to Cheltenham, or when you can let me know that such is there, I will be happy to give my nieces introductions.

I had a letter from Walter a few days since, in excellent health and spirits, and entering with laudable zeal into the *esprit de corps* which induces military men to mention with so much emphasis the important designations of *We* and *Ours*. I expect Walter to do great things, if it pleases God to preserve his health. His hand is getting firmer and better, and indeed I agree with you that it might still be amended, an observation which extends itself to the Oxonian Charles, whose Latin is said to be good, but whose English would *thole a mend*. Walter the larger writes also with a happy resemblance to a partridge scratching in the dust below a hedge. It is very odd all the girls write good hands, Anne pre-eminently so. Walter has got a good house in Dublin and is living quietly there. He is recommended for purchase, and there is a prospect of his getting a troop, as I hinted before. But I must needs say it is a hopeful profession, when a man buys an annuity on much worse terms than he could get it upon Change, binds himself to be a slave to the commands of others, and occasionally to spoil his annuity bargain by putting himself in the way of being killed,—and after all to be told he is very lucky, and has got high promotion. If his Majesty's officers were to wear snuff-coloured clothes, with pig-tail wigs and square buckles, do you think the mere spirit of patriotism would make commissions sell as highly? However, whether Walter becomes a Captain or remains good master Lieutenant, I intend to go and pay them a visit of a week or ten days at Dublin, to see how they carry on the war. I think I shall be tempted to return, if my time will permit, by Cheltenham, for the purpose of seeing you all, as I cannot expect my Christmas visit when it is taxed with so long a journey, in bad travelling weather. . . .

Pray let me know that this has reached safe, and let me know what folks you have at Cheltenham, in case I should know some of them, though my fashionable acquaintance is much decreased of late years. When you are lazy yourself, Anne can write me a line.

TO HIS SON WALTER.

7th June 1825.

I RECEIVED your letter at Abbotsford, whither I had retreated on the 4th June to spend the time betwixt that day and yesterday, which I did, as Robinson Crusoe says, "to my exceeding refreshment." The country is looking beautiful, though the weather has not been warm, an easterly wind predominating. The only news is that Tom Purdie's daughter (the pretty one, Jenny) is to be married on Friday to George Fairbairn, a hind at Loch Breast, one of a family that have been long servants to my uncle and my grandfather. So that being a bridal among *our ain folks*, I send the bride this morning a present of a set of tea-things with spoons corresponding. The bridegroom is the lad that used to fiddle to us for want of a better.

I have left Anne and Mama in the country till Saturday sennight, when I propose to fly out per mail and fetch them in till the Session rises. In the meantime my Saturdays are well filled up. On next Saturday, being the 11th, I go on our usual skirmish to Blair Adam, where the good-natured Chief Commissioner proposes to lay off an entrance to the grounds and house of Lochore along his own lands, which will be a great matter for the property. . . . Upon Saturday, 18th, I mean to go to

Abbotsford, as already said. On the 25th I will go to Tyningham to see the old peer and learn a few more of his stories.

Yesterday I gave a smart party in the character of Bachelor Bluff to some of my big-wigged friends and my very old acquaintance Lord Forbes in particular. Our new housekeeper sent up everything very smart.

I expect to be able to set off for Glasgow on Saturday 9th July. Next day we will go to the kirk, like good bairns, and spend the day with Dr. Lockhart, and set off next day by the steamer for Belfast. So with any luck of a tolerable passage, Anne, Lockhart, and I will be in St. Stephen's Green on the evening of the 12th, or morning of the 13th July. . . .

Amidst the casualties which you mention of the canal, you do not mention an incident which has figured in all the papers announcing you by name and surname as having fished up a certain Miss Bergen out of the said canal, and thereby, like Hotspur, "fished up pale-faced honour by the locks;" perhaps we should read *from the lock*, viz., the lock of the canal. We are dying of curiosity to know whether this be true or no, as both your silence and Jane's induce us to doubt the fact.

On Saturday we had wellnigh made a neat paragraph ourselves, for a stupid blockhead of a postillion took fright in the ford, the water being rather heavy, and wisely proposed to turn, which would unquestionably have swampt us. I kept him to his tackle though, and we went on without danger, though the water came through the carriage, and I was obliged to open both doors. Mama was horridly frightened; but Anne joked the whole way, which makes me hope she will be a bold traveller. Do you think you will be able to get leave for Killarney? I should like much to see that celebrated scenery.

My kind love to Jane, and pray take the utmost care

of the gig. I have a holy horror for these vehicles, and more than one accident has happened to young married women in my time which has been the cause of distress for a lifetime. Speaking of vehicles, I intend to have a light barouche for the journey, which two horses will trundle along like a bowl.

To whom do Messrs. Coutts pay the cash in their hands when you are gazetted? Let me know, that I may give orders accordingly. It would be awkward to have it unsettled while I am rambling about.—I am always, your affectionate father,   WALTER SCOTT.

TO HIS SON CHARLES

BLAIR ADAM, 12th June 1825.

MY DEAR CHARLES,—You have been so long of answering my letter, as to leave little time to determine on a plan which I thought of for your pleasure and advantage, how to employ some part at least of this vacation. Shakespeare says that homebred youths have ever homely wits, and besides, as you think of something diplomatic, the sooner you have a glimpse of foreign parts the better. Now, suppose you had any intelligent friend, Mr. Surtees for example, willing to take such a tour with you, I should have no objections to your going over to Paris, running as far as the verge of Switzerland, then descending the Rhine, and returning by Brussels and Holland. I would do this the rather that our family will be much dispersed this year, as Walter cannot get over, and Anne, Lockhart and I have settled to go to Dublin as soon as the Session rises (9th July). Now if it be too late, as I fear it may be, for you to think of arranging your foreign excursion, you can come down here and be with us during the interval, and while we are absent you could make a little tour through the Highlands and see something of your own country, or

if we can arrange room, which I think we may do, as
I intend to take for the tour a little light barouche, which
will hold four, we can all go jollily together to the land of
Erin. I should not be afraid of the visit incommoding
Walter, because he has a largish house, and I can make
the matter of the *ménage* quite easy. Mama and Sophia
promise either to remain quiet at Abbotsford or to go to
some sea-bathing quarter. Mama dare not trust ferry-
boats and Irish travelling.

Perhaps this may do as well as the foreign trip, and
next year you will have studied the French and German
a little, in order that you may make your journey conveniently and usefully. Remember at least to keep up
what you have of modern languages, for readiness in
speaking and composing in them is like to be of the
last consequence to you, as is English composition. Think
my plans over, and decide for yourself whether you would
like to go abroad this year, so soon as necessary arrangements can be made, or to scour the Highlands, or to storm
Walter in his camp at Dublin. Either will, I think, form
an agreeable divertisement after the hard reading.

Walter is very well. We are at present divided—Anne
and Mama being at Abbotsford for ten days, but next
Saturday being the 18th, I go to fetch them all in upon
the Tuesday or Wednesday following, when we will be
together until our final dispersion in the beginning of
July.

In case you should want cash for travelling, etc., I
have advised Messrs. Coutts to honour your Draft for
£20. . . .

TO HIS DAUGHTER-IN-LAW.

EDINBURGH, 17*th June* 1825.

MY DARLING,—You are doomed to have long answers,
even to postscripts, but you deserve them were they worth

anything, for you have been a most excellent correspondent. We will certainly be with you on the evening of Wednesday, 13th July, or the morning of the next day. I find the steam-boat does not sail till Tuesday 12th, which makes this change in our motions. Do not put yourself to any trouble about us; Walter will tell you that my delight is in plain fare and kind welcome, and as I am sure of the one, I venture to command the other. When you were at Abbotsford we were, you know, somewhat in gala; it was high holiday with us, and occasion called on us to be a little *en seigneur*. But you have never seen us quietly, when we are *very quiet* from choice as well as propriety.

I was at Blair Adam and Lochore the other day. I am very anxious to secure a good access to your mansion there. I think I can make you understand what I mean. You remember the bridge over the brook, about half-a-mile to the west of your farm-house of Chapel—very well, a road made and *metal'd*, as it is called, communicates from the bridge with the high road through Lord Moray's lands there, and I have no doubt we can get the use of the road as well as Mr. Syme,—we then cross the bridge, and my proposal would be, to carry the road along the left bank of the brook eastward to join that road which communicates with Chapel from the west, and which is a very good one. Some part of the road from the bridge to the Chapel farm would be through Mr. Syme's grounds of East Blair, for the greater part through your own property, and it would be equally useful almost to both estates and permit the farmers of both to communicate with the high road to the Roscobie lime-works, which would be of great consequence.

You will then have a level access (comparatively) to Lochore House, without climbing up the sides of Benarty merely to come down again, by driving past Chapel and coming round by the east avenue. This will serve present purposes. But you will also secure the power of making, when you so please, a very beautiful avenue, from the south-west, by entering your own woods just after you pass the march between East Blair and Lochore, and winding gradually through them till you gain the level of the mansion-house. This may be made a most beautiful thing, but there is no hurry in it. On the other hand, it would be quite necessary to make an agreement with Mr. Syme's agent, while they are desirous (as Lord Chief Commissioner seems to think they are) to engage in such a beneficial transaction. If young Walter had been the surveyor, instead of old Walter, he would have given you a sketch of the ground to assist your comprehension. You will always have the present approach as an entrance to the place from the north-west or Kinross direction. If you approve of what I am recommending, I will manage the expense for you, for you cannot be expensive in rural economy and improvements while -you have so many cormorants to feed.

So Walter's laurels in the case of the drowned fair one are transferred to the head of Hamilton Dundas. I think the tailor of twenty stone has a right, both in regard to his size and his spirit, to pass for something more than the ninth part of a man. I am glad there are still tailors in the 15th. It was chiefly composed of such worthies when it was raised and called Elliot's Light Horse, and when the regiment suffered so severely (at Minden, I think), they gave rise to the well-known joke, that the King had neither lost *men* nor *horses*, the riders being *tailors* and the chargers *mares*.

Let me know, my love, what I can fetch for you from Scotland. Mrs. Jobson promises me a parcel. She had the goodness to dine with me in my widowed state the day before yesterday, and is in high health and spirits. I have the vanity to think myself a great favourite. I have made an arrangement that permits me to go to the country (Abbotsford, of course) to-morrow after twelve o'clock, and stay there till Wednesday, which will be delightful in this hot weather.

I wrote Walter fully about his money matters, and although I was positively certain of what I then stated, yet I looked into the banker's shop to-day and saw the letters advising that £1500 was paid for Major Lane's use. I have written to him, and expect the Gazette will make you a Captain's lady—a *real* Captain's lady—very soon. —Adieu, dearest Jane, and God bless you.

WALTER SCOTT.

TO MISS EDGEWORTH.

WE are rather lonely here, having nobody but Lady S., Anne, and myself at Abbotsford. Lockhart's business detaining him in town, the want of Sophia and little Johnie is rather annoying. I have given Johnie a pony so very small that it is less than many dogs, otherwise so beautifully made and so active that it might serve the king of Lilliput, God save his grace! Johnie, with a little assistance, rides into the hall and dining parlour, and like the ministrels of old, "up to the fair board's head," and the pony perfectly understands the value of a dainty piece of bread. When I write about these trifles you may be sure I have little else to say. The people are all mad here about joint-stock companies, and the madness which possesses John Bull has caught his speculative brother Sawney. No man can commit the extremity of folly with so grave a countenance and under the influence of such admirable reasoning as a Scotchman; the whole nation, indeed, bears out the character given to the sapient monarch of old,—" that of the wisest fools in Christendom." Such folly however has a better chance to pass unnoticed, as the perpetrator completely possesses his own self-opinion; they treat laughers as the Newcastle keelmen did the owl. The keel (a particular boat for carrying the coals down the Tyne) had run ashore under the ruins of the old abbey of Jarrow, and the shock startled out an owl from her place of strength; the hand who was ashore, having never seen such a bird in his life, concluded from its appearance and cry that it must be a spirit, and exhorted his comrade to come ahead and speak to it, which he did to this purpose; the supposed ghost, you must understand, had treated them with two or three shrieks. " Hoo! hoo!" said the keeler, who thought the expressions of the owl's wonder too strong for the occasion, " What's thee hoo-hooing about, didst never see a keel ashore before ? " I believe we shall see a few keels ashore before the play is played out, whether we are all [able] to laugh at them or no. We are endeavouring to profit by the mania to get a railroad brought up from Kelso, which would accommodate a valuable tract of country with coal and lime, from which we are twenty miles distant. We had a meeting of our committee here on Tuesday, on which occasion Anne (who is a decided punstress), hearing more of the undertaking I suppose than she relished, observed, if our conversation was deficient in wit there was no want of raillery. She begs her kindest respects to you and has written a letter to Miss Harriet, which I enclose. My kindest compliments attend Mrs. Edgeworth and all your kind family.—Always, my dear Miss Edgeworth, most respectfully yours, WALTER SCOTT.

TO WILLIAM STEWART ROSE.

ABBOTSFORD, *29th June* 1825.

MY DEAR ROSE,—I think it is about the time when good men arrange their country parties and inquire after the motions of their friends. How sets the vane (I will not say the weathercock) of your inclinations ? Due north

I hope, with a westing towards Abbotsford when the moorfowl season sets in.   I mention the moorfowl, not only
on account of your further delectation, but because I am
going for a week or two to Ireland in the beginning of
July, and shall scarce, if I visit Killarney as I purpose, get
back before the first week of August. . . .   Pray let the
Author of the *Wilderness of Monkeys* [1] know I expected he
would send me a copy of the work, especially as I think
he has got some of my tales, and being generally read and
admired, I might as well quote the best-thumb'd page of
our friend Joe Miller, as again attempt to tell what is
generally known, so I ought in all justice to have a copy
of the record.   Mr. and Mrs. Stewart Mackenzie are here
for a day, and talk of having seen you at Morritt's, and that
both of you were very well.   I think I must see Johannes
Mauritanius as I return through England, that is, if I do
take that route.   Anne and Lockhart are to be my travelling companions.   Lady Scott, Sophia, and little Johnie
Hugh, as he calls himself, go to Helensburgh I believe, to
sea-bathing quarters.   Perhaps we might manage somewhere or somehow to pick you up on our return northward.   After August I shall be stationary as usual, and
the Chapel [2] awaits you.   Adieu, dear Rose; all at Chiefswood and Abbotsford hope you will not sadden autumn
by your absence.   Address Edinburgh, as I came here
only for a day.—Yours, with most sincere regard and
affection,   WALTER SCOTT.

TO HIS NEPHEW.

EDINBURGH, 29*th June* [1825].

MY DEAR WALTER,—You have been long silent, which
is not right.   You ought to let me know how your studies

---

[1] Mr. Stewart Rose had lately
published a little book called an
*Apology addressed to the Travellers'
Club*, being anecdotes of monkeys.

[2] See *Life*, vol. v. pp. 8-9, for
an account of "the Chapel" at
Abbotsford.

are going on, and what your motions are like to be. Our family undergoes a dispersion in the beginning of next month, which is rather unusual. I go to Ireland with Lockhart and Anne—Lady Scott to some watering-place yet unsettled, with Sophia and little Johnie. Charles, who is now here, proposes a tour to the Highlands. So there will be only empty walls at Castle Street and Abbotsford for the space of four weeks. Now, we would be most happy to have you with us upon either of these parties, but that I am strongly impressed with an idea that your time might be more usefully employed in endeavouring to make yourself acquainted, however superficially, with the principles of civil engineering. The rapid progress of knowledge in this country does not soon or easily transmit itself to distant colonies, and an acquaintance with the means of making gas, applying steam, constructing roads, bridges, etc., might be the means of very rapid advancement. You have not, unhappily, had anything like a regular course of this important study, but by exertion on your own part you might get some general insight into what may be of infinite consequence. You are now no boy, my dear Walter, and having stated my proposition generally, I must leave it to yourself to consider, after advising with Colonel Pasley, or any other qualified person who may take the trouble to advise you, the proper means of carrying it into execution as far as circumstances render it possible. It occurs to me that a residence in London for some weeks might be the best way of attaining the necessary information, although it has its inconveniences for young people, abounding with temptations, both to trifle away valuable time and to indulge in excesses which are fatal to health and to morals. But you are a good and steady boy, and must be sensible how much the happiness of your mother and sisters, and the good opinion and affection of myself and all your other friends, which you possess in no ordinary degree, must depend upon your continuing to maintain the same steadiness of character which you have always shown, and which entitles me to express my warm hopes that you will be a credit to the name you bear, and a comfort to us all. I only hint at these matters as you are now entering in some degree upon the system of self-management, which must always be one of self-control.

I will be also desirous that you should possess such books on Engineering, Mathematics, etc., as may be of most practical advantage to you. I will also remit any money that may be necessary for your comfort and for the facility of advancing your studies either in London or else-where. It may be necessary to say that I leave this on the 10th, and therefore would wish to hear from you on these matters as early as you can fix on anything. When you have laid your plans, I daresay I will be able to get you introductions to Mr. Rennie, Mr. James Watt, or some leading person wherever you may go.

This pursuit of knowledge cannot of course exclude a visit to your mother and sisters, or one to Scotland. We shall be at Abbotsford the whole season after August. Let me know for what time your departure for India is actually fixed, if fixed it is, and believe me always, my dear boy, your affectionate uncle,   WALTER SCOTT.

CHAPTER XXII

1825

July—August

IRISH EXCURSION

Now for the land of verdant Erin,
The Emerald Isle where honest Paddy dwells,
The cousin of John Bull as story tells.
For a long space had John with words of thunder,
Hard looks, and harder knocks, kept Paddy under
Till the poor lad, like boy that's flogged unduly,
Had gotten somewhat restive and unruly.
Hard was his lot and lodging, you'll allow,
A wigwam that would hardly serve a sow ;
His landlord, and of middlemen two brace,
Had screw'd his rent up to the starving-place ;
His garment was a top-coat and an old one :
His meal was a potato, and a cold one ;
But still for fun or frolic, and all that,
In the round world was not the match of Pat.

The Search after Happiness.

" Let merry England proudly rear
  Her blended roses, bought so dear ;
  Let Albin bind her bonnet blue
  With heath and harebell dipp'd in dew ;
  On favour'd Erin's crest be seen
  The flower she loves of emerald green."

Rokeby, canto v.

CHAPTER XXII.

EDINBURGH, 1st *July* (1825).

I HAD the great pleasure of your letter of date 27th, and believe me, I am *at least* as much delighted with your being a real *bona fide* Captain as if I had been made a Captain myself. With respect to money matters, I have the pleasure to tell you the advance has been rendered quite easy to me by the favour of my bold and very gullible friend, the Public, who through their Prime Minister, Mr. Constable, have been far more liberal than I had any title to expect. Your income will be advanced without any interest being paid on your part during my life for the advance of £1500; and it will depend upon circumstances whether you are ever called upon, after the event which must necessarily take place within a certain period, even to replace any part of the principal sum.

We will talk of this at meeting, but you will be pleased to know in general that I have been able to make arrangements which render the advance no earthly inconvenience. While I see you the affectionate, considerate, and steady fellow you have always been, what have I to do with money, that can be more agreeable to me than to assist your reasonable views ? A little hospitality at Abbotsford and my country improvements are my sole expenses.

Major Lane was so good as to spare me any anxiety about the delay of gazetting, for in an answer to a letter of mine saying that all was right, he was so attentive as to add that the promotion was to go in the regiment as he had learned at Horse Guards. . . .

I will have the greatest pleasure in dining with the mess of the regiment, and certainly design for Wicklow and Killarney. These, with Edgeworthstown, comprise my sole plans, and with what time I hope to pass at No. 10 Stephen's Green fill up my hopes of pleasure from the expedition. . . .

I have got a barouchette for the expedition, shabby enough, which is of little consequence, so it be but sound and convenient, as it seems to be.

Twenty loves to sweet Mrs. Anne Page. Do not let her plague herself about her household concerns on our account.—Yours affectionately,

WALTER SCOTT.

TO MRS. HUGHES.

EDINBURGH, *July 2d*, 1825.

MY DEAR MRS. HUGHES,—This will find you, I suppose, returned from your rambles either in Amen Corner or your more pleasant residence in Berks. It is high time I should thank you for a thousand instances of kindness both to Charles and myself. He is returned full of his obligations to you for your maternal attentions; and I sincerely believe and hope they are not thrown away. He is a good deal grown and greatly improved; he is at present in great embarrassment, and indeed it is "*l'embarras des richesses*," for he has more than one tour of pleasure offered to him: he may go to the Highlands and shoot red deer with Glengarry; or he may go to the seaside with Lady Scott and Sophia and little Johnie, and study the geography of the field of Largs; or lastly, he may go, if he likes it, with Lockhart, Anne, and me to Ireland, where I intend to be Walter's guest for a fortnight, and see Killarney and the scenery of Wicklow. He is a real *Captain* now—no travelling name—and it must be a fine thing to be one, judging from the pleasure it seems to give.

The anecdotes from Mr. Bowdler's note-book are extremely curious.[1] The letters between Grafton and Monmouth have been published, but I never saw so curious and detailed an account of the villainy of Sunderland in cutting off the interest of the unfortunate Monmouth with the King. You will observe that Sir J. Dalrymple alludes to it in a note in his *Annals*, but in a manner which expresses doubt of the authenticity of the transaction. Mr. Bowdler's narrative removes such doubt. Indeed it consists well with the more plausible account of what Monmouth meant when he offered to purchase a pardon by revealing a secret of the highest importance. This was no doubt the correspondence between Sunderland and the Prince of Orange, and perhaps some instigation of his own enterprise from the same perfidious quarter. It was a great shame to King William to take into his confidence that shameless traitor; the other anecdote is also very curious. I cannot help thinking that Cromwell was right. His power was almost too great to keep, yet it was still more perilous to resign it. A man may stand safer on the most giddy precipice than he can descend from it,—such are the laws to which ambition subjects its votaries.

I am pleased with the spirit of the Welch in asserting the superiority of their great Chieftain to the high Northumbrian Duke, his relation; but it has been an old use, if our Shakespeare may be credited, of the Percy to treat the Cymric as upon an unequal footing, and our Northern Britons may be pretty sure that the two brothers were

---

[1] "An account which Mr. Bowdler received from the mouth of Colonel Scott, who had been in the service of James II. It proved that Lord Sunderland had suppressed a letter sent to James by the Duke of Monmouth the day before his execution.' —Note to transcript. See Dalrymple's *Memoirs of Great Britain*, part I. bk. 2, pp. 65-67.

on better terms than Hotspur and Glendower.[1] Pray tell your son I am much gratified by the views of Provence: No. 5 safely received and as beautiful as the former. It is really a charming quality to be thus able to steal a country's beauties for the amusement of another. As for your Devil's Bridges, and your Menai Pass, and all such *pontifical* matters, I have long done with riding over seven-inch bridges upon a trotting horse, like Mad Tom, although I once thought there were few, not slaters or sailors by profession, who could have boasted more steadiness of brain when such feats were in question.

I am just setting off for Abbotsford, to return on Wednesday, which would be a feeling much like that of pulling out a tooth, only that I am going to see my young folks in Ireland. I do not intend to stay above a month in the green Isle; but I must see my friends at Edgeworthstown, and I must see Wicklow, and if possible Killarney. I am not so fond of seeing sights as formerly, yet one has heard so much of this scenery that it would be sin and shame to omit seeing them, being so near. . . . But I must bid you good-bye, with kindest wishes to the excellent Doctor: I hope his health continues well. My kindest remembrances to your son. Our matters seem to be settling propitiously for our various purposes of locomotion.—Believe me ever, my dear Mrs. Hughes, your honoured and affectionate friend,   WALTER SCOTT.

TO MISS EDGEWORTH.

ABBOTSFORD, *3rd July* 1825.

MY DEAR MISS EDGEWORTH,—My objects in Ireland besides Dublin and Edgeworthstown are Wicklow and

---

[1] At the coronation of the King of France, which took place in May 1814, Sir W. Watkin Wynn accompanied his brother-in-law the Duke of Northumberland, who was ambassador extraordinary. The Welsh thought their prince had the best right to be ambassador himself, and an old Welsh lady said she did not think it decent for Sir Watkin to go in the tail of any man.

Killarney. How to attain them I cannot fix till I am in Ireland, not knowing distances and routes or being certain of your motions.

Walter is just gazetted Captain, and breaks off a letter to me on the occasion of seeing his promotion in the papers, to say he must hasten down to the Barracks to remonstrate against mounting a subaltern's guard.

This rapid assumption of his new privilege puts me in mind of the officer mentioned by Swift who used to rail against the assumption and the oppression practised by the commanding officers of regiments, but being asked what he thought of it when he was himself promoted, confessed that he felt the *spirit of Colonelcy coming fast upon him.*

Walter's prospects of getting leave to go to be our guide at Killarney must be a check on our engagements. He writes me he has been securing what little privileges he can claim in that way by giving close attendance; but if you will write me a note to St. Stephen's Green, No. 10, Dublin, where I expect to be on the 14th current, it will enable me to regulate my motions. I wish much to see my cousin, Peggie Dallas, by marriage Lady Foulis, but on applying to her brother I could only learn she had given up her residence in Dublin, and was with some friend—he knew not whom—at a town called Kells, which I see is in the County of Kilkenny. I must see her, if I can, to talk over auld lang syne, about which she can say more to me than most. My best respects attend Harriet and your brother, and all the less known, but not less respected members of your kind family. I hope to greet them all soon in green Erin, though for the matter of that, Abbotsford is just now as green as George-a-green's jacket.   WALTER SCOTT.

TO JOHN RICHARDSON.

Monday, 4th July, ABBOTSFORD.

AGREEABLY to my last, I went up to Newhall this day, excellent road, and not five miles from this place. In point of annual return it cannot fairly be estimated according to current terms lower than from £150 to £160 supposing it out of lease, and is very improvable. To pay £5000, or even five thousand guineas, for this annual return is not amiss in the present age, and you will not buy land at a much cheaper rate in Scotland. I think 5000 guineas will be accepted in lieu of £5500 asked. As to its capabilities, they are much greater than you would apprehend from the present condition of the subject, unplanted and unimproved, and disfigured by large cross dykes of stone, which cut through height and hollow in every direction save the right one. But it comprehends a beautiful and varied outline of hill and holm, along a charming stream varied by a number of banks and acclivities, where Nature cries to a purchaser "*Come, plant me,*" as loudly as Sancho's dish of cow-heel cried "*Come, eat me.*" It is enclosed with large swelling hills on all sides, and looks a little world of itself,—as sequestered a spot as can be found, and yet a quarter of an hour's ride places you in a London or Edinburgh mail, and bating distance you may carry on your business as well as at Hampstead, so regular is the intercourse with London. The present lease endures for three years after the present season, but I have little doubt that £100 would purchase it up, or that a moderate sacrifice would command any pieces of ground you might wish to plant in the meantime. There is a park belonging to Torwoodlee of about thirty acres. The obtaining this or a few acres of it might be a considerable advantage. I daresay this could be managed, but it is not indispensable. There is another bank of no value, belonging to

Pringle of Whytbank, which should be planted to close
in the gaze of the long vale, but indemnity could be given
to Whytbank off the moor-ground at another place, or
I have little doubt that to oblige a good neighbour he
would plant the ground himself. If you make this purchase, you must consider yourself as buying a bare doll,
the dressing of which, your children will tell you, is the
best part of the fun; but I can safely assure you the
expense and trouble will not be thrown away, since, were,
Newhall properly fitted up for a shooting or fishing lodge,
it would have a very ready currency either for lease or
sale, if you tired of it. I will own I may be a little sanguine about my scheme, but I have the counsel and
backing of an admirable judge, George Craig, writer,
Galashiels, for whose judgment, sagacity, and even for
whose taste, I have much respect. I took him with me,
as knowing the country and the place well, and he
anxiously recommends the purchase as safe and reasonable. For myself, I am afraid of saying too much, for
I am conscious that the first view of the premises will
disappoint Mrs. Richardson, or perhaps even yourself.
But *Time* and *I* against any two, saith Don Diego. Let
my planting but rise a little, and if you can show me a
sweeter thing between Leader Haughs and Yarrow I will
eat the farm-house (which is a decent cottage in a sweet
enough situation), and pick my teeth with one of the stout
ash trees which go round it. I own also I may have
some selfish motives from the pleasurable hope of more
frequent meeting. But yet I say it again, that laying
romantic scenery of forest, rock, and cascade out of the
question, I think you will find fewer spots more capable
of being rendered exactly what you wish at a moderate
expense, which expense will add proportionably to the
value of the place. Being all large proprietors around
you, you can be envied by no one. I have told Nairne

you will write him your mind, and the post is going off. If you offer 5000 guineas I think you are pretty sure. If you are off, tell him so. "And for my love, I pray you, scorn me not."—Yours in haste,   WALTER SCOTT.

TO MISS EDGEWORTH.

ABBOTSFORD, 5th July 1825.

MY DEAR MISS EDGEWORTH,—I like to be as precise as possible in my appointments, having incurred much disgrace for neglecting them in my youth; and all the world knows that a prudent old age, with no passions to disturb its tranquillity, makes an easy amends at least, if not an ample one, for the erratic courses of a wayward youth. My friend Hartstonge may, like wisdom, uplift his voice in the streets of Dublin; but there is not the least purpose on my part to enter into any society. Then, I must dine with my son's Mess, I suppose, one day, and with said Hartstonge another, if he asks me; but as I do not intend to be above a week at Dublin in all, the remaining days will be few enough to spend with my son and daughter in a quiet way. My purpose is certainly for Killarney, and I am happy to learn from your letter that I can make my route by Edgeworthstown. I wish to heaven you would make some arrangements to go to Killarney with us. Walter and his *Cara Sposa* will also make it out. Indeed, I have long tired of seeing fine places alone; and though I could dispense with the company of Lady Jocunda,[1] I find my excursions go on much better now-a-days with good company by way of sauce: once I loved my beef-steak best without pickles, and my romantic scenery was most enjoyed in solitary blessedness. Not hearing from you about the dog, I was afraid he might be rather a troublesome present, and gave him away to Chantrey the

---

[1] Lady Jocunda Lawler—a high-bred romp; one of the characters in Miss Edgeworth's *Ennui*.

sculptor, who fell in high fancy with him. But I will keep as fine a puppy for you next spring—that is, if you really wish to have one, for I never bring up more than one or two puppies for fear of weakening the dam. In fact, that designed for Edgeworthstown was put out to nurse; but I will keep a fine puppy for you next spring.

To speak of a puppy of a different litter, I know well that Walter is deeply impressed with that sort of *mauvaise honte* which makes people uncivil, when they are only bashful and awkward. He has a holy dread of anything which he considers as highly gifted with talent, and has not yet learned the simple fact that clever folks are in reality the least to be found in the shape of criticals.

I fancy you have Jane's answer, for the last time I heard from her she was sitting down with much apprehension, and I daresay after a most careful mending of pens and folding of paper, to write a side to Miss Maria Edgeworth. You are not aware of the terrors of your own reputation; but you are an old acquaintance of Jane's, for I found almost all your works in her little boudoir at Lochore, reasonably well thumbed. Walter's regimental leave of absence is difficult to be obtained, and keeps him short by the halter; and until I learn how that stands, I can form no definitive plan. He has hopes, but no certainty, of getting with us to Killarney; but field-days and reviews are things which interfere much with the plans of young officers. This is the reason that there is such rapid promotion in these light corps, considering the times. A young man of fortune enters, smitten with the delight of ploughing the earth with a sabre and sweeping heaven with a plume, and in a few months he finds himself *gêné* by the severity of the discipline: exit Dandy, and there is a step in the regiment.

I have little to add, except kindest love to Mrs. Edgeworth, Harriet, and all friends, known and unknown.

We must manage to see Mr. W. Edgeworth. I regret to say our limited stay gives us no hope of seeing my charming young friend, Mrs. Fox Lane, or making her husband's acquaintance.

Lady Scott begs kind love.—Always yours, with equal respect and sincerity,   WALTER SCOTT.

TO LADY LOUISA STUART.

EDINR., 7th July 1825.

. . . I PROPOSE going for Ireland on the 12th to spend a week or two with my young folks at Dublin, and take a peep at Killarney, if time and circumstance will admit. My youngest daughter Anne and John Lockhart go with me—the latter to save me all the plagues incident to travelling, by acting as what gentlemen call *Boots*. Sophia stays to take care of her little delicate baby, and of Lady Scott. Charles, whom by the way I must one day introduce to your Ladyship's notice, proposes making a tour in the Highlands during our absence, so we are a family unusually dispersed. Charles is very different from Walter—has a turn for literature, as the other has for the exact sciences which apply to the art of war; and, although a modest boy, he is not indisposed to profit by those advantages which my connection with literature may afford him. Walter, on the contrary, conscious that the gods have not made him poetical, is much distressed by the attentions which he sometimes meets with under the impression that the Lion's whelp is to be honoured after the Lion himself; and he wants the experience of such an often-hunted and experienced Lion as myself to get gracefully and composedly out of the toils. This has been a besetting grievance with the young soldier ever since he fought deadly battle at the High School with the boys who called him "The Lady of the Lake," and I scarce think he has yet learned to reconcile himself to the reflected dignity of his literary descent; although he should praise the bridge, in old phrase, that has carried him over, for I do not know by what other roads I was to seek out for him a lairdship and a troop of horse. I have my own internal qualms about Dublin, where I am told the Lion Hunters are already preparing stake and net. However, as Marshal Macdonald will be there at the same time, it will be hard if I cannot skulk unheeded. . . . I am however famed for bearing my faculties meekly, and this is only a private groan of apprehension in a friendly ear,

> "For if I should *as Lion* come in strife
> Into such place, 'twere pity of my life."

So says Snug, the best and discreetest of Lions.

I am heartily glad that you think well of the volumes I had sent your Ladyship.[1] I say heartily glad, because I had sinkings of the heart about them both while writing and when they were finished. I never read them a second time till printed, and it does strike me there was a flatness and a labour about some passages which savoured of the Bishop of Grenada's apoplexy. But if *you* did not discover them, I would fain hope they are not so discernible as I had feared, since although I have the vanity now as a friend of long standing to claim some portion of your partiality, I am not afraid that it would baffle your penetration or disarm your sincerity.

If I find any news from Ireland worth sending, I will volunteer it; but I am not now, as I was forty years since, convinced that in changing countries I shall find much that is new. I neither expect to kill myself with laughing at Pat's jests and blunders, nor to be beat on the head with Pat's shillelah, nor to jump out of the boat and drown

---

[1] *The Tales of the Crusaders. Talisman* and *The Betrothed* were published in June.

myself with sheer delight, as my road-book says folks are apt to do, at the Lake of Killarney.

I will put this sheet of nonsense, as Win Jenkins says, under Lord Montagu's own *kiver*. I am delighted to hear the Miss Morritts are well, both for the young ladies' sakes and their uncle's, who has been drawn, I think, to hang up his happiness on frail supports.—Ever, dear Lady Louisa, believe me, your truly obliged, honoured, and grateful,   WALTER SCOTT.

FROM MR. LOCKHART TO HIS WIFE.

TUESDAY, 12th July.—3 P.M. left Greenock. The *Swift* is a large and well-arranged steamboat, 5 or 6 times bigger than that you were in from Glasgow. The Captain, a sturdy old seaman, ex-master of some *sailing* authority, I don't know what, in the King's Navy. His life must be horrid. He had, he said, made 36 such voyages day after day, never being above 4 or 5 hours either at Glasgow or Belfast, except on Sundays, when unfortunately the time of repose meets him at Belfast, where he is *not* at home. Think of being entirely out of bed, and almost entirely I think without sleep, six nights out of seven. Yet he seemed gay and glorious enough, in his white waistcoat, etc., which he retained until after dinner. He said he had been sixty years at sea. Take forty as the fact. The dinner good, very good for the place and price, 2s. a head. Sir W. of course extremely kind to all the damsels, etc., which gave huge delight. Old Bailie —— announced himself seventy-five years old—said grace and talked wisely about the herring fisheries and the police of Glasgow. The hooknosed daughter and the Lady Anne got very intimate *apparemment*—a regular *tea-pot* as Davidson and John Hugh have it. A shocking night. John alone was snug in the carriage, which I did all I

could to make Anne occupy, but she dreaded the *rags*,
mountains of which were piled about that part of the deck.
Her Ladyship did not suppose the steam coming across
them would at all resemble the sweet South, and the bed
of violets (my love to Violet *en passant*). The whole night
through it rained, and I was afraid Anne might seriously
suffer. But she behaved wonderfully, both heart and
stomach, and appeared then as afterwards neither sick nor
sorry, but only sleepy. We were very uncomfortable, but
the poor soldiers' wives and children presented a sight of
real and picturesque misery when day broke. We got
into Belfast about nine—Donegall Arms: excellent breakfast, and most luxurious toilet. Paid four guineas for the
Carriage's passage (besides *rails*), only a guinea a-piece for
ourselves. Warned by a Mr. Hutcheson (apparently a
squireen) not to travel on the Drogheda road after 7 P.M.
on account of robbers. It is not easy for us to believe
in this, but it is as well to act as if we did, until we have
means of judging. This Mr. H. gave grand slang to the
Porters, etc., who crowded the vessel on our anchoring,—
"Your fingers are all thumbs, I see,"—"Put that (portmanteau) in your mouth, you gumpus," etc. etc.

The Duke of Hamilton seems to have a great castle
with fine woods at Brodick in Arran. Lamlash *ibidem* is a
capital bay and harbour. Belfast a thriving, bustling place,
surrounded with gentlemen's houses, and trees, and built
very like a second-rate English town, yet here we saw the
use of the imported rags forthwith. One man, apparently
happy and gay, returning to his work (a mason I thought)
from breakfast, with pipe in mouth, had a coat of which I
do not believe any three inches together were of the same
colour, yea, or stuff, red, black, yellow, cloth, velveteen,
corduroy—the complete image of a tattered coverlid, originally made, on purpose, of particularly small patches; no
shirt, and almost no breeches; yet this is the best part of

Ireland, and the best population. What shall we see in the South? The Unknown says he wonders none of the Antiquarians refer the tartan of the Highlands to an imitation of the tatters of the Parent race of Erin.

Erin deserves undoubtedly the style of Green Erin. We passed through high and low country, rich and poor, but none that was not greener than Scotland ever saw. The husbandry to the North seemed rather *careless* than bad—I should say *slovenly*, for everything is cultivated and the crops are fine, though the appearance is quite spoiled by the *bad*, or oftener the *no*, fences, and above all, to unaccustomed eyes, by the human wretchedness everywhere visible even there. Your Papa says, however, that he sees all over the North marks of an *improving* country,—that the new houses are better than the old, etc. I believe he is right as to the towns and even villages; but I cannot imagine the huts—the newest huts of the peasantry—to have been preceded by worse, even in the days of Malachi and the collar of gold. They are of *clay*, without chimney, and very often without any opening for light, except the door, and the smoke-hole is in the roof. When there is a window, it seldom has even one pane of glass; and I take it the opening is only a summer luxury, to be closed up with the ready trowel whenever the winter comes. The filth, darkness, and squalor of these dens and their inhabitants are beyond imagination, even after travelling the wildest of our highland glens; yet wonderful to say, I have not observed one face decidedly careworn and unhappy; on the contrary, an universal good-humour and merriment, and to us every sort of civility, from the poor people. As yet, few beggars. An old man at Dunleer having got some pence from Anne while the carriage stopt, an older woman came forward to sell gooseberries, and, we declining these, she added that we might give her an alms too then, for she was an old *struggler*. Anne thought she said smuggler, and dreamt of potheen, but she meant that she had done her best to resist the waves of Evil, "the sea of trouble," whereas her neighbour, the professed mendicant, had yielded to the stream too easily. We shall recollect the word. We slept at Dundalk, a poor little town by the shore, with a magnificent Justice-hall and Jail in the midst, a public building superior I think to any in Edinburgh, in the midst of a place despicably dirty and miserable. We saw, in passing, Newry—a lively manufacturing place, and on this side of Dundalk; break-fasted at Drogheda, which is on the Boyne, and two miles below King William's ground. This coast has been fought over every inch by Danes and Irish, by Normans and Irish, then by Royalist and Republican, and lastly by Jacobite and Orangeman. We saw several of the famous round towers, the age or even purpose of which nobody has settled to the satisfaction of mankind, tho' if I had baby kind here I could make grand use of them. We reached Dublin yesterday (Thursday) at four, and found Walter established in a very large and stately house in Stephen's Green, which is an immense square of a quarter of a mile each side, irregularly,—and what's worse,—unimposingly built of brick, but containing very fine houses, of which his is one. I have a bed at a neighbouring hotel, where I now write (I mean in bed). Walter and Jane are very well, the latter quite easy, full of conversation, and doing the honours remarkably well. They gave us a good round of beef, and Scotch broth for dinner, and some capital cham-pagne, Mozelle, etc., all which affairs the Captain gets for a mere song from the Mess cellars. They don't pay above half the usual duties you know, so we may punish his claret without much remorse. When we called for a little whiskey at Dundalk, they fetched what looked like an in-judiciously decanted *bottle* of Sauterne, but here they have not a single gill for love or money.

This appears to be a very magnificent city. The streets we came through are like the best of London five or six years ago, and contain a number of public buildings of the finest architecture I have seen anywhere in Britain. But I shall say no more until I have seen things at leisure. Meantime I think I have set you a good example : so write to me a full and particular narrative of the tour from Greenock, and description of the *terra incognita* of the Largs. My best respects to Lady S., and a kiss from me to Johnny.—Always, my dear Sophia, yours affly,

J. G. L.

DUBLIN : Friday morning : 15*th July* [1825].

P.S.—I forgot to say that *literally* we had not sat down in Walter's house ere Mr. H. arrived with a 4to book of Transactions of the Royal Society, and (I think) an invitation to the Unknown to a public dinner of that body, which, whatever it was, he declined.

Friday, 15*th.*—This morning met Sir Humphry Davy, in the highest glee, and a spick and span new *white* waistcoat, on his way to Connemara, etc., to fish. Broad brim white Beaver, lined green as of yore. He told a story of an Irish steward of a steamboat from Holyhead, who was endeavouring to be very polite to a distressed lady passenger. He said the best thing was whiskey. The lady said she had an idea that whiskey *could* not agree with her stomach. "And is that against it ?" quoth Paddy, "won't your ladyship have all the pleasure of tasting it over again in its way up ?" Sir H. was bitter against the Royal Society of Literature,[1] as also the London University. He mentioned a plan Peel is said to approve, viz. : —a college in or near London where *all* the Catholic Priests, etc., for Britain and Ireland are to be educated.

[1] See Sir Walter's letter to Hon. Mr. Villiers, April 1821, in Appendix No. II. p. 399.

Sir H. much doubts whether this plan will be carried into effect, but is of opinion it is a wise one. He told *once more* the story of the late Pope asking him in 1814 if he thought there was anything in his (the P.'s) power to do for the good of the Government of England in testimony of his gratitude. Sir H. wrote Mr. W. Hamilton to tell Castlereagh now was the time if they wished to get the Pope to give the King the nomination of the Catholic Bishops of Ireland; but they were busy, and nothing done. Probably "Sromredevi"[1] overrated the value of his holiness's pretty words; but it may be otherwise. "H." carried off the Unknown all the morning. I went and saw Walter's Regiment, with the 3d D. Guards, and some Artillery in "the 15 acres." The Phœnix Park very noble. Admired again the outside of the Bank, Post Office, Custom House, etc. I have never seen so imposing a group of modern edifices. Dublin has even at this season a decidedly metropolitan air, which I never saw about Edinburgh, except when the King was there in 1822. I take it the Irish gentry who do live in Ireland are mostly resident here, or at most in villas about Wicklow. Many carriages *approach* to the style of London, as do also the horses, even of inferior equipages. Lackeys, etc., pretty much as with ourselves. Merrion Square, etc. etc. *Porte-cochères* to the chief houses.

Dined again *en famille* with the Captain and his Lady. They expected in the evening a number of people, and among the rest Sir H. Davy: but nobody came, except the joint occupants of the house, Captain and Mrs. Macalpine, owing to illness, pre-engagements, etc.,—"He a hero famed for arms, she a matron of peerless charms,"—the beauty of the 15th. The Captain played tolerably on the violoncello, and sang a verse or two of their regimental song, the composition of a private Trooper of the Peninsular period.

[1] Sir H. Davy.

It seemed good, indeed superb (for the Captain)—witness the chorus:—

> " Then fill a bumper and let us sing
>   Long life to the fifteenth, and God save the King
>   For the battle of Sagune."

I almost suspect the Captain of having been the author.

Saturday.—Hartstonge ready at breakfast in the same brown surtout he wore when in Scotland. We went to St. Patrick's. The Cathedral has a very *old* appearance, extremely rudely worked, outside coarse and almost shapeless, inside however imposing, and in parts even grand. The choir is fitted up both as the Cathedral Church, and as the Chapel of the Knights of St. Patrick, the Dean's seat being also the King's, and fifty of the rest. One or two old monuments of the Cork family, etc., but in fact one can think of nothing but Swift there. The whole Cathedral is merely his tomb. The famous inscription is in gilt letters on black, and over it—far too highly placed— is what seems to be a bust by Roubilliac,—so far as I could judge a very capital bust. This was presented by Faulkner (his printer I suppose; Hartstonge knew not). Swift had a prodigious double chin according to this, and the severity of the whole countenance is much increased by the absence of the wig, which in the prints conceals much of the brow and temples, and the firm way in which the head joins the shoulders behind. The Epitaph on Stella is on the next pillar: Sir W. seemed not to have thought of the matter before (or to have forgotten if he had), but to judge merely from the style that Swift himself wrote it. She is described as " Mrs. Hester Johnson, better known to the world by the name of Stella, under which she is celebrated in the writings of Dr. Jonathan Swift, Dean of this Cathedral." This, said Sir W., the Dean himself might say; any one else would have said more. She died in 1727,

Swift in 1745. His monument appears to have been recently regilt, etc. Just by the entrance to the transept is
Swift's tablet in honour of his servant, who behaved so well
about the secret of the Drapier's letters. We then saw the
St. Sepulchre's Library—a monastic-looking place, very
like one of the smaller College libraries in Oxford. Here
they have the folio Clarendon, with Swift's marginal
remarks, ☞'s, etc., mostly in pencil, but still quite legible.
Very savage as usual upon the poor Scots everywhere.
We then went into the Deanery (the one Swift inhabited
has been pulled down), and saw the picture of him, which
it is satisfactory to have seen. The print in Sir W.'s
edition is very good, but the *complexion* is, in the picture,
black, robust, sanguine, a heavy-lidded, stern, dark-blue eye.
The figure is not very intelligible, except the long square-
pointed shoes with gold buckles. An idiot who showed
the place entertained us with reading some complimentary
speeches of the *present* Dean to his Clergy, written out in
very small hand.

We then saw the Bank,—late Parliament House, all as
per road-book. Then the Dublin Society's Museum, where
the Unknown was sadly mobbed. Charles Griscoke, in a
little ribbon, showed the things, which are not worth seeing, except a perfect skeleton of the gigantic Moose-deer,
the horns fourteen feet wide from tip to tip, and high in
proportion. At all these places a terrible rushing to see
the Bart., but the theatre in the evening completed the
scene. I *never* heard such roaring. The players might
as well have had no tongues. Miss Foote twice left the
stage, and at last Abbott the manager came forward, cunning dog, and asked what was the cause of the uproar. A
thousand voices roared Sir W. Scott, and the worthy
Lion being thus bearded, rose, after an hour's torture, and
said with a kindness and grace of tone and manner *these
words* :—" I am sure the Irish people (a roar), I am sure

this respectable audience will not suppose that a stranger can be insensible to the kindness of their reception of him, and if I have been too long in saying this, I trust it will be attributed to the right cause—my unwillingness to take upon me honours so distinguished, and which I could not, and cannot but feel to be unmerited." I think these are the very words. The noise continued, but he would take no hints about going to the stage box, and the evening closed pretty quietly. Horribly hot. A nice woman there, a Mrs. Ede, and several officers of the 15th, Captain Studd and Mr. Rose, very pleasant young men.

Mr. Plunkett called in the morning on Sir W.: I was present. He is a very pale and gentlemanlike old lawyer, said Swift did little good to Ireland, but by *accident*, and invited us all to his seat near Wicklow this day week. Bought Irish Ballads, prints, etc.

The University of Dublin have made Sir Walter LL.D.

P.S. Sunday Morning.—Plunkett said how much better men and greater statesmen would Fox and Pitt have been, had the one spent half his time in power, the other half of his in opposition.

Abbott and Foote were a very vulgar and romping Benedick and Beatrice. The theatre here is very handsome, the scenery, dresses, etc., capital, the players as bad as can be. My best respects.—Yours always.

J. G. L.

Kiss my man for me.

FROM MR. LOCKHART TO HIS WIFE.

Sunday, 17*th July.*—Breakfasted at my hotel. Walked with Walter to see his barracks and stables, and smoked a segar with some ediles under the tent among the officers, all of whom seemed particularly agreeable and

gentlemanlike, especially Lyndesay, son of the late
Bishop of Kildare, and the Major (Philips). The rooms
and style of life and manners all put me strongly in
mind of Oxford. *E.g.*, they seemed to have everything
but tooth-brushes in common, and almost none of them
had a penny in hand. The Captain and I joined the
ladies and Sir W. at St. Patrick's, where there was a
great crowd of well-dressed people to see the Bart., and
infinite politeness from the Dean and his Lady. The
Dean showed us the cast of Swift's face taken after death,
which they have ever since kept in the Chapter-house.
He does not seem to have been reduced in flesh when he
died: a large broad massive face, solemn but not stern.
The music here was exquisite, both the boys of the choir
and the singers of the Anthem, among the latter of which
Terry M'Grath holds but a subordinate place. Terry, however, seems well shaved and in high heart. We dined at
Walter's, and in the evening drove to Donnybrook—the
scene of the famous fair which is now, I believe, dissolved
and abolished,—a charming ride, thick with villas and
all the insignia of ease and opulence—in fact not to be
distinguished from the environs of London, but by the
beautiful hills on the right, and the innumerable hosts of
jaunting cars ploughing the fine road in every direction, at
a speed apparently most cruel—one poor horse often
cantering with a whole family of nine or ten at his heels.
We came home by the Black Rocks, where the same confusion covered the whole of the coast. The tide coming
in *blue* upon the *yellow* bay; never was a more glorious
sunset. This is the great resort of the citizens, especially
on Sundays. Countless taverns, and pipe and pot in full
play on every green place, and under every green tree.
Sunday not over discernible in Dublin. At the Cathedral
nobody seemed to think of the service—scarcely a prayer-
book open—nor did I hear a single response but from the

officials. Dr. M'Crie would die if he could see the streets full of fruit, fish, fiddles, etc., etc.

Monday, 18.—Young Maturin breakfasted at Walter's, a fine lad apparently, quick and easy, and very Irishly gentlemanlike. I observe the Protestants here have what we would call a Presbyterian aversion to the *saintly* titles of the Catholic Church. He called St. Patrick's, Patrick's —and St. Stephen's Green has been Orangeised into Stephen's. We then went to the Bank, where we were almost stewed alive, seeing the beautiful machinery by which the paper is prepared, wet, cut, etc., printed, numbered, etc., —in fact all but signed. This steamwork is managed so neatly, that the whole might go on in a drawing-room and not a spot come of it. The Governor and Directors were there, and as Sir W. himself was forced to say, treated him as if he had been a Prince of the blood. I do believe that just at the time the Duke of York *might* be treated as well: he could not be better. We then went to the College. The Provost, Dr. Kyle, received S. W. in a splendid drawing-room, and then carried him to the library, which is a very large and handsome place—a considerable crowd of eager students, intelligent-looking but sorrily drest for the most part. I never before saw the Academic costume in tatters, and with accompaniments of foul linen. In the MS. room saw Dr. Brinkley, a very pleasing man, the great astronomer, and Dr. Macdonnell, Maginn's friend, the Greek Professor, and a very agreeable person, etc., etc. A superb *déjeuné* in the Provostry. Review in the Phœnix Park, 15th Hussars, 3d Dragoon Guards, a regiment of Foot Guards very fine, the 28th and the 42d in grand order. Saw Rev. Mr. Turner and his wife at O'diennes, whence Marshal Macdonald had just gone. Dined with Col. Blacker, Under Treasurer of Ireland, grand affair but rather dull: saw there Col. Sutherland, the Ashantee conqueror, a fine-looking young man, I think brother to Mrs. B.

S. W. told the story of Lord Abercorn's answer to Johnson's
sneer about oats, " Well, where are there better horses or
better men ? "—in return for which Col. Blacker gave not
a bad one of a French officer who was abusing the English
uniform as tasteless, and concluded with taking out his
pencil and caricaturing one of our people in full fig. A
British officer present made no answer, but merely shuffled
the picture to him, and drew a Waterloo medal on the
breast of the figure.

Sir Stewart Bruce with his grand snuff-box; Sir
Colin Campbell; the Master of the Rolls, Sir W. Mac-
mahon, a tall spare figure; all great Orange people, with
" Old glorious " and his spouse, as large as life upon the
wall.

Tuesday, 19th.—Returned the Archbishop of Dublin's
visit, but were unfortunate enough to miss him again:
walked with Dr. Macdonnell; drove to Phœnix Park, to
see the Lodge and gardens of the Viceroy, where Sir C.
Campbell did all the honours; a pretty place, but nothing
royal. The Marquess Wellesley at Malahide at present.
Sir W. is now well known, and cannot go along the
streets without tokens of respect. The shopkeepers and
their wives bow and curtsey as he passes. It has much
elevated the Irish in my opinion to see them so capable
of *honouring* (which implies *understanding*) the merits
of a non-military greatness. Ridiculous paragraphs about
the Bart. in the Dublin papers. Every word almost
false. Anne is so unfortunate that one half the people
call her " Mrs. Lockhart," and the other " Lady Scott."
This is too bad, for the young lady's eye may shoot
less effectual beams; but we do what we can to proclaim
the fact.

Dined in great form at Mr. Hartstonge's. Brinkley,
Kyle, etc., a blow of ladies in the evening, but unfortunately, no Lady Morgan. A house full of knick-

knackery, a little painted glass-window, a back-green
ornée, etc. etc.

Wednesday.—College again. Library and two halls
very handsome. Chapel handsome too. I desiderate
the air of antiquity. We then saw old Major Sirr, illus-
trious for the capture of Ld. E. Fitzgerald,—a very noble
old head,—and a house full of curiosities; a few fine
pictures, many queer old Irish arms and ornaments.
Then to the Master of the Horse (Col. Gore) and the
Castle Chapel—the best by far of all modern Gothics.

I am very sorry to find by your letter just received
that you have been bothered in plans and otherwise.
Abundant as diversion is, I wish from my heart I saw
our noses turned homewards.

I trust nothing prevents you from receiving this in
comfort at Abbotsford, for I hate to think of any more
tossing about and discomforts. Kiss my dear little boy
for me, and give my best compliments to Lady S.—Yours
affectionately, my dear Sophia,   J. G. L.

DUBLIN, *Wednesday.*

ON Friday week, I hear, this moment, we are to be at
Killarney. Be assured I will do *mon possible* to cut the
travels short.

This is the *third* part of my *Gurnal.* The first was
addressed to you "at the Post Office, Largs, Ayrshire,"
the second at "Ardrossan Hotel, Ayrshire." I mention
this because I suspect from your saying you have got no
letters, that you have neglected to take order about having
them properly sent after you. If so, be so good as to lose
no time in rectifying the matter.   J. G. L.

TO SIR ADAM FERGUSON.

10 STEPHEN'S GREEN, *18th July* [1825].

MY DEAR ADAM,—Here we are in Pat-land, and almost
killed with kindness. The emphatic personal pronoun *we*

comprehends on this occasion, Lockhart, Anne, and my own self. I write chiefly to tell you, what I am sure you and Lady Ferguson will be pleased to hear, that I find Walter and Jane living most respectably and moderately in a little circle of friends, of good fashion, by whom the young folks seem to be held in much regard. Jane's shyness is much worn off. She does the honours with a very modest matronly little air, and it is good fun to see her chaperon Lady Anne, who is more of a dasher than herself. They are very fond of each other, and *draw kindly*, as the coachman says in the play. They have got a great large house divided between them and a brother officer and his lady, and furnished out with a great deal of antiquated finery, all of which stands our young friends about £150 a year, cheap enough for the extensive accommodation. The Irish have been most flatteringly kind in their reception. I have been made LL.D. and a double S. by Trinity College, almost worried by crowds and acclamations. In short, I begin to think there is something about me which I never suspected before, and give Pat great merit for having discovered it.

Walter, Jane, Anne, and Lockhart beg a thousand kind remembrances. The two former are in hopes of seeing you here, where they can give you excellent quarters, and Jane's *cuisine* is by no means to be sneezed at. She is a very managing little person, and overhauls all her accounts with laudable accuracy. Walter's late promotion is subject of much congratulation here.—Always, with kindest love to your good Lady, most truly yours,

WALTER SCOTT.

Thermometer up at the heat of old Nebuchadnezzar's fiery furnace.

TO MISS EDGEWORTH.

10 ST. STEPHEN'S GREEN,
DUBLIN, *July 18th*, 1825.

MY DEAR FRIEND,—I did not trouble you with an immediate answer to your kind letter which I found lying here for me, because I should have forfeited my character as a man of business by sending you a very diplomatical and consequently unintelligible account of our motions. There are wheels within wheels, it seems, visits which must be paid, regimental *leave* which may not be obtained, in short, a sort of negotiation which I certainly could not have anticipated any more than the kindness of those who have chosen to make my motions of some consequence, or would persuade me at least that they are so. At last we have been able to fix our plans. We have dinner engagements in Dublin till Friday 22nd July. On that day we go down to Wicklow with a friend and patron of Walter's, Mr. Crampton, the Surgeon-General to the Army. Next day we are to see scenery in Wicklow, visit Mr. Attorney-General, in whom unexpectedly I find an old acquaintance, and return about Monday at farthest; and here begins my diplomatic deficient, for Sir John Campbell has intimated to me that the Lord-Lieutenant wishes to see me, and as a King's man back and edge, I must show proper respect to the representative of Majesty. I intimated however to my friend Sir Colin, that, saving the pleasure of his Grace, I wished to be at Edgeworthstown about Friday 29th. We would reach you "time enough to go to bed with a candle," or about 8 or 9 o'clock. I speak for security, for ladies are rarely early starters, and though I can make Anne and Jane be as exact to time as the guard of a mail-coach, yet Jane has a Scotch Mrs. Petitoe [1] who may manage the whole of us should she be of the party. The result therefore is that Lock-

---

[1] Lady Clonbrony's maid in Miss Edgeworth's *Absentee*.

hart, Anne, and I, with Jane for certain, and Walter by possibility, will descend on you, time and place above mentioned, unless you please to say, which I am sure you will do frankly, that we will overcrowd you. Anne is dancing with joy at the idea of Harriet going along with us, and as an old quarter-master of dragoons, I have taken it upon me to arrange our mode of travelling. We have for our own necessary transportation two low, light carriages, which defy injury, each capable of carrying four insides of the most respectable dimension, with two dickies one for a male and female domestic, and one for the gentlemen cavaliers when they chuse to smoke segars.

Now our whole party being five insides, exclusive of the two dickeyites, it follows that we have three seats to dispose of, and as Miss Harriet and you can only occupy one each, you will make the most delightful addition to the spirit of the party without adding anything of consequence to its weight. The inns I have seen here are all better than we have at home, and a cloak and a hay-loft are neither new nor unpleasant resources to either Walter or Lockhart or myself, and we will only want the same number of Knockecrogheries,[1] which would be indispensable for our own march. Having been here *three* days I am of course *au fait* of all the particulars affecting the state of the country, and prepared with a stock of infallible remedies for the grievances of Ireland, but I will reserve them for a personal triumph. Dublin is splendid beyond my utmost expectations. I can go round its walls and number its palaces until I am grilled almost into a fever. They tell me the city is desolate, of which I can see no appearance, but the deprivation caused by the retreat of the most noble and most opulent inhabitants must be felt in a manner a stranger cannot conceive. As Trinculo

---

[1] See *Ennui*, chap. vi. for Miss Edgeworth's description of the Irish hack horse.

says when the bottle was lost in the pool, "there is not only dishonour in it but an infinite loss."[1] It is a loss however which time will make good, if I may judge from what I have heard old people say of Edin[r] after 1707, which removed the crown from our Israel,—an event which, had I lived in that day, I would have resigned my life to have prevented, but which, being done before my day, I am sensible was a wise scheme. So says the advising ape whose tail was cut off 120 years since, to the ape whose tail has not had time to cicatrize since its abscission. Perhaps it is like the Priest to the Gascon upon the scaffold :—

> "Courage, friend, for to-night is your period of sorrow,
> And things will go better, believe me, to-morrow."

Walter and spouse tho' unknown, Lockhart and Anne, send all love and respects to the known and unknown of Edgeworthstown, particularly Mrs. Edgeworth and your brother. I have a hint from Sir Colin Campbell that Walter will be allowed his leave, but we must manage not to *commit* him by getting it in any way disagreeable to his commanding officer, as these gentlemen are apt to be punctilious.—Yours, my dearest Miss Edgeworth, with sincere pleasure at the hope of again meeting one for whom I have so much respect and regard,

WALTER SCOTT.

FROM MR. LOCKHART TO HIS WIFE.

Thursday, [21*st July*].—The newspaper says (and for once truly) that one of the College librarians fishingly told Sir Walter, "I have been so busy that I have not yet had time to read *your Redgauntlet*," to which replied the Bart., "I have not happened to meet with such a book." An absurd letter about —— being the author of

---

[1] *Tempest*, Act IV. sc. 1.

Waverley is also in the Irish paper, evidently with the same purpose. We dined yesterday with the mess of the 15th, and had a very sumptuous entertainment, not the least part being the introduction of half-a-dozen hussars, who were ranged after dinner by the sideboard, and sung the Sagoon ditty with a gravity and soldierlike coolness of attitude, etc., quite delightful: Col. Gore, Abbott, Sir Grenville Temple, Col. Clitheroe, Col. Aitcheson (brother to my acquaintance George) of the Guards, etc., etc. Lots of everything good. The windows crowded all the evening with pretty faces, which is improper on the part of the commanding officer. Came home early with Sir W. and Col. Gore—Walter at 2 o'clock, and *Jane says*, sober, but she is young. This morning went with Sir W. to the Oil Gas Co., where we had stink enough and a pretty collation from some very well-bred gentlemen, the directors. Of course they wanted a puff of their own concern. Drove to Lucan amidst dust indescribable, which allowed us no more than casual glimpses of a most beautiful country. Fine streams: banks clothed with magnificent trees: *some* rocks too.

Saw Milliken's copy of the Magna Charta embellished *à outrance* by one Whitaker of London—price 300 guineas! The purchaser is self-cognosced. We all dined at Mr. Blake's (Chief Remembrancer), a Catholic. Very good everything. B. a very pleasant man, and told sundry stories of the Rt. Honble. Denis Browne's hanging a tailor. etc., in the time of the French Invasion, of his *wishing* to hang Hubert, etc., etc., and of B.'s own adventure with a comical postillion near Ballymena. The Provost of Trinity frying lest we should believe these stories, and take them as fair samples of Irish manners—A. S. S.

Mr. Plunkett, very unaffectedly agreeable,—an old Hutchinson, "blood relation to my Lord Donoughmore," his brother in fact, amusing and conversible,—the first specimen I have seen of the real old Irish insolence in his way of speaking *to servants* and *of* common people. Qy.— What the pedigree? The name no great sound. Lord Meath, a handsome man in a fine star. This is the finest set-out altogether we have as yet encountered.

Friday, [22*nd*].—At noon set out for Wicklow by Rath-farnham, Lough Breagh, etc., along with Mr. Crampton (Surgeon-General), a very lively, clever, and agreeable man; in face, manner, and even I think in style of talk, strongly resembling Sir H. Davy. Magnificent view of Dublin and the bay as we ascended the hill. Savage desolation equal to anything in the Highlands, except the comparative lowness of the hills about Lough Breagh. Rowed there and saw Crampton's fishing cottage just begun. Down the valley to Powerscourt, a grand domain with very grand trees. The Dargle—superior even to its fame—an indiscriminately beautiful mixture of wood, water, rocks, hill, valley. One side Ld. Powerscourt's, the other Mr. Henry Grattan's part of the estate, purchased by the (Irish) Parlt. for £50,000 for his father. Dine and sleep at Mr. C.'s, Willford, near Bray, a neat, smallish house. Secy. Goulbourn and his wife (prettyish); he a poor rat, I take it. Sir Colin Campbell: a pleasant (nameless) M.D.; Mrs. Bushe (Chief-Justice's Lady), an agreeable woman; Mrs. and Miss C., pretty. Mem.—Crampton's Tony Lumpkin squire, who sat in the *centre* of the back room at a fifth-rate inn with a jug of porter and no newspaper, and being asked if he would not have a book, remarked it was *tadious* to be reading *always*. Burke said to Fox one day, " How charming this is, country air, a green tree, a bottle, a friend, and a book." Fox answered : " But why the book ? "

Saturday, [23*rd*].—Drove by Dunran to the Devil's Glyn, which is a glen with wooded crags and a stream brawling below, not unlike many in Scotland, though I think rather on a more extensive scale than any I can remember there.

Passed through the grounds of several gentlemen, and of course saw the exterior of many charming places. Kilruddery, Lord Meath's seat, a new Gothic chateau surrounded with very fine antique gardens, the scene of " the Irish hunt."[1]   Rosanna, the scene of Miss Edgeworth's tale, a singularly beautiful lane with oak-boughs reaching clear over it.   Luncheon at Newrath,[2] and dinner (late) at Old Connaught, near Bray, the house of the Attorney-General Plunkett.   He had in addition to his own large family the Blakes, who are now quite friends.   Plunkett, an excellent domestic character, surrounded with four unaffected lively girls (one married to a Revd. Sir Francis Blosse), and I know not how many sons and sons' sons. William is " Vicar of Bray."   Robert, a young doctor, likely to be in Edinburgh.   The champagne here in quality and quantity superior to all praise.

Sunday, [*24th*].—Went to church at Bray.   Bathed in the sea.   Smoked with Robert P. and Walter in the garden, and *dined*.   Missed, by my bath, a visit to Kilruddery, where Sir W. was much pleased with the gardens and the picture of the famous hunt.   Mr. Burroughs, Insolvent Judge, entertained us with the Dublin history of Baron Hoffman.   That scamp is still in D., but fallen into the lowest degradation.

Monday, [*25th*].—Off by ½ p. 6, with 2 carriages, the four Plunkett girls, and 2 young men being with us, as also their old groom, Brian (the *Cream-saver* so honoured by C. W. Wynne), went by Grattan's place and Powerscourt, etc., over the hill to Roundwood, where we breakfasted, and conversed with Judy, an original character, who says vir for *virtue*, consola for *consolation*, etc., etc., " tol lol," and much more slang, picked up, no doubt, from tourists —a queer hag.   We then proceeded to Glendalough, a wild valley with a small gloomy lake surrounded by black

---

[1] The Kilruddery Fox-hunt.   [2] Newrathbridge Inn.

desolate hills,—the scene not unlike St. Mary's, but *savage* in addition to *desert*. Here are the ruins more or less entire of *seven churches*, and 110 feet still remaining of one of the celebrated Round Towers. The *Cathedral* is roofless. In that called St. Kevin's Kitchen, Mass was daily performed within these eight months. Appearance of extreme antiquity farther back than any church I have seen in England—*far*. The 4 original windows, about the size of pigeon holes,—long before the days of glazing. A wall and remains of gateway round about these ruins, and traces certainly of a considerable town for those old times. Danes or Celts? Some sculpture of wolves, etc., that looked very northern. The Belfry tower, an obvious imitation of the great round one, and nearly, but not quite, united to the stone roof. That roof made of stones equally like the walls, set in edgeways, and resembling nothing so much as an overgrown cairn. I wish you had seen this, and am sure it would have pleased you more than half Ireland. It makes me wish to see Iona. The bed of St. Kevin is a hole in the sheer rock, in which 2 or 3 may sit. It is the scene of the fate of Kathleen celebrated in Moore's ballad, "By that lake whose gloomy shore skylark never warbles o'er," etc. The difficulty of getting into this place has been exaggerated, as also the danger, for it would only be falling 30 or 40 feet into very deep water. Yet I never was more pained than when your papa, in spite of all remonstrance, would make his way crawling along the precipice. He succeeded and got in,—the first lame man that ever tried it. After he was gone Plunkett told the female guide he was a poet. Kathleen treated this with high indignation: "No poet, but an honourable gentleman, and gave me half a crown." Swam, rowed, dined off a tombstone, drove to Luggelaw, a very fine lake, where Latouche keeps a house *pro bono publico*; fine trees on one side, and a marvellously naked cliff on the other.

Rowed again, got back to Mr. P.'s by 10, where we dined over again.

Tuesday, [*26th*].—Took leave of this very pleasant and very Irish family, and came back to Dublin. Sir W. went to Malahide to see Lord Wellesley. I dined with Walter at his mess. . . . Got your letter from Abbotsford. I hope and trust the ancle will soon be well. At the same time I confess myself still very anxious; so do write often and fully. On Friday we are at Edgeworthstown, from which I shall give you another of these letters.—God bless you, my dear Sophia,   J. G. L.

All well. Anne a capital traveller. Best compts. to Lady S., and a kiss to John Hugh.

TO MISS EDGEWORTH.

STEPHEN'S GREEN, 27*th July* 1825.

MY DEAR FRIEND,—I am just returned from Wicklow delighted with all I have seen; the mere wood, water, and wilderness have not so much the charm of novelty for a north as for a south Briton. But these are intermingled with an appearance of fertility which never accompanies them in our land, and with a brilliancy of verdure which justifies your favourite epithet of the green isle. The ruins at the seven churches are singularly curious; the oldest places perhaps where the Christian faith was taught, and which still remain standing. I fear they will not stand long unless measures are taken to preserve them.

I was seized with a return of a spirit of enterprise— once the most familiar of my attributes—and scrambled up into St. Kevin's bed; my Kathleen on the occasion was an old soldier's wife of the bloody Connaughts, as she called them. . . . At the risque of saying *Monseigneur vient* once too often, I drop you this line merely to say that we begin our journey nominally at seven o'clock on Friday as per former advice, and hope to be at Edgeworthstown (Knockecrog-heries being bespoken) by your dinner hour. The Surgeon-General talks of coming with us for a day. We can easily give him room with us, and undoubtedly he knows better than we whether he is like to incommode you for lodging room. In every other respect he must be an addition. My womankind hold out gallantly upon forced marches, long walks, and so forth. I never feared for Anne, and my new daughter seems alert at everything but talking much. A good listener is no bad thing however, and she always laughs in the right place. Yesterday I had the honour to lunch with the Viceroy's own self, and, " King's chaff being better than other folk's corn," his Excellency's lunch served me for my dinner, and I had a long chat with Jane in the evening about all her little matters of business and her plans, which I thought very prudent. They are living comfortably, but without extravagance of any kind ; but this is *hors de propos*. Walter's leave is not yet arranged, but I trust to attain it.

I wish we had a good route from Edgeworthstown to Killarney. I matter not going out of the way to see what is worth seeing. I am informed Cashel is well worth a visit, and can be brought within our route; the great matter is not to attempt more than we can accomplish, and to see things well and leisurely. Perhaps you may be able to procure us some light on the subject.—I am, with the pleasant expectation of seeing you all in the space of two days, very much your respectful and obliged friend,

WALTER SCOTT.

FROM MR. LOCKHART TO HIS WIFE.

EDGEWORTHSTOWN, *August 1st*, 1825.

MY DEAR SOPHIA,—To resume my letter-writing in the old way, I forget if I carried it down to Thursday, when we visited in the morning Palmerston, a beautiful seat of Ld. Donoughmore on the Liffey, inhabited by his brother Francis, and where we saw the son of the said Francis, Colonel Hutchinson, who took the share in liberating Lavalette. . . . We had the same day at dinner poor old withered toothless Lady Foulis, sister to Henny Dallas, and as unlike her in everything as may be. Also Colonel Ferguson, who, we all thought, looked very stupid and lonely, besides a little lameness to set him off. I dare-say we shall fall in with him again at Killarney. On Friday we all came to this place, but I was of the second carriage, with Walter and his wife and her maid, and did not leave Dublin until 11 A.M.; whereas the Bart., Anne, and Mr. Crampton had been off by seven. We, therefore, dined on the road at Kinnigad, and did not reach our *gîte* until eleven, when we had just time to be introduced and so to bed. The country between this and Dublin is dull and flat, with much bog; but one fine lake—Loch Oel I think —was seen in the gloaming not far from Mullingar. This is a large house, patched and added to with considerable taste by the Papa, and all full of knicknack locks, bells, bolts, clocks, doors, windows, walls, etc.[1] The family consists, besides Miss E. and Curly, of Mrs. Edgeworth, a very pleasing lady-like and intelligent woman, rather younger than Maria, and apparently a great friend of hers; then Honora, daughter to one of the Sneyd wives, a woman of thirty, pleasant enough and has been rather pretty; then old aunt Sneyd, a poor old powdered body to whom they are all very kind,—lame and helpless, and has had some paralytic touch evidently; then the Laird Lovell himself, . . . quite a character, far too much so for being

[1] For a fuller account of Edge-worthstown, its surroundings, and the remarkable group of men, friends of the proprietor, see Miss Seward's curious *Life of Erasmus Darwin*, also *Memoirs of R. L. Edgeworth*, 2 vols., and a very bitter Croker-like criticism of the latter biography in the *Quarterly Review*, vol. xxiii.

described thus and now. He has a school of 240 boys, half Protestants, half Catholics, and, the teachers being men of sense, I believe the imbecility of the supervisor is not able to prevent this from being an useful establishment. But who shall paint the absurdity of the bugle horns, the band of music! the marching to this music up and down the school stairs, and after dinner over the lawn at the big house; above all, imagine leap-frog to "its ain tune" solemnly performed by 240 boys before the drawing-room windows! What a farce might be made of Owen and this man, whom I take to be an Owen, as far as a gentleman and a squire can be such a matter.

Sunday, August 7.—Killarney. I was interrupted in the above this day week, and have never since had leisure to get a pen into my fingers again. I heard mass at the Chapel at Edgeworthstown, and was pleased with the Priest's address to his people, and afterwards to church, where we had a capital sermon from a clergyman in red slippers. This was Mr. Jephson, a great friend of Miss E's., and really a very superior man, both in parts and in appearance,—a sad martyr to gout, which laid him up the same evening in complete style. Monday we went to see Loch Gaunack, a tame piece of water, but reckoned the gem of Longford, Mr. Dopping's place,—a descendant of the Bishop. Luncheon the second at Mr. O'Farrell's, a gentleman who had the extreme civility to send us about all this day with his own capital horses. Dined at E.-town again. Mr. Whitney, a proud, purple man, ass enough not to patronise " the Queen's " (which is their way of express-ing *smuggled*, in opposition to the King's). Mr. Butler, my old Balliol acquaintance, now vicar of Trim, was here, a Mr. and Mrs. St. George, etc. On Tuesday morning, we commenced our journey by Mullingar, and reached in time for dinner Lamberton, the seat of Judge Moore, near Maryborough. King's and Queen's counties full of beautiful scenery, a very great allowance of castles and churches in ruins; above all, Dunamak Castle on its grand rock, built by Strongbow.   Lamberton a capital house, and a good-humoured family.   Judge on Circuit. Son, a parson, officiates.   Mrs. Ede, the daughter, a pretty, foolish widow.   The Blakes meet us here.   *N.B.*—Blake's story of Hannah Jones's mother, etc., excellent; some neighbouring nameless squires and squireens, excellent venison, champagne, etc., etc., and we are off next morning.   We reach Rosecreagh in Tipperary in safety, and are then *like* to be murdered altogether with the mob of people, some thousands, filling up the whole streets during our bother about horses.   I can't forget the scene ever, nor describe it now.   Miss E. declared she had lived all her days in Ireland without seeing anything the least to be compared to it.   However, after a variety of annoyances, we do at last reach Limerick,—Sir W. and Anne at 9 p.m. the rest of us about 3 in the morning.   The bridge over the Shannon has still houses on it.   Mr. O'Kelly, a bard of Limerick, waits on Sir W. in the morning, and repeats this epigram—

> " Three poets, of three different nations born,
> The United Kingdom in our age adorn,
> Byron of England, Scott of Scotia's blood,
> And Erin's pride, O'Kelly, great and good."

In one of his printed poems (which he made us buy) was this line of lines—

> " Scott, Morgan, Edgeworth, Byron prop of Greece."

The Cathedral singers came in a body, having sounded Sir W.'s advent, and expecting a crowd.   A very wet day; we saw, however, the ruins of two very fine monasteries at Adair, the churches being occupied still, one by the Protestant Rector, the other by the Priest on Sunday, and through the week by the Popish school of 400 boys and girls.   Extremely clean and well-behaved they were.   The

teacher said he had many Protestants too, and allowed
them to use their own books, and lamented over the
poverty of the establishment, owing to which they have
no stoves in the church, and can't keep school after the
winter is set in. A pretty little cloister at the other Abbey.
We sleep miserably at Listowell, where is a ruined castle
of singular architecture in some respects. Sad, wet
weather, and Walter and I quite soaked. Next morning
(Friday) we breakfast at Tralee, the capital of Kerry, and
reach this about two in the day; and being favoured with
a divine afternoon we go to Mucross Abbey, and ride along
the shores of Mr. Herbert's demesne. The abbey small, and
without ornamental architecture, but the most perfect, and I
think *by far* the most impressive specimen 1 have ever seen.
It is absolutely clothed with ivy, and mantled with giant
trees, and being the holiest burying ground in Ireland
among the Papists, there is an air of mortality and misery
heaped upon the original wildness and gloom of the place,
the like of which I have never imagined. The resort for
burial is so great that they decompose the bodies by means
of lime, and then after but a year or two (*on dit*) take out
the bones and pile them up to make room within the
small vaults for more Tybalts green in earth. The whole
place is strewn with skulls and bones, and some cockneys
have written Hamlet's address to Yorick's head-piece on
half a dozen of them.

We were much gratified with this, and with the fine
scenery of the lower lake: and yesterday all but Jane
(who took fright at starting) visited in a boat the whole
both of the upper and the lower lakes, dining on one
of the islands. The things are very fine, but they
are exactly of the same character with the highlands,
without being comparable either for beauty or grandeur to
the best of that region. To-day we repose here, and
to-morrow go to Cork. I have left me no room to say

anything, but that owing to some mistake our letters are
detained in Dublin, which annoys me sadly; but I *hope*
we shall be out of Ireland by this day week, and all
together in happiness on or about this day fortnight.
Your father, however, varies his plans. At all events, you
shall have a long letter from Dublin as soon as we get
back to it. At present we are astir by six or seven every
day, and dog-weary every night, so I must needs be excused for brevity. My best respects to Lady S. and kisses
to my little man. All here as well as possible.—Yours
ever affectionately,   J. G. LOCKHART.

FROM MR. LOCKHART TO HIS WIFE.

DUBLIN, *Sunday morning, August 14th,* 1825.

MY DEAR SOPH,—I think I brought you down to
Sunday last, the 7th. Ever since we have been kept in
motion so continually that no one but Miss Edgeworth
could ever find a moment for pen-work. She, to be sure,
is a being by herself as to that matter, and well might
Joanna Baillie say she would be scribbling at Almack's.
I don't think we ever stopped ten minutes but she was
at it,—what, why, or to whom, God only knows. . . . On
the whole, our expedition has been a very pleasant one,
and it is much that the seven members have gone through
it all without anything even like a single flash of *glum.*
Right weary and worn, however, did I feel myself last
night, when we once more found ourselves in a place where
one can lie in a bed like a Christian till nine o'clock, and
where I, poor I above all, have nothing to do with the
bills or the baggage of anybody but myself. But to the
Journal. Sunday we spent in rowing again on the lake,
and the weather being quite calm Jane was of the party.
Inisfallen, a charming island, where of yore was a great

abbey. Holly trees here larger than anywhere I have
seen,—quite like moderate-sized oaks. We saw the rock
entitled the "bed of honour," in scrambling near which
Hallam fell t'other day and broke his thigh. Sir W. went
to call on the invalid, who is doing well, and we had much
ado to parry reiterated assaults of M. Alexandre, the
ventriloquist. On the whole, Killarney disappointed us
all. So much the greater should be the damnation of the
road-book and tour-makers. O'Donoghue, the boatman, a
character. A Catholic gentleman had died the day before,
and we observed that men in mourning scarfs, etc., kept
watch at his door. Miss E. said this was new even to her,
probably the custom of one county or district only. The
widow, who was acquainted with Mr. Wm. Edgeworth,
sent him a note inviting him to the funeral, and remarking
that she was *the more* in distress, as the circumstances
prevented her the honour of seeing Miss E. and Sir W. S.
Killarney Club rooms, very poor affairs.

Monday, 8th.—We were early astir—dined at Millstreet,
where Capt. Blomfield called, and pitied our poor fare, and
proceeded to Mallow, where we slept—a pretty English-
like town, and a very fine old Castle. We breakfasted
next morning at Cork, a town which by no manner of
means came up to my expectations. But the river and
country were beautiful. We drove to Blarney. The Castle
is a noble one, all sunk into utter disrepair, owing to very
recent folly or profligacy. No remains of the glorious
statues[1] could we discover—the groves alone preserve
their character. We dined at Cork, and slept at Fermoy,

---

[1] See Milliken's song, *The Groves of Blarney* :—

> "There are statues gracing this noble place in.
> All heathen gods and nymphs so fair,
> Bold Neptune, Cæsar, and Nebuchadnezzar
> All standing naked in the open air."

Also "Plea for Pilgrimages" in *Father Prout's Reliques*, vol. i. pp. 47-96, with Maclise's very clever vignette representing Sir Walter kissing the stone.

a fair town and inn at the foot of mountains. The
country finely diversified all here, and some considerable
improvements going on, particularly at Lord Mount
Cashel's. We went through one village, where misery
unparalleled appeared, a beggar at least from every
hovel. . . . Wednesday the 10th we saw Cahir on the Suir,
a fine place every way, and the remains of a very grand
Castle of the Glengall Butlers ; and so on to Cashel, where
we soon found we must pull up for the day, in order to
examine at some leisure the magnificent rock with its
cathedral, castle, etc., etc. By far the most splendid
antiquities we have met in Ireland are here. The Church
has been one of the very first *order*, and is full of most
singular inscriptions, etc., few of which seem to have been
as yet deciphered. The most curious thing is the Chapel
of Cormack, a building of the old, small, black, Saxon
taste, which has been allowed to remain under the shelter
of the Gothic edifice. On its walls the traces of old
paintings are still quite visible. One of the Round
Towers, in high preservation, is also attached at one
corner to the Gothic Church, and we could see to the roof
of it clearly. The ferocious Price, who unroofed the
Cathedral, attempted to pull this down also. I should
like to know more of that blackguard's history, for it
seems as if all this ruin were modern, and of his making.
The situation is most noble, commanding a view as fine
and as wide as Windsor ; and I know nothing in England
better worth seeing than Cashel. Next morning, we went
by the old Abbey of Holy Cross, where we saw the apart-
ments of the Priests, in wonderful preservation—the
marks of book-shelves, etc., quite distinct, and delightful
snuggeries some of them had been ; and the very splendid
monument of an O'Brien King of Munster, who founded
the Abbey. Major Armstrong and his ladies wished us to
breakfast, but we went on to a bad inn in a dirty village,

from which, advance to Kilkenny. There we have Squire
Duffy, a Catholic dandy, and Mr. Barnes, an English
barrister (married to a daughter of old Gatch's at Oxford),
and agent to the Commissioners on the Ormonde estates,
to show us the honours. The castle is a most ducal pile
in appearance, having three towers built by Strongbow.
These, and indeed the whole, had been sadly Frenchified
by the first Duke; yet I question whether the restored
Gothic of the present Earl will in a hurry have an air of
so much grandeur. All in disrepair and confusion. The
Cathedral, a wide, large building, with some fine tombs of
Butlers and De Grases. We saw also a Nunnery, where
the Nuns educate numbers of little girls—apparently a
very comfortable place, but the ladies were "in retreat,"
and we could only see them walking, pretending to read,
in their little garden. Next morning, we all went to the
cave of Dunmore, which is vast without dignity, and
dangerous without terror,—a black, slippery, dirty hole.
The Unknown got safe out, minus his breeches, which
were all torn. The ladies had the wit not to attempt
beyond the entrance. Slept at Naas, and yesterday fore-
noon reached once more Dublin. Dined at Mr. Blake's.
In the evening Miss E. came, with her sister Sophy, two
brothers, boys, and Fanny, who she told me is her
favourite; and who, I rather think, might be mine too, if
I had time to get acquainted with her, but this will not
be, as they are all off for Edgeworthstown to-morrow.
Miss E. always talks of *you* with singular affection, and I
really think we must visit this place some day together.
If you don't go to E.'town, she won't forgive you. On
reaching Dublin, I had the satisfaction to receive your
letter, which had not been forwarded after us. I assure
you, I am heart-sick of wandering, and would fain have
persuaded Sir W. to make a short-cut home. But he is
determined on being a day at Cheltenham. I hope and

trust we shall be free of Ireland by 8 o'clock on Wednesday morning; and, as travelling through England is light work, that a few days after that will bring me once more home. Meantime, I shall write whenever we halt. Give my best respects to Lady Scott, and kiss many times for me the young equestrian.—Yours affectionately always,   J. G. L.

FROM MR. LOCKHART TO HIS WIFE.

[AT SEA, WRITTEN ON THE OFFICIAL PAPER, WITH LIST OF PASSENGERS ON BOARD HIS MAJESTY'S PACKET "THE HARLEQUIN."]

THIS is the 18th [17th] of August (I think), Wednesday, and the paper will sufficiently show *where* I take up my pen again. I brought the party to Dublin in safety on Saturday. We dined at Mr. Blake's, and met the Edgeworths again in the evening; but I think I told all this before. The Sunday morning I for one had a long and comfortable sleep, and lounged over a few calls. Dined at Walter's, where we had again the three sisters of Edgeworthstown, and where and when I still more admired Fanny, and regretted to find that she was very much failed and old-looking. She is agreeable and intelligent, perfectly mild and ladylike, and she has been very pretty. Your cousin . . . and our friend dined with us,—two cold, dull bores, but otherwise of different breeds, and I prefer the Paddyland specimen, for he has good champagne, and gave us yesterday a very gay luncheon; but this is anticipating—a fault to be eschewed in gurnalizing.

On Monday I did nothing but drive about with Sir W., making P.P.C. visits too numerous to mention. We drove then four or five miles to the observatory, where Dr. Brinkley had a capital haunch of venison, and everything suitable, except the company, which was rather insipid. Nevertheless, we had some good narrations of the Emmet

Row and the like from Mr. Ellis, M.P. for Dublin, and a
grand Orangeman,—a *very* handsome man, and, *apparemment*, one that has really done yeoman's service.   Dean
of Ardagh, a very civil old apron-wearer, etc. etc.   Dull,
and rather sleepy.   The view of Dublin, etc., from the top
of the house most superb.   Ditto, I suppose, the Grand
Circle, etc. etc., which the Dr. showed us.   *N.B.*—I do not
inherit the passion of that distinguished Astronomer,
Dr. L., President of the Astronom. Society of Glasgow:
but Dr. Brinkley's Hock was very good.   To wind up
beautifully, I was taken home in Hartstonge's Carosse.   His
sisters are good souls, and speak the broadest Irish I
have met with above the "struggling" order.   The elder
told me this day that champagne was a gentale wine, but
she liked port better far, for the teest of it, and also becaas
it is not so wake.   Sir W. exchanged 1745 stories about
Invernachyle, etc., with Ellis's Wicklowiana.

Tuesday.—We visited again; and among other matters
had an audience of half-an-hour of the Lord-Lieutenant,
at the Phœnix Park; very clever-looking, very old, bright,
bright eyes—a dandy of the first water, full of humour,
good and *bad*; told excellent stories, among the rest how
Pitt outquizzed George Ellis the day Ellis was introduced
to him at Lord Melville's, after the Rolliad libels.   Full
of spleen about Magee, and praising Lawrence highly.
Evidently curious to hear about Miss Edgeworth, and
pleased to hear of her pro-catholicism.   Blake told us it
was himself that first mentioned and recommended Magee
to Lord Wellesley.   We dined, *a finale*, at our friend
Blake's, where we met Mrs. Paterson, the American flame,
on dit, of Wellington, and peradventure of Canning.
She is much made up in manner, and maybe in person,
but has been an eminently fine woman.   The sister's
name I could not catch—nor cared I.   Sir John Burke,
a Catholic Bart. of note, a very smooth, *but* polished,

gentleman; CoL Shaw, and after dinner, the Surgeon-General came in.   I have ordered one of Chantrey's busts of Sir W. for this admirer, who was *in tears*, says Anne, at the parting.   We really had reason to be sorry in parting from him and the Blakes; but I will confess that I was pebble-hearted, and glad to see myself with my face fairly turned homewards once more. . . . Here we are about half-way over the sea.   To-night we sleep at Bangor.

HOLYHEAD, 3 *o'clock*.

Here we are in safety.   Sir W. has written to say that he dines on Windermere on Saturday; so I hope our return is not to be very far off now.—Ever yours affectionately,   J. G. L.

CHAPTER XXIII

1825

ENGLAND AND ABBOTSFORD

"Once again,—but how changed since my wanderings began
I have heard the deep voice of the Lagan and Bann,
And the pines of Clanbrassil resound to the roar
That wearies the echoes of fair Tullamore.
Alas! my poor bosom, and why should'st thou burn!
With the scenes of my youth can its raptures return?
Can I live the dear life of delusion again,
That flow'd when these echoes first mix'd with my strain?"
The Return to Ulster.

Flows Yarrow sweet ! as sweet as sweet flows Tweed,
As green its grass, its gowans yellow,
As sweet smells on its braes the birk,
The apple frae the rock as mellow !

Hamiltoun of Bangour.

CHAPTER XXIII.

TO MRS. THOMAS SCOTT.

[HOLYHEAD], *August* 1825.

MY DEAR MRS. SCOTT,—I am thus far on my return to Scotland, having left Ireland under a warm sense of the kindness of the inhabitants, who gave us a very cordial reception. I found my young folks in great comfort, living modestly and rationally, and keeping very good society. They went with us a long tour to the Lakes of Killarney, going by Limerick and returning by Cork, so that we saw a very great part of Ireland, a country which wants nothing but internal quiet to render it almost the richest portion of the Empire. This it is now likely to obtain, under the constabulary, who are by no means the Dogberries to whom the charge of the police is committed in London and Edinburgh, but troops of mounted and dismounted soldiers, armed and dressed like our yeomanry, and quartered all over the country. We passed much of the country which was about two years ago much disturbed, and found all tranquil; and a most plentiful harvest waited only the hands to cut and house it, about which, to our Scotch eyes, the natives seemed unaccountably slow. The worst is that we have left ourselves too little time to fulfil our proposed visit to Cheltenham, to which I had looked forward with so much pleasure, for my affairs call me hastily back to Scotland. My wife is grumbling, and I must see a gentleman on the road on business, if I can. Besides, I think my dear Eliza would not be the better of our being with you, unless she was perfectly recovered. . . . So on the whole, I think it best and wisest

to give up the idea of seeing you and the girls, in hopes
that next year will make us meet under better auspices.

FROM MR. LOCKHART TO HIS WIFE.

ELLERAY, *Sunday, August* [21], 1825.

MY DEAREST SOPHIA,—I have no doubt you have
heard something of our movements since my last writing
(from Holyhead). Yet, not to stop after having gone on so
regularly,—we slept that Wednesday evening at Capel Curig,
which Sir W. supposes to mean the chapel of the crags;
a nice inn, in a most picturesque situation certainly, and as
to the matter of toasted cheese, quite exquisite. Next day
we advanced through, I verily think, the most perfect
gem of a country I ever saw, having almost all the wildness
of Highland backgrounds, and all the loveliness of rich
English landscape nearer us, and streams like the purest
and most babbling of our own. At Llangollen we waited
on " the Ladies," as they are called, and found them and
everything about their habitation odd, extravagant, crazy
beyond even report, not to speak of imagination. Imagine
two women, one apparently 70, the other 65, dressed
in heavy blue riding-habits, enormous shoes, large men's
hats, more for show than use, a world of brooches, rings,
etc., and Lady Eleanor Butler positively *orders*, stars,
crosses, and a red ribbon exactly like a K.C.B.; and to
crown all, crop-heads, shaggy, rough, bushy, and as white
as snow, one with age alone, the other (Lady E.) partly with
age and partly with a " tait o' powther." The elder lady
is almost quite blind, and twaddles fearfully; the other is
very pleasing. But, O Lord! the prints, the dogs, the
cram of *bijouterie*, and cabinets, and glass cases, and
books, and whirligigs of every shape and hue, and the
whole house, outside and in, *covered* with carved oak, very
rich and fine, much of it, and the illustrated copies of
Sir W.'s Poems, and the joking compliments about

Waverley, and the anxiety to know who MacIvor really was, and the absolute devouring of the poor Unknown, who had his dose of butter to carry away, including one small bit of butter dug up in a cask lately from the bottom of an Irish bog! Great *romance*, *alias* absurd innocence, of character visible in these old girls; high—very highly bred—but queer, and indeed the elder mad beyond all dreaming. Such curiosity and such an enormous knowledge of the scandal of all towns and villages, even among the Antipodes, I believe. Their luncheon was more beautiful than satisfactory; however, having swallowed it, and taken the tenderest of adieus, we proceeded by the magnificent aqueduct bridge of the Ellesmere Canal, along which Sir W. and I walked,—I think the greatest human edifice I have seen,—and so to Chester, in which ancient city we had barely time to stare a little at the galleries and piazzas of which we have all heard or read, and to make up by a good supper for a very poor luncheon, for *dinner* would be absurdity here.

Friday, we jogged over bad causeways to Burton-in-Kendal, where we slept, having run through Lancaster in the full cry of the Assizes. Yesterday morning we breakfasted at Kendal, and came to Bowness immediately after, where we found Professor Wilson in readiness at the White Lion. He seized Sir W., etc., for the day, and took us out on the Lake in his barge, where we spent many delightful hours—the weather, according to Sir W.'s usual luck, getting fine the moment we wished to have it so. We called at Storrs, where we saw Mr. Canning, Charles Ellis, and the poet Wordsworth, who desires his best compts. to Lady S. and to *you*, and agreed to dine there as to-day. The Professor gave us a good dinner and plenty of champagne, and we were well pleased, all of us I believe, to have these in quiet style for one day after our tossing, instead of grappling at once with that chateau full of lions and jackals, to say nothing of females of any order. Lady Fred. Bentinck, daughter to Lord Lonsdale, a very pleasant woman indeed, and some misses, went with us for a while on the water, as also Wordsworth, who is old and pompous, and fine, and absurdly arrogant beyond conception—evidently thinks Canning and Scott together not worth his thumb. What a change!—bowing and smirking here—from Wordsworth, as your Papa describes him, the first time he saw the lakes, with the little cottage and the sister and wife dressing the mutton leg in the same room where it was to be eat. That was what Byron calls "Wordsworth yet unexcised, unhired, seasoning his pedlar poems with democracy."[1] But he has been better and done better, and is well where he ought to be, would he only drop a little of his airs, and his preaching above all, for that is the devil, particularly when two such anti-prosers as your Papa and the Secretary are in the room. The Professor here is in the new house, which commands certainly the most splendid panoramic view of all Windermere, and is besides a clean and cheerful place enough; but I prefer the old cottage, and desiderate the shadow of the sycamore.[2] To-morrow the Professor musters all the boats on the Lake for a regatta in honour of the Unknown. I suppose there is a dinner again at Bolton's. Tuesday we breakfast at Mr. Wordsworth's, visit Mr. Southey, and return to Ambleside to sleep. On Wednesday we go to Lowther Castle; on Thursday, to Rokeby, and, your Papa bids me say, reach Abbotsford for certain on Sunday afternoon—which grant were come, for I am thoroughly home-sick, in spite of novelties and interesting ones à discrétion. I think these letters will serve to jog my memory as to many stories I have not time to

[1] *Don Juan*, canto iii. 94.

[2] The famous sycamore of Christopher North still flourishes in great beauty, overshadowing the old cottage. See Wilson's *Winter Rhapsody* in *Blackwood's Magazine*, Dec. 1830.

set down in penwork. Canning looks ill, but not so bad
as I had expected,—jaded and fatigued; and then the man
is allowed nothing but Seltzer water at present. This fore-
noon Sir W. and I went to Church at Bowness, and the
ladies afterwards joined us to go to Calgarth. . . . I shall
write one more letter ere I come home, but I think it likely
I may be the bearer of it myself. So kiss Johnny red and
blue for me, and expect us patiently till Sunday. On
Monday I hope to find myself once more in " pretty Chiefswood."—Yours always affly.,   J. G. L.

TO HIS DAUGHTER-IN-LAW.

[Storrs, *August* 22, 1825.]

It is almost a week since your visitors have left Dublin,
and I think Walter and you may be desirous to know how
we got on.   Our passage was excellent, and we passed
with all manner of success through England, regretting
most things we had left behind us in Ireland, excepting
the Strugglers.   It was quite refreshing to travel without
the everlasting chorus of " Good luck to your Honour "—
" May the Lord preserve and be kind to a poor miserable
creature."   I think I still hear their song in my ears.

We arrived at this celebrated Lake on Saturday, and
spent the day with Professor Wilson at Elleray.   Yesterday, we came after church to this beautiful villa, where
Canning and his party are living in clover, the guests of
Colonel Bolton, a man of great wealth and respectability.
You may believe our old luck of claret and venison, not
to mention champagne, does not fail us in such a berth.
When you see the Attorney-General, or Blake, you may
assure them of Mr. Canning's good health. . . . It is always
knowing to have the last news of a Minister of State.   But
then people must not fall into the error of talking of such
folks too long or too often.   No occasion for such maxims
to Jane, who is not given to sounding trumpets.

Here is this beautiful lake lying before me as still as a mirror, reflecting all the hills and trees as distinctly as if they were drawn on its surface with a pencil. I wish you were with us, love, for we expect a grand show upon the Lake. Wilson has ordered out the whole flotilla, and being a sort of High-Admiral of Windermere, we shall have very gay doings. I am told the last regatta consisted of seventy boats of various descriptions. We shall want a little breeze of wind to manœuvre with, but that, were you here, is the last thing you would wish for.

To-morrow I go down to Keswick to see Southey, who is unwell. Wordsworth I saw yesterday, much the worse for wear; he looks so old that I begin to think that I must be getting old myself—a secret which I am by no means fond of prying into. On Wednesday, we go over to Patterdale, down the Lake of Ullswater, and so to Lowther Castle, where I found myself obliged to pass a day. Next day to Morritt's, at Rokeby, and from thence *home*, where we will arrive on Saturday or Sunday. We have tarried so long, that I am apt to doubt we will be received with a good scolding.

I hope to hear from you soon, directed to Abbotsford. You can be at no loss for subjects of correspondence, for I am quite *en pays de connaissance* when you talk of the regiment and of our Dublin friends. I long to know whether Mrs. Thackwell proves a strict disciplinarian amongst the ladies of the 15th.

My love to Walter. I do not say how sensible I am of all your affectionate kindness during the last pleasant weeks, because that you will easily suppose. I hope circumstances will permit us to pass much of our time together, as far as Walter's military duties will permit.

Finding Lord Frederick Bentinck here—an old and intelligent soldier—I asked him the question about the aide-de-camp business. He asked if my son were im-

mediately expecting regimental promotion; and when I
replied that I could not expect it for some years, he said,
in that case he considered his taking the situation as
highly advisable, since he could hold it for a little time
and afterwards join and serve with the corps long enough
to secure his share in any promotion which might occur.
. . . You and Walter will judge of all this better than I
can. I have some fears of your being ill accommodated
and uncomfortable in these little country towns, if Walter
and his troop are sent there in summer. I am called to
breakfast. Anne sends kind love. Adieu, my dearest
child. Direct, Abbotsford.   WALTER SCOTT.

FROM MR. LOCKHART TO HIS WIFE.

LOWTHER, THURSDAY, *August 25th*, 1825.

MY DEAR SOPHIA,—On Sunday morning we heard a
bad sermon at Bowness, and then went to Calgarth. . . .
Dined at Storrs, where Canning was very languid, and the
champagne very bright. Mrs. Canning *espiègle*, like a
Frenchwoman all over, with very fine dark eyes, wicked,
M. G. N. C.—the Liverpool ladies only so-so in this company. Lady Fred. Bentinck (one of the Lowthers) a very
pleasing woman indeed. The Unknown seemed to me to
take the command of the Secretary without much scruple
—indeed without being in the least aware he was doing so.
Wordsworth told Wilson yesterday he thought Canning
seemed to have no mind at all. Other people might find
an easier explanation of his worn and exhausted state.
Besides, would not he be a goose to indulge Wordsworth
with speechification, not only *pro* but *con.*, on the principles
of poetry, etc., on which humbugs alone the Stamp-master
has the power of oral communication.

I went home to sleep at Elleray, and next morning the
Professor was up with the lark to set his boats in order.
About noon, 35 or 40 rowing boats, decorated with flags of

all sorts, and conveying an enormous population of lion-hunters, together with two execrable bands of music, set off from the bay of Bowness, the Prof[r] leading in his barge, which he had crammed with Watsons, Pennys, etc. etc., all females; his own wife holding the seat of honour with a grand *turban and streamers*. I was in the boat of some good Cambridge lads now studying mathematics at Ambleside. At Storrs Mr. Bolton's barge, having in her the Secretary, the Unknown, etc. etc., came off, and was hailed with three cheers, and then joined the procession, which moved round the islands and on to Bowness Bay, etc. etc. during about 3 hours' time; little cannons pluffing and the two bands lilting at different tunes almost always all the while. Cheers repeated at different points. Then the Storrs boat returned. Bolton's and Wilson's sailing boats were out latterly, a breeze having sprung up. The sight altogether was really a beautiful one, gay, elegant, and very new to *us*. As for the Professor he was quite in *alt* all the while—his beard, neckcloth, etc. etc., all truly horrible. The Secretary says W.'s carelessness as to these things really distresses him; but 'tis hopeless now. Lady F. Bentinck has fallen in love with him as he is, quoth the Lady Anne.

This day Wordsworth was in the sailing-boat with Mr. Bolton, and remained to dinner, when he was very pleasant after his fashion. Canning too, having had a holiday, cheered up a little, and if he had taken a little wine would, I doubt not, have proved a man. But it is terrible odds Champagne against Seltzer. Mr. Dennison is a clever fellow, and has had his eyes well about him among the Yankees. The wine circulated pretty gaily in spite of the minister's discountenance. The Prof[r] and I rowed home by moonlight (not much) to Bowness, where we both slept.

Tuesday morning Sir W., Anne, and Wordsworth picked me up there, and Wilson attending on horseback, we all went to Rydal Mount to breakfast. A large assemblage of vulgar women and men,—little Quillinan, "the heavy dragoon,"[1] the only genteelish figure. Wordsworth knew all about his history in Scotland, and spoke gaily thereof. The Professor, who had not been in W.'s house for 6 years, made up for his lost time, by eating a Breakfast which absolutely thunder-struck the Stamp-master and all the strangers that were within his gates. He and young Wordsworth went to Coniston to a regatta; and we with Wordsworth and his daughter went to Keswick,—he spouting his own verses very grandly all the way. It was a fine sunshiny day, only too hot, and we certainly saw and heard many fine things. This I remark once for all, that during all these rides, etc., the Unknown was continually quoting Wordsworth's Poetry and Wordsworth *ditto*, but that the great Laker never uttered one syllable by which it might have been intimated to a stranger that your Papa had ever written a line either of verse or prose since he was born. Wordsworth spoke kindly I think, on the whole, of Hogg, which is more than I should have expected after the story of "Poets, where are they?"[2] being blabbed in print, especially as I knew Wordsworth took mighty offence at that matter,—of Byron contemptuously—of Shelley well and rightly, saving that (as is the custom of all one-edition

---

[1] Edward Quillinan, who married Wordsworth's daughter Dora, published in 1819 a heroic poem entitled *Dunluce Castle*, which *Blackwood* made great fun of in a witty article called "Poems by a Heavy Dragoon." Quillinan replied in 1821, in a poem entitled *The Retort Courteous*.

[2] It was reported of Hogg that on meeting Wordsworth for the first time he exclaimed, "Lord keep us a', there's nae want of poets here the day at ony rate." To which Wordsworth replied,

"*Poets*, Mr. Hogg? Pray where are they, sir?" "*Poets*," quo he (deil mean him!), etc. etc. See *Noctes Ambrosianae*, No. xvii., *Blackwood*, vol. xvi. p. 592. We must not forget the generous tribute which Wordsworth paid to his brother bard on hearing of his death in November 1835, beginning:—

"When first descending from the moor-lands,
I saw the stream of Yarrow glide
Along a bare and open valley,
The Ettrick Shepherd was my guide."

clubs) he said Shelley was a greater genius than Byron (*i.e.* a less successful one).

We found Southey rather pale and sickly in looks; he has been stung by a venomous insect in the Netherlands, and suffered seriously for many weeks in consequence, but his eyes bright, and the folios and the portfolios of beautiful MS. open before him as usual, in the midst of all the ladies. Mrs. Coleridge, a pleasing person, and has been pretty; ditto, ditto, Mrs. Laureate, and all very neat and prettily dressed. To be sure they were as Don Juan says, "Two pretty sisters, Milliners at Bath." Miss Southey is a tall, strapping, and comely lass, and some of the younger sisters promise to be very beautiful: but the cousin, Miss Coleridge, *is* really a lovely vision of a creature, with the finest blue eyes I ever saw, and altogether, face and figure and manner, the very ideal of a novel heroine. They say she is very clever and accomplished. We could see nothing except extreme ignorance of the world. She talked to Anne, as if she was sure she had found a congenial spirit, about books, bards, and "the literary females of Edinburgh." Southey was very civil. A little sherry and cake, and so back to our inn, where we eat a little dinner, and then drove back to Rydal, [where] was a *fresh* party of abominables to stare at Sir W.; so he cut it short. We drank tea at Ambleside with Baron and Misses Hume, who have been rambling here for some weeks. Miss Hume is an ecstatic Wordsworthian, and is to go to see him one of these days in the flesh. They send you their love.

Yesterday, being Wednesday, Wordsworth joined us again at 7 A.M., and we came over Kirkstone to Patterdale, Mr. Quillinan driving Mary in a gig, and Dora riding in our rear. The same sort of talk; poor old Crabbe would have been worried clean outright had the Unknown not been there to quote "Sir Eustace Grey," and to say sensible and true things in his favour. Both right, as usual in

disputes with men of sense. Wordsworth says Crabbe is
always an addition to our classical literature, whether he
be or be not a poet. He attributes his want of popularity
to a want of *flow* of *feeling*—a general dryness and
knottiness of style and matter *which it does not soothe the
mind to dwell upon*; Scott, to the painful truth of his
pictures of human life, especially for the lower order of
society, who cannot butter their bread and sigh over the
description of a crust. Wordsworth quoted some lines in
which Crabbe sums up the object of his writings as being
to convince the high that they are only worms and dust
like the poor, the poor that, miserable as they are, they
shall one day have the Lords of the Earth for their bed-
fellows in the dust; and to be sure this is a rather anti-
poetic result to aspire to. By-the-by, is not it odd what
a total want of religion there is in all the writings of the
political parson? I mean all religious feeling.

The ladies were rather disgusting with their aping of
the Stamp-master's enthusiasm both as to nature and
verse. We parted at Mr. Marshall's, a pretty place on
Ullswater, where we saw Allan's "Jewish Wedding." We
saw Lyulph's Tower and Ary Force in W.'s company, and
saw Dorothy as yellow as a duck's [foot] at Mr. Marshall's.
Took leave of the Lakers and fell in with Lady Frederick
B. at Emont Head, with her boy; and the Unknown taking
her Ladyship and the youth into the carriage, because the
boy wished to be near the post-horses, Anne and I followed in Ld. Lonsdale's barouche, which had four horses,
not posters, to this place, which is very grand, and surrounded with a most noble old garden of yews and pines,
and a terrace quite majestic. The family all very polite
and talkable. Lady L. and the Earl not at home. Sir H.
Vivian, Lord Pocklington, who imitates ducks and pea-
cocks, Mr. O'Callaghan, a real Paddy who sings the "Castle
Hyde" song admirably.—Yours aff^ly,   J. G. L.

TO MORRITT.

LOWTHER CASTLE, *25th August* 1825.

MY DEAR MORRITT,—I am disappointed at finding no note from you at Penrith, and conclude my letter from Holyhead or thereabout has not found you at home, or has otherwise miscarried.[1] It is of the less consequence, as we could only have stayed at Rokeby to-day and to-morrow, which would have been but a shabby visit, and our wishes as well as our duties begin to point homewards after so long an absence from Scotland. I had half a mind to have taken the height of Stainmore on a venture, but as it would be forty miles going and as much returning out of our road, and as every chance is against your being at home, I must take this way of sending kind wishes, and reserve my personal greetings till another time.

The loss is, you will not have my Irish news in their racy freshness. They are of a pleasant description, as I think the country is settling fast, notwithstanding the exertions of factious men to set matters in a blaze. Men of property begin to feel that the public eye is upon them, and are lightening the burthens of the lower orders, giving them more wages, and apparently considering them as entitled to something better than dogs' allowance—a crust and a kennel. On the other hand the lower classes are restrained in the excesses to which wretchedness and evil counsellors are driving them, by a very strict police, which reminds me more of the Gendarmerie of France than any other institution. These are taken from under the authority of the local magistrates, who seem to have jobb'd the matter sadly, and are commanded by special inspectors and regulators named by Government, and connected with and corresponding with the administration directly. This would seem a violent and unconstitutional proceeding in Britain; but in Ireland it works well.

[1] Scott had misdirected his letter to Abbotsford instead of Rokeby.

We passed in absolute safety through the parts of the country where 18 months since a mail-coach could not travel without the escort of a corporal and five soldiers, and was sometimes robbed and the passengers murdered notwithstanding. I own one felt a little gruse at a pass called Shanes Inn, near Millstreet, where they cut an unfortunate Inspector of the Mail Coaches, who had come out in defiance of the insurgents, to pieces with scythes, especially as we know the very same Paddies who were joking and laughing with us had been all in the affair. One of them described the man that was murdered as he that hanged the men at Carlow, meaning he for whose murder they had been hung. A savage old mine host of an Orangeman described the battle of Skibbereen, subsequent to the murther in 1823, if I mistake not, in which his sons and he and other *two* protestants of the loyal town or village of Millstreet had been active on the King's side. He spoke before the whole kitchen household of the Papist dogs, as if killing them had been the natest thing in the world. They are certainly a very odd people, and but for that ugly humour of murdering, which is in full decline, they would be the most amusing and easy to live with in the world.

Anne sends love to the young ladies, in which Lockhart and I sincerely join. I saw Canning at Storrs for two days. He seemed much fagged by public business, but was picking up by dint of quiet and exercise. I came here yesterday with the purpose of leaving this morning for Rokeby and breakfasting at Appleby; but neither yesterday's nor this morning's post bringing any news from you, I shall remain in these hospitable halls for this day and be off to-morrow by six o'clock and sup at Abbotsford.—Adieu, dearest Morritt; it is a great satisfaction for me to entertain the strong confidence that it is no cause of health which prevents our meeting.—Yours ever,   WALTER SCOTT.

TO TERRY.

17th September 1825.

MY DEAR TERRY,— . . . I left Ireland with a mind much enlarged by the information which I collected concerning that fine country, and the comfortable conviction that it is every day becoming a more valuable part of the empire. I had also the domestic satisfaction to leave my son and daughter well and happy, attached to each other, living with prudence, and at the same time in good society and with the best-informed people. There is a haunted house in the fine square they inhabit, one of the most striking mansions you ever saw. If I had time I would write you out the story, for it would make an admirable incident in a romantic drama or pantomime, but on consideration there are too many living people of high birth and circumstances implicated in the tragedy. It was the tale of an Irish Don Juan.

Pray do you ever look into the book-shops now? Pray keep in mind the drama. I have always a £10 to spend on good bargains of that sort. There is a song-book I would much like to see again called the *Roundelay*, with a frontispiece of Mrs. Bellamy (I think) and the motto—

" Marinetta
Claimed the merry, merry Roundelay."

The collection is curious, and contains some good songs now out of fashion. It was published about 30 or 40 years since. You are so capital a grubber that I have little doubt you will light upon it sooner or later. . . .

TO HIS SON WALTER.

NEWTON DON, *Saturday*.

I AM afraid Jane and you have forgot your late guests, or are so glad to get rid of them as not to think of inquir-

ing any more about them. Surely, with ten pair of fingers
between you, you might find ten minutes to let us know
what you are doing, even though you should chuse them
just when the post is going off. I wrote to Jane very
shortly on arrival in England, and Anne tells me she has
written since.

We know so much of Dublin and of Ireland now that you
can be under no trouble to find subjects for a letter, as you
can tell us about the Blakes, Plunketts, and all our late
and kind friends. I hope the stone lion of the Whalleys
has not been shaking the square with its howlings since
our departure. We have been constant at Abbotsford
since our return, and it may be my vanity, but I think it
as convenient and comfortable a dwelling as we saw in
our travels. The weather is now breaking, but not without
fine intervals of sunshine. Old Nicol[1] still talks to every
one of selling his land to me, but the proposition must
come directly from himself and at a different price from
that which he held out, otherwise I will not touch collar.

Our harvest has been most abundant, and everything
seems to promise quiet and prosperity. I hope Pat keeps
in good order; he is a capital fellow, and I think another
score of years will lead him to a very different point of
estimation among the British subjects. Let me know if
you have heard any more of the Aide-de-camp business and
what you have determined about it, whether there is any
news of your regiment moving in spring, and so forth; also
whether Rebecca has cast any more *real aspersions* upon
Mrs. M'A.'s Abigail. Charles is here pelting away daily
at blackcock and partridges with indifferent success, worse
I think than last year. He has got a new fowling-piece

---

[1] Readers of the *Journal* do not
require to be told that this refers
to Mr. Nicol Milne, the proprietor
of Faldonside, a valuable estate
covering about a thousand acres,
situated to the westward of Abbotsford, which Scott had long desired
to purchase, but which still remains
in the possession of Mr. Milne's
family.—See *Journal*, vol. ii. p. 461.

from Jedburgh.   Pray did you bespeak one from Forrest, for there is one there supposed to be for you, unless he had got two orders from different people for one gun ?

Mama and Anne are quite well; they are with me on a visit to Sir Alex. Don and his new lady,[1] who is a very pleasant woman, and plays on the harp delightfully.   The Lockharts are of the party.   Sophia is looking better than I have seen her this many a day, and positively is getting fat again.

Tell my little Jane I am tiring for a letter from her. Mrs. Jobson is, I believe, with Sir Adam and Lady F. in Dumfriesshire.   I hear the merry knight is already looking back to his old quarters, and heartily tired of his new. Young Lyon has given up thoughts of building at present, in which I think he acts wisely; a young man of twenty-one can scarcely know what sort of a house is like to suit him, and Sir Adam might have found the task of building a mansion for another person a very troublesome one, and thankless after it was done.

If Nicol and I were to agree, perhaps Sir Ad^m would like to take new Faldonside, as you I think would prefer the upper for a shooting-box.   But I fear the glories of Gattonside would prevent their being comfortable in a house so much smaller, though it is a good one.   The Colonel has not yet appeared, but has written that he is going to Lincoln or to York—he is not sure which—and to return by the Lakes.   He has been both at Oxford and Cambridge, but has been made a Doctor at neither University.   I believe his mode of travelling is to get into the first coach where he sees a place vacant, and after he has had his umbrella and portmanteau accommodated, and himself comfortably fixed, asks which way they are going.   He would be an admirable subject for the *barkers* who ply at the Gloucester Coffee-house and White-

---

[1] Miss Grace Stein, who married, secondly, General Sir J. Wallace.

horso collar,—a sort of natural prey to these vociferating animals.

Remember me most kindly to all my friends in the King's Hussars, young Rose especially, and to all our other friends civil and military. All join in love to you and your *sposetta* (an elegant diminutive of *sposa*), and I beg you will write immediately.

When you want a troop your correspondence is much more regular.—Yours affectionately, notwithstanding,

WALTER SCOTT.

TO THE SAME.

ABBOTSFORD, 11*th October* 1825.

I HAD duly your letter with an account of your late proceedings, and congratulate you on your escape after breaking your sword in single combat with a post. I must conclude Monsieur Du Bois behaved handsomely, and took no advantage of an accident which might have been fatal if you had had to do with a more active antagonist.

Winter is now coming seriously upon us; I really thought it was going to forget us, the weather was so exquisite down to a late period. Charles left us last week for Oxford, and Lockhart is gone to London on some special business, which is not however to detain him long. I suppose he will take up his abode at the Blue Posts.

I am very glad you are fixed for a while in Lord Wellesley's family. He is so very well-bred a person that I think it must be very pleasant to make part of his society. As for the riding-horse and the tandem, I have so little mettle left that I would rather hear that Jane had a couple of decent horses to your chariot to "carry her through the dub and the lairie." The household appointment at least secures you from the comforts of an out-

quarter, where you might live and *diet* with as little comfort as our friend the Dandy at Shaw's Inn, or what do
they call the place ? . . .

We have a large houseful just now, Lord and Lady
Gifford, Lord Chief Baron[1] and Lady Shepherd, besides
two friends of Lord Sidmouth. If it were good weather
all is well enough, but one's friends are not so easily entertained on such a sulky day as this. There is the Solicitor[2]
too, by-the-bye. However, this will be so far [good], that
they will find a frank among them.

I cannot say Mama has been very well this season; she
had a severe attack of something like a determination of
blood to the head. From knowing her constitution this
alarmed me extremely.

We had the Russells with us for ten days. Their
brother[3] is coming home, and there is a letter from him
dated from Tiflis in Georgia; he will be here this month.
It must be with curious and bewildering sensations that a
man of fifty and upwards returns to the country which
he last [saw] at fifteen. All objects on which the mind has
dwelt are so much magnified by imagination that generally there is great disappointment. The mountains seem like
molehills, the houses like ruinous huts, the rivers like
kennels, and what is worse than all the rest, old friends
left in the bloom of youth have ceased to be as strong as
Samson, without becoming as wise as Solomon, and have
become in a few words *doited* old bodies. You know this
was not unlikely to have been your own lot, and you
should be thankful it is ordered otherwise. Mr. Milliken
is a treacherous man, though a member of the house-

---

[1] Sir Samuel Shepherd, of whom there are frequent notices in the *Journal*, see vol. i. p. 51 *n.* After his retirement from the Bench in 1830, he lived at Streatley, in Berkshire, where he had built a cottage, but he saw no one owing to his increased deafness. He died in 1840.

[2] John Hope was Solicitor-General for Scotland at this date.

[3] Afterwards General Sir James Russell of Ashestiel.

hold. He has not sent me my box of books, at least I have not received it, nor the picture neither. I beg you will with the least possible delay inquire into this matter. Fifty pounds worth of books is too much to lose.

Anne is very well and sends kind love. I advise her to set her cap at Cousin Colonel, but she seems to think he must be an ugly old Quihi. Give my dear Jane all love from me, and ask her what has happened to her little fingers, that she does not write me a line. Anne had a long letter the other day, and I will begin to take the pet. There is now to be no dissolution till next year, but I have settled that it is best on all hands that you should make such a stay in Ireland as will entitle you to make us a comfortable visit of two or three months. Travelling is always both troublesome and expensive, and one likes to have pennyworths for money and fatigue.

TO MRS. THOMAS SCOTT.

ABBOTSFORD, 12th October 1825.

MY DEAR MRS. SCOTT,—I slide a note under Anne's cover to say that I have been rather disappointed about Walter, as I had hoped to get him down to some engineer of eminence, where he could see Civil Engineering in some at least of its branches. I fear he must now trust to doing what he can for himself, under advice of Colonel Pasley, for after all I am not a competent adviser on a subject on which I am very ignorant. I only know that dedicating some time to these studies is likely to produce rich fruit in India. I must therefore trust a good deal to his own sense in employing the interval which he is to spend in Britain to improve himself in useful knowledge. Of course it will be his wish and duty to spend some time with you, but your own good sense and his must determine time and space. We shall also wish to see him here to bid him, poor fellow, a long farewell. I have little doubt that he will make the best use of the confidence which leaves his time much at his own command, and I will write to him to correspond with you about the time he should be at Cheltenham. I am grieved our poor dear Eliza is not yet quite stout again, but I trust she is getting round. Love to her and to Anne.—Always your affection-ate brother,   W. S.

TO HIS NEPHEW.

12th October [1825].

DEAR WALTER,—I have been expecting to hear from you some time past, but you seem to stand upon regularity of correspondence, and like a ghost are determined not to speak till you are spoken to. But you should remember that you have more to tell me than I can have to say to you. You are aware that the way in which I wish you to pass as much as possible of the time you are to remain in Scotland is to make yourself generally acquainted with some of the most useful branches of civil engineering; but I am ill qualified to direct how this is to be done, and should wish you to advise with some competent person. I know my friend Mr. Watt, son of the celebrated Mr. Watt of Soho, would give his best advice, but I do not know where he now is. But you have Colonel Pasley to advise with, and all I can say is, that I will pay with pleasure any ex-pense which may attend your endeavouring to gain this sort of information, as I am sure it may determine your future.

Your mother will of course expect a visit, and so shall we. But you must regulate these both as to date and duration so as to interfere as little as possible with your studies, for you are now to sow the seed of which I hope you will one day reap a good harvest.

Let me know what you think can be best done to attain this object, and remember I trust to you as a young man of prudence and sense, who knows the value of time and has shown himself desirous to collect the means of information. Every hour is precious to you just now. Let me know also what things you have bought, and I will make remittances for the payment. Lady Scott sends best love. Anne was with me in Ireland and made a capital traveller. She sends kind compliments.—Believe me, dear Walter, yours with much affection,   WALTER SCOTT.

TO WILLIAM STEWART ROSE.

ABBOTSFORD, *October 12th*, 1825.

MY DEAR ROSE,—I have just received your letter, and but that it is a proof of your continued and inexhaustible kindness, I should have been sorry that Goosequill had the trouble of writing out the ballad, as I knew it well, am possessed of the book you mention, now very rare, and knew the editor intimately. He was a grim old Antiquary of the real Scottish cast, all feu-parchment, snuff, and an occasional deep glass of whisky toddy; this wight was benempt David Herd, an accomptant by profession, by taste a collector of old songs and ballads. The story of the Flowers of the Forest is well known; the only good stanzas beginning, "There was a lilting, at our ewes milking," were written by Miss Elliot, aunt of the late Lord Minto, in imitation of an old song now forgotten. I have spoken to her about it; she said the first verse was original, and that there were others, but she only remembered one line:

> "I ride single on my saddle
> Since the flowers of the forest are all wede away."

Dr. Somerville,[1] still alive, was in the house of Minto tutor of the late Lord, when the imitation was written;

[1] The venerable parish minister of Jedburgh, whose autobiographic memoirs were published in Edinburgh in 1861. Dr. Somerville died at the age of 90, in 1830. His niece and daughter-in-law was the distinguished author of the *Mechanism of the Heavens*, etc.

apparently some indifferent poetaster patched up the
ballad by adding the stanzas "From Spey to the border,"
which are a few years later than Miss Elliot's beautiful
song.[1] It does not end there, for Mrs. Cockburn, my old
friend and my mother's relative, wrote another fine set of
verses to the same tune. She was born Miss Rutherford
of Fairnalie, and when a great deal of distress and misfortune came upon the Forest by seven Lairds becoming
ruined in one year, she composed the fine verses beginning,

> "I've seen the smiling of fortune beguiling."

David Herd [incorporated] all together. He could not, or
would not, tell me who wrote what may be called the historical part of the ballad, but I believe it must have been
himself, for old Graystiel, a name which I gave him, and
which he loved to be called by, was a bit of a poet. His
collection was a curious one for the time, and I have had
in my hands a large collection of songs and ballads from
which he selected it. I took one or two for the *Border
Minstrelsy*, and you will see it quoted as from Herd's
Manuscript in that work, where I think you will find, so
far as the Flowers of the Forest are concerned, the saddle
put on the right horse, or rather the *right mare*; I never
thought it ancient, though *ben trovato*. I could tell you
many funny stories of Graystiel, but as they chanced over
a bottle of wine or a tumbler of toddy (which he rather
affected) or a welch rabbit and a tankard of ale, which he
liked best of all, they require the atmosphere of a cigar
and the amalgam of a *summat* comfortable. He was a fine
figure, with a real Scotch face of the hawk, but manly and
intelligent, and a profusion of grey hair—a determined
misogynist, and always stipulated for the absence of my
womankind when he came to see me, and the presence of
Constable the bookseller.

[1] See Johnson's *Musical Museum* (Stenhouse), vol. iv. p. 129, and
Herd, vol. i. pp. 45-49.

How could you stay from the North this whole season ?
No wonder you are afraid of the devil; however, if it has
done you good we will forgive you. Here has been a visitor
of Lockhart's, a sprig of the root of Aaron, young D'Israeli.[1]
In point of talents he reminded me of his father, for what
sayeth Mungo's garland ?—

> " Crapaud pickanini,
> Crapaud himself,"

which means a young coxcomb is like the old one who got
him. He said he was known to you, and gave me an
account of your having lost a Canto of *Orlando* in MS.,
which I hope is not accurate.

Sincerely, Walter's filiation gives me much pleasure; it
was done by Lord Wellesley kindly and without solicita-

---

[1] Mr. Disraeli had come to Scotland as Mr. Murray's envoy, bringing with him the following note— a remarkable instance of confidence in so young a man :—

WHITEHALL, *Sept.* 12, 1825.

MY DEAR SIR,—Do me the favour to receive with kindness my most particular and confidential young friend Mr. B. Disraeli, son of my oldest friend his worthy father. Any communication which he may make, I beg of you to entertain as if it were given to you in person by myself. — Remaining always, my dear sir, most sincerely yours,   JOHN MURRAY.

J. G. LOCKHART, Esq.

The object of this visit was to secure Mr. Lockhart as editor of a London daily newspaper which Mr. John Murray, Albemarle Street, tempted by the desire of becoming owner of a great Conservative organ, and driven on by the unremitting importunity of his young friend Disraeli, then only twenty years of age, started in 1826 and carried on for six months at a loss of £26,000. The paper was named the *Representative*, and its history has been so fully told in the 26th chapter of Murray's *Memoir* that no more need be said of it here than that the proposal led to Mr. Lockhart's engagement as editor of the *Quarterly Review*.

We can judge of Mr. Disraeli's powers of persuasion even at that early age, when we see that he was able to induce the shrewdest publisher of his time to enter upon such a hazardous undertaking, and almost to convince Scott that Mr. Lockhart would do well to join in it. Sir Walter, however, had had his own experiences in newspapers, and advised his son-in-law not to engage in the *Representative* scheme further than as a contributor.

Mr. Disraeli made two journeys into Scotland during the autumn, and the extracts from his letters given in Appendix III. afford an idea of his energy.

tion, and goes I believe for something in the service; but besides this, Lord Wellesley has excellent good-breeding, and to be at his table varies the Tom and Dick stile of a military mess; moreover, it dispenses with out-quarter commands where the accommodation is wretched, and *still-hunting*,—that is, not perpetual hunting, but hunting of stills,—the predominant amusement. I learned to know your nephew at Dublin, who is extremely good-humoured, and *tout à fait le gentil hussard*. I will subscribe for *Dante* with all pleasure, on condition you do not insist on my reading him. . . . All here are well and desire love.

I hear Calantha is loose again; my authority is the Chew lad aforesaid. Young Pringle of Haining has brought a bear to teach us manners, and a wolf to instruct us in moderation.[1] Here is a sheet of nonsense to put under the Chevalier's cover, for it is not worth postage.—Yours fraternally,   WALTER SCOTT.

I hope the Gander is in good health. Glengarry's helmet is true enough; but why speculate on what can come either *in* or *on* such an extraordinary head?

TO LOCKHART.[2]

ABBOTSFORD, *15th October* 1825.

MY DEAR LOCKHART,—I received a letter from Mr. Murray distinctly to the same purpose of that which you wrote to Sophia on Thursday, viz., proposing £1000 a year for editorship of the *Review*, which he calculates may, with writing articles, be easily raised to £1500; also contributions to the intended paper, to be ensured £1500. The first of these is quite certain; the

---

[1] In allusion to the laird of Haining's private menagerie. The bear's den and the wolf's cage are now used as dog-kennels. This gentleman's death a few years later, the result of a sad accident at his own stable-door, is noted in a touching entry in the *Journal*, vol. ii. p. 404.

[2] Mr. Lockhart was in London at this date.

paper may not answer their object, but yet I think, with the care necessary to stamp an independent, manly, and national character on the publication, may be also rendered effectual. Another thing I certainly believe, namely, that personal violence and abuse is now stale and tiresome, and though its novelty took at first, yet I have a notion people are disgusted with it, and that a controversialist had better shoot balls than pelt with rotten eggs. A general tone of manly candour and civility gives much vigour to occasional severity. I conclude you will see Ellis as you proposed, and be made acquainted with the interior machinery proposed to carry on their grand engine. You may be sure I have no desire to know more of the *unbekannten Obern* than that Murray is their sword and D'Israeli their shield; but *your own* information should be complete, of course.

Two things I am anxious about—both are in your power—the one is your health, for which you should keep a pony and ride, not once a week, but regularly; the other is your society. You will have great temptation to drop into the *gown and slipper* garb of life, and live with funny, easy companions, whose company, like Lucio's, is fairer than it is honest, and whom you can slip on or off at pleasure. But *noscitur a socio* is a maxim very generally adopted in London society. Many eyes will be on you, and some of them malignant; and if you fraternise too much with our friend Theodore,[1] you must be content to be set down as altogether one like himself, and not fit therefore for very good society. You will not, I know, misconstrue what I say at this anxious moment, when I recommend great circumspection concerning this point, for the outset at least. It will save you much mortification and even distress hereafter,—nay, will have no inconsiderable influence on the success of your under-

---

[1] Theodore Hook, editor of *John Bull*.

taking, which will never do if considered merely as a second part of *John Bull*.

I have written to Murray [1] stating that I cannot object to your changing scenes upon the very advantageous prospects which he holds out, and particularly the editorship of the *Review*. But I mentioned to him, both on your accompt, Sophia's, and your present and future family, I held it my duty to suggest the propriety of matters being legally arranged before you left London. I shew'd him that your sacrifice of views here would be completed the moment the transaction was known, and that your new prospects must therefore be put beyond question. I added that you might have delicacy in entering into these details of business, but that we should be perfectly content with such arrangements as might be made under the eyes of our mutual friend Mr. Wright.

There is nothing about the seat in Parliament in Murray's letter. It would be no doubt very desirable if you would bend your brows and speak like a man, and give Abercromby and Tom Kennedy a little dry rubbing, which God knows would be no hard task. But it would be useless to sit there as a mere *dumbie*. Indeed, I am a little afraid the late hours and hard work of the House might add too much to your other heavy duties.

On the subject of finance, I should think if these views are realised, you would get on well enough. The editorship of the *Review* is a sure card; the other lasts for three years, and supposing it fails, I think there is little doubt that something else will cast up; for as the failure would set your time at liberty, it must be hard if you could not make £1000 or £1200 besides carrying on the *Review*; and out of such an income, with other odds and ends to help it, you might live at the rate of £2000 a year or less, and lay by the balance, which, even if the newspaper

---

[1] Murray's *Memoir*, vol. ii. p. 197.

should *not* turn out as expected (of which I cannot help having doubts), will make a tolerable nest-egg.

Wright's plans of the law are not to be neglected. Yet I picked up one unfavourable opinion from Lord Gifford the other day. Coleridge[1] was mentioned, and his situation in the Review. Lord Gifford said it might be better for him to lose it, as it would prevent his progress in his profession, in which he had fair prospects. I said we had an instance of law and literature being successfully pursued by the same person, Jeffrey. He said he did not think that would do in England,—the prejudices of attornies would be too strong. And there the conversation stop'd.

I think it will not be amiss that I trouble Mr. Wright with two or three lines to serve as a sort of authority to him to enter upon the subject of a legal settlement, in case Murray should propose speaking to him. . . .—Yours affectionately, WALTER SCOTT.

TO HIS DAUGHTER-IN-LAW.

ABBOTSFORD, *25th October* 1825.

I WRITE soon to say that I am *very* angry that your kind letter did not arrive sooner. It gave me much pleasure when it *did* come, and I hope the next will be a little earlier. I do not ask for long letters, nor care a farthing about choice phrases. Tell me your domestic news, and you will always do me a great happiness.

I am likely to be rendered more dependent than hitherto upon epistolary amusement, for a change is about to take place in my family which I rejoice in, for the advantages which it promises to those principally interested, though to me individually it must be a great deprivation.

Our friend Lockhart's talents are about to call him into a much more enlarged field of exertion than he has

[1] Afterwards Sir John Taylor Coleridge. See notes, pp. 213 and 374.

yet acted.   Proposals have been made to him to undertake a very important literary concern, which is combined
with personal and professional engagements of considerable emolument.   In short, he is ensured about £3000
a year, and has his own little fortune and other advantages
besides.   In consequence of this very tempting offer, he
went up to London to examine the proposal more closely,
and see the principal persons concerned, and the issue is
that he changes his residence from Edinr. to London, and
goes to the English bar instead of the Scotch.

You are aware what a sufferer I must be, as you know
very well that Lockhart always shewed me the duty and
affection of a son, and that Sophia was a most kind and
attentive daughter.   But there is an end of all our Sunday
dinner-parties *en famille*, and my rides over to breakfast
to Chiefswood, and so many other comforts which their
society afforded me, and which was the more precious to
me as both Walter and Charles are like to be little at
home during my time.   I ought not, however, to admit
of selfish regret upon this occasion, but rather to be happy
that Lockhart's extraordinary talents have brought him
into a situation by which his ambition may be gratified,
and his income advanced.   I suppose if he made £1000
a year here it would be the utmost.   Sophia managed, by
economy and attention, to live very decidedly within that
income, and though London is more expensive, yet their
income is so much as to give room for saving upon £3000.
I think it likely Lockhart will go into Parliament next
General Election.   He will have it in his power at least;
and then we will all get franks. . . . To conclude this subject,
the Lockharts do not propose to go to Edinburgh, which
would engage them in a round of farewell visits to little
good purpose.   They remain fast at Chiefswood till the
New Year, and then weigh anchor for their new residence.

We expect the great Mrs. Coutts here to-day, bringing

in her train the Duke of St. Albans and his sister; the former, the newspapers will have it, is slave to her *beaux yeux*, or more properly the *beaux yeux de sa cassette.* . . . I could heartily have wished to have forfeited their good company on this occasion, being by no means in the humour to entertain strangers. His Grace shall give me a frank (as Lockhart is not yet in Parliament), and so you will be 2/6 the better for the visit, and that is more than I shall.

I am glad you like your Colonel's lady and your new horse. I beg pardon for putting them together, but I have turned my fourth leaf and must be concise. I am also glad you have courage; but courage, as Bob Acres says in the play, will come and go, so do not be over venturous, lest it fail you in some moment of emergency. I never saw a lady ride but with a secret sense of insecurity, and yet I have known the best horsewomen of my time—have seen old Lady Salisbury ride, and Lady Anne Hamilton break a restive and runaway horse—a sort of *Spring* with a side-saddle on him.

I would rather somehow you had a quiet pair for the chariot. Walter's duties as a courtier seem long of commencing. I shall be curious to hear how he performs in his new capacity. Make my best compliments to the Blakes, the good-humour'd Hartstonges, whose voices still ring in my ears, and all our kind friends of merry Dublin. "Ballinrobe," says the *Gazetteer,* and he ought to know, "is a town in Ireland where assizes are sometimes held"— (you have a luck to assizes, Jane)—"15 miles south from Castlebar, 112 miles from Dublin." This hath a sound of banishment about it. I hope you will get good accommodation. Let me know all about it.

We expect Sir Adam and my Lady Eve almost every day in this corner, but the Colonel has concluded his rounds of travels and dissipation with a fit of the gout, which luxurious visitor, I suppose, detains them at Tinwald House.

Lady Scott and Anne send their best love. Anne proposes to write immediately—quære, what space of time does the word *immediately* intimate when it is the expression of a young lady? I will keep the frank open however.—Always, my dear love, your affectionate father,

WALTER SCOTT.

TO HIS SON.

Oct. 26, 1825.

DEAR CHARLES,—I had your short letter, and heard of you again through Anne, from which I observe you are at College and working hard. *Incumbite remis*—men labour to most advantage in the morning of life.

I have a piece of news for you which will surprise you, as it has done us all. Lockhart and Sophia leave Scotland to settle in London. This is in consequence of a negotiation about the Editorship of the *Quarterly Review*. It would be absurd in him to decline appointments of so valuable a description, and in a line where he can distinguish himself so highly, as take literature, talents, and good sense altogether, he certainly is as likely as any man to play his part well. But it is a sore deprivation to us who remain behind, and I cannot help feeling it as such personally. Sophia pleases herself with the idea of coming down to Chiefswood Cottage for a few weeks every year, but that she will find difficult after a season or two, and I fear it will be *Cha till ma tuille*,—we return no more. It would be very selfish, however, to see their removal with selfish sorrow. I am and ought to be more interested in my children's advantage than in that which I myself derive from their society. . . .

Anne is downcast at the idea of losing Sophia, Mama faces it better than I could have expected, and we all look at the bright side as well as we can, and turn from the separation.

I must add that the precise nature of Lockhart's views is yet a secret, because the *Review* remains under the present management for a season longer, namely, till 1st January, and any annunciation of the change would be premature. You will be benefited by Sophia coming to town, as I suppose she will afford you a bed at a time.

Adieu, my dear Charles; work hard and you will qualify yourself to enjoy good fortune in your turn. Wind and tide—mere chance, I mean—may be in one man's favour more than in another's, but if he cannot hand-reef and steer he will make little of the voyage. All here send love. In the enclosed letter to Surtees, I have mentioned Lockhart's views only generally, as being literary and professional.

TO HIS NEPHEW.

1st *November* 1825.

MY DEAR WALTER,—A fault fairly confessed is always its own best apology, and therefore what I am about to say to you must be considered, not with reference to the past, but to the future. Your poor father's affairs have first and last embarrassed me a good deal, and without very advantageous circumstances of a different kind I could not have had the pleasure of assisting considerably in the support of your mother and sisters. I do not claim any merit for doing so—it is the duty of an affectionate relation. But this state of matters renders it indispensable on your part, that by every honourable exertion and every sacrifice and self-denial that may be called for, you ought to get into a situation,—one which may be useful to your family. This cannot be without strict economy, for let a man's talents and acquirements be what they may, he will fall into disrespect unless he is independent; and he who grasps at means of indulgence to-day without considering the wants of to-morrow never can be so.

When you land in India you must make your pay answer your support. You must therefore practise in time that method and order from which you have a little departed. To close the lecture I send a note payable to your order for £60, which will clear out your debts. I do not even deduct the £12, because I wish you to start free and with a few guineas beforehand.

I expect almost daily to get an introduction to you to Mr. Telford, who I hope will permit you to attend in his office. He is now the first engineer in the civil line, and Dr. Brewster has applied for his permission. I hope it will be granted, and that you will use all industry in availing yourself of it.

Your list of necessaries seems very moderate, and you may proceed to get them, and to send me the exact amount, which I will remit. . . .

Let me know when this arrives to hand, and how I am to direct to you when you leave Brompton. I wish your uncle Robert would invite you to live with him. It might be dull, but these must be months of labour, and folks that are industrious do not tire for want of amusement.

Adieu, my dear Walter; I should be cruelly disappointed if I should ever be deceived in the high hopes I have formed in you. You have, I believe, peculiar talents for the profession you have embraced. You have besides a quick observation, (a little too satirical, which is a woman's fault,) good sense, and a good disposition. I will endeavour to procure you the best recommendations; therefore there is no fear of you if you be your own friend, as I trust and hope will be the case.—Always, my dear Walter, your affectionate uncle,   WALTER SCOTT.

Lady Scott and Anne join in kindest regards.[1]

[1] Walter, Thomas Scott's son, went to India in 1826. He attained the rank of general in the Indian army, and died in 1873. He was considered to bear a great resemblance to Sir Walter.

CHAPTER XXIV

1825

EDINBURGH AND ABBOTSFORD

" I 've seen the forest
    Adorned the foremost,
With flowers of the fairest, most pleasant and gay ;
    Sae bonny was their blooming,
    Their scent the air perfuming,
But now they are withered and weeded away.
    I 've seen the morning
    With gold the hills adorning,
And loud tempest storming before the mid-day ;
    I 've seen Tweed's silver streams
    Shining in the sunny beams,
Grow drumly and dark as he rowed on his way."
                     Flowers of the Forest (Ritson).

"Ah me! the flower and blossom of my house
The wind has blown away to other towers."

CHAPTER XXIV.

TO HIS SON WALTER.

I PROMISED Mr. Crampton a model of an engine for lifting stones, but I cannot get a right one here. When I go to Edinburgh I will take care to forward one. We have his friend Tom Moore here, singing like a Cherubim.

I hope in God you will not break Jane's neck with your horsemanship experiments. I would rather have heard you had got two useful brutes for the carriage. I do pray you to be cautious, and remember she has not been brought up to horse-play, and as you are strong be merciful.

Lockhart and Sophia are in Edinburgh, letting their house and preparing for their grand remove to London, which takes place at Christmas. Soph seems to take it much more discreetly and quietly than I could have anticipated; but why should she not? Lockhart has high talents, and is ambitious. The road to wealth and fame is as open to him as to most young men, and why should he not press forward in the path that lies open? He wishes some house about Westminster, and if possible looking on to the park.

I am more afraid of little Johnie than any of the party,—he has been so well accustomed to fresh air and the side of the little burn, and is such a delicate creature. But it is all in God's hands. After all, it is a doleful change on all sides.

Sir Adam and Lady Ferguson are at Huntlyburn just

now, and dined with us twice to hear Moore sing, which is really a delightful treat.

I like your last way of writing very well—I mean your beginning a letter and filling it from time to time as occasion furnishes more subjects. I suppose the vice-regal marriage[1] may afford a paragraph, for I see you and Jane came in for a share of the wedding supper,—always supposing that the newspapers are to be trusted on this *blissful* occasion, as one of them calls it. I am not apt however to place implicit trust in the said publick intelligencers, because if I did, I must needs suppose that I am at this moment in Paris, whereas the evidence of my senses assures me I am seated in my black arm-chair in my own room at Abbotsford. These things are hard to be reconciled.

I have discontinued the Abbotsford Hunt this year; the crowd became rather too great, and so many of the old stagers are gone, besides that I have no young folks to head the field.

My kind love attends my dear Jane, with that of Mama and Anne. We go to Edinr. next week, so pray direct, Castle Street. Love to the Blakes, Mr. Crampton, etc., and do not forget my respectful duty to the Viceroy, which is really due from me.—Always yours affectionately,

WALTER SCOTT.

TO LOCKHART.[2]

EDINBURGH, 17 *November* 1825.

MY DEAR LOCKHART,—I have written to Murray[3] as you desire, and will also write to one or two of the others. But I cannot conceive what the object of all this is. If merely to remove the prejudices of Barrow or others, I

---

[1] Lord Wellesley's second wife was Marianne, daughter of R. Caton of Maryland, U.S.A., and widow of R. Paterson of Baltimore.

[2] Then at Chiefswood.

[3] See letter published in Murray's *Memoir*, vol. ii. pp. 220-224.

think a Number or two will do that more completely than any argument which I could use. I almost wish you had come to town to state distinctly the nature of the charge to which I am to frame an answer. To your general disposition to take advice I can bear ample testimony, and I can assure them that you have not in your disposition a grain of petulance. But I really do not know how much or how little you have been concerned in Blackwood, which is the only distinct charge. I remember well your undertaking, when your marriage was in treaty, to break off that sort of satirical warfare. But I have always felt a delicacy in inquiring how far that was strictly complied with, or how far your roguery carried you again among the Ambrosians. It is necessary I speak with certainty and exactness when I interpose my testimony on such a subject, and in behalf of so near a connection. But what is to be the upshot of this ? Mr. Murray[1] cannot surely expect that you will break off a contract in which you have acted so far as to make a retreat positive ruin. The thing is now fixed, you must mount the box, and for my part I am not for personally using any kind of intercession, which, too generally and anxiously employed, might lead men to think that your appointment depended on the pleasure of these people. Nothing is more valueless than the opinion of literary people of London coteries, although it is unnecessary to tell them so.

They quickly take the tone from the public instead of giving it, and are never to be feared, unless they can stop you at the starting. You will find them troublesome

---

[1] Mr. Lockhart's position as regards Mr. Murray was quite secure, as they had on the 19th of the previous October signed two separate agreements in the presence of Mr. B. Disraeli, one of which binds Mr. Lockhart to edit the *Quarterly Review* for three years at £250 for each number, the editor to have the power to issue five numbers in the year ; and in the other Mr. Lockhart, in consideration of the sum of £1500 per annum, undertakes to assist Mr. Murray in the publication of a daily newspaper for the same period.— See letters in Appendix No. III.

enough if you play the old man and his ass, and defer to their judgment too submissively; and I really think that after the situation has been offered, and even pressed on you when you were not thinking of it, by those who were most interested in bestowing it on a fit person, there would be something ridiculous in going about to half the world to explain that you are not subject to failings which, if they existed, ought to have excluded you from the situation altogether.

You must harden your face against all this nonsense, or consider it as " penance for past folly." You must mount the box, and when you have driven a stage or two folks will know what to think of you on better grounds than mere rumour. . . .

If this makes you really unhappy, far the best way is to accelerate your going to town. When on the spot you know what is to be admitted or contradicted.—Ever yours,

WALTER SCOTT.

You know I told you to expect this. For my part, if Barrow were to wheel himself to the North Pole, I can't see the work would be less saleable. Love to Sophia and Johnie.

Nov. 18.

I have some reason to conjecture that it is not altogether Blackwood's concern, but some idea of your having *liaisons* with " John Bull " or Theodore Hook which is working against you. You must take devilish good care of your start in society in London. I do not look on Theodore as fit company for ladies, and if you haunt him much yourself you will find it tell against you, especially when the paper comes to be read. He is *raffish, entre nous.*

TO SOUTHEY.

EDINR., *22nd Novr.* 1825.

I HAVE intended for some time to write to you about the change about to take place in the management of the *Quarterly*, which is about to devolve upon my son-in-law, Lockhart, to whom your aid and counsel will be most acceptable and most useful. There have few things come upon me more suddenly than this unexpected change, which withdraws from me two persons in whose society I have received so much satisfaction, and whose removal from this country I had never contemplated as even a possible event. When I had the pleasure of seeing you at the Lakes, I had not the most remote idea that such an idea had entered into the head of any one, or indeed that any change was intended. On the contrary, I was exerting what influence I had to secure for Lockhart the Sheriffdom either of Caithness or Sutherland, which would have added £300 or £400 to an income of about £1000, on which my daughter and he were living very comfortably and economically. In the course of October a friend of John Murray came down with some very flattering and advantageous proposals to Lockhart, which inferred however his removing to London. Neither he nor I considered that upon the whole the advantages presented counterbalanced the great comfort of dwelling amongst our own people. Lockhart agreed however to go to London to see Murray, when he heard for the first time that there was decidedly to be a change in the management of the *Quarterly*, and the situation of Editor was offered to him, coupled with such views as to his profession, etc., as made the offer a very tempting one. A letter from Lockhart from London was the first intimation that I had of the subject, and as the advantageous character of the transaction was sufficient, I had no right, to whatever privations I might be subjected, to prevent my young friend from following where his better fortunes called him, or seemed to call him. And in the end of October the transaction was regularly concluded. I mention these particulars, because you might think it odd that when we spoke together at Keswick on the subject of the *Quarterly*, I never hinted at this transaction, in which I was so nearly connected; still less would I like you to entertain an idea that either Lockhart or I had thought of soliciting or manœuvering for such a situation while it was in the hands of another and most respectable gentleman. The most distant idea of such a thing never crossed my head, until I had Murray's answer from London, in answer to one of mine stating that my son-in-law's views were sure, though moderate. I believe Lockhart's scholarship (of which however I am no great judge), his ready powers of composition, and willingness to labour, his general knowledge, and especially his docility and tractability of temper, may make him as proper a person as could well be found to take this weighty matter in hand, since a change was to be. Some satirical follies in *Blackwoood's Magazine*, ere he was twenty-four years old, will doubtless be remembered to his prejudice. When he married my daughter six years ago, I pointedly objected to this application of his talents, as what was not respectable in itself, and tended to compromise my daughter's happiness. He promised me to forbear, and accordingly never did afterwards mingle in that species of personal warfare waged in *Blackwood's Magazine*, nor was there the least foundation for supposing that he had any the least interest in that work as a proprietor, editor, or regular contributor of any kind. I have not the least reason to think that the man of thirty and upwards, a most affectionate husband and father, is likely to relapse into the satirical and freakish humours of his inexperienced youth. Still, however, the early follies of his pen, added to the continued effusions of the same kind by some of his friends, must lead him to be suspected by some, and accused by others, of this species of imprudence and indifferent taste, until his own course of acting shall prove these accusations false. This he must lay his account with. But I wish him to stand *rectus in curia* with you, and I need scarce tell you that without the most perfect belief in this steadiness which I ascribe to him, I know no worldly bribe would have induced me to consent to his holding the situation in question, since I should have thought it likely to be attended with nothing save discredit and loss to himself and all his friends.

I cannot tell you with what pleasure I saw your fair young ladies and Miss Coleridge. It had been so long since I saw them absolute children, and they are now fine young women. I trust your own health is better. Mine is stouter than even in my best days, but I am no longer able to take the same exercise, either on foot or horseback.

A thousand thanks for the tale of Paraguay. I am sure you can almost at once illustrate the history of a country, and enrich its poetry; it is felling the jungle with one hand and gathering flowers with the other.—Believe me, dear Southey, yours very truly, WALTER SCOTT.

TO LOCKHART.

MY DEAR LOCKHART,—I have just received both your letters. You have taken exactly the ground you ought to stand upon as a man and a gentleman. If you were to mind Murray's backshop, the thing would never do. Before Barrow and such gentlemen, who like Tristram Shandy's bull gain a character by going gravely through their business, think of giving up the *Review* or correspondence with it, they will do well to consider whether they have served its turn, or whether it has not rather served theirs. . . .

I shall certainly write to Gifford and Heber, but on the general footing of kindness to you and friendship to them, touching very briefly on the case in hand. I do not see what dearer pledge you can throw into such a concern than your whole income, or nearly so, your friends, and your future hopes. All these stand pledged to warrant your doing your best, and is it to be supposed you will permit them to be rashly or idly forfeited ?

Though it is against my own interest, as I wish you could have spent this Christmas *en famille*, yet I really think your own presence in London will spare you some uneasy reports. . . . You will of course spend Sunday with us, and will part without leave-taking. I may perhaps see you in spring; at all events summer comes round fast enough in its turn, and we will write often.

I admire your good-natured way of getting rid of Maginn. Let us know if we can do anything for you here, as you must be a little hurried.—Always yours,

WALTER SCOTT.

Love to Sophia and Johnie. I cannot say how I shall miss you all.

I think it will be highly indelicate, nay imprudent, in Murray to delay a decisive settlement with Mr. Coleridge. If your journey to London were to precede his dismissal, his friends would say you had urged or hastened it, and we have too many misrepresentations to omit prudent means of avoiding others.[1] Besides, the work will be injured by the least uncertainty in the line adopted.

[1] When Scott wrote this letter to his son-in-law he was not aware that Mr. Coleridge undertook the editorship of the *Review* without any intention of holding it permanently. It suited him at the time to take it, but as his professional duties increased it is understood that he made no secret of his intention of giving up the editorship. Murray knew this, and hence his action in the matter.

TO MRS. THOMAS SCOTT.[1]

EDINR., 26th Nov. 1825.

MY DEAR MRS. SCOTT,—I received your letter this morning and was greatly relieved by it, as I began to entertain some apprehensions for Eliza. I delight to hear she is so much better, and am not alarmed at any nervous symptoms which may remain, since the consequences of so severe an attack cannot pass away at once. I am glad this will find Walter with you, and should wish him to stay there till he hears from me. Dr. Brewster has written a fortnight since to Major Colby, who is at the head of the National Survey, to ask his advice in the case, and both he and I are impatient for an answer. Assure yourself I deeply sympathise with you in parting with Walter, who I trust will behave so as to be a credit to us all. I feel it the more, that I am myself like to be lonely enough as my day draws to evening. If any fitting person should take a fancy to Anne, the old couple would be left to comfort each other as they could. . . . My kind compliments to Mr. David M'Culloch. I have begged Tom Moore to call on you should he come to Cheltenham. He is a very pleasant creature, and has most excellent manners. If your brother's health allows him to match *sang about*, I don't believe there were ever two such singers in the same room, and both of the kind which addresses itself to the heart. He spent two or three days at Abbotsford, and I being a Jacobite, and he a Jacobin, we agreed to a T. But as I see the papers have got my joke, it is scarce fair to duplicate it upon my friends. I sincerely hope my dear nieces will reap in future life a reward for the troubles in which their career has begun, poor bodies. I sincerely hope that the worst is past, and the habit of patience is in fact its own best reward. Just as you surmise, I will be

[1] At Cheltenham.

in London in spring, and will certainly make out Cheltenham at all rates. Sophia starts about the 8th or 10th for
the great city,

> " Not stranger like, or sojourner,
>   But to inhabit there,"

as our precentor Lawrie Lothian used devoutly to scream
through the Auld Greyfriars. It is a sad separation after
all, but I shrug my shoulders and think as little as I can
about the disagreeable part of it. Lady [S.] is indifferent
well, but begs with Anne a thousand kind remembrances.
. . . Walter, you are aware, is also an aide-de-camp and
courtier in a small way, which is in his favour, and particularly in his wife's, as it gives habits of good society and
varies the gossip of regimental ladies and the Tom Dick
of a military mess. Kiss my dear nieces for me, and believe me always, your affectionate Brother,   W. S.

TO SOUTHEY.

EDINBURGH, 28*th November.*

I RECEIVED your letter this morning, and have to
thank you both for its frankness and its kind expressions
as far as I am concerned. Believe me, they are perfectly
reciprocal, nor is there occasion for them being otherwise.
Whatever you may have to complain of with respect to
Murray's conduct, was totally unknown to me. Till the
middle or rather the end of October, I had no more
idea of Lockhart's being manager of the *Quarterly* than
of my being to-night on the top of Skiddaw. Neither do
I know at this moment with whom the plan originated, or
how many or how few of those connected with the Review
were concerned. Indeed, I neither wrote nor spoke to any
friend that I have in the world on the subject, until I
wrote on the same day to Heber and yourself—to both
my old friends, and literary men, and to you as a most

valuable contributor to the work. I was by no means
anxious on the subject of his getting the situation, fore-
seeing some difficulties, and feeling sufficiently strongly
the pain of parting with my son-in-law, daughter, and
grandchild. So that whatever has been done or left
undone by Murray, I neither had nor could have the
slightest accession to it. If I had wished to make an
interest among friends of the *Review*, I would have
written to you among the foremost, being aware of the
title you had to be consulted in the matter, and having
the highest confidence in your kind feelings towards myself. In respect to Mr. Coleridge, nothing would give me
more pain than the idea that either Lockhart or I were
edging him out of a lucrative and honourable situation.
The situation was offered to Lockhart by Mr. Murray as
open and *disengaged*; he put the question whether Mr.
Coleridge's retiring was a thing determined on, and he
received a positive answer in the affirmative. He had no
access to Mr. Coleridge personally, but never doubted that
a full explanation had taken place between Mr. Murray
and him.

The first question I asked was concerning Mr. Coleridge's connection with the *Review*, and I was assured it
terminated with the new year's commencement. An
accident would have confirmed me in this belief had I
doubted it for a moment. Lord Gifford, in my house, and
in conversation, mentioned Mr. Coleridge's prospects of
rising at the bar, and his Lordship expressed a regret that
his management of the *Quarterly* was like to interfere
with them. This seemed perfectly to explain *why* the
situation was open. The fact I own I never doubted. I
have only to add that Mr. Coleridge has most handsomely
offered to continue his support to the *Review* by the contribution of articles—a circumstance which is valuable of
itself, and will be most grateful to Lockhart's feelings.

It is possible, as you say, his friends may resent what he himself has no cause for resenting. But I should think it improbable, because I have observed that in such cases there are usually some private motives of the resenters' own, which are conveniently carried by affectation of zeal for a friend, and I know no ground for the existence of such motives in this case.

The circumstances mentioned by your fair correspondent are such as I doubt not will be the sentiments of many, and disseminated by more than believe in or feel them. But there is nothing which some experience with letters has brought me more to despise than the puffing of friends, or the rumours circulated by enemies. I would as soon buffet with the snow-flakes which are falling on my window at this moment, as I would try to contradict idle rumours and combat unfounded imaginations. A work like the *Quarterly* is *sure* to have the fair play of perusal, and then the public at large, who care for neither our friends nor our enemies, will judge for themselves.

With respect to Murray's undertaking a newspaper, I suppose it is by no means unlikely; but I am certain Lockhart will not accept an office so toilsome and laborious as that of Editor, and that he will have no connection with that or any other speculation which can interfere with doing his duty to the *Quarterly*.

As for Joannes de Moravia, I think his conduct to you is indefensible, but I am perfectly convinced it arose out of a constitutional timidity, and I am sure it could not be any depreciatory feeling of the great services you have rendered to the *Quarterly*, to which we can all bear witness, or a want of sense of the great loss which the work would sustain by your withdrawing, which occasioned his putting off the proper communication to you on the subject, but that in fact he anticipated objections on your part to a greater degree than I hope you will find cause for, and put

off apprising you, as men are apt to delay encountering
an apprehended difficulty, however that very delay may
increase it. I am sensible that it requires an effort, however, to overcome the very natural feeling arising from
ill-treatment, whether it arise from the weakness or the
malice prepense of him by whom it has been offered. I
am at the same time truly affected with your kind message
overcoming that effort, in consequence of our old and
mutual friendship. Believe me, you will not repent it. It
requires some time to know John Lockhart, and you have
been accustomed to associate his name with disagreeable
matters. But when you do know him, remember I tell
you beforehand, you will like him.

If I had not occasion to know him to be both safe, well-
tempered, and competent, with a high feeling of honour
and public principle, I would rather put my hand in the
fire than accept of your generous offer to continue on my
account your support to the work which he must in future
manage. I shall mention to him when he comes to town
this week, that although you are not satisfied with the
manner in which the change of Editorship has been intimated to you, yet in consideration of our old friendship,
you are not disposed to withdraw from the work an assistance which I know Lockhart will highly appreciate. If
you would have me say less or more, or wait till a future
season for saying anything, you will have time to write, as
Lockhart does not come to town till Friday, to receive a
parting entertainment from some of his young friends here,
which, Whigs excepted, comprehend the first young men
at our bar. It was not Sophia but Anne who was called
Madame French,—the black-eyed lass you saw at Keswick.
—God bless you, my good friend, WALTER SCOTT.

Lockhart has had the most flattering assurances of
support from the literary patrons of the *Quarterly*. Barrow
had some doubts, which are satisfied.

TO LOCKHART.

27th Nov. 1825.

MY DEAR LOCKHART,—I have your letter of yesterday.
. . . You are welcome to my best exertions for *Pepys*,
and I think of a gay trifle—a review of the account of
Cranbourne Chase, which may be made funny enough.
I fear my services cannot be made very useful to you
unless *ventum est ad Triarios*,[1] when I never flinch. In
ordinary cases I never write about politics or literature of
a serious kind. I think the last is unfair in one who
writes so much himself. It is as if I swept away the snow
to prepare smooth ice for my own cast. If you are a
curler you will understand this simile; if not, I must refer
you to Captain Ormiston.

I chiefly write to beg that if possible Sophia and you
will anticipate your visit to Edinburgh one day, and dine
here on Friday next, to meet a few family friends and one
or two of your own,—as Admiral Wilson and Cay; I intend
to ask them at all events, knowing that if possible you
will give us that day also. We have a bed for Sophia, and
can secure one for you in the vicinity. The Keiths and
Col. Russell will form our family forces. Pray come if you
can possibly. The dinner hour will be six o'clock.

This is Sunday and we have dined quite alone. But we
will get used to this while we know you and Soph are well
and prosperous.

On Sunday next we will be quite alone, and I will
submit to you the few ideas which occur to me about your
new and important task,—not that I think I can suggest
any which will not occur to yourself, only it is not altogether useless to know how a *vieux routier* like myself
thinks on such matters.

I have had the readiest and kindest assurances (unsoli-

[1] The *Triarii* were a class of Roman soldiers who formed the third
rank.

cited, of course) from Lady Melville and Mr. Dundas, of
their wish to shew civility to Sophia in her new sphere,
and the same warmly offered by Lord and Lady Montagu.

Mama and Anne join in kindest love to Sophia and
poor little Johnie.—Affectionately yours,　　　W. Scott.

TO HIS SON WALTER.

Edinr., 29th November 1825.

I take the opportunity of Charles Purdie going to
Dublin to send you a letter. It is always good to save
postage. Charles is going to be a gardener somewhere
near the sweet town of Limerick, to which you made your
advances by that famous night march. He is a clever fellow,
and I hope will do. He has a book from me to give to
the head-gardener at the Lodge, who I suppose will have
no objection to let him see the gardens there. If you can
give him quarters in your hotel for the day or two he
must stay at Dublin, I am aware you will do it for old
Tom's sake. I also intend to give him the superintendence
of a box containing some copper and bronze implements
for Dr. Tuke, your neighbour in the square, who has so
beautiful a museum. I promised to add one or two
articles to it, and now send these old rattle-traps, as Capt.
John would call them, to make my word good. Will you
be so good as pay for the carriage of the box, if it has cost
Purdie anything?

Since we came to Edinburgh, I have been asked to
meet Lord Melville at several parties, which has made me
more of a junketter than usual; but as it was chiefly among
old friends, it was not so tiresome as such [things usually
are]. On Thursday, Lockhart and Soph come to town, alas!
to take leave, which will make our future life the sadder.
He has a rough sea before him, for many will envy and
abuse him for his own sake, some perhaps from thinking

the world has given me more than my due, and many more from political hatred. But he is very clever and sufficiently hard bitten to make him indifferent to much of this sort of petty warfare. And then his talents are of a kind that must [tell], now that he has fair scope for exertion. He has, besides the good backing of Canning, Ellis, Heber, Bishop Blomfield, and all the contributors, I believe, of the review; so that, *Vogue la Galère!* I hope he will dissolve the good-natured club, except when the original members have the happiness to meet. Seriously, his satirical propensities make him enemies which his good-nature does not deserve. But, as Corporal Nym says, things *must* be as they *may*.

We have had bitter weather here; Sunday and yesterday the ground was covered with snow, and the snow was falling till ten o'clock at night, when I returned from Melville Castle; this threatens an early and severe winter.

Colonel Russell, my cousin, has come home a fine, dashing, soldier-looking fellow, who has suffered less from India, though he has been there near thirty years, than most folks. I know his manners are not very elegant; but he is a kind-hearted, warm-feeling man, and I have been heartily glad to meet him again. . . .

We are very desirous to have your Court news. The Viceroy is a person so particularly well bred, that I think it must be comfortable to be near him sometimes. I hope the Marchioness gives satisfaction. I think she will bear her style bravely. But I do not suppose brother Jonathan would like much so large a fortune passing out his continent to gild a Marchioness's coronet in Britain; I should rather think it would gall his republican pride.

How does the riding come on? But I will ask Mrs. Jane herself about that matter; only I fear my correspondence will be none of the brightest just now, for I am writing in the Court, very cold and very dull, and little warmed or enlivened by the thrumming of two very dull pleaders.—Your affectionate father,   WALTER SCOTT.

Our Xmas vacation begins on 24th December; our festival will be an awfully dull one this season.

There will be no dealing with Nicol in these times, for the money market is in such a state of agitation that I would not like to embark in so large a transaction. . . .

Concluded this letter 4 December.

TO HIS DAUGHTER-IN-LAW.

EDINR., *29th November* 1825.

... I TAKE the opportunity of sending a few lines by the son of my old and faithful bottle-holder, Tom Purdie, who has got a place as a gardener in the sweet county of Limerick. I saw Mrs. Jobson two days since, and let her know of this opportunity. She was very well, and Lady Ferguson staying with her. The worthy Knight is himself at Meigle, visiting his old friend and mine, Peter Murray of Simprim. I hope all goes on well, that the palfrey ambles easy, and the Colonel's lady carries her dignities meekly towards the ladies of the regiment; that the parties are gay, the *snacks* better ordered than at Lucan, and laughing as merry as it was wont to be. Above all, how do you like your Vice-regal mistress? You are, I suppose, one of the little stars which wait upon her Majesty the Moon of Ireland. We had little Moore with us about three weeks since. He and I went to the play once, when it happened to be a pretty good house. Moore was discovered, and received a great deal of applause, at which I was particularly pleased, as Saunders was, in giving him a good reception, paying part of my debt to Paddyland.

All our thoughts are turned to our approaching parting

with the Lockharts. Knowing how intimately we all
live together, you will have no difficulty in supposing
that this must be an unpleasing anticipation. But what
is thought best for the young folks must satisfy the old.
They come on Thursday, remain till Monday or Tuesday
next, then back to Chiefswood, and from thence immediately to London. It is time they were there, for Lockhart
must have much to do in his new departure. Sophia
has all her domestic establishment to arrange ; and as to
our losing them a few days sooner, one must piece it out
with the old proverb, " Better a finger off than aye
wagging."

You would see a notice in the newspapers that I had
gone to the Maréchal Macdonald's at Paris.[1]   There was a
letter from him yesterday to Hector MacDonald, which is
a very funny one. He complains very politely that while
he had *not* the pleasure, and so forth, of receiving the
person in question, he had a whole host of literary ladies,
some begging scraps of handwriting, some locks of hair,
and several sending verses, which they wish the Scottish
author should revise and criticise.

We are in tolerable good health, and walking through
the world in its old fashion, eating, drinking, scribbling,
and waking and sleeping, without much to interfere with
our very mechanical operations. Only, Lord Melville
being down here, I have been more about than lately,
being asked to meet him. About 24th December we crawl
out to Abbotsford, and wish we had Prince Houssain's
tapestry to transport you there to eat your Christmas pie.
We must comfort ourselves with the hope of seeing you
in better travelling weather—worse, it cannot well be, for
as the old hunting-song says,—

" My dear, it hails, it rains, it blows."

All which elemental discords, clattering against the win-

[1] See letter to Walter, *ante,* p. 360.

dows of our old halls of justice, do not at all relieve the dulness of a November day, or enliven the eloquence of two or three drowsy advocates; so, if I am dull, there is a reason for it.

I hope your maids have found a more agreeable mode of amusing themselves than by keeping the house literally in *hot water*. When such accidents happen, it is now I believe agreed that cotton (supposing the skin is broken) is the most effectual application. Vinegar and lime-water is a specific, and oil is also good; but I should greatly doubt *salt*, though the favourite recipe of your Abigails.

I beg my particular regards to the Surgeon-General, Attorney-General and family, the Blake family, and Dr. Brinkley.—Always, my dear little woman, your affectionate father, WALTER SCOTT.

TO HIS SON WALTER.

5th December 1825.

MORE last words of Mr. Baxter after all. Lockhart's friends gave him a dinner on Saturday, a very stylish one. About fifty people were present, Solicitor-General Preses, Robt. Dundas of Arniston, Croupier, and much wine shed. Many songs and speeches to the honour and glory of the said Don Giovanni, who fell asleep in his chair about one in the morning to the sound of his own praises. Mr. Williams wakened him and the whole company, with bouncing sentences of Latin, that sounded like a discharge of artillery, and I suppose was by that time nearly as intelligible to most of the company. These things I only know by report, having left at ten, as a sober man should. Yesterday Lockhart dined with us, consuming little meat and much small beer.

This morning Sophia and he took French leave, de-

camping about seven in the morning. I was glad of it, for
as the song says

> " What argufies snivelling and piping one's eye ? "

I hope the parting is for their advantage; and that
must make me acquiesce in it, although it is hard to be
separated from almost all my children. But we hope to
see Jane and you in a few months.—Yours affectionately,

WALTER SCOTT.

TO MRS. HUGHES.

EDINBURGH, *Nov.* 23*d*, 1825.

MY DEAR MRS. HUGHES,—I have owed both you and
Mr. Hughes a letter for a long time, but I am, as you well
know, terribly dilatory in matters of correspondence, and
particularly since my eyes have begun to make writing
inconvenient to me, and more troublesome in necessary
consequence to the reader than it formerly used to be. I
have been besides under some anxiety at the thoughts of
parting with Lockhart and my daughter, whose good
fortune (I hope at least it is to prove such ultimately)
brings me sore discomfort in the outset. I have not the
slightest idea who or what determined Murray on a change:
I only know that the offer of the situation was not made
till the end of October, when without a word of previous
information, the situation was offered to Lockhart, who
had not the most distant thought of it: the surprise
was equal to me, who was at that very time engaged in
soliciting a situation in this country on which Lockhart
had some claims. We were then given to understand distinctly that Mr. Coleridge retired from the situation, though
why or wherefore we were not told. Mr. Coleridge has
behaved as handsomely as possible, and continues I hope
his assistance to the *Review.* I am sure nothing could
be more agreeable to Lockhart's feelings, for altho' he

neither had nor could have the least accession to Mr. Coleridge's giving up the critical sceptre, yet if Mr. C. had behaved otherwise under the circumstances, the good-natured world would have accused Lockhart of wrenching it out of his hands, whereas he only succeeded to it when it was unswayed. I have little doubt that Lockhart will do the business well: but he had in his own country and among his old friends enough for all the comforts and most of the elegancies of life, and sadly does my mind misgive me that he may one day repent the exchange of his quiet life at Chiefswood for the feverish and ambitious occupation which he is about to assume. I have been entirely passive in the matter: I could not exert any influence to prevent my son-in-law from an honourable mode of distinguishing himself in the eyes of the world, and which was offered to him in a manner so creditable to his character in literature; and frankly I feel more and more, as the moment approaches of separation, circumstances which make it peculiarly painful to me.

I wish to bespeak your affection for Lockhart. When you come to know him, you will not want to be solicited, for I know you will love and understand him, but he is not easy to be known or to be appreciated as he so well deserves at first; he shrinks at a first touch, but take a good hard hammer (it need not be a sledge one) break the shell, and the kernel will repay you. Under a cold exterior Lockhart conceals the warmest affections, and where he once professes regard he never changes: at least he will not change with *you*, and I will burn my books if you are not good friends very shortly. I have not the least apprehension of Lockhart's getting on well, as he has passed the age when his superior talents for satire might have led him a little too far: but I am most anxious for the health of Sophia, and still more for the poor, frail, little child in whom they are so much wrapt: he is very, *very* delicate, and I fear the spine is affected: in which case—but it is needless to write about it. . . .

My wife, who is rather better, is much obliged by your inquiries; asthmatic complaints are of a very tedious kind, and her fits of breathlessness return very often. We have had real northern weather of late, the snow lying deep on our mountains, and I question whether the Lockharts, who are coming to Edinburgh to-day to bid their friends adieu, will get through the Moorfoot Hills, and I shall be glad to see them safe.

December 5th.—They *have* arrived, and have parted too, this morning, without any formal adieus, for which I thank them. They were off before daybreak. And now, dearest Mrs. Hughes, let me bespeak your love—your *maternal* friendship for Sophia. She will have many young and gay associates, but I wish to secure her a faithful and experienced friend. Love her for my sake till she can make her own claim good; advise her if she wants advice, treat her as you would a daughter of your own, and be assured she will love you in return. I need not tell you how glad she will be to see you in London, where, poor soul, she will be like a cow in a *fremit loaning*: (this will try your Scotch, Madame).

Pepys has had bad luck, for I made some scratches about him for Lockhart's use last week: this *entre nous*: I certainly would not have interfered with my friend, Mr. Hughes.[1] My kind compliments to him and to the kind Doctor.—From him that is lonely, dowie, and wae, but always truly yours,   WALTER SCOTT.

TO LOCKHART.

EDINBURGH, *8th December* [N.Y.].

I RETURN the sheets revised, most anxious as you may believe to hear from you. I send a letter from that weary

---

[1] John Hughes had been engaged by Mr. Coleridge to review Pepys, and had made some progress with the article.

wight Gillies. I will try to do him some accompt of
Molière's life, but nothing will thrive with him. He is
the sloth who gets up into a tree, eats up to the very last
leaf, and then begins to grin and howl so as to deafen
the whole neighbourhood. But I think I said this of
the poor fellow once before to you, so I will rather hail
him in the language of the ballad—

> Now up there spake a good fellow
> That sate at John o' the Scales' board,
> Said, "Welcome, welcome, Heir of Linne,
> Some time thou wert a right good lord.
>
> Some time a good fellow thou hast been,
> And neither spared thy gold nor fee,
> Therefore I'll lend thee twenty pence,
> And other twenty if need should be."

It is, however, very dangerous for a petitioner whom
that sole quality renders bore enough, to be a *bore* on
his own account. Miss Edgeworth might have made a
good chapter on Beggars who are bores otherwise than
by their profession.

Anxious to hear from you, and with love to all, 1
am yours,   WALTER SCOTT.

TO THE SAME.

EDINBURGH, 14th Dec. 1825.

MY DEAR LOCKHART, — This will find you, I trust,
temporarily if not comfortably settled. I have been
thinking much of Sophia and Johnie during the gloomy
weather, which must have made Stainmore doubly
desolate, especially as you wanted the kind welcome and
friendly countenances of Rokeby. Yours from Catterick
Bridge did not reach me until yesterday. . . .

Sophia or you can write at a time, and let us know the
gossip, especially how Johnie likes London and if he talks
of Abbotsford and Chiefswood and Ha-papa.

I have a very kind letter from Lady Stafford with kind

offers of all attention to Sophia. She does not come to London till May, but wishes to see you at their Villa. I think with Ditton Park and Cleveland House, you will have as good backing as folks need desire who do not wish above a *genteel competence* of the great world. . . .

I enclose a note to Allan Cunningham. By the way, poor Fanny escaped from the servants at Leith, came up to Castle Street, and scratched at my room door, which was rather an affecting circumstance.[1] She sought about and whined a good deal, but did not offer to leave the house, so was contented with us as a *pis-aller*; we kept her till Friday morning when the smack was about to sail, and then sent down John as the most experienced head of the party *to deal with* the Steward in her behalf. I hope she has reached safe. . . .

Barrow's letter was in the kindest possible terms towards you; all assistance to be at your service at all times, etc. So that blast is blown by, but you will always have to remember what a freakish unsettled being you have to do with, and how certain you would be of his deserting if he could, supposing any pinch to occur, as an examination before the House or the like, which will render it doubly incumbent on you to keep out of scrapes, for you will have bad backing except in the way of backing *out*.

May I trouble you to settle with Allan Cunningham for Wordsworth's bust,—I mean my bust sent to Wordsworth, and let me know amount. I am told the little Pepper has run away from Newton; I hope this is not true.

I send you under cover to our friend Mr. Croker a whole host of letters, and pity your having the trouble to open and read them. It will be ill luck if you find another as difficult to read, as little worth the trouble of decyphering.—I am, with kindest love to Sophia and Johnie, affectionately yours,

WALTER SCOTT.

[1] Mrs. Lockhart's dog.

TO HIS SON WALTER.

ABBOTSFORD, *29th December* 1825.

I HAVE not been quite idle. I have sent a song to Jane, which I think dashing enough. If you think it will interest at your head quarters, you may give the Marchioness a copy; only beg it may not become public. My letter to Jane will . . . explain the subject of the ditty. I will not say a word to her about the Sahagoon dinner, and indeed should have done it at any rate with the greatest unwillingness. Married folks' little disputes, —and such must happen until husbands and wives are angels,—are always best accommodated among themselves. Poor Jane's heart is so sincere and good, that one must make considerable allowance for the narrowness of her situation.

I hope you will be able to come over here some time in winter or spring. There wants something to be done in thinning the woods at Lochore, which will improve the plantation, save wood for repairing the enclosures, and even perhaps put a little money, though not much, in the Laird's pocket. You will be able best to judge how this can be.

We keep a wretched Christmas here. The Scotts of Harden came to-day, but I was not able to sit with them. Harry also called, who is a real honest lad and my favourite of the young people, but I could not ask him even to stay dinner. This is not illness, but the unpleasant and depressing consequences of calomel.

Lockhart and Sophia are occupying a comfortable house in Pall Mall. I wrote to little Jane, so don't send my love through you.

I have got my freedom from Cork, and am, I conclude, entitled in future to button my coat *behind*, though I shall not intimate that to the kind donors. A Cork lady, a sister of the paymaster of the district, has sent as a rider on my freedom, a long letter wretchedly spelled and worse expressed, asking me to get her ten pounds for a novel which I am obliged to decline, as of course it cannot be worth ten pence.   Pray get a frank at your levee, as it would concern me to cost the poor woman postage besides her disappointment.

TO HIS DAUGHTER-IN-LAW.

ABBOTSFORD, *29th December* 1825.

MY DEAR JANE,—You will be sorry I think to learn that the cause of my silence has been sudden and severe indisposition.   None of my misfortunes happen like those of any one else, for I always break down at the top of my gallop, and when I least expect it.   So I was in a manner shot dead on Christmas day, within half an hour after dinner, mince pies in my very throat.   The pain was very great, but it proves to be what is called a *chronic* disease, which learned word means, I believe, it is not a disorder which one immediately dies of, but only which, if it visits you frequently, renders life little worth having.   But as our friend Dr. Dickson [1] would say, shall we receive good at God's hand and shall we not receive evil ?   If I am a bad divine and a worse philosopher, I hope I am not ignorant of the advantages I have enjoyed, or unreasonably impatient under the increasing infirmities which must attend old age, and which in my case have been longer delayed and less severely inflicted than in that of many contemporaries. Besides, have I not all of you, my dear children, loving each other and affectionate to me, to comfort me under such circumstances ?

I hope besides, by caution and attention, to avert the return of this cruel complaint, and though I write out of spirits more than usual, you must, my love, impute it to

[1] The Rev. David Dickson, for forty years the worthy and benevo- lent minister of St. Cuthbert's, Edinburgh.

the depressing effects of calomel, which I have been obliged
to take in a quantity which does not agree with me at all.
Well—but we will talk of something more agreeable. You
know, among my foibles, I am a most incorrigible Jacobite,
and the other day I lighted on the passage in Baron
Dalrymple's *Memoirs of Great Britain* (not Dalrymple
Lord Hailes's *Annals of Scotland*) in which there is a very
spirited description of the Viscount of Dundee leaving
Edin[r] to go north to raise the Highlands.[1] He headed, you
know, the clans in the battle of Killiecrankie, and died in
the moment of gaining a complete victory. My great-
grandfather was with him, I believe, in his retreat, and
certainly in the battle in which Dundee fell. And you
remember the picture of old Walter with the beard which
we always look on with a sort of family reverence, for he
was a staunch old Carle. Well, these things running in
my mind, and having no spirits for serious business, I have
thrown off the verses I enclose to the tune of " Bonnie
Dundee." There are three sets of words to the tune. The
one is *rather free* and begins—

> " Oh wha hae I burned, or wha hae I slain ?
> Or how hae I done ony *injurie* ? " etc.[2]

The other is a common song—

> " Oh where got ye that haver-meal bannock ?
> Ye silly blind body, and dinna ye see
> I gat it out of the Scots laddie's wallet
> Atween Saint Johnstoune and bonnie Dundee."

The third is in the Beggar's Opera—

> " The charge is prepared, the judges are met,
> The jury all ranged—a terrible show."

Under one or other of these heads I think you will
find out the tune, and I enclose you a beautiful and
illigant copy of new words for it. Don't make them public
but if you find that giving a copy to the Marchioness

---

[1] Sir John Dalrymple's *Memoirs*, vol. i. p. 221.   [2] Herd, vol. ii. p. 202

Wellesley, or our friends the Cramptons, or the Plunketts, or in short where you like, and where they will think it a kindness, you are under no restraint. The meaning is that you should make a compliment where you like it, only it is always best to make it a sort of little mystery and favour —*no copies to be given*, and the like. What people think they cannot easily come by they always consider as a compliment, though it is not worth having. It requires almost no setting, for I, who have no ear—or almost none—for *tune*, have a perfect ear for *time*, and never wrote a verse in my life for a measure with which I was familiar which was not quite adapted to it. You will observe the tune is usually sung, like most Scotch tunes, too slow, and as a sort of dirge. It is this which makes Scotch music be thought generally to want spirit, whereas by singing a Scotch tune with more spirit you always have the power of giving feeling to pathetic passages by dwelling on and prolonging them.

Sir Adam was here and sang the " Bonnets " with great spirit. I trust I will be able to go to Huntly Burn on next Monday, and make him perfect in the melody. What a different season is this Christmas from the last! But each had its advantages and its doubts and perplexities. We will see no one here but the Scotts of Harden and the Fergusons. The former family have Newenhams with them, who will be our guests one day next week, hoping that I shall, please God, be able to receive them.

I hope Walter and you will get over in spring, just to let you both take a look of your property and friends here. It is now a long time that, excepting his pleasant scamper with us through Ireland, Walter has not stirred from his regiment, and he surely should have leave in his turn like other folks.

We are dull enough here. I am sitting in my little room off the library with Ginger and Spice (you remember them, I hope) to keep me company. *Nota Bene,* Spice got into one of the flues of the garden wall to-day after a *cat,* and we thought we should have to have opened the wall to get out the little spit-fire alive. However, she was poked out at last. Then Mama and Anne sit at the other end in the little breakfast parlour over the fire, and there is our merry Christmas—an't please ye. Mama and Anne desire kindest love and all the happiness of the New Year. —God bless you too, says old papa, and believe me, my dear little body, your most affectionate father,

WALTER SCOTT.

APPENDIX.

No. I.

Extracted from Mr. Gifford's letters to Scott.

Feb. 20th, 1809.—You have acquitted your promise nobly; yet nothing less was requisite to enable us to complete the first No. Without your uncommon exertions we must have failed.

Nov. 20th, 1809.—If you desert us, I do not think we can stand, and my hopes, which were once pretty sanguine, begin to fail me. . . . Pray take our case into your pitiful consideration. This is now the 2nd No. which, as my acquaintance at Cam. says, has *desiderated* you.

Dec. 30th, 1809.—But what, my dear friend, will you do for us this time? I should grow cold at the heart if you abated of your kindness and zeal to serve us.

Feb. 17th, 1810.—I have been looking northward for some time, and now with increased anxiety, for we are collecting our materials for the next No. . . . Our last No. has done us much good. If we can keep to it, and we may by your assistance, which I have always looked to as the *sine quâ non*, we should gain the press to our side,—an object of transcendant importance to our friends, who indeed—(I speak, of course, of C[anning] and those you know)—are always asking me what I have from you, and rely not a little on your friendship and assistance.

April 30th, 1810.—I am proud to tell you that you underrate our success. Our regular sale is already between 4000 and 5000, and on the increase. Add to this, that we have a "local habitation and a name," and are looked up to with confidence. We are pitted by every one against the Edin^r Rev^rs, and with a more active and efficient editor should in a few numbers, I am well convinced, rival them not only in credit, but in sale. Poor Rogers is in labour, and it is lamentable to witness his throes. He visits me, he asks folks to dine with him, he bows to the Irish cousins of criticks—the babe, therefore, is at hand.

May 9th, 1810.—I beg that henceforth you will select from the whole catalogue whatever may strike your fancy, and I seriously engage that not a single instance of interference with your choice shall again occur.

Sept. 24th, 1810.—I earnestly hope you will be able to help us in the *next* No.; this is now out of the question; your two little articles in our last were a great relief to us, and extremely well liked. . . . After all, my kind friend, we want a little, no, not a little, of your pleasantry and spirit. Pray look out for something. . . . But you, my dear Scott, *must* stir. Mark his absolute *must*, this triton of the minnows! you will say. . . . Send me something as soon as you can, for we must absolutely in our coming No. (that is the 8th) make up our lost time and be out by the middle of Dec^r.

Oct. 27th, 1810.—We are out at last, and I grieve to think, without you, "the best feather of our wing," as Iachimo says. Verily this ought not to be, for I consider you, George [Ellis] considers you, and the world considers you as the triple pillar of our state. . . . In future I will take care that the choice shall always be with you. You know your forte, or at least I do,—it is fun and feeling. Whatever will admit of both is better still, and there are many subjects which will. . . . Meanwhile, what will you do, or what will you have?

Dec. 29th, 1810.—A thousand and a thousand thanks to you for "Kehama." It came too late, but to do away both your regret and mine, it could not have found a place in this No. had it come a month sooner. . . . Southey has so much feeling, and every now and then such woful delinquencies of taste and sense, such talents and such genius, that he is altogether the most singular creature imaginable. But the man is a great man, and if he would harmonise, or rather socialise himself, and live among men, he would be greater.

July 6th, 1811.—Your propitiation came in pudding time to disarm me; for I was about to send a file of musqueteers to apprehend you as a deserter. For *homme d'honneur* I waited to the last moment for a review of the old romances, but none came, as you doubtless know. Pray be more alert in future, or I will complain to Parliament of you, which now seems the place for noticing all enormities; and if Mr. Whitbread and one or two others live, I do not despair of seeing the day when no country schoolmaster shall turn up a little brat's posterior without having a petition against him in that Honourable House, which has so wisely turned its attention to these things lately.

Oct. 6th, 1811.—But what have you done for us?—or, what will you do for us? Or have you quite run away from us? I am something in the condition of Falstaff after his distresses. I don't want you to sing me " a bawdy song to make me merry," but to give me some of your lively articles to make my readers merry.

Oct. 30th, 1811.—Why are you all so careless of us? An article from Scotland " peeps out " in our Review, as Pope says of souls, " once an age." This is not what was promised me both by the Government of Scotland and England when I undertook the care of it. Here am I, a miserable invalid, old in years, older in constitution, without eyes, without strength, without anything, grubbing on, while the mighty men of war are satisfied with looking at me.

No. II.

TO HON. JOHN VILLIERS, AFTERWARDS THIRD EARL OF CLARENDON.[1]

MANCHESTER, *April 6th* [*7th*], 1821, 10 *at night.*

MY DEAR SIR,—I have been thinking on the scheme you had the goodness to mention to me, and as the objections which occur to me are of a very strong character, I am about to lay them before you more fully than our hasty conversation permitted. God knows, I should be sufficiently diffident of my own opinion in most cases where it stands in opposition to those for whom I entertain so much respect, and to whom, in almost all other instances, I should be most willing to defer. But this is a matter in which my experience as an author who has been twenty years before the public, maintaining during that long space a much higher rank of popularity than he deserves, may entitle me to speak with some opportunities of knowledge to which few others can lay claim; and to be silent merely out of politeness or false modesty would in the circumstances be a folly, if not a crime, since it is obvious that the measure, if not eminently successful, would be a marked

---

[1] During Scott's visit to London he had been " consulted by several persons in authority as to the project of a Society of Literature for which the King's patronage had been solicited." Scott did not approve of the plan, and he wrote this remarkable letter while halting at Manchester for the night on his way home. See *Life,* vol. vi. p. 303, where Mr. Lockhart states that he had failed to recover a copy.

failure for malignant satire to fix his fangs upon, and that the noble purpose of the Sovereign would be made the means of heaping on all concerned ridicule and calumny and abuse. My personal feelings would naturally determine me against becoming a member of such an association. These however I might unwillingly set aside. But convinced as I am that the scheme will be hurtful at once to the community of letters, and to the respect due to the Sovereign, my own feelings are out of the question, and it becomes only my duty to consider the measure, as these are implicated. In the first place, I think such an association entirely useless. If a man of any rank or station does anything in the present day deserving the patronage of the public, he is sure to obtain it. For such a work of genius as the plan proposes to remunerate with £100, any bookseller would give ten or twenty times that sum, and for the work of an author of any eminence, £3000 or £4000 is a very common recompense. In short, a man may, according to his talents, make from £500 to as many thousands, providing he employs those talents with prudence and diligence. With such rewards before them, men will not willingly contend for a much more petty prize, where failure would be a sort of dishonour, and where the honour acquired by success might be very doubtful. There is therefore really no occasion for encouraging by a society the competition of authors. The land is before them, and if they really have merit they seldom fail to conquer their share of public applause and private profit. It will happen, no doubt, that either from the improvidence which sometimes attends genius, or from singularly adverse circumstances, or from some peculiar turn of temper, habits, or disposition, men of great genius and talent miss the tide of fortune and popularity, fall among the shallows, and make a bad voyage of it. It would highly become his Majesty, in the honourable zeal which he has evinced for the encouragement of literature in all its branches, to consider the cases of such individuals; but such cases are nowadays extremely rare. I cannot, in my knowledge of letters, recollect more than two men whose merit is undeniable, while I am afraid their circumstances are narrow. I mean Coleridge and Maturin. To give either or both of them such relief as his Majesty's princely benevolence might judge fitting, would be an action well becoming his royal munificence, and of a piece with many other generous and benevolent actions of the same kind. But I protest that (excepting perhaps Bloomfield, of whose circumstances I know little) I do not remember any other of undisputed genius who could gracefully accept £100 a year, or to whom such a sum could be handsomely offered. That there would be men enough to grasp at it would be certain, but then they would be the very individuals whose mediocrity of genius and active cupidity of disposition would render them undeserving of the Royal benevolence, or render the Royal benevolence ridiculous if bestowed upon them.

But the association is not merely unnecessary and useless. It will, if attempted, meet a grand and mortifying failure; and that from a great concurrence of reasons. In the first place, you propose (if I understand you rightly) to exclude Byron, Jeffrey, Tom Moore, etc., for reasons moral or political. But allowing these reasons their full weight, how will the public look on an association for literary purposes where such men, whose talents are undisputed, are either left out or chuse to stay out, or what weight would that society have on the public mind? Very little I should think, while it would be liable to all the shots which malice and wit mingled could fire against it. But besides these, I think (judging however only from my own feelings) that few men who have acquired some reputation in literature would chuse to enroll themselves with the obscure pedants of universities, and schools-men, most respectable doubtless, and useful in their own way, excellent judges of an obscure passage in a Greek author, understanding perhaps the value of a bottle of old port, connoisseurs in tobacco, and not wholly ignorant of the mystery of punch-making, but certainly a sort of persons whom I for one would never wish to sit with as assessors of the fine arts. There are many men, and I know several myself, to whom this description does not apply. But to one who has lived all his life with gentlemen and men of the world, to mingle his voice with men who have lived entirely out of the world, and whose opinions must be founded on principles so different from our own, would be no very pleasing situation. Besides, every man who has acquired any celebrity in letters would naturally feel that the object, or rather the natural consequence of such a society, would be to *average* talent, and that while he brought to the common stock all which he had of his own, he was on the contrary to take on his shoulders a portion of their lack of public credit. Now this is what no one will consider as fair play; and I believe you will find it very difficult to recruit your honorary class on such conditions with those names which you would be most desirous to have, and without which a national institution of the kind would be a jest. But we will suppose them all filled up, and assembled. By what rule of criticism are they to proceed in determining

the merits of the candidates on whom they are to sit in judgment? The Lake School have one way of judging, that of
Scotland another, Gifford, Frere, Canning, etc. a third, and
twenty others have as many besides. The vote would not be
like that of the Institute, for in science, and even in painting
and sculpture, there are conceded points on which all men
make a common stand. But in literature you will find people
entertaining as many different opinions upon that which
is called taste, in proportion to their different temperaments,
habits, and prejudices of education. They *could* only agree
upon *one* rule of decision, and that would be to chuse the
pieces which were least *faulty*; for tho' literary men do not
agree in their estimates of excellence, they coincide in general
in condemning the same class of errors. But the poems,
though unexceptionable, belong in general to that very class
of mediocrity which neither gods, men, nor columns, not even
the columns of a modern newspaper, are disposed to tolerate,
and which assuredly are sufficiently common without being
placed under the special patronage of a society. As to the
men who are to be stipendiaries of £100 a year, on what
decent footing can they, receiving a pension not more than is
given to a man-servant in a large establishment, hold an open
and fair front with the public, or with the other classes of
the association? I declare they will only be regarded as the
badged and learned almsmen of literature, and sooner than
accept it, were I in a situation to need it, I would cut my
right hand off, and beg for bread with my left, when I had
thus given assurance that I could never again commit the
sin of using a pen. How is it possible, I repeat, for the
stipendiaries to hold anything like a fair and open front with
the patrons or honorary classes? and if you destroy equality,
you debase all the generous pride of a young author. Besides,
we are, by habit and character, an irritable race; leave us at a
distance from each other and we may observe decorum, but
force into one body a set of literary men, differing so widely
in politics, in taste, in temper, and in manners, having no
earthly thing in common except their general irritability of
temper, and a black speck on their middle finger, what can
be expected but all sort of quarrels, tracasseries, lampoons,
libels, and duels? Fabricio's feast of the author in Gil Blas
would be a joke to it. It would give rise, supposing the
whole association did not fall into general and silent contempt, to a sequence of ridiculous and contemptible feuds, the
more despicable that those engaged in them were perhaps, some
of them, men of genius. Lewis the Fourteenth, in his plenitude

of power, failed to make the Académie respectable; nor did it ever produce any member who rose above mediocrity. Those of genius who were associated with it made their way at a late period, and rather because the Académie wanted them than because they required any honours it could bestow. In England such a monopoly of talent would be ten times more misplaced. We all know John Bull, and that, from mere contradiction's sake, he will overlook what is admirable rather than admire upon anything resembling compulsion. Every judgment of the proposed society would be the subject of a thousand wicked jests, merely because it appeared in shape of an injunction which seemed to impose on the public a particular creed of taste; and a happy time would the patrons honoraries have of it, betwixt the internal dissensions of the hive of wasps they had undertaken to manage, and the hooting and clamouring of the public out of doors. I have still to add that this society, like some well-meant charitable associations, would go far to occasion the discontinuance of that private assistance which is so much more useful both to the individual and to the public. Let me speak a proud word for myself. I have not for several years, and even when money has been scarce with me, given less than from £50 to £100 a year to the aid of unfortunate men of literature, in various ways. Your proposed society would relieve me of this burthen; but could it distribute the relief with such secrecy or attention to the feelings of those who receive it? There is no merit in my doing this, for I work up to it; that is, I labour some hours more in order to gain the means of this charity, than I would do on my own account, and I know it is a common practice with many literary men to do the same, from the same very natural motive. But all this would fall if the matter were taken up by a privileged society, and the poor devil, in his necessity, would be sent there as naturally as you give a beggar a mendicity ticket. I was very sorry to hear you intimate that matters had gone so far in this affair as to render a retreat difficult. But be it ever so difficult, a timely retreat is better than a defeat; and what can be said after all save that the king had, in his eagerness to advance literature, listened to a plan which upon mature examination was found attended with too many objections to be carried into execution? The circumstances so well known to a veteran hack of letters like myself could not possibly occur to the sovereign or those with whom he at first consulted. I would have his grace flow directly from himself, and his own knowledge, taste, and judgment, rather than through the interposition of any society. His Majesty's kindness, and the honourable and gratifying distinction of those who have cultivated letters with success, has been illustrated by very many examples besides those conferred on one individual, who may justly say of the marks of royal favour that they "were meant for *merit,* tho' they fell on *me.*" If his Majesty should be pleased to relieve the wants of the two or three men of acknowledged talent who are subject to them, or if he would condescend to bestow small pensions on the wives and families of men early cut off in the career of letters, he would show his interest in literature, and at the same time his benevolence. The assistance of young persons in education (provided they are selected strictly with a view to proper qualifications) is also a princely charity; and either or all of them might be gracefully and naturally substituted for the present plan. If a device could be fallen upon to diminish the quantity and improve the quality of our literature it would have an admirable effect. But the present scheme would have exactly the contrary tendency. The number of persons who can paint a little, play a little music, or write indifferent verses is infinite in proportion to those who are masters of those faculties; and their daubing, scraping, and poetastering is, to say the least, a great nuisance to their friends and the public; and the misfortune is that these pretenders never have tact enough to detect their own insufficiency. A man of genius is always doubtful of his best performances, because his expression does and must fall infinitely below his powers of conception; and what he is able to embody to the eye of the reader is far short of the vision he has had before his own. But the *modérés* in literature are teazed with no such doubts, and are usually as completely satisfied with their own productions as all the rest of the world are bored by them. All such will thrust their efforts on the proposed adjudgers of the prizes (and who on earth would have patience to read or consider them?), while from modesty or pride real genius would stand aloof from competing with such opponents. Your invitation would have the effect of the witches' incantation—"all ill come running in, all good keep out." I would besides call your attention to the extreme indelicacy of authors practising the same art, sitting as judges on each other's performances, a task which, with all its unpopularity and odium, few would undertake who had the least capacity of performing it well. In a political point of view, the proposed plan is capable of being most grossly misrepresented. It would be no sooner announced than the Jacobin scribblers would hold it forth as an attempt on the part of the sovereign to blind and to enslave his people by pensioning their men of letters and attaching them personally to the crown. No matter how false and infamous such a calumny, it is precisely the kind of charge which the public beast would swallow greedily, and from that moment the influence of any individual connected with that society on the public mind is gone for ever. Absolute independence is of all things most necessary to a public man, whether in politics or literature. To be useful to his king and country he must not only be a free man, but he must stand aloof from everything which can be represented, or misrepresented, as personal dependence. And the bounty of the Crown also, when bestowed on men of letters, should be so given as to shew that it was the reward of merit, and not the boon given to a partisan. But I should never end were I to state the various objections which occur to the practicability and utility of the proposed association. I am sensible I have stated them very confusedly, but some excuse is due considering I have just travelled 200 miles without a moment's stop; yet the matter being on my mind, it is of the last importance that you should have all that the experience of my calling suggests, before you come to a final determination, and therefore I write this before I sleep. I beg my best respects to Mrs. Villiers. I will have "Hey tuttie tattie" copied out for her, whenever I get to Edinburgh, to which place you may have the goodness to address, should any part of my letter require answer or explanation. My kindest and best respects attend my Lord Clarendon; and believe me ever, etc. etc., WALTER SCOTT.

No. III.

LETTERS FROM MR. MURRAY AND MR. DISRAELI TO MR. LOCKHART, RELATING TO *The Representative* NEWSPAPER AND THE *Quarterly Review.*

FROM MR. MURRAY.

CHICHESTER, *Sept. 25th*, 1825.

MY DEAR SIR,—I left my young friend Disraeli to make his own way with you, confident that, if my estimation of him were correct, you would not be long in finding him out.[1] But as you have received him with so much kindness and favour, I

[1] Mr. Disraeli was at this date, and for some days later, Mr. Lockhart's guest at Chiefswood.

think it right to confirm the good opinion which you appear so
early to have formed of him, by communicating to you a little
of my own.   And I may frankly say, that I never met with a
young man of greater promise, from the sterling qualifications
which he already possesses.   He is a good scholar, hard student,
a deep thinker, of great energy, equal perseverance, and indefatigable application, and a complete man of business.   His knowledge of human nature, and the practical tendency of all his
ideas, have often surprised me in a young man who has hardly
passed his twentieth year, and above all, his mind and heart
are as pure as when they were first formed; a most excellent
temper too, and with young people, by whom he is universally
beloved, as playful as a child.   I have been acquainted with
him from his birth, but it is only within the last twelve months
that I have known him.   I can pledge my honour therefore
with the assurance that he is worthy of any degree of confidence
that you may be induced to repose in him—discretion being
another of his qualifications.   If our great plan should take
effect, I am certain that you will find in him a most invaluable,
trustworthy friend, from whose energies you may derive the
most valuable assistance.   But he is yet very young.   I approve
entirely of your objections and views, which cannot, I assure
you, go beyond the notions of exaltation of character which
have been long fixed in the contemplation of Mr. Disraeli and
myself, and I do solemnly assure you that I never should have
thought of communicating with you upon any undertaking
which I did not verily believe to be every [way] worthy of Mr.
Canning himself, when not in office; it is worthy of, and indeed
requires, the highest degree of moral and intellectual endowment.
I have written fully to Mr. Disraeli, to whom I refer you.   I
thought it a duty however, to add some pledge to you and Sir
Walter Scott for the integrity of all that may pass between you
and my valuable friend.

Do me the favour to offer my compliments to Sir Walter
Scott.   Assuring you of the esteem which I have ever retained
towards you, I remain, my dear sir, your faithful servant,

JOHN MURRAY.

FROM MR. DISRAELI.[1]

Oct. 26th, Wedy. 1825.

DEAR LOCKHART,— . . . I have been engaged at the *magnum
opus* unceasingly since we parted, as well as Murray, who is
perfectly indefatigable.   I have received six letters from differ-

[1] Mr. Disraeli and Mr. Lockhart left Chiefswood for London early in
October, and the latter returned to Scotland after the 19th.

ent correspondents in the Levant and Morea, who all appear very intelligent. I have written to them fully. Mr. Briggs, the great Alexandrian merchant and the agent in this country for the Pashaw of Egypt, has engaged to furnish us with information from that quarter. By his account, Egypt is now one of the most flourishing countries in the world, and his detail of the policy and conduct of the reigning Pashaw certainly proves him one of the most enlightened of modern rulers. Besides letters, Briggs receives by every ship a journal of the public occurrences of the kingdom, and he has pledged himself to give us this regularly.

I have not yet engaged Maginn, but I hope shortly to inform you of this business being arranged.

I inform you, *au secret* of course, that Copleston is also engaged on the subject of Universities. As in the present state of affairs, there is every appearance of the opinion of the Church party upon this important subject being extremely varying, Mr. Powles has written to the Bishop to arrange that on his coming to town a council, consisting of two or three Churchmen and as many laics, should be instituted, and that they should immediately take into consideration the whole affair, and settle upon some system to be adopted, and that their plans should be developed in our journal; that they should also invite Copleston to send in his ideas, and that you should, if in London, form one of the council, and if not, assist them by your advice. If this plan be adopted I will immediately let you know. It seems rational. I am vigorous in my researches after a *maison* for you, and hope I shall succeed very shortly. Two or three are upon the *tapis*.

Do me the favor of presenting my best compliments to Mrs. Lockhart, and believe me with great regard, yours,

B. DISRAELI.

FROM THE SAME.

Saturday night.[1]

DEAR LOCKHART,—I should have written to you before this, but have waited with the expectation of receiving a letter from you as mentioned in your last. I hope you received mine directed to you at Edinburgh and dated somewhere about the end of last month—the subject, your house. I am the last person who could ever wish to make a bore of correspondence, nor have I the least desire that you should write to me a single letter, unless you have something to communicate which may

[1] Written early in November, before Mr. Disraeli made his second visit to Scotland.

authorise the great trouble of your writing and my reading a
letter; but I confess *for Murray's sake*, I rather wished to have
a line as to the feeling *now* existing at Abbotsford on the grand
plan. A communication of this kind infuses new life and
energy into the Emperor.[1] It is perhaps foolish to mention this,
but the truth is Murray has long been accustomed to look up
to authority, and the approbation of such a man as Scott is to
him "meat, drink, and raiment."

Much, my dear Lockhart, has happened since we parted, I
think of importance. In the first place *Maginn is engaged.* I
called upon the Dr. shortly after your departure. It is impossible for me to give you any adequate idea of our interesting
interview: to present you with a few of the leading features,
you must know that M. speedily came to the point and told me
that £300 to £350 per ann. was the regular salary for the
services we required, but that it would not suit his views to go
for a less income than £500 per ann., *but that he felt bound in
honour and candour to tell us that he did not conceive that our paper
could afford or justify such an expenditure.* He then went on
backing Barnes against us, ridiculing the attempt generally,
swearing there was only one way to conduct a newspaper, that
a newspaper *was* a newspaper, and other of these sage truisms.
He "ventured to predict that with all our system, in six months'
time we should be doing the same thing as the Old Times;"
that he was "*the most experienced man as regards newspapers in
London*," that he knew what the system was capable of, etc. etc.

As I did conceive him to be decently honourable, and as I
felt the importance of arguing the question with a man, who
might fairly be considered a very prosopopœia of the public
press, I thought the experiment might be hazarded of giving
him a slight and indefinite sketch of our intentions. This I did
with great caution, and mentioning no names. To give you an
idea of the effect which I produced is utterly impossible. The
Dr. started from his chair like Giovanni in the banquet scene,
and seemed as astounded,—as *attonitus*—as Porsenna when
Scævola missed him. A new world seemed opened to him, and this
sneering scribe, this man of most experience, who had so smiled
at our first mentioning of the business, ended by saying that as to
the success of the affair doubt could not exist, and that a year
could not elapse without our being the very first paper going.
Upon my faith, Lockhart, I consider this a most important
interview, because really after all, it is becoming acquainted, as
it were, with the private opinion of Barnes, etc. In brief, the
Dr. goes to Paris, and Murray acquits him (this *au secret*) of his

[1] Mr. Murray.

little engagement. He sets off some time in December, that he may have six weeks clear in Paris before we commence our operations; but his salary commences *from this time* and he is to assist us by his general advice and exertions until he goes off. Have I managed this well? It has come to our knowledge that the Bishop of Durham, spirited on by his able council in the North (Philpotts, Townsend, and Co.) is contemplating some move in the press. We intend to write to them informing them of our plans and requesting their co-operation.

I am most unceasingly employed about this business. The following is a sketch of our correspondence *at present established* :—

S. A.	N. A.
All South America.	All the North American news-papers, and private intelligence from a family of distinction at Washington by every packet. Mexico.

All the Morea. All the Baltic. All the Levant. Smyrna. Constantinople. Greece.	Making about 27 correspondents.
Paris.	A general agent.
Florence. Rome.	Correspondents.
Netherlands.	Two Correspondents — both men of intelligence.
Germany.	Vienna, Berlin, Munich, Dresden, Stuttgardt, Weimar, Coblentz, Frankfurt, Hamburg, and Treves.

I have been very much assisted in this grand coup of Germany by Mrs. Wm. Elliot, who, when devoid of humbug, is very clever. All the letters which we have written to these places are not answered, but we do not anticipate the *slightest* doubt of their success. I have heard this day of a most admirable man at *St. Petersburg*. In addition to these we must put down

The West Indies   Teneriffe.

I have no doubt that in a few days I shall get a most excellent correspondent at Cadiz; but I have not yet succeeded in Madrid, which is most important. We have established also

at Liverpool, Glasgow, Manchester, Birmingham, etc. etc.—
actually established. I see no visible obstacle to our beginning
the first day of February, for our mechanical part, such as
reporters, printers, building, etc. goes on as well as the other.
Pray present my kindest compliments to Mrs. Lockhart, and
remember me to John.—Yours ever faithfully,   B. D.

I should think it most desirable for you to write a *serious*
letter to Maginn.

FROM THE SAME.[1]

Nov. 21, half-past 5 o'clock.

MY DEAR LOCKHART,—I have arrived after a most fatiguing
journey. I went immediately to the Emperor, and my reception
was most unfavourable. I would use a harsher word if I
remembered one. He has spoken to Coleridge, and nothing
could go off better; it is perfectly settled. But as to my unhappy mission. He swears that he understood I undertook to
go to Sir W. *au secret*, and not to you;[2] that I have ruined and
mêléed everything, etc.; that he only wanted Sir W. to write a
few letters in consequence of the spirit evinced against you, etc.
etc. I was too ill to answer him, and I trust to the course of
events to settle all things. He swears also that I ought not
to have mentioned Barrow's name, etc. All these things, I
need not tell you, appear to me very extraordinary, as I am not
aware of having violated any confidence or instructions whatever. Stewart Rose has made a miserable business of it;
instead of calling on Murray, he wrote to Barrow, and the
latter has called on Murray in great ire.

I hope all things will turn out well. Murray writes by to-
morrow's post to Sir W. Scott. I will write by to-morrow's
post fully and positively.—Yours ever, B. D.

You will not, of course, come to town upon this letter. I
only write that you may be prepared.

---

[1] Written to Mr. Lockhart from
London after the writer's second
visit to Scotland. See *Journal*,
vol. i. pp. 21-23.

[2] On 21st November Mr. Murray
wrote to Sir Walter that Disraeli
had totally mistaken the object of
his mission, "which was to tell
you alone the apprehensions which
had been expressed by the most
valuable friends of the *Quarterly
Review* at the appointment of one
who had so long been connected
with *Blackwood's Magazine*, but
which could be instantly dissipated
by the influence of your name,—by
writing to three persons, Canning,
Croker, and Heber. Mr. L. was
not to have been told of it by any
means." Sir Walter in sending
this letter to Lockhart mentioned
that he had written to Heber and
Southey, but that this was all he
could do in such a matter.

Nov. 22, 1825.

MY DEAR LOCKHART,—Forget the letter, which, in a moment of great agitation about your business, and utterly exhausted in mind and body, I wrote you yesterday evening.

I rose this morning, having previously sworn by the God of the Silver Bow to slay the mighty Python of Humbug, whose vigorous and enormous folds were so fast and fatally encircling us. Thank the God, I have succeeded! You will now come to London in *triumph.*—Yours ever, B. D.

Give my best compliments to your lady, and your visitors, with whom I regret my too short acquaintance. Murray is desirous of writing you as to all that has happened. I could not refrain giving you the gratifying result, but consider this letter as *perfectly confidential.*

Wednesday, November 23rd, 1825.

MY DEAR LOCKHART,—I think I have kept my word, and am pestering you with communications right sufficient. I am quite alarmed for the postmaster's bill, which, by the bye, will not be the less light for the by no means slender sums incurred by my own postage during my two visits, and which, I am ashamed to say, your fascinating conversation prevented me from daily remembering and reimbursing.

The Emperor is writing you a long and full letter, but his morning has been so broken into that he has desired me again to write, lest you might imagine that all was not right.

I feel that a day should not pass without your having a somewhat more definite idea of what has passed than my last communication afforded. I confess it is a very difficult subject to handle on a sheet of paper. You must know that I called on Tuesday morning at Murray's, and finding that he was in a more temperate humour, I determined to bring matters to a crisis. What I said in our three hours' uninterrupted conversation it is difficult to detail. My communications were the results of what I had seen, of what I had felt, since we had become acquainted. I detailed my sentiments as to your character, my experience of your disposition, my knowledge of your views in life. The result you are acquainted with.

Do not think Murray's conduct in this last affair wavering and inconsistent. His situation has been very trying. You and he have never rightly understood each other. When such connections were about to be formed between two men, they should have become acquainted, not by the stimulus of wine. There should have been some interchange of sentiment and feeling. The fault I know was not yours; the result however was bad. All men have their sober moments, and Murray in his is a man of pure and honourable, I might say elevated, sentiments. He wanted only to understand you. He wanted only to be told what has now made him esteem the happiest incident in his life his connection with Mr. Lockhart.

I am speaking soberly and seriously. The trash which has been too long bandied about as to your character, your feelings, your society, can only be effectively repelled by your conduct as really known by an acquaintance with yourself 'in spirit and in truth.' The Baronet's letter has opportunely assisted me. When I say it was worthy of him I say sufficient.

When you come to London, you will be introduced on the best-understood terms, not only to all the regular supporters of the Q. R., but to Coleridge himself, who will feel honoured by your acquaintance, and will be most happy to assist you in the mechanical detail.

As to your coming to London, it cannot be too speedy. I expect in less than eight-and-forty hours to have arranged everything about your house. Many are offered, and all suitable.

The other affairs are prancing on in such prosperity that a strong desire is expressed by all parties to commence operations sooner. The Emperor will write how. When you come to town, it will be advisable for us to have some *private* conversation before you see him, as I think it proper for both of you that you should be put in possession of what has passed without obliging him to detail.

My compliments to all, and my best respects to Sir W. when you write.

I shall not add to the unpleasant sensations which you may have already experienced by presuming to offer you advice from a young gentleman aged twenty. I may however, my dear Lockhart, indulge in the hope that your destiny may be crossed no more, and that no indiscretion may prevent your splendid talents from having their full and fair play. If so, the result will be as honourable to yourself as it will be gratifying to your very attached friend,   B. DISRAELI.

MY DEAR LOCKHART,—I received your letter of Monday enclosing one for me this morning. I immediately put yours in an envelope and forwarded it to Murray without comment. He has this moment left me, having called in consequence. He tells me that he wrote to you last night. I did the same and have troubled you with epistles every day since I left Chiefswood. I hope you have received them all.

I have often complained to you of Murray's inconsistency, vacillation, and indecision. I have done more, I have complained of them to himself. I regret it. Had I had any conception of the utter worthlessness of the intriguing, selfish, and narrow-minded officials by whom he has been so long surrounded, I certainly would have restrained my sentiments, and have pitied the noble and generous-minded being who was subjected to such disgusting thraldom. When I tell you that in the whole of this business Murray does really appear to have behaved in a manner more correct and more conscientious than I did previously consider human nature to be capable of, I feel that there is no person in the world to whom it can give such pleasure as yourself. It is impossible in a letter to give you any idea of the agitating and curious scenes which have taken place during these last days. The scales, however, have at length fallen from our friend's eyes, and the walls of the Admiralty have resounded to his firm and bold but gentlemanly tones. He is now in no state of excitement to which any reaction can ensue. His mind has undergone a revolution which it has taken ten years to bring about, and which I honestly confess I did conceive could never have occurred. You would not know him for the same man. Thank God I did not postpone my departure to town one other second !

On the whole, my good and excellent Lockhart, I do most sincerely rejoice that our affairs have taken this turn. Some ill blood may for a moment have existed, some intemperate expressions may have perhaps on both sides been uttered, but after all, without these mental purges, where should we have been? Half confidence, hollow friendship, and wavering councils are of all things the most terrible, and I cannot see, that if this affair had not happened, you could have come to London without these being your welcomers. I am most obliged to you for the frank and straight-forward manner in which you have delivered yourself in this day's letter. Honour me with your perfect confidence always, and I hope you will have no cause to repent.

We are most nervously anxious to see you in London. Affairs assume a most important aspect; I need not say what place you hold now really in Murray's confidence. He says without any violent protestations and with a coolness which I never remember to have witnessed in him, that he listens to no more *opinions* on these affairs, and that while he has cash in his pocket and blood in his veins he stands by John Gibson Lockhart, even unto the death. You know my former opinion of the Emperor; you know I have had some little experience with him, and you have sometimes expressed your opinion that I was not utterly ignorant of this world's ways. Now I deliberately and solemnly declare that I have as much confidence in the permanency of Murray's present disposition as I have in your honor.

But to your coming to town—Murray is most anxious to know whether you and Mrs. Lockhart, her maid, and your son and his peculiar suite will not come up immediately to Whitehall Place. Everything is already prepared for your presence, *actually* prepared, and allow me to hope that you will come. Before that time I very probably shall have a house for you, but it appears to me by no means undesirable that Mrs. Lockhart should not be bored by novel domesticities immediately on her arrival. I do most sincerely hope therefore, that you will comply with the imperial request.

There is one thing which I again mention; it is *absolutely necessary* that you and I should have a conversation before you see Murray. I have no objection to his knowing it, but mind me it is absolutely necessary.—Yours ever,

B. DISRAELI.

It is in vain to give you any details; I keep them till we meet.

FROM MR. MURRAY.

WHITEHALL PLACE, *Nov. 23rd,* 1825.

MY DEAR SIR,—In the hasty lines which I sent in acknowledgment of, rather than in answer to, the kind and satisfactory letter of Sir Walter Scott, I stated simply that the arrangements between you and me remained unaltered. I have yesterday and to-day listened to Mr. Disraeli's admirable details of his conferences with you and Sir Walter, and I can now state with my whole heart that nothing could have proved more completely gratifying; it has put me into complete possession of your views and character, and I can only repeat what I told him to say to you, that after this, Heaven and Earth may pass away, but it cannot shake my opinion, and I am prepared to go on with you with every good feeling, and with every exertion of which my nature is capable.　Your plans respecting the Review are noble and just, but the conception of the State Paper, and the first Number of the Paper are magnificent, and very far beyond my previous conception.　This deserves all your thoughts, study, and talents, and if done as we expect it, success is certain and instantaneous, and the public mind must capitulate at once.

Nothing can be more noble than the conduct of Mr. Coleridge, to whom I am very desirous of introducing you, and from whom you may expect every help that he can communicate.　In a note from him yesterday he proposes to give you an article on the W. Indies, from Mr. W. H.'s notes, if you like it for your first number; indeed everything is moving most satisfactorily, but your presence would still, we think, make them more complete.

Don't trouble yourself an instant about Mr. Rose's communications with Mr. B[arrow].　I have settled all that, but I have to regret very much indeed that Mr. B. should have mentioned the Newspaper to him, but it can't be helped.

Write me your plans about the Review and tell me all that you think I might do.　Mr. Croker has given up the Pepys Papers, and Mr. Bankes, the Member for Cambridge, wrote to undertake them a few days ago.　Of course you will induce Sir Walter to persist in his kind intentions.

To conclude, think of nothing now but that I am, my dear Lockhart, faithfully and devotedly yours,

JOHN MURRAY.

FROM THE SAME.

WHITEHALL PLACE,
[In haste and confidential.]　　　*Nov. 24th*, 1825.

MY DEAR LOCKHART,—I have far more satisfaction in writing to you this day than I had even yesterday, because your letter to Mr. Disraeli proves to me that you are determined to have no reserve, and had you been ten times more severe it would only have increased my pleasure in geometrical proportion when the occasion should be renewed.　Luckily I did beforehand, when in London, warn you of the deceitful conduct of a certain individual, and I then told you that he would avail himself of any means in his power to divert you from our

course have pressed your immediate coming to town had I been aware of the circumstance you mention. The sooner you arrive after, the better. Indeed the experience of every moment makes me the more urgent for your presence. As to the paper, everything goes on swimmingly. The terrific agitation in which the city and the whole commercial interest has been thrown, during the last three weeks, may have prevented Powles from writing to you, but I know that he is attending to the points you mention.

As to the *Review*, Coleridge, if possible, is more friendly. I mentioned I believe to you about my father. I have called at Wright's three or four times and have kept him up to the sticking point. The Chancery Commissioners publish their report at the commencement of this year, and it is therefore very important that you should have a first-rate article on the subject. Means might be taken to get a previous view of the report, and place it at the head of the article. I have attended to this. Palgrave came to town last week and called on Murray yesterday in consequence of the *Q. R.* reports. He was delighted at hearing you were to be editor, and inquired whether his assistance would in future [be] acceptable. He was of course not a little pleased when he found that his services had been already desired.

Merivale[1] (a gentlemanly Whig) called immediately after to congratulate M. on the *coup* he had made in bringing you up to London, etc. etc. Great Unknown, etc. etc., such a father-in-law, etc. etc. etc. In short, all goes right, and you have only to come to London to take advantage of affairs; and indeed, as the Marchioness of Hastings says in the letter which Mrs. Lawrence Lockhart would not let me bring to town, " who the devil ever heard anything against you ? " which, considering all we know, was rather an odd observation. In g^t haste,

B. D.

Chenevix will be in London as soon as yourself. I have had immense trouble about the Burke, and I am flattered to-day with the prospect of success.

I have heard nothing from Maginn and am most anxious to see him.

I send you "The Age." Is it credible that it has come to this ! ! !

[1] Mr. J. H. Merivale, one of the Commissioners of Inquiry into Chancery abuses.

Friday, Nov. 25, 1825.

MY DEAR LOCKHART,—I have just received your letter of
Tuesday evening. God grant your communion with " *my father-
in-law* " may lead to no ill consequences. You are perhaps, by
this time, convinced that you have been on a wrong scent. As
for Murray, he has done more in eight-and-forty hours than if
he had been sweating at the business as many weeks, and
actually, the *Prince of Pluck and Count of Confidence* must now
be added to his numerous titles. I shall not show however
to him the letter I received from you to-day, because I think
when all goes right I may as well be silent.

As to other matters, my father sends you his compliments,
and says, if you think an article on Charles First worthy your
attention, he will *pledge himself* that you shall have it for your
first number ; as he has of late years cut the Q. R., he begs it to
be understood that he now resumes his labours merely because
you are its conductor ; and that if at any time *circumstances may
arise from which you may deem it desirable for your interests that
this fact be known, you are perfectly at liberty to say so.*

I have had a view of the gubernatorial article, and I must
say—although I hope I am the last fellow in the world who
has a foolish penchant for parental effusions—that for exquisite
philosophy, beautiful feeling, intense interest, and profound
research, it was never equalled.

Your fear that Murray may be endangered by a conference
with Croker makes me smile. Perhaps you smile too at my
remark, but, my dear fellow, as ye showman says, ' you will see
what you will see.'—In the greatest haste,   B. D.

I have just received a letter from Powles, and shall dine
with him to-day. I must again impress upon you the mighty
importance of your presence in London. May the next post
bring news of your movement southward. Compliments to
Mrs. L., etc.

WHITEHALL PLACE, *2nd December* 1825.

MY DEAR LOCKHART,—Nothing could have been more
gratifying to me than your letter. We now know each other,
and I hope no one will be allowed to come between us. We
are doing all we can to get you a *house,* for I am fully aware
that we can settle to nothing until our Study is comfortably

arranged. Every moment I expect an answer about a capital house in Pall Mall, which also enters from St. James's Square—the best situation in all respects in London. I feel it to be of the greatest consequence to keep inviolate any connection with the Editorship of the Paper. Everything goes on well. The *Times* had offended every one so much last week that Mr. P. told us there was scarcely a knot of Merchants,—Rothschild was at the head of one knot,—which did not talk of setting up a Paper. It was therefore thought desirable to circulate in the city that one was on the point of being commenced by me, and it has been electrical. I have all kinds of classes calling to thank me for it. The Daily Editors and proprietors are in dismay. Yesterday Dr. Stoddart called and wished to join on any terms I would propose, and he was astonished at my *mad deafness* to his proposal. Barnes has written to Mitchell to dissuade his friend Murray from so ruinous an attempt!!!!! I saw your most excellent friend's letter. I have urged him with all my power to come up for six months, Book and Bookage. I agree about Byron, etc. A very important communication waits you about Sheridan's Life by Moore; a letter from Chenevix, all promising all that we can wish. Gifford in great spirits about all our arrangements.

Kindest compliments to Sir Walter Scott, and thanks for his kind letter.

Offer Mrs. Murray's and my compliments to Mrs. Lockhart, and mind if you should drive to our door everything *is* ready, and I am, faithfully yours, JNO. MURRAY.

INDEX.

FINIS. LAUS DEO.

Nov. 4, 1893.

Printed by T. and A. CONSTABLE, Printers to Her Majesty,
at the Edinburgh University Press

Lately published in one volume, Crown 8vo
and in two volumes, Demy 8vo

THE JOURNAL OF
SIR WALTER SCOTT
1825-32

FROM THE ORIGINAL MANUSCRIPT
AT ABBOTSFORD

ΝΥΞ ΓΑΡ ΕΡΧΕΤΑΙ

'I must home to work while it is called day; for the night cometh when no man can work. I put that text, many a year ago, on my dial-stone; but it often preached in vain.'—SCOTT'S *Life*, x. 88

EDINBURGH : DAVID DOUGLAS : 10 CASTLE STREET

OPINIONS OF THE PRESS.

Quarterly Review.
"Although many of the details are melancholy, yet the interest of the whole is entrancing, and the 'Journal' is a most precious relic of Sir Walter Scott."

Times.
"The story is as thrilling as any tragedy. . . . Those who read the 'Journal' will clearly understand what he was as a man, and such a man as he is the more beloved the more intimately he is known. He reveals himself with perfect candour and completeness in his 'Journal,' and he appears even greater in its pages than in other works from his pen which are prized as English classics."

Irish Times.
"It will be read everywhere and by every one with the deepest curiosity and interest."

Spectator.
"This book is one of the greatest gifts which our English literature has ever received."

Scotsman.
"Reads like a romance."

Scots (National) Observer.
"What we have there is Sir Walter's confession to Sir Walter—a piece of self-revelation, that is to say, unique in literature, and as absolutely assured of immortality as the best and bravest of those admirable achievements in romance which mark an epoch in the literature not only of Britain, but of Europe and the world."

Athenæum.
"Sir Walter keeps nothing back, and his admirers have no reason to be ashamed of his frankness. . . . This final work by Sir Walter Scott is as instructive and welcome as any which he penned."

Saturday Review.
"The portion of the public which only looks at new books will assuredly find the diary perfectly new to them. The students of Scott will take pleasure in observing the pages which Lockhart for various reasons omitted."

Speaker.
"Quite as fascinating as some of his romances."

Academy.

" On the whole, Lockhart presents an admirably true portrait ; it needs no varnishing ; it admits of no retouching. But it is a portrait ; and here in the 'Journal,' printed in full from the MS., we are in presence of the original : we see Scott in his hours of strength and in his hours of weakness : we feel the touch of his hand ; we become acquainted with the very beatings of his heart."

Pall Mall Gazette.

" Certainly all who read these volumes will rise from their perusal with a deepened admiration for one of the noblest and best of men."

Morning Post.

" As a picture of what has been described as the noblest sight conceivable—that of a brave man struggling with adversity —nothing more remarkable can readily be imagined than the journal, which now for the first time is given to the world in its entirety."

Guardian.

" But few men, whose lives have been open to the public, have shown more consistently and loftily how a brave man may bear heavy adversity, with full sense of its weight, and of its being partially deserved by imprudence, but yet without vain anger against the world or himself, with patient and genuine cheerfulness."

Birmingham Post.

" Those who know and love the Waverley Novels will cherish this 'Journal' as not less to be prized'than *The Antiquary* or *The Heart of Midlothian*."

Manchester Guardian.

" In the whole range of British literary history there are few nobler figures, few men who have devoted splendid powers to higher purposes than Sir Walter Scott, and the least that can be said of this latest of his many legacies to a grateful posterity, is that it reveals even more vividly than before the strength of his character, the sweetness and gentleness of his disposition, and the greatness of his soul."

Glasgow Herald.

" Deep-seated already as is the memory of Sir Walter Scott in the affection of all Scotsmen, and indeed of all the English-speaking race, these Journals will endear him still more. They show us the humble-minded, strong-souled, large-hearted man as he was, and they let us see, if not for the first time, at least more fully than before, the true meaning and the nobility of that fight for honour with which he crowned a wonderful career."

Harper's Weekly.

"The 'Journal'—immensely valuable for its copious variety of thought, humour, anecdote, and chronicle—is precious most of all for the confirmatory light that it casts upon the character of its writer. It has long been known that Scott's nature was exceptionally noble, that his patience was beautiful, that his endurance was heroic. These pages will disclose to his votaries that he surpassed even the highest ideal of him that their affectionate partiality had formed."

Tribune (New York).

"The 'Journal' as it stands is full of interesting glimpses into the great author's mind, and reveals in a striking manner the inextinguishable buoyancy with which he encountered misfortune, the iron perseverance with which he set himself to clear away the mountain of debt with which he found himself burdened when his best years had passed, the keen sense of honour and duty which marked even his most private communings with himself, and the gay humour which characterised him whenever the clouds parted for a moment and permitted the sunshine to pass."

Leisure Hour.

"It is a wonderful book, the most pathetic work of a great master of pathos, and a beautiful revelation of a character more worthy perhaps of study than the author's finest works."

Atlantic Monthly.

"The 'Journal' is a book to last. No king in literature has such a chronicle, and as Scott in his 'Novels' has made his principal characters now and again serve as heroes of the tale without being conscious of their heroism, so here, without egotism, without pettiness, yet with minute detail, he has drawn his own superb figure with a strength which is ineffaceable."

Macmillan's Magazine.

"Even those, then, who have long ranked Lockhart's great work among their most precious possessions will miss much if they miss this book. What a book! What a man! It is indeed no reproach to it, no reason against its existence, to say that it leaves Scott where he stood before. Higher he could not stand. And of how many a one of the world's heroes could every thought of his brain, every beat of his heart, be thus laid bare, and leave him no lower?"

EDINBURGH: DAVID DOUGLAS.

ARCHITECTURAL
ARCHÆOLOGICAL AND HISTORICAL WORK

RECENTLY PUBLISHED

By DAVID DOUGLAS

*Five Volumes, Royal 8vo, 42s. net each volume, with about
500 Illustrations in each volume.*

THE

CASTELLATED AND DOMESTIC

ARCHITECTURE

OF SCOTLAND

FROM THE TWELFTH TO THE EIGHTEENTH CENTURY

BY

DAVID MACGIBBON AND THOMAS ROSS

ARCHITECTS

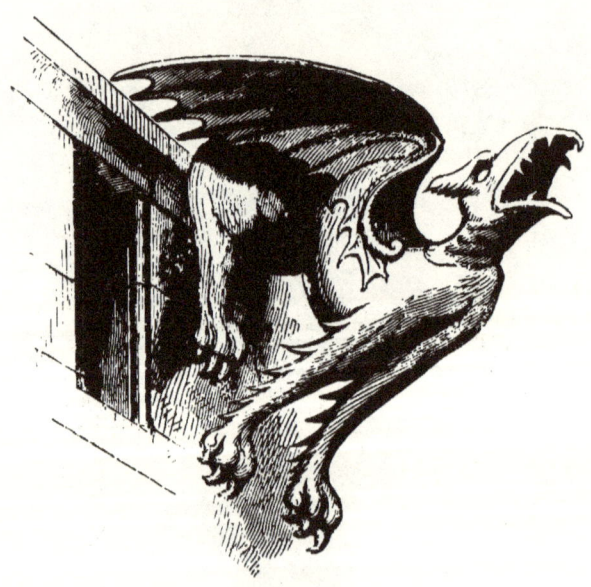

"One of the most important and complete books on Scottish architecture that
has ever been compiled. Its value to the architect, the archæologist, and the
student of styles is at once apparent. It consists almost exclusively of what may be
called illustrated architectural facts, well digested and arranged, and constituting a
monument of patient research, capable draughtsmanship, and of well-sustained effort,
which do the authors infinite credit."—*Scotsman.*

EDINBURGH: DAVID DOUGLAS

One Volume, 8vo, 21s., with nearly 300 Illustrations.

THE ARCHITECTURE OF
PROVENCE
AND
THE RIVIERA

BY

DAVID MACGIBBON

AUTHOR OF "THE CASTELLATED AND DOMESTIC ARCHITECTURE OF SCOTLAND"

EDINBURGH: DAVID DOUGLAS

Two Volumes 8vo, fully Illustrated, 12s. each (sold separately).

SCOTLAND

IN

EARLY CHRISTIAN TIMES

THE RHIND LECTURES IN ARCHÆOLOGY—1879 AND 1880.

By JOSEPH ANDERSON, LL.D.

KEEPER OF THE NATIONAL MUSEUM OF THE ANTIQUARIES OF SCOTLAND

EDINBURGH: DAVID DOUGLAS

One Volume 8vo, fully Illustrated, 12s.

SCOTLAND

IN

PAGAN TIMES

The Iron Age

THE RHIND LECTURES IN ARCHÆOLOGY FOR 1881

By JOSEPH ANDERSON, LL.D.

KEEPER OF THE NATIONAL MUSEUM OF THE ANTIQUARIES OF SCOTLAND

—

EDINBURGH: DAVID DOUGLAS

One Volume 8vo, fully Illustrated, 12s.

SCOTLAND

IN

PAGAN TIMES

The Bronze and Stone Ages

THE RHIND LECTURES IN ARCHÆOLOGY FOR 1882

By JOSEPH ANDERSON, LL.D.

KEEPER OF THE NATIONAL MUSEUM OF THE
ANTIQUARIES OF SCOTLAND

CONTENTS OF VOL. II.

EDINBURGH: DAVID DOUGLAS

One Volume 8vo, fully Illustrated, 15s.

THE

PAST IN THE PRESENT:

WHAT IS CIVILISATION?

By SIR ARTHUR MITCHELL, M.D., LL.D.

Contents.

EDINBURGH: DAVID DOUGLAS

William F. Skene.

Celtic Scotland. A History of Ancient Alban. By
WILLIAM F. SKENE, D.C.L., LL.D., Historiographer - Royal for Scotland.
Second Edition, carefully Revised by the Author, with a new Index to the
entire work. 3 vols. demy 8vo, 45s.

> Vol.   I.   HISTORY AND ETHNOLOGY. 15s.
>
> Vol. II.   CHURCH AND CULTURE. 15s.
>
> Vol. III.   LAND AND PEOPLE. 15s.

" Forty years ago Mr Skene published a small historical work on the Scottish
Highlands which has ever since been appealed to as an authority, but which has long
been out of print.   The promise of this youthful effort is amply fulfilled in the three
weighty volumes of his maturer years.   As a work of historical research it ought, in
our opinion, to take a very high rank."—*Times.*

E. W. Robertson.

Scotland under her Early Kings. A History of the
Kingdom to the close of the Thirteenth Century.   By E. WILLIAM ROBERTSON.
2 vols. demy 8vo, cloth, 36s.

Historical Essays, in connection with the Land and the
Church, etc.   By E. WILLIAM ROBERTSON, Author of "Scotland under her
Early Kings." 1 vol. demy 8vo, 10s. 6d.

Rev. James B. Johnston.

The Place-Names of Scotland. By the Rev. JAMES B.
JOHNSTON, B.D., Falkirk. 1 vol. crown 8vo, 7s. 6d.

This book, for which the author has been collecting materials during the
last five years, contains an introduction, general and philological, followed by a
list of the important place-names in Scotland, with explanations of their meaning,
and with their old spellings, each dated so far as known.

Lord Cockburn.

Circuit Journeys. By the late LORD COCKBURN, one of the
Judges of the Court of Session.   Second Edition, 1 vol. crown 8vo, 6s.

"One of the best books of reminiscences that have appeared."—*Morning Post.*

"Delightful alike for its pleasant landscapes ; its sound criticisms on men, law,
and books ; for its sharp things said in a good-natured way."—*Academy.*

"Valuable for their topographical descriptions ; and they form an indirect contribution to the social history of Scotland."—*Scotsman.*

Sir Daniel Wilson.

The Lost Atlantis and other Ethnographic Studies. By Sir
DANIEL WILSON, LL.D., F.R.S.E. 1 vol. demy 8vo, 15s.

Contents.—The Lost Atlantis—The Vinland of the Northmen—Trade and
Commerce in the Stone Age—Pre-Aryan American Man—The Æsthetic Faculty
in Aboriginal Races—The Huron-Iroquois: a Typical Race—Hybridity and
Heredity—Relative Racial Brain-Weight and Size.

EDINBURGH: DAVID DOUGLAS.

Two Volumes, Demy 8vo, Illustrated, 25s.

THE HEREDITARY
SHERIFFS OF GALLOWAY

THEIR "FORBEARS" AND FRIENDS
THEIR COURTS, AND CUSTOMS OF THEIR TIMES

WITH NOTES OF THE EARLY HISTORY, ECCLESIASTICAL
LEGENDS, THE BARONAGE AND PLACE
NAMES OF THE PROVINCE

BY THE LATE

SIR ANDREW AGNEW, BART.
OF LOCHNAW

EDINBURGH:
DAVID DOUGLAS, 10 CASTLE STREET
1893

Two Volumes, Demy 8vo, with Maps and Plans, 28s.

THE NJALA SAGA

BURNT NJAL

FROM THE ICELANDIC OF THE NJAL'S SAGA

BY

SIR GEORGE WEBBE DASENT, D.C.L.

Graysteel

Small 4to, with Illustrations, 7s. 6d.

THE GISLI SAGA

GISLI THE OUTLAW

FROM THE ICELANDIC

BY

SIR GEORGE WEBBE DASENT, D.C.L.

EDINBURGH: DAVID DOUGLAS

Demy 4to, Illustrated, 42s. and 84s.

THE

HISTORY OF LIDDESDALE

ESKDALE, EWESDALE, WAUCHOPEDALE

AND THE

DEBATEABLE LAND

Part I. from the Twelfth Century to 1530

BY

ROBERT BRUCE ARMSTRONG

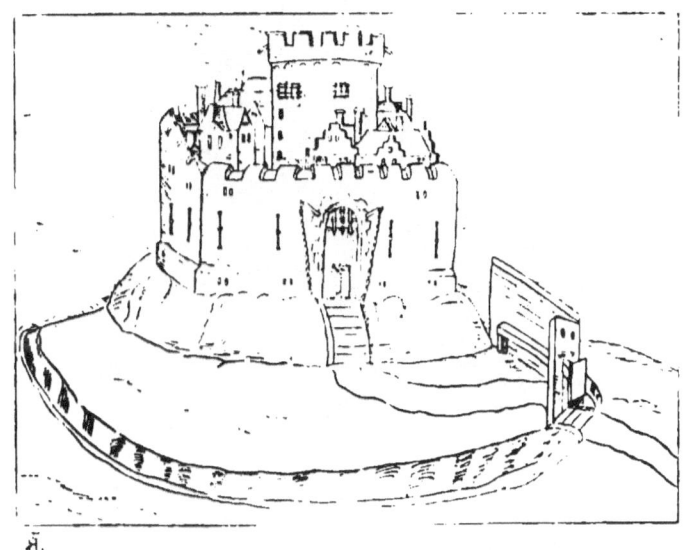

CRUKILTON CASTLE

EDINBURGH: DAVID DOUGLAS

One Volume 8vo, Illustrated, 7s. 6d.

SCOTLAND

AS IT WAS AND AS IT IS

BY THE

DUKE OF ARGYLL

RON ROY'S HOUSE, GLENSHIRA

**A HISTORY OF RACES, OF MILITARY EVENTS,
AND OF THE RISE OF COMMERCE**

EDINBURGH: DAVID DOUGLAS

Two Volumes 4to, 21s.

ARCHÆOLOGICAL ESSAYS

BY THE LATE

SIR JAMES Y. SIMPSON, BART.

EDITED BY THE LATE

JOHN STUART, LL.D.

AUTHOR OF THE "SCULPTURED STONES OF SCOTLAND"

ANCIENT ORATORY IN THE ISLAND OF INCHCOLM

CONTENTS.

EDINBURGH: DAVID DOUGLAS

Two Volumes, Demy 8vo, 19s. 6d.

SOCIAL LIFE

IN FORMER DAYS

CHIEFLY IN THE PROVINCE OF MORAY

Illustrated by Letters and Family Papers

By E. DUNBAR DUNBAR

LATE CAPTAIN 21ST FUSILIERS

THUNDERTON HOUSE.

EDINBURGH: DAVID DOUGLAS

One Volume, Demy 8vo, price 14s.

EARLY TRAVELLERS
IN SCOTLAND

1295-1689

EDITED BY

P. HUME BROWN
AUTHOR OF 'THE LIFE OF GEORGE BUCHANAN

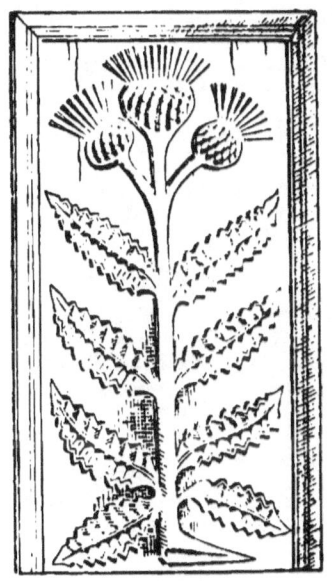

EDINBURGH:
DAVID DOUGLAS, 10 CASTLE STREET.

P. Hume Brown.

George Buchanan, Humanist and Reformer: a Biography.
By P. HUME BROWN. Demy 8vo, 12s.

"There is, perhaps, no eminent Scotsman who has stood in better need of an impartial and scholarly biography than George Buchanan; and Mr Hume Brown is to be congratulated on having in the present volume produced a model of its kind."—*Scotsman*.

Tours in Scotland, 1677 and 1681. By THOMAS KIRK and RALPH THORESBY. Edited by P. HUME BROWN. Demy 8vo, 5s.

A lucky accident having brought these two interesting narratives to light since the "Early Travellers in Scotland" was published, it was thought desirable to reprint them uniform with that book.

Scotland Before 1700. From Contemporary Documents.
Forming a Companion Volume to "Early Travellers in Scotland." By P. HUME BROWN, Author of "The Life of George Buchanan," &c. Demy 8vo, 14s.

Bishop Forbes.

Kalendars of Scottish Saints. With Personal Notices of those of Alba, etc. By ALEXANDER PENROSE FORBES, D.C.L., Bishop of Brechin. 4to, price £3, 3s. A few copies for sale on large paper, £5, 15s. 6d.

"A truly valuable contribution to the archæology of Scotland."--*Guardian*.

Thomas S. Muir.

Ecclesiological Notes on some of the Islands of Scotland, with other Papers relating to Ecclesiological Remains on the Scottish Mainland and Islands. By THOMAS S. MUIR, Author of "Characteristics of Church Architecture," etc. Demy 8vo, with numerous Illustrations, 21s.

Sir Samuel Ferguson.

Ogham Inscriptions in Ireland, Wales, and Scotland. By the late SIR SAMUEL FERGUSON, President of the Royal Irish Academy, Deputy Keeper of the Public Records of Ireland, LL.D., Queen's Counsel, etc. (Being the Rhind Lectures in Archæology for 1884.) 1 vol. demy 8vo, 12s.

Miss Maclagan.

The Hill Forts, Stone Circles, and other Structural Remains of Ancient Scotland. By C. MACLAGAN, Lady Associate of the Society of Antiquaries of Scotland. With Plans and Illustrations. Folio, 31s. 6d.

"We need not enlarge on the few inconsequential speculations which rigid archæologists may find in the present volume. We desire rather to commend it to their careful study, fully assured that not only they, but also the general reader, will be edified by its perusal."—*Scotsman*.

Prof. Baldwin Brown.

From Schola to Cathedral. A Study of Early Christian Architecture in its relation to the life of the Church. By G. BALDWIN BROWN, Professor of Fine Art in the University of Edinburgh. Demy 8vo, Illustrated, 7s. 6d.

The book treats of the beginnings of Christian Architecture, from the point of view of recent discoveries and theories, with a special reference to the outward resemblance of early Christian communities to other religious associations of the time.

Patrick Dudgeon.

A Short Introduction to the Origin of Surnames. By PATRICK DUDGEON, Cargen. Small 4to, 3s. 6d.

EDINBURGH: DAVID DOUGLAS

www.ingramcontent.com/pod-product-compliance
Lightning Source LLC
Chambersburg PA
CBHW052344110726
47901CB00005B/1359